ALBERT G. GIORDANO is on the Business Division Faculty at Monterey Peninsula College. He holds a Ph.D. from the University of Ottawa, Canada, and is a former head and professor of Business Education at the University of New Mexico, Albuquerque. Dr. Giordano is Executive Vice-President of the Howard Corporation of Atlanta, Georgia, and Vice-President of Condominium Living International, Chicago, Illinois. In addition Dr. Giordano is a former Assistant Director of the Bureau of Business Services, School of Business Administration, Tempe, Arizona. He is the author of six other books published by Prentice-Hall, Inc., including *Business Machine Calculations* (Vols. I and II), *Basic Business Machine Calculation*, first and second editions, *College Business Mathematics*, and *Business Mathematics/Electronic Calculation*.

Dr. Albert G. Giordano

CONCISE DICTIONARY OF BUSINESS TERMINOLOGY

A SPECTRUM BOOK

PRENTICE-HALL, INC., Englewood Cliffs, New Jersey 07632

Library of Congress Cataloging in Publication Data

Giordano, Albert G
    Concise dictionary of business terminology.

    (A Spectrum Book)
    Bibliography: p.
    1. Business—Dictionaries. I. Title.

Hf1001.G56   650'.03'21   80-26749

ISBN 0-13-166553-7
ISBN 0-13-166546-4 (pbk.)

Prentice-Hall International, Inc., *London*
Prentice-Hall of Australia Pty. Limited, *Sydney*
Prentice-Hall of Canada, Ltd., *Toronto*
Prentice-Hall of India Private Limited, *New Delhi*
Prentice-Hall of Japan, Inc., *Tokyo*
Prentice-Hall of Southeast Asia Pte. Ltd., *Singapore*
Whitehall Books Limited, *Wellington, New Zealand*

FOREWORD

The ability to communicate ideas effectively is an essential characteristic of all leadership. Business leaders have consistently listed the acquiring of communication skills at the top in all surveys when asked to recommend curricula for those aspiring to business leadership. Business educators have long recognized that the understanding and use of language in both written and oral form is vital to those preparing for major responsibilities in the business world. A knowledge of the language and terminology of business is a basic prerequisite in the acquisition of the ability to communicate in the world of economic enterprise.

This book, *A Concise Dictionary of Business Terminology*, is a comprehensive coverage of the language used in many diverse areas of business. Words, abbreviations, and acronyms are explained in a simple, clear, descriptive manner that is equally useful to the practitioner or the student. Availability of the dictionary to those beginning professional study in business should provide a useful tool not only during the years of study, but also after entry into the world of work.

The author of this valuable addition to the literature of business has had many years of successful experience in teaching, research and publication. His understanding of business and educational methodology has enabled him to compile an educational reference book that should be widely adopted in either beginning or advanced business courses. It will become one of the books the student will retain after graduation and keep in a convenient place for frequent reference as he climbs the ladder of success in business.

The compact form of this book makes it easy to keep on the desk, in the bicycle basket, on the patio table, in the classroom or in the car. Although its primary use will probably be as a classroom textbook, it will also serve as an ideal gift or a part of the personal library of those who recognize the need for improved skill in oral and written communication in the field of business.

Glenn D. Overman, Dean
College of Business Administration
Arizona State University

A

ABANDONMENT: the act of relinquishing ownership of property.

ABATEMENT: a reduction; often a reduction of taxes provided by statute.

ABATOR: one who gains illegal possession of an estate.

ABC LAW: Alcoholic Beverage Control Law regulates the sale of alcoholic beverages.

AB EXTRA: from outside (Latin).

ABEYANCE: a temporary suspension of title to property before the correct owner is determined.

AB INITIO: from the beginning (Latin).

AB IRATO: in anger (LATIN).

ABILITY TO PAY THEORY: a theory of taxation advocating that individuals pay taxes according to their ability to pay.

ABJURE: legally to renounce.

ABOVE PAR: at a premium.

ABOVE THE LINE: the promotional expenses associated with advertising in one of the media.

ABROGATION: the process of annulment by some authority such as the enactment of a law.

ABSCISSA: in graphs, the horizontal distance from the vertical axis.

ABSENTEE OWNER: a property owner who does not reside on his property, leaving management in the hands of others.

ABSOLUTE ADVANTAGE: the ability of a particular country or organization to supply a product or service at a cost lower than that of its competitors.

ABSORB: to merge by transfer all or portions of an account with another account, resulting in the loss of identity of the first account.

ABSORBED: designating a security, no longer in the hands of an underwriter, and now with a shareholder.

ABSORPTION: acquisition of one business by another.

ABSORPTION COSTING: a method of cost accounting in which fixed manufacturing expenses are included in inventory valuation in addition to direct materials, direct labor, and variable overhead expenses.

ABSORPTION POINT: the point at which the securities market rejects further offerings unaccompanied by price concessions.

ABSTRACT OF TITLE: a document containing the history of a particular piece of land which evidence affects title to the land.

ABUTTING: joining or adjacent; contiguous to another property.

ACCELERATED DEPRECIATION: the allowance of depreciation to be charged against income for tax purposes earlier than would otherwise be the case.

ACCELERATION CLAUSE: a provision requiring the immediate payment of an unpaid amount upon breach of contract.

ACCELERATION PREMIUM: the increasing rate of pay allowed workers with increasing production.

ACCEPTANCE: promissory notes issued and offered for sale by finance companies.

ACCEPTANCE LIABILITY: the total liability which the bank assumes when accepting negotiable instruments drawn upon it by its customers.

ACCEPTANCE SUPRA PROTEST: following a protest, the payment of a bill to preserve the reputation or credit of the drawer or endorser.

ACCESS: the process of obtaining data from or placing data into computer storage.

ACCESSION: the process whereby property that belongs to one person becomes the property of another by reason of its being added to or incorporated with the property of the latter.

ACCESS RIGHT: the right of an owner of property or another person with the owner's approval to enter, enjoy, or leave the property without obstruction.

ACCESS TIME: the length of time it takes a computer to locate or use data.

ACCIDENT PRONE: applied to workers who are involved in an unusually large number of accidents.

ACCIDENTAL DEATH: the death of an insured resulting, directly and independently of all other causes.

ACCOMMODATION ENDORSER: a second signer to a promissory note who also guarantees it.

ACCOMMODATION PAPER: a promissory note that has been signed on the back in order to help a person with weak credit to obtain the loan.

ACCORD: an agreement to accept a smaller amount or a different payment plan than a creditor is entitled to legally.

ACCORD AND SATISFACTION: an agreement between two parties changing the terms of an original contract.

ACCOUNT: a statement summarizing transactions over a given period; a formal accounting record of a particular (or type of) asset, liability, revenue, or expense.

ACCOUNTABILITY: the act of holding a manager liable for carrying out activities for which he or she has the necessary authority and responsibility.

ACCOUNT DEBTOR: an individual who is obligated on an account, contract right, or general intangible.

ACCOUNT EXECUTIVE: an employee, particularly of an advertising agency, who is responsible for all matters relating to a specific client.

ACCOUNTING: recording, classifying, summarizing, and interpreting the financial transactions of a business.

ACCOUNTING CYCLE: the period during which the books of account are opened, transactions recorded, financial statements prepared, and the books of account are closed.

ACCOUNTING PRINCIPLE: a rule which has developed and evolved in guiding the measurement, classification, and interpretation of activity and information in terms of money.

ACCOUNTING PROCEDURE: the method, chosen by an organization from acceptable alternatives.

ACCOUNTING RATE OF RETURN: income for a period divided by the average investment made in that period.

ACCOUNTING RECORDS: books of account, vouchers, and any other documentary evidence used in the accounting function.

ACCOUNTING SYSTEM: the combination of accounting principles, procedures, and records used by a particular organization.

ACCOUNTS PAYABLE: amounts due to creditors; usually refers to short-term debts for goods and services rather than long-term liabilities such as bank loans or mortgages.

ACCOUNTS RECEIVABLE: amounts due from debtors; usually refers to short-term receivables in respect to sales of goods and services rather than long-term debts such as mortgages receivable.

ACCRETION: growth by addition; in business, accretion usually refers to growth of wealth or growth by acquiring other companies.

ACCRETION ACCOUNT: records the increase between the acquisition value and the face value of bonds purchased at a discount.

ACCRUAL ACCOUNTING: the recording of revenue and expenses as they are earned or incurred rather than when they are received or paid.

ACCRUAL BASIS: the method of keeping accounts that shows expenses incurred and income earned during a given period without regard to date of payment.

ACCRUE: to be gained or obtained; such as a profit or loss.

ACCRUED ASSET: a receivable that is accumulating with the passage of time or the rendering of services, but that is not yet collectible.

ACCRUED DEPRECIATION: the difference between the cost of replacement of a building new as of the date of the appraisal and the present appraised value.

ACCRUED DIVIDENDS: dividends due but not paid.

ACCRUED EXPENSE: an expense which has been incurred in an accounting period but for which no claim for payment can yet be made.

ACCRUED INTEREST: interest accumulated since the last interest payment due date.

ACCRUED LIABILITY: a debt which is accumulating with the passage of time or the receipt of services, but that is not yet payable.

ACCRUED REVENUE: revenue that has been earned in an accounting period although no claim for payment can yet be made.

ACCUMULATED DEPLETION: the total to date of periodic depletion charged against income in respect to wasting assets.

ACCUMULATED DEPRECIATION: the total to date of periodic depreciation charged against income in respect to depreciable fixed assets.

ACCUMULATED DIVIDENT: a dividend not paid when due.

ACCUMULATION: purchases made in anticipation of rising prices.

ACCURACY: the certainty with which a value is known or can be measured.

ACHIEVED PENETRATION: a marketing measure of the ratio of existing users (or buyers) to current potential users (or buyers) of a product class.

ACHIEVEMENT TEST: a measure of proficiency level determined by testing performance displayed in a particular field.

ACID TEST: the ratio of total cash, accounts receivable, and marketable securities.

ACKNOWLEDGMENT: confirmation of the receipt of a document, such as a letter, order, or check.

ACQUIRED SURPLUS: surplus arising from changes of the capital structure or purchase of one or more businesses.

ACQUISITION: a taking over of one company by another, usually accomplished by purchasing a controlling portion of the other corporation's common stock.

ACQUIT: to formally declare the innocence of a person previously accused of a crime; to release a person from a duty or obligation.

ACQUITTANCE: in law, a written agreement to release one from the payment of money.

ACRE: a measure of land equal to 43,560 square feet; there are 640 acres to a square mile.

ACRE-FEET: a measurement for large volumes of water as stored behind dams; an acre-foot of water is an acre in area by one foot in depth.

ACRONYM: a word, frequently a commercial name, formed from the initial letters or syllables of the successive words of a compound term.

ACROSS-THE-BOARD: applying to everyone or everything.

ACTION IN PERSONAM: a court action that seeks a judgment against an individual or person as distinguished from a judgment against property.

ACTION IN REM: a court action that seeks a judgment against property, such as a quiet title action.

ACTIVATION: putting a prepared facility into operation.

ACTIVE ACCOUNT: a bank account that has frequent deposits or withdrawals.

ACTIVE MARKET: characterized by numerous transactions in securities trading.

ACTIVE TRADE BALANCE: a balance of trade that is favorable.

ACTIVITY: a sign that a record in a file has been moved or used for reference.

ACTIVITY CHARGE: a bank service charge imposed on a checking account depositor for check or deposit activity.

ACTUAL VALUATION: the true value of a shipment at the time of delivery to the carrier.

ACTUALS: commodities on hand, ready for shipment, storage, or manufacture.

ACTUARY: a mathematician who determines insurance rates from known data.

ADAPTATION: a design reflecting the dominant feature of a style that inspired it, but is not an exact copy.

ADDED VALUE: the value that is attached to the cost of unprocessed resources.

ADDENDUM: added matter; in a signed agreement, frequently initialed by both parties.

AD DIEM: at the day appointed (Latin).

ADD-ON CLAUSE: a clause in an installment contract that allows new purchases to be put on the contract from time to time.

ADD-ON CONFERENCE: a system that enables a third person to participate in a telephone conversation without operator assistance.

ADDRESS OF RECORD: the official or primary location for an individual, company, or other organization.

ADDRESSER: a device used in stores in connection with the "charge plate" or "credit card" to imprint customer's name, address, and other data, on the salescheck.

ADDRESSOGRAPH PLATE: a metal device bearing customer's name, address, and other details from which monthly statements and direct mail are addressed.

AD HOC: for this purpose (Latin).

AD IDEM: to the same effect (Latin).

AD INFINITUM: indefinitely (Latin).

ADJACENCIES: the programs that precede or follow a specific broadcast time period.

ADJUDICATION: the decision of a judge.

ADJUNCT ACCOUNT: an account that adds to another existing account, represented by transfers from another account.

ADJUSTABLE PEG: a system permitting changes in the par rate of foreign exchange after a country has had long-run disequilibrium in its balance of payments.

ADJUSTER: one who determines damages under insurance policies.

ADJUSTING ENTRY: a correcting entry; before closing the books for an accounting period, items of revenue or expense may be apportioned to accounting periods or various classifications or accounts.

ADJUSTMENT BOARD: an agency designed to deal with labor-management problems.

ADJUSTMENT PREFERRED SECURITIES: preferred stock that has resulted from an adjustment of claims in a restructuring of the company.

ADMASS: high pressure advertising and promotion, found in the media, to increase sales, with damaging impact on the culture of the society.

ADMINISTERED PRICE: the price established under situations of imbalanced competition wherein one business has some degree of control.

ADMINISTRATIVE EXPENSE: an expense of an organization relating to the overall management of its affairs rather than to a particular function.

ADMINISTRATOR: in business law, a qualified individual or bank who is appointed by a court of law to manage and distribute the estate of a person who died intestate or left a will that fails to name an executor.

ADMIRALTY LAW: national and international law covering maritime affairs.

ADOPTION PROCESS: a five-stage procedure by which an individual makes a decision to buy a new product.

AD REFERENDUM: indicating that although a contract has been signed, specific issues remain to be considered.

AD REM: to the point (Latin).

ADULTERATED: the failure of a product to meet minimum standards of purity and quality.

ADULTERATION: the introduction of unwanted impurities into a product, such as food.

AD VALOREM: assessment of taxes according to value (Latin).

ADVANCE: a payment which is to be accounted for at a later date; a loan.

ADVERSE POSSESSION: a method of acquisition of title to property based on hostile use and occupation of another person's property for a continuous period of five years and on payment of taxes.

ADVERTISING: the communication of signed, paid messages to influence people.

ADVERTISING AGENCY: a company that prepares and places advertising and promotes distribution of products and services for others.

ADVERTISING ALLOWANCE: a discount in price or payment given to a store to help meet the expense of the store's advertising of a product.

ADVERTISING CAMPAIGN: the planned use of varying media and advertising methods to solicit acceptance for an idea or item.

ADVERTISING CREDIT: the mention of a store's name in the advertisement of a producer.

ADVERTISING MEDIUM: a means used to carry advertising messages to the general public.

ADVERTISING MIX: the proportions of various media used to make a total advertising campaign.

ADVERTISING SPECIALTY: a low-cost item on which the seller's name, address, and telephone number are printed, to give visibility.

ADVICE NOTE: a supplier's statement listing items sent to a customer prior to an invoice either accompanying merchandise or preceding it.

ADVOCATE: a supporter, in particular, a lawyer, who pleads on behalf of a client or, an accountant, who gives testimony on behalf of a client.

AFFIANT: a person who makes an affidavit.

AFFIDAVIT: a statement in writing and under oath.

AFFILIATE: the relationship between two companies when one partially or wholly owns the other or both are subsidiaries of a third.

AFFINITY: relationship by marriage, to be distinguished from consanguinity.

AFFIRMATIVE ACTION: positive steps taken by firms or other organizations to remedy imbalances in their employment of minorities.

AFFLUENT: wealthy.

AFLOATS: commodities loaded on vessels or in transit not yet at port of destination.

A FORTIORI: much more so (Latin).

AFTER SIGHT: a phrase used in a bill of exchange indicating that the period for which the bill is to be calculated from the date on which it is first presented to a drawee for acceptance.

AGAINST THE BOX: in a short sale of stock, a person selling against the box who owns the security sold short but prefers not to or who cannot deliver the stock to the buyer.

AGENDA: a scheduled program, as for conducting a meeting.

AGGLOMERATION DISECONOMIES: an imbalance of scale occurring when a large number of individuals live close together.

AGGREGATE: total.

AGGREGATE DEMAND: the total quantity of goods and services demanded in a period of time, including both consumer goods and producers' goods.

AGGREGATE SUPPLY: the total dollar output of goods and services produced in an accounting period by private firms and public agencies.

AGGRESSIVE PORTFOLIO: a portfolio of stocks and bonds usually held for appreciation.

AGING: a listing by age, as of accounts receivable; maturing of a product, as tobacco or whiskey.

AGIO: a premium paid for the exchange of one nation's currency for that of another's; the sum given above a nominal value; the rate of exchange among all countries of the world.

AGRARIAN: pertaining to the land, its crops, or the people who work the crops.

AGREED VALUATION: the value of a shipment agreed upon in exchange for a reduced liability.

AGRIBUSINESS: the activity of farming as a major force of the economy.

AIDED RECALL: a method to survey the impression made by an advertisement, in which an interviewer presents an advertisement or other aid to memory.

AIR CHECK: a permanent record of a broadcast, program, or commercial to determine the quality of production and delivery time or date.

AIR POCKET: noticeably extreme weakness in a specific stock.

AIR RIGHTS: the rights to utilize open space above a property, or conversely, the right to control the air space by preventing construction that will block out light and air.

AIRWAYS: air transportation companies; airline routes.

ALCOHOLS: products and by-products of chemical processes, notably ethyl (potable) alcohol and methyl (wood, poisonous) alcohol.

ALGORITHM: a series of logically consistent steps that outline a progression of actions which, if followed in order, will lead to the final result.

ALIAS: also known as, otherwise called.

ALIENATION: the transfer from one person to another.

ALIEN COMPANY: an incorporated company formed and operating under the regulations of a foreign nation.

ALIMONY: periodic payments, made under a court order, for support of a divorced or separated spouse.

ALIQUOT: a part of the whole, a subdivision or unit of the entire.

ALKALI: caustic; principally caustic soda, lime, or caustic potash.

ALKYD: synthetic resin, principally used as a paint base.

ALLEGATION: a statement, often sworn, accusing another or others of damaging or criminal act or acts.

ALLOCATION: assigning one or more items of cost or revenue to one or more segments of an organization according to benefits received, responsibilities, or other logical measure of use.

ALLONGE: a paper on which an endorsement is written, attached to, and made part of a promissory note.

ALLOTMENT: a portion set aside, referring at times to a portion of a seller's merchandise set aside for a buyer under scarcity conditions.

ALLOWANCE: in the settlement of a debt, a deduction permitted by the seller for damage or shortage, but not discount.

ALLOWANCE FOR BAD DEBTS: evaluation account; recording the estimated amount of receivables that will ultimately prove uncollectible.

ALLOWANCE FOR DEPRECIATION: evaluation account; reflecting the gradual loss of usefulness of a fixed asset.

ALLOWED TIME: for incentive workers, time set aside for tool care, fatigue, and personal needs.

ALPHANUMERIC: pertaining to or describing characters that may be letters of the alphabet, numerals, or symbols.

ALTERED CHECK: a check on which the date, payee, or amount has been changed or erased.

ALTERNATE SPONSORSHIP: two sponsors sharing a program.

ALTERNATIVE RATE: in transportation, the lower of two or more rates applicable to the same shipment.

AMALGAMATION: a merger.

AMENDMENT: a change or addition after the approval of a document.

AMENITIES: things that are desirable or enjoyable rather than necessary; in employment terms, amenities could include an extra vacation or a luxury office.

AMICUS CURIAE: literally, a friend of the court; for example, a lawyer who gives information on points of law on which the judge is doubtful (Latin).

AMORTIZATION: a gradual and

systematic apportioning of an amount over a period of time.

AMORTIZED COST: the original cost of an asset less amounts written off as expenses or losses.

AMPLITUDE: the distance from the highest to the lowest points of a curve.

ANACHRONISM: the misplacement in time of an event or custom.

ANALOG COMPUTER: a computer which uses physical quantities, usually voltages, to represent values.

ANALYSIS: the examination and division of anything into its major parts.

ANALYST, PROGRAMMER: an individual possessing talent in creating a set of instructions for a computer, in addition to analysis of problems, systems, and specific specialties as requested.

ANALYTICAL AUDITING: an audit technique based upon an appraisal of an organization's systems of internal control and accounting, that relies on a system of flow charting and limited testing of transactions.

ANARCHISM: a concept that formal government is unnecessary and wrong in purpose; the elimination of ownership of private property by a coercive government.

ANCILLARY: auxiliary, subsidiary.

ANIMUS QUO: the intention with which (Latin).

ANNEX: to join a smaller or subordinate thing to a larger or more dominant thing.

ANNEXATION: permanently affixing, such as a city increasing its size by adding additional land in its jurisdiction.

ANNOTATE: to make marginal notes.

ANNUAL EARNINGS: the total of all monies received during a year.

ANNUAL REPORT: a printed report to stockholders incorporating various financial statements for the company's latest fiscal year usually with comparisons to previous periods and prospects for the future.

ANNUAL RETURN: the rate of return on the purchase price of a security.

ANNUAL WAGE: a guaranteed minimum income and/or hours total during a year.

ANNUAL WAGE PLAN: an approach designed to give continuous income to workers throughout the year.

ANNUITY: payments to an insured based upon an annual rate.

ANNUITY PERIOD: the period after retirement during which an annuitant receives payments.

ANNUL: to make void.

ANOMALY: a feature that does not conform to the regular order.

ANONYMITY: without name.

ANTE: before (Latin).

ANTEDATE: to put a date on a document which is earlier than the date on which it was actually issued.

ANTICIPATION: payment in advance of due date, usually to reduce interest charges.

ANTICIPATORY BREACH: the informing of the seller by a buyer before closing of title that the buyer plans to terminate any involvement in the transaction.

ANTIPROTECTIONISTS: those who oppose a protective tariff.

ANTITRUST: referring to federal laws limiting competition through acquisitions, mergers, collusive pricing, and other similar actions that may inhibit public choice and bargaining power.

AON: all or none, used to identify a lot of goods which cannot be broken.

APHORISM: saying, adage.

A POSTERIORI: from the effect to the cause (Latin).

APPEAL: the motivation from which a sales pitch is directed with the expectation that the potential customer will become favorably disposed toward the product or service.

APPEALS SUBSYSTEM: the consciously designed process in the glacier theory which enables grievances of managers and workers to be adjudicated before an elected body of representatives.

APPELLANT: one who appeals, as from a judicial decision.

APPELLATE COURTS: courts that hear appeals from the general trial court level.

APPELLEE: the individual or stated party in a cause against whom an appeal is made.

APPLICATION: the problem or business situation in relation to which a computer is used.

APPLIED ECONOMICS: using economic theory to assist in the solving of economic problems (See positive economics).

APPLIED OVERHEAD: overhead costs that have been allocated to a particular product or activity.

APPLIED RESEARCH: research concerned with solving practical problems.

APPORTION: to assign a cost factor to a person, unit, product, or order.

APPORTIONMENT: division into parts according to some guide or formula.

APPRAISAL: a valuation made by qualified experts.

APPRAISE: to determine the cost, quality, or value of an item.

APPRECIATION: increase in value.

APPRENTICE: a person who has contracted to work for an employer for a fixed period of time in order to learn a skill and gain practical experience.

APPROPRIATED EXPENDITURES: purchases made by a governmental agency which are covered by appropriations.

APPROPRIATION: a sum of money approved for spending for a specific purpose.

APPURTENANCES: expense-allowed luxuries pertaining to a style of living of an employee or office holder.

A PRIORI: from the cause to the effect (Latin).

APRON TRACK: a railroad track built for the transfer of freight between a ship and railcar.

ARBITRAGE: a simultaneous purchase and sale of identical commodities, foreign currencies, or securities in different markets in order to profit from price differences.

ARBITRAGEUR: an arbitrage dealer.

ARBITRATION: a method of settling disputes out of court through the intervention of a third party (or parties) whose decision is final and binding.

ARBITRON: an immediate technique for acquiring television program measurements by means of an electronic apparatus placed in multiple homes and connected to a central measurement unit.

ARITHMETIC ELEMENT: the portion of the computer system where all calculations take place.

ARITHMETIC MEAN: the value obtained by adding all the individual values of a series of items and dividing by the number of items.

ARTICLES OF AGREEMENT: any contract between two or more people that is reduced to a written instrument.

ARTICLES OF ASSOCIATION: any instrument that is similar to a corporate certificate, usually used with nonstock corporations.

ARRAIGN: legally, to call an accused person to the bar to plead to the charge made against him.

ARRAY: a listing of items by size, either from the smallest to the largest or largest to the smallest.

ARREARS: interest or dividends that were not paid when due.

ARROGATE: to assign.

ARSON: illegally setting a fire to destroy property.

ARTICLES OF INCORPORATION: a paper drawn up for the formation of a corporation, including the name, the purpose, and the location, as well as any other items that are considered necessary.

ARTICULATE: to join.

AS IS: a condition of sale under which the buyer accepts the property in the exact condition existing at the time of the sale.

ASKING PRICE: the price asked for goods, frequently shares of stock.

ASSAY: to estimate the value of something, usually of mineral ore by test.

ASSEMBLY LANGUAGE: machine-oriented language.

ASSEMBLY-LINE PRODUCTION: procedure used in mass-production industry, where the materials and parts are conveyed on mechanical belts and the worker performs the appropriate task.

ASSESSED VALUATION: value, usually of real estate, determined by assessors for tax purposes.

ASSESSMENT: evaluation of property for tax purposes; a levy on members of some group, such as stockholders or club members, for the purpose of raising additional capital.

ASSESSMENT ROLL: the list of taxable persons and property in a particular jurisdiction compiled by the official assessors.

ASSESSOR: one who estimates values for tax purposes.

ASSET: property, cash, or other tangible or intangible items of value owned by someone.

ASSET-POOR: the condition of being short of money because of owning an excess of properties that don't produce income.

ASSETS, ACCRUED: assets arising from revenues earned but not yet due.

ASSETS, CURRENT: assets that are readily convertible into cash without substantial loss.

ASSETS, DEFERRED: assets that are not readily convertible into cash or subject to current settlement.

ASSETS, FIXED: assets of a long-term character which are intended to be held or used on a continued basis, such as land, buildings, machinery, furniture, and other equipment.

ASSETS, LIQUID: those assets, generally current assets, which may be quickly turned into cash.

ASSET TURNOVER: the ratio of sales to total assets available.

ASSIGNED RISK: a risk that underwriters do not wish to insure but must because of state law or regulation.

ASSIGNEE: one to whom an assignment is granted.

ASSIGNMENT: the transfer of property to another by written agreement.

ASSIGNOR: an individual making an assignment.

ASSIMILATION: the completed distribution of new shares of securities to the public by the issue's underwriters and syndicate members.

ASSOCIATE: one who works in the same organization or on the same project as another; part of a title.

ASSUMED LIABILITY: an obligation for payment accepted by another person.

ASSUMPSIT: a type of legal action at common law for money damages resulting from a breach of contract.

ASSUMPTION: bank loan payments accepted by a party other than the original maker.

ASSUMPTION OF MORTGAGE: in taking title to a property, the assumption of personal liability for an existing mortgage.

ASSURANCE: a synonym for insurance.

ASTERISK: a star (*) often used to call attention to a footnote.

ASYMMETRIC: not symmetrical.

ATOMISTIC ECONOMY: characterized by the competition of small independent manufacturers in each industry.

AT OR BETTER: in a purchase order for securities, to buy at the price specified or at a lower price; in a selling request, to sell at the price given or at a higher price.

AT SIGHT: a term used in the body of negotiable instruments indicating that payment is due upon presentation or demand.

ATTACHED ACCOUNT: an account against which a court order has been issued, permitting disbursement of the balance only with the consent of the court.

ATTACHMENT: a seizure of property by judicial process while a court action is pending.

ATTEST: legally to aver the truth of another's statement.

ATTESTATION CLAUSE: a clause in an instrument or writing stating that the persons therein named have affixed their names as witnesses.

AT THE MARKET: at the best price obtainable at the time an order to buy or sell is executed.

ATTORN: to accept and acknowledge a new landlord, following foreclosure of a trust deed on the fee title, for instance.

ATTORNEY-IN-FACT: a person holding a power of attorney as an agent for another person.

ATTRITION: a reduction through natural causes.

AUCTIONEER: one who conducts a sale by bids in which the highest bidder purchases the offering.

AUDIMETER: an electromechanical unit used by A. C. Nielsen Company to record which radio and television stations receivers are tuned to in sample homes to give a national average.

AUDIT: to examine and check accounts or claims; to attend a college class or classes as a listener receiving no credits.

AUDITING PROCEDURES: the steps carried out by an auditor in applying auditing techniques to particular circumstances.

AUDITING STANDARDS: standards that have evolved against which the appropriateness of auditing procedures are measured in relation to the desired objectives of the audit.

AUDITING TECHNIQUES: the methods of obtaining audit evidence.

AUDITOR: one who performs an audit.

AUDITOR'S CERTIFICATE: a synonym for auditor's report.

AUDITOR'S REPORT: formal expression of the auditor's opinion of whether the financial statements of an organization present fairly its financial position in accordance with generally accepted accounting principles.

AUDIT TRAIL: the means by which the processing of data can be traced through the processing cycle.

AUTARCHY: self-sufficiency in an economic sense.

AUTHENTICATION: a certification that the document authenticated is genuine or a true copy of the original.

AUTHORITY TO PURCHASE: used in Far Eastern trade, a substitute for a commercial letter of credit.

AUTHORIZATION: preapproval or an act or expenditure.

AUTHORIZED CAPITAL: the number and par value, if any, of shares of each class of the capital stock that a corporation can issue in accordance with its documents of incorporation.

AUTHORIZED DEALER: a middleman who has received a franchise to represent or sell a manufacturer's products.

AUTHORIZED STOCK: the maximum number of shares that a company may issue according to its articles of incorporation.

AUTOCRACY: an organizational structure in which one person has power over all others in the organization.

AUTOCRAT: a person who exercises power over all others in an organization.

AUTO DIN: a telephone transmitter-receiver that allows remote transactions with a centralized main computer over telephone lines.

AUTOGESTION: organization and management by committee of workers, in factories, farms, etc.

AUTOMATED: involving the complete performance of a complex mechanical act without human intervention during the process.

AUTOMATIC FISCAL STABILIZERS: nondiscretionary approaches that automatically cushion recession by assisting in creating a budget deficit and curb inflation by helping to create a budget surplus.

AUTOMATIC PROGRESSIONS: automatic pay increases at set time intervals until a maximum rate for the job is reached.

AUTOMATIC STABILIZER: a tool

of economics used to compensate for shifts in the business cycle without the involvement of a government official.

AUTONOMOUS CONSUMPTION: consumption independent of income.

AUTONOMOUS TRANSACTIONS: the transactions among nations that arise from factors unreleated to the balance of payments as such.

AVAIL: the amount remaining following a discount or expense deduction.

AVERAGE COST: the sum of all output costs divided by the quantity of production.

AVERAGE DAILY BALANCE: the average amount of money that a customer keeps on deposit.

AVERAGE HAUL: the average distance in miles one ton is moved.

AVERAGE LOAD: the average number of tons of freight per loaded vehicle.

AVERAGING: a benefit allowing individuals to average taxable income for four preceding years over a five-year period.

AVULSION: any shift of land from one property to another caused by forces of nature without change in ownership.

B

BABY BOND: a US government bond of small denomination, such as $25 face value.

BACKDATING: placing on a statement a date prior to the date on which it was drawn up.

BACKDOOR FINANCING: the practice enabling a government agency to borrow from the US Treasury instead of relying on congressional appropriations.

BACKER: an individual who provides financial support for a project or person.

BACK FREIGHT: freight payable when delivery is not taken within a reasonable period at the discharge point.

BACKGROUND PROCESSING: the automatic execution of lower priority computer programs when higher priority programs are not using system resources.

BACKING UP: a second press run, printing the reverse side of a page after the front has been completed.

BACKLOG: unfilled orders.

BACK ORDER: the unfilled portion of an original order for goods or services.

BACK PAY: wages due for past services.

BACK SPREAD: a condition in which the price for identical items in two markets is less than the normal difference.

BACKSTAMP: to make an impression with a postmarking device on the back of a piece of mail, indicating date of receipt/dispatch or that the item was improperly sent.

BACK-TO-BACK: describing adjacent time slots for programs or commercials.

BACK-TO-WORK MOVEMENT: a return of strikers to their jobs before their union has declared the strike to be ended.

BACKUP SYSTEM: systems that contain error detection and correction techniques.

BACKWARD INTEGRATION: expansion activity in which facilities that provide parts, supplies, or raw materials are accumulated.

BAD DEBT: an uncollectible receivable.

BAD DEBTS RECOVERED: amounts collected after being written off as bad debts.

BAD DELIVERY: a delivered item not conforming to the original terms of agreement; an improperly prepared or transferred security or certificate.

BAIL: the security given for the release of a prisoner from custody.

BAILEE: the person to whom goods are committed in trust.

BAILIFF: a court official who is responsible for committed prisoners during a trial, or a sheriff's deputy who serves warrants or other court papers.

BAILMENT: a property or chattel pledged as bail.

BAILOR: one who delivers goods to another in trust for some particular purpose.

BAILOUT: utilizing corporate monies to provide to shareholders payments that are taxable at desirable capital gains rates.

BAIT ADVERTISING: advertising exceptional prices or terms of a specified product to attract prospects to a store.

BALANCE: the difference between total debits and total credits in an account.

BALANCED BUDGET: a condition or system in which receipts attributable to a particular period equal or exceed expenditures attributable to that period.

BALANCED ECONOMY: a condition of national finances in which imports and exports are equal.

BALANCE DUE: the total amount needed to equalize the debt and credit sum of an account; the amount owed.

BALANCE OF PAYMENTS: the net result of a nation's transactions with the outside world over a particular period of time.

BALANCE OF POWER: the excess of the greater potential force of two adversaries over the lesser.

BALANCE OF TRADE: a statement of the value of merchandise exports and imports.

BALANCE SHEET: an itemized statement listing the total assets and the total liabilities of a given business to portray its net worth at a given moment in time.

BALANCING: the act of bringing two sets of related figures into agreement.

BALLAST: a cargo of much weight and no merchandise value placed in the hold of a ship to decrease its motion from wave action.

BALLOON NOTE: a note calling for periodic payments not large enough to pay off the note in full.

BALLOONING: price manipulation used to send prices beyond safe or real values.

BALTIMORE METHOD: a formula for appraising corner lots in which the lot is determined to be worth the total value of the inside lots on each of its sides.

BANK ACCEPTANCE: a draft drawn on a bank and accepted by the bank.

BANK ACCOMMODATION: a short-term bank loan to a customer, either on the individual's own note or on the endorsement of another's note owed to the individual.

BANK CALL: the demand made upon a bank by a supervising authority for a sworn statement of the bank's condition of a certain date.

BANK CONFIRMATION: a statement an auditor obtains from a client's bank detailing the position of the client's balances, loans, and other matters as of a particular date.

BANK DEBITS: the sum total of all debits drawn against deposited funds of individual, partnership, corporations, and other legal entities.

BANK DRAFT: a check drawn by a bank against funds deposited to its account in another bank.

BANK EXAMINER: a person who, as the representative of a federal or state bank supervisory authority, examines the banks under its jurisdiction.

BANKING POWER: the strength of investing possessed by a bank, as determined by the bank's excess reserves.

BANK NOTE: a promissory note released by an authorized bank which is payable on demand to the bearer and can be used as cash.

BANK POST REMITTANCE: the conversion into cash or a money form of a foreign bill of exchange and subsequent mailing to the payee.

BANK RATE: the rate of discount established by the national bank of a country for the rediscounting of eligible paper.

BANK RECONCILIATION: a statement accounting for the difference between a bank balance per the bank statement and the balance for the account as reflected in the books of the bank's customer.

BANKRUPTCY: a state of conditions in which the financial position of an individual, corporation, or other legal entity is such as to cause them to be actually or legally unable to pay their debts.

BANK SERVICES: the services customarily rendered by banks, such as checking, savings, loans, discounts, and collections.

BANK STATEMENT: a statement of deposits, withdrawals, and balances within a given period rendered by a bank to a depositor.

BANK-WIRE SYSTEM: a private, computerized message system that links about 250 banks in about 75 cities, used to transmit funds, and transfer information, and also relay other data.

BARGAIN BASEMENT: the below-ground-level floor of a store, where special prices are offered on merchandise.

BARGAIN COUNTER: describing stocks offered for sale at prices below their intrinsic value.

BARGAIN HUNTER: an individual who seeks out items at the lowest possible price.

BARGAINING AGENT: a union designated by legislation as the exclusive representative of all employees in a particular bargaining unit for the purpose of collective bargaining.

BARGAINING, INDIVIDUAL: a situation in which each worker individually bargains with management, as distinguished from collective bargaining.

BARGAINING RIGHT: the legal rights of workers to bargain collectively with their employers; the right of a specific union to represent its members in collective bargaining.

BARGAINING UNIT: a group of workers who have been determined under legislation as appropriate for purposes of collective bargaining.

BARGAIN STORE: a store that sells merchandise at a submarket price.

BAR GRAPHS: a graph in which quantities are represented by vertical or horizontal bars of length proportional to the quantities.

BAROMETERS: the business indexes that are used to evaluate the condition of a market or economy.

BARRATRY: the misdemeanor of habitually starting quarrels or nuisance litigation.

BARREN MONEY: currency that does not earn interest or other forms of income.

BARRISTER: an attorney admitted to plead at the bar in British courts of law.

BARTER: an exchange of goods or services for other goods or services rather than for cash.

BASE: a reference value; the number of characters of use in the digital positions of a numbering system; a number that is multiplied by itself.

BASE DATE: the period upon which a price index number of any given year is calculated.

BASE PAY RATE: wages paid, exclusive of overtime, premiums, and bonuses.

BASE PERIOD: an extent of time used as a reference period in presenting statistical data.

BASIC CROPS: clearly identified farm items subject to government price support.

BASIC STOCK: merchandise that is in constant demand, thus requiring perpetual inventory throughout the year.

BASIC YIELD: the return per year which would be produced by an investment that carried no risk of default.

BASING POINT: a geographical point from which uniform prices are figured.

BASIS: the grade, weight, size, or other specification accepted as standard and from which deviations are figured.

BASIS BOOK: a book of tables used to convert bond prices expressed in terms of yield to maturity (a rate) into the price of the bond in dollars.

BASKET PURCHASE: the purchase of a group of assets for one price.

BATCH: a number of records or documents considered as a single unit for the purpose of data processing.

BATCH PROCESSING: a mode of operating a computer facility in which jobs are processed sequentially, one at a time.

BATTEN: a wood strip attached to a structure to reinforce it.

BATTERY OF TESTS: a group of tests used in screening and testing.

BAUD: a speed unit in data processing equal to one binary digit per second.

BEAR: one who believes that prices will fall and sells in anticipation of that event.

BEARER: one in possession of a demand note or check payable to the possessor.

BEARER SECURITY: a security not registered in the name of a particular owner.

BEAR HUG: an unnegotiated corporate takeover proposal, made privately or publicly to directors.

BEARISH: a market in which the prevailing trend of prices is downward; an attitude that prices are about to fall.

BEAR MARKET: a ceiling stock market.

BEAT DOWN: slang, to bargain to lower the cost of an item.

BEHAVIOR MODIFICATION: the increase of desired behavioral patterns or the decrease of undesirable behavior, brought about by utilizing rewards and/or punishments.

BELOW PAR: at a discount; less than face amount.

BELOW THE LINE: an item of revenue or expense of an unusual character, usually used in connection with large amounts.

BELOW WAGE PLAN: a type of contract exempt from the wage-and-hour law.

BELT LINE: a short railroad, usually found moving within or around a city.

BENCHMARK: a measurement by which others are compared.

BENCH SCALE PRODUCTION: the manufacture of a small number of units before the development of normal production techniques.

BENEFICIAL OWNER: the real owner of something.

BENEFICIARY: one who receives benefits, profits, or advantages.

BENEFIT: the gain or advantage received by an individual; the amount of indemnity to be regularly paid; that which fulfills a need.

BENEFIT-BASED PENSION PLAN: a plan under which the pension benefits are determined in accordance with years of service and amounts earned by the employee.

BENEFIT PRINCIPLE OF TAXATION: the rationale for taxation based on the benefits received from the government by the taxpayer.

BENEVOLENT ASSOCIATION: voluntary groups formed not for profit, but to render financial or other aid to their members.

BEQUEATH: to devise or give in a last will and testament.

BEQUEST: a gift of personal property by will; to be distinguished from devise.

BETTER BUSINESS BUREAU: a voluntary agency of business executives created to improve business practices and to define fair standards and ethics in the conduct of business activity.

BETTERMENT: an improvement made to property that increases its value more than would ordinary repair or maintenance work.

BIAS: an attitude that may influence an individual's feeling, resulting in a leaning toward or away from a particular idea, thing, or person.

BID: the price a prospective buyer offers for a stock, bond, or other asset.

BID AND ASKED: "bid" is the quotation of a prospective buyer for the purchase; "asked" is the quotation of a seller for the sale of a trading unit or other specified amount of security.

BIDDING UP: the activity of raising the price bid for a security, in fear of failing to have an order executed before an upswing begins.

BIG BOARD: a nickname for the New York Stock Exchange.

BIG EIGHT: the eight largest public accounting firms.

BIGELOW PLAN: a wage-incentive approach providing for a step bonus between the minimum wage and standard wage.

BIG STEEL: the United States Steel Corporation.

BIG THREE: the three largest automobile manufacturers in the United States.

BIG-TICKET ITEMS: merchandise that is large in size and high in price.

BILATERAL CONTRACT: a contract in which a promise is given by both parties.

BILLBOARD: a poster panel in outdoor advertising; the opening routine of a broadcast program.

BILL CHECK: a payment system in which a debtor, on receipt of an invoice or statement, authorizes the creditor to obtain payment directly from the debtor's deposit account.

BILLED ESCROW: the amount of escrow payment that represents a total of the regular escrow payment plus arrears or minus prepaid escrow amounts.

BILLED PRINCIPAL: the amount of principal payment that represents a total of the regular escrow payment plus arrears or minus prepaid escrow amounts.

BILLED WEIGHT: the weight of a shipment shown on the freight bill, not necessarily the actual weight.

BILLER: a person trained in operation of bookkeeping or billing machines.

BILL OF ADVENTURE: a shipper's written statement that a shipment is the venture or property of another individual and that the shipper is responsible only for its delivery as consigned.

BILL OF CREDIT: an individual's written request to a bank asking for the delivery of money to the bearer on the credit or account of the writer; used as if it were a state's currency.

BILL OF EXCHANGE: an unconditional order in writing

requiring the person to whom it is addressed to pay a certain sum of money to, or to the order of, the bearer or any other specified person.

BILL OF LADING: a document executed by common carriers acknowledging the receipt of goods, and which serves as a document of title to the goods consigned.

BILL OF MATERIALS: a specification of the quantities of direct materials allowed for manufacturing a given quantity of output.

BILL OF PARTICULARS: legally, a statement in writing, made in the course of litigation, in which a party sets forth in detail the particulars of his cause of action.

BILL OF SALE: an instrument for conveying title to merchandise sold; an invoice.

BILL OF SIGHT: a temporary entry permit, authorized by a custom's official, for imported items, allowing the goods to be unloaded from a carrier to permit examination by a customs agent.

BIMETALLISM: the principle of using two metals, particularly gold and silver, as backing for currency.

BINARY: referring to the mathematical base of two, instead of the more familiar base of ten.

BIN CARD: an inventory card showing the actual quantity of goods in a bin or other receptacle or on a shelf.

BINDER: a sum of money tendered as a deposit on a transaction.

BIRD DOG: to seek data to assist in studying a firm's position and potential earnings; an individual paid to obtain business.

BIRTHRATE: the number of births per year per thousand population in a stated geographic area.

BIT: the smallest unit of computer information.

BLACK CAPITALISM: an attempt to increase business ownership among the blacks.

BLACK FRIDAY: September 24, 1969, the day of a business panic resulting from an attempt by financiers to corner the gold market.

BLACKING: during a union action, the refusal by employees to perform any work that they conclude will hurt their cause.

BLACKLIST: to place on a secret list of proscribed persons to whom employers will deny job opportunities.

BLACK MARKET: traffic in illegal, illegally obtained, or illegally sold merchandise.

BLACK MONEY: income that is not reported for tax purposes because of its illegal origin.

BLANK CHECK: a check which is signed by the maker but which does not have an amount filled in.

BLANK-CHECK BUYING: the practice of a retailer to place an open order with a supplier with requests to be made throughout the season as needed.

BLANKET AGREEMENT: a collective bargaining agreement based on an industry-wide negotiation or large geographic areas within an industry.

BLANKET BOND: a bond usually secured by a mortgage on a number of pieces of property, each of which may have other and prior mortgages.

BLANKET INJUNCTIONS: injunctions prohibiting future acts or violations that have not actually been committed in a case presently before the court.

BLANKET MORTGAGE: a mortgage covering all the property of a corporation and given to secure a single debt.

BLANKET ORDER: a preseason order to meet expected buyer demands.

BLANKET POLICY: an insurance policy that covers several different properties, shipments, or locations under one item, rather than under separate items.

BLIGHTED AREA: an area in a community or neighborhood which is about to become a slum.

BLIND ENTRY: a bookkeeping entry stating only the accounts and the amounts debited and credited, but not giving other data or accounting

factors essential to an accurate record.

BLISTER PACKAGING: a type of plastic packaging, permitting visual inspection of the merchandise.

BLOCKADE: the act of preventing commercial exchange with a country or port.

BLOCK BUSTING: the unethical real estate practice of creating fear by renting or selling units in a neighborhood to families of a religion or race different from that of the current residents.

BLOCKED ACCOUNTS: in times of war, the accounts, such as those of enemy nationals, on which payment is suspended by order of the President of the United States.

BLOCKED CURRENCY: currency which by force of law cannot be expatriated or exchanged for the currency of another country.

BLOCK TRADE: a transaction involving an unusually large number of shares.

BLOOD BATH: a horrendous loss suffered by investors when the stock market declines sharply.

BLUE-CHIP STOCKS: shares in well-established companies, normally with a long and satisfactory dividend record and all the attributes of a perfectly safe investment.

BLUE-COLLAR WORKERS: a term applied to production and maintenance workers, in contrast to office and professional personnel.

BLUE LAW: any state or local law restricting business activity on Sunday.

BLUE SKY: having no value, though offered for sale at a price.

BLUE-SKY LAW: a term for a law regulating the issue of securities.

BLURB: a brief but highly laudatory statement to be used in promotional activities.

BOARD: a standing committee of high rank or importance.

BOARD LOTS: the number of shares in a corporation which represents a regular trading unit as decided on by a stock exchange.

BOARD OF DIRECTORS: the group of persons elected by the stockholders to set policies, engage officers, and operate a corporation.

BOARD OF TRADE: business executives who operate a local commodities exchange or a chamber of commerce.

BOARD ROOM: a room for registered representatives and customers in a broker's office, where opening, high, low, and last prices of leading stocks are posted.

BOBTAIL: a small truck used for deliveries, or a trailerless tractor.

BOBTAIL STATEMENT: an abbreviated statement prepared for demand deposit accounts.

BOGEY: efforts by employees to restrict output by setting up an informal standard that the employees do not exceed; the standard of performance.

BOGUS: false, counterfeit, nonexistent, or fraudulent.

BOILER ROOM: the peddling of stocks, usually of doubtful value, over the telephone.

BOILER-ROOM TACTIC: selling of very speculative and often worthless securities through the use of high-pressured and misleading literature.

BONA FIDE: in good faith.

BONA VACENTIA: describing property of which there is no apparent owner or claimant.

BOND: a certificate of indebtedness, usually implying that assets have been pledged as security; an indemnity against loss caused by a third party.

BOND, BEARER: bonds whose proceeds (principal and interest) are payable to the bearer, that is, to whoever has physical possession.

BOND, CALLABLE: bonds that the issuing corporation or body may redeem before their maturity.

BOND, CONSOLIDATED: a debt instrument issued to take the place of two or more previously issued bonds.

BOND, CONVERTIBLE: bonds having the special provision for being converted into stock at a certain time and at a specified price.

BOND, COUPON: bonds to which are attached coupons representing the interest payments; as the interest becomes due, the coupons are clipped and presented for payment.

BOND, DEBENTURE: bonds that represent a company's funded debt, backed only by its credit and not secured by a pledge or mortgage of property.

BOND, DEFERRED: a debt instrument in which a due payment has been postponed until some future time.

BOND, INDEMNITY: a written instrument under seal by which the signer, usually together with his surety bondsman, guarantees to protect another against loss.

BOND, REGISTERED: a bond which is registered on the books of the issuing company in the name of the owner, and which can be transferred only when endorsed by the registered owner.

BOND, SURETY: a bond or guarantee usually given by a bonding company to answer for the debt, default, or miscarriage of another.

BOND DISCOUNT: the amount by which the selling price of a bond is less than its face value.

BOND FUND: in government accounting, a fund established to account for bond sale proceeds.

BONDED: referring to an employee on whom bond has been obtained.

BONDED GOODS: goods on which excise or customs duties must be paid.

BONDED WAREHOUSE: a warehouse in which goods are stored without excise or customs duties being paid until they are removed from the warehouse.

BONDHOLDER: the purchaser of a bond; a lender who receives a bond to document his loan.

BOND INDENTURE: a contract describing the interest and maturity date and other important terms under which bonds are issued.

BONDING COMPANY: an organization whose business is the forming of contracts of surety and the providing of bonds.

BOND PREMIUM: the amount by which the selling price of a bond exceeds its face value.

BOND RATING: appraising and rating by a recognized financial organization, such as Moody's Investors Service; the worth of a bond as a sound investment.

BONDSMAN: one who posts bond for another.

BONIFICATION: the return of a tax paid but later found to be not due.

BONUS: extra compensation because of high productivity or contractual agreement, or similar reason.

BOODLE: money received through corruption in public activities.

BOOK DEBT: a synonym for an account payable or receivable, as the case might be.

BOOK INVENTORY: inventory arrived at by adding the units and the cost of incoming goods to previous inventory figures and subtracting the units and cost of outgoing goods.

BOOKKEEPER: person who makes entries on the general ledger of a business.

BOOKKEEPING: the classification and recording of business transactions in terms of money.

BOOK OF ORIGINAL ENTRY: a book of account in which transactions are recorded for the first time.

BOOK PROFIT: an unrealized profit.

BOOK VALUE: the amount at which an item appears in the accounting records or on financial statements.

BOOM: a period of rapidly rising prices, characterized by substantial excess of demand for goods and services, full employment, and sharply increasing demand.

BOOMERANG: an international program to minimize the practice of goods dumping by returning such items, duty free and exempt of quantity restrictions.

BOONDOGGLING: a term used to criticize any of the government's programs for being wasteful and unproductive.

BOOT: something given in addition.

BOOTLEGGING: illegal movement of items, which themselves may or may not be prohibited by law, in order to avoid payment of taxes on such items.

BOOTSTRAP: a technique designed to bring about a desired state by internally generated means; a method for getting the first few instructions into memory when a routine is initially loaded.

BOROUGH: a political subdivision of a city, having authority over certain local matters.

BORROWER: one who borrows cash or buys something on time.

BOTTLENECK INFLATION: a rise in the price level with an increase in aggregate demand or in the money supply.

BOTTOM LINE: a phrase indicating the final result, such as the net profit after taxes.

BOTTOM OUT: as market prices, to sink to a low level and remain there for a while, establishing a new base before rising.

BOTTOMRY: a loan secured by a lien on a vessel.

BOUNDED DISCRETION: the limits imposed on a manager for making decisions that are conditioned by social norms, rules, and organizational policies.

BOUNDED RATIONALITY: the principle that a decision maker doesn't attempt to discover optimum solutions.

BOUNTY: a payment offered for performing an act well, such as completing a structure by a given date.

BOURGEOISIE: the middle-class group in society.

BOURSE: a European security or commodity exchange.

BOXCAR: an enclosed freight car.

BOYCOTT: an organized movement not to purchase from a specific store or source and the attempt to prevent others from doing so.

BRACING: the process of supporting contents in a package to prevent damage through movement and/or to distribute the weight on all sides of the container.

BRAIN: a shrewd businessman; an electronic computer.

BRAINSTORMING: a sudden inspiration, idea, or plan.

BRANCH: a set of instructions in a program consisting of a series of changes from the normal sequence of steps.

BRANCH BANKING: any banking system where there are few parent institutions, each having branches operating over a large geographic area.

BRAND AWARENESS: a buyer's realization of the existence and availability of a branded product.

BRAND FRANCHISE: describing the extent to which a brand has attracted a substantial and loyal following.

BRAND LEADER: an item that is looked on as number one in the field, or is marketed with that assumption.

BRAND LOYALTY: the strength of a buyer's preference for a particular brand, which suggests a refusal to purchase a substitute.

BRAND NAME: any combination of letters or words used by one manufacturer or supplier to distinguish his goods and services from those of other companies.

BRAND RECOGNITION: the perception by buyers, when confronted with a product, that they have been exposed previously to that brand name.

BRASS: key executives in a business.

BREACH OF CONTRACT: not fulfilling one's part in an agreement; breaking a promise.

BREAD: money.

BREAK: a sudden, steep, broad decline of prices.

BREAKAGE: an allowance for losses resulting from breakage of merchandise.

BREAKDOWN: an analysis.

BREAK-EVEN POINT: point in time where revenue equals expenses.

BREAKING BULK: the practice of some middlemen to take the large economical shipment from a manufacturer and divide it into small units for sale at greater profit; the point when cargo is first unloaded.

BREAKUP VALUE: the net amount that would be realized upon the winding up of a business.

BRIBE: something of value offered to another for an illegal or improper favor.

BRIDGE FINANCING: an interim loan made for a short period during which the borrower is arranging long-term financing.

BRIEF: a legal document submitted in support of one side of a court case.

BROAD-FORM INSURANCE: a term generally understood to describe the combination of, at a special discount, various real and personal property coverages and comprehensive personal liability.

BROAD MARKET: describing a time when there is a considerable volume of buying and selling in stocks and bonds.

BROAD TAPE: the Dow Jones news ticker tape displayed in brokerage houses as a large rectangular screen with lines of copy rolling upward.

BROCHURE: a well-printed booklet or folder, the good appearance of which adds institutional value to its message.

BROKEN LOT: goods offered for sale in smaller numbers than usually constitute the unit of sale.

BROKER: generally an agent who acts for both parties to a transaction.

BROKERAGE FEES: the fees, usually a commission, charged by a broker.

BROKER'S LOAN: a loan made to a stock broker and secured by stock exchange collateral.

BROKER'S MARKET: a condition when the investing public is generally inactive at the same time that brokers are trading quite heavily with their own accounts.

BROKER'S TICKET: a written statement of all buy and sell orders executed by a broker.

BROOM CLEAN: in real estate language, used to describe the condition of a building turned over to a buyer or tenant with the floors swept and completely free of debris.

BROTHERHOOD: a union, federation, guild, or association.

BROWN GOODS: a retailer's term given to television sets and radios.

BUDGET: an estimate of future transactions.

BUDGET DEFICIT: an excess of expenses over revenues.

BUDGET LOAN: a mortgage loan that requires a proportionate amount of tax, insurance, and assessment to be held in escrow, in addition to interest and principal payments.

BUDGET SURPLUS: an excess of revenues over expenditures.

BUFFER: a mechanism that permits the temporary excess supply of one instant to offset the temporary shortage of another instant.

BUFFER STOCK: the merchandise kept on hand to prevent a shortage resulting from an unexpected increase in demand for the items.

BUILDING PERMIT: a permit granted by a local government enabling the holder to construct or renovate a building.

BUILT-IN STABILIZERS: countercyclical factors that automatically come into play when the business cycle rises or falls, such as income tax.

BULGE: a rapid advance in prices.

BULK: unpackaged; in large quantities.

BULK CARGO: cargo that consists entirely of one commodity.

BULK DENSITY: the weight of a unit of volume of a substance, expressed in pounds per cubic foot or other equivalent units.

BULK DISCOUNT: a reduced charge for quantity or multiple purchases.

BULK FREIGHT: liquid or dry freight not carried in packages or individual containers and usually shipped in flowable or fungible form.

BULKHEAD: a cargo-restraining separation in a vehicle.

BULK MAIL: second-, third-, and fourth-class mail, including parcel post, ordinary papers, and circulars.

BULK SALES: substantial quantities of a publication bought for redistribution.

BULK ZONING: division of an area by the size and number of buildings, their shape, and other characteristics.

BULL: one who trades in securities or commodities in such a way as to be affected favorably by rising prices.

BULLETIN BOARD: wall space for the display of messages or information

BULLING THE MARKET: speculator trading purporting to force the level of prices upward.

BULLION: bars of precious metal, such as gold or silver.

BULLISH: a market in which the prevailing trend of prices is upward; an attitude that prices are about to rise.

BULL MARKET: an advancing stock market.

BUMPING: in labor language, the practice under which one worker is allowed to replace another worker in a job because the former has greater seniority.

BUNCO GAME: one of a variety of methods of swindling.

BURDENED VESSEL: a vessel not having the right of way which is required to yield to another ship.

BUREAUCRACY: the concentration of authority in administrative groups; a written statement of the procedures and regulations in an organizational structure.

BURSAR: school official responsible for collection of receipts.

BUSHEL: a measure of capacity (approximately 1 1/4 cubic feet) used in commodities.

BUSINESS: the buying and selling of goods and services; the activity of an individual, partnership, or organization involving production, commerce, and/or service; one's occupation or employment.

BUSINESS AGENT: an elected or appointed representative of one or more local unions, with responsibility for negotiating contracts, administering existing contracts, and adjusting grievances.

BUSINESS BAROMETER: a weighted average of a variety of economic indicators.

BUSINESS CYCLE: the progression of prosperity, recession, depression, and recovery.

BUSINESS DAYS: all days other than Saturday, Sunday, and legal holidays.

BUSINESS INTERRUPTION INSURANCE: insurance against continuing expenses or loss of earnings resulting from interruption of business.

BUSINESS LOGISTICS: a set of activities dealing with the control of incoming and outgoing materials.

BUSINESS MANAGER: the individual responsible for overseeing a firm department, or other unit, to ensure smooth operations; a business agent.

BUSINESS TRANSFER PAYMENTS: transfers from business to persons which are charges against business product but for which no services are rendered currently.

BUSINESS TRUST: an unincorporated business organization in which title to the property is given to trustees to hold, manage, or sell; a Massachusetts trust or common law trust.

BUST: a drop in business activity to an exceptionally low level.

BUTTERFLY SPREAD: the simultaneous purchase or sale of three futures contracts in the same or different markets.

BUYER: in retailing, an executive responsible for purchasing and other duties of departmental management.

BUYERS' MARKET: when supply exceeds demand.

BUYER'S MONOPOLOY: a market situation characterized by many sellers and one buyer.

BUYERS' SURPLUS: the difference between what a buyer actually has paid for a good and what he would have been willing to pay.

BUYING BY SPECIFICATIONS: submission of specific requests for delivery rather than purchasing standard merchandise available from the manufacturer.

BUYING IN: a condition in which a seller does not hand over his securities at the expected time, so the purchaser obtains shares wherever he can find them.

BUYING LONG: buying stocks, bonds, or commodities outright with the expectation of holding them for a rise in price and then selling.

BUYING OFF THE PEG: the purchase of ready-to-wear merchandise, to be taken home or delivered immediately, thus involving no adjustments or alterations.

BUYING ON BALANCE: condition in which a stock broker's orders to buy exceed his or her cumulative orders to sell.

BUYING ON MARGIN: condition in which items are bought without the purchaser paying the whole price immediately; margin refers to the proportion of down payment made by the purchaser.

BUYING POWER: in margin securities accounts, the total dollar volume of new purchases the broker will authorize without a further increase of the investor's balance.

BUY OUT: to purchase all the assets, stock, and so on, of an ongoing organization; to purchase the interests in a firm that is owned by another.

BY-BIDDER: a person who makes fictitious bids at an auction, on behalf of the owner or seller of the items, to obtain a higher price.

BYLAWS: the rules and regulations adopted by an organization to regulate its internal operations.

BYPRODUCT: a marketable product of lesser importance produced incidentally with a major product.

C

CABINET CROWD: the section of the bond trading unit of the New York Stock Exchange which handles trading in inactive bonds.

CABLE ADDRESS: a coined code word of ten or less letters which serves as a complete name and address for cablegrams.

CABLE TRANSFER: the transfer of funds in a foreign country through instructions sent by cable.

CADASTRE: an inventory of the appraised value of real estate which is used for the purposes of apportioning taxes in the district.

CAESAR MANAGEMENT: a demanding, autocratic, power-oriented leadership.

CALCULATING MACHINES: manual, electric, or electronic machines usable for multiplication, division, and simple arithmetic problems.

CALCULATOR: a device that performs arithmetic operations based on data and instructions.

CALENDAR SPREADING: the simultaneous purchase and sale of options within the same class having different expiration dates.

CALL: a transferable option to buy a specific number of shares of a particular stock at a stated price at any time during a stated period.

CALLABLE: of bonds, giving to the issuer the privilege of repayment at prices and times stated in the indenture at time of issue.

CALLBACK: the technique used by a sales representative on a second or subsequent effort to induce a potential customer to buy.

CALL-BACK PAY: premium wage to an employee who has been asked to return to work after completing his or her regular work shift.

CALL COMPENSATION: guaranteed monies for a worker who reports for assignment and is informed that there is no work for him or her.

CALL CREDIT: credit given for the price of an item when merchandise is picked up from a customer and returned to the store.

CALLIGRAPHY: artistic writing of letters, numerals and associated shapes.

CALL LOAN: a loan payable on request.

CALL MONEY: brokers' demand loans to customers secured by collateral.

CALL OF MORE: the right to call again for the same amount of goods previously bought.

CALL PRICE: the price at which a corporation or other obligor is permitted to redeem securities containing call provisions.

CALL PURCHASE: the buying of commodities when the seller has some option of pricing at a later date.

CALL STATION: an area at which a pickup and delivery service is available, although there are no dock or warehouse facilities.

CALL TRANSFER: relocating a call to another person inside or outside a telephone system without using an operator.

CAMBIST: a specialist in foreign exchange or a publication tabulating rates of foreign exchange and associated regulations.

CAMPAIGN: a marketing plan; advertisements of a single related series appearing in a planned program.

CAMP-ON-BUSY: a system that allows a telephone operator to inform you that another call is coming in while you are using your phone.

CANCELED CHECK: a check that has been honored by the bank on which it was drawn and on which evidence of payment is stamped or otherwise indicated.

CANCELLATION: the annulment or rendering void of any instrument upon payment; the termination of an insurance policy or bond before its expiration.

CANNED PRESENTATION: a prewritten and usually memorized presentation by a sales representative.

CANVAS: to call upon individuals, personally or by phone for the purpose of conducting fact or opinion polls; selling merchandise or service; survey.

CAPABILITY: the ability to perform satisfactorily.

CAPACITY: volume of storage space; ability of an individual.

CAPACITY, COMPUTER: the amount of information that can be stored in a computer drum or memory.

CAPITAL: in a corporation, that portion of the equity which is contributed by the shareholders; the excess of assets over liabilities.

CAPITAL ACCOUNT: an account maintained in the name of the owner or owners of a business and indicating his or their equity in that business — usually at the close of the last accounting period.

CAPITAL ASSET: an asset intended for long-term use.

CAPITAL BUDGET: the formal estimate of anticipated sales and purchase of capital items as compared with ordinary income receipts and expenditures.

CAPITAL CONSUMPTION ALLOWANCES: a measure of the plant and equipment worn-out, damaged, or rendered obsolete during a given period of time.

CAPITAL COST ALLOWANCE: the income tax term for depreciation.

CAPITAL FLIGHT: a massive transfer of currency out of a country because of adverse economic, political, or military policies.

CAPITAL FORMATION: the development or expansion of capital goods as a result of savings.

CAPITAL GAIN: excess of proceeds over book value from the sale of noninventory assets; for purposes of income tax, the excess of proceeds over net cost of securities and other assets.

CAPITAL GOODS: commodities, such as raw materials, which are used to produce other goods, either consumer goods or other capital goods.

CAPITAL-INTENSIVE INDUSTRY: an industry that utilizes extraordinarily large amounts of assets in relation to its labor force.

CAPITAL INVESTMENTS: a collective term representing the amounts invested in capital, fixed assets, or in long-term securities.

CAPITALISM: an economic system that encourages privately owned and directed production, distribution, and marketing.

CAPITALIST: loosely, a wealthy person; an individual who owns or shares in the ownership of the means of production and employs others; an individual investor in a business.

CAPITALIZE: to treat an expenditure as a capital asset rather than as an expense.

CAPITALIZED VALUE: the asset value (principal) of a given number of income dollars determined on the basis of an assumed rate of return.

CAPITAL LIABILITY: a fixed liability that is created to acquire fixed assets or for purposes of funding.

CAPITAL LOSS: the opposite of capital gain.

CAPITAL MARKET: a place or system in which the requirements for capital of a business can be satisfied.

CAPITAL OUTLAY: expenditures for the acquisition of or addition to fixed assets.

CAPITAL RATING: a rating given by a mercantile organization when appraising the net worth of a firm.

CAPITAL REQUIREMENTS: the total monetary investment essential to the establishment and operation of an enterprise.

CAPITAL STOCK: the ownership interest in a corporation as authorized by the terms of its incorporation.

CAPITAL SUM: the original amount of an estate, fund, mortgage, bond, or other financial dealing.

CAPITAL SURPLUS: paid-in surplus, donated surplus, and revaluation surplus, that is, surplus other than earned surplus.

CAPITAL TURNOVER: the rate at which an organization's assets are converted into cash.

CAPRICE: a value, not economic, created by a special circumstance, such as a particular location.

CAPTION: explanatory text accompanying a drawing or photograph.

CAPTIVE AUDIENCE: people exposed to commercial messages while passengers on carriers whose use of media they cannot control.

CAPTIVE MARKET: purchasers who have little latitude in choosing the vendor of a product or service.

CAPTIVE SHOP: a manufacturing facility whose production is used solely by the company owners.

CARD PUNCH: a device for punching cards from data in a computer memory.

CARD READER: a device for reading punched cards into a computer memory.

CARGO INSURANCE: insurance covering goods being transported, as on ships, planes, trucks, or by railroad.

CARLOAD: a shipment occupying an entire freight car.

CAR MILE: a unit of railroad statistics representing one freight car moved one mile.

CARNET: a document of international customs permitting temporary duty-free import of specific items into certain nations.

CARRIAGE CHARGE: the charge made by a carrier of freight for carrying items from one place to another.

CARRIER: a railroad, truck line, barge line, or other facility that transports freight.

CARRY: to enter or post; to supply funds to a customer; to hold stocks; to be "long" of stock.

CARRY BACK: to apply a loss to lessen a previous year's stated profit for tax-reduction purposes.

CARRY FORWARD: to apply a loss to the reduction of a subsequent year's stated profit to reduce the tax liability in the subsequent year.

CARRYING CHARGE: the interest on unpaid installments on retail purchases; warehouse charges, insurance, estimated weight loss.

CARRY OUTS: items bought in a store that are not shipped but are taken from the store by the customer.

CARTAGE: transfer of goods by wheeled vehicle from common carrier to destination or from shipping point to common carrier.

CARTE BLANCHE: without restriction.

CARTEL: a group of separate business organizations which has banded together and agreed to institute measures that will effectively control competition.

CARTOGRAPHY: the art and science of mapmaking and chart drawing.

CASE: a legal matter brought to trial; a container, often of wood, for shipping large objects or many cartons.

CASE STUDY: an account of events and factors relating to a particular business problem.

CASH: in a balance sheet, not only money but also negotiable money orders and checks and balances on deposit with banks.

CASH-AND-CARRY WHOLESALER: a wholesaler who demands that when the buyer picks up his merchandise he pay for it on the spot, without credit, or the wholesaler will not make delivery.

CASH AUDIT: an examination of cash transactions during a given time period to determine whether all received cash has been documented and that all other cash is accounted for.

CASH BASIS: a method of keeping accounts whereby revenues and expenses are recorded when received and paid.

CASH-BASIS ACCOUNTING: the recording of revenue and expenses as they are received or paid, rather than when earned or incurred.

CASHBOOK: a book of original entry used for recording cash received and cash paid out.

CASH BUDGET: a schedule of expected cash receipts and disbursements.

CASH BUYING: the purchase of securities or commodities outright for immediate delivery of the item.

CASHCARD: a card given by a retailer or store owner to a customer guaranteeing a discount for a cash payment.

CASH COMMODITY: an actual physical product, as distinguished from a commodity for future delivery.

CASH DISCOUNT: a reduction in payment allowed for prompt settlement of a debt arising from a sale.

CASH DISPENSER: a machine capable of giving out cash, representing a withdrawal from a deposit account or an extension of credit.

CASH DIVIDEND: declared dividends payable in cash, usually by check.

CASH FLOW: the cash position of an enterprise determined under cash-basis accounting.

CASH-FLOW PROGRAM: a special insurance company concept devised for large risks that in effect defer customer payment of part of the insurance premium.

CASHIER'S CHECK: a check drawn by a bank against itself rather than against the customer's account.

CASH POSITION: the percentage of cash to the total net assets; the net amount after the deduction of current liabilities.

CASH RESERVE: an amount of cash, or very liquid securities quickly convertible to cash, kept in reserve for special purposes or to protect against sudden emergency need.

CASH-SURRENDER VALUE: the amount that would be received upon cancellation of an insurance policy.

CASTING VOTE: an additional vote granted to the chairman of a meeting to be used if the votes cast for and against a particular resolution are tied.

CAST UP: to add up a total, as "to cast up an account."

CASUALTY INSURANCE: insurance primarily concerned with the losses caused by injuries to persons and legal liability imposed on the insured for such injury or for damage to property of others.

CATS AND DOGS: highly speculative stocks; items that do not have satisfactory sales turnover and accumulate in inventory.

CAVEAT EMPTOR: "let the buyer beware" (Latin).

CAVEAT SUSCRIPTOR (VENDITOR): "let the seller beware" (Latin).

CEASE-AND-DESIST ORDER: order issued by a court or government agency directing a business, employer, or union to end an unfair or illegal practice or policy.

CEILING: an upper limit on prices.

CENSORSHIP: the power and practice of reading and deleting material from another's message.

CENSUS: a counting and the publication of tabulated information derived from the counting.

CENTENNIAL: the one hundredth year.

CENTER SPREAD: a single sheet of paper that forms the two facing pages in the center of a publication.

CENTRAL BANK: a bank set up by a government to transact government business and to recommend and implement the government's monetary policy.

CENTRAL BODY: a geographical gathering of local unions for political, legislative, and other purposes.

CENTRAL BUYING: a popular approach with chain stores whereby all purchasing is done through the central or main office.

CENTRALIZATION: the bringing together of operations or functions of similar types into a common grouping.

CENTRAL LABOR UNION: a grouping of local unions in a specific geographic area.

CENTRAL PROCESSOR: the heart of a digital computer which performs arithmetic and controls the flow of its stored program and input and output operations.

CENTS PERCENT: usual form of quoting marine rates of insurance.

CERTIFICATE OF BENEFICIAL INTEREST: a statement of a share of a firm's business, when such ownership has been deposited with a trustee.

CERTIFICATE OF DEPOSIT: a fixed-income debt security issued by chartered banks for terms normally of one to six years.

CERTIFICATE OF INDEBTEDNESS: a short-term note issued by a governmental agency, describing the current debt.

CERTIFICATE OF INSURANCE: evidence that an insurance policy has been issued, showing the amount and type of insurance provided.

CERTIFICATE OF NO DEFENSE: when a mortgage is sold, the certificate signed by the borrower that identifies the mortgage indebtedness.

CERTIFICATE OF OCCUPANCY: a permit issued by a building department verifying that work on a structure meets the local zoning ordinances and the structure is ready for occupancy.

CERTIFICATE OF ORIGIN: a certificate declaring that goods purchased from a foreign country have been produced in that country and not in another.

CERTIFICATE OF RELEASE: a certificate signed by the lender, indicating that a mortgage has been fully paid and all debts satisfied.

CERTIFICATE OF TITLE: a title company certification that the seller possesses sound, marketable, and/or insurable title to the property.

CERTIFIED CHECK: a check bearing evidence on its face that payment of it is guaranteed by the bank on which it is drawn.

CERTIFIED MAIL: first-class mail on which the post office, for an extra fee, certifies delivery.

CERTIORARI: writ from a higher court for records of a case tried in a lower court.

CESSION NUMBER: a number assigned by an underwriting office to identify reinsurance premium transactions.

CHAIN DISCOUNT: a series of discounts taken on a base lessened successively by the amount of the preceding discount.

CHAIN OF COMMAND: the organizational design for the flow of communications outlining direction toward authority, peers, and subordinates.

CHAIN OF TITLE: the succession of conveyances from some accepted starting point whereby the present holder of real property derives his title.

CHAIN STORE: a unit in a group of retail stores of the same general type, commonly owned and with a degree of centralized control over operations.

CHAIRMAN: the highest ranking officer in most corporations.

CHAMBER OF COMMERCE: an organization of businessmen in a particular area formed to promote commerce and industry in that area.

CHANGE: money returned following a purchase.

CHANNEL: in marketing, the course taken by merchandise through wholesale and retail channels to the consumer.

CHANNEL OF DISTRIBUTION: the route a product follows from an original grower, producer, or importer to reaching the last consumer.

CHARGE: a demanded price; a cost of expense allocated to a specific account; a judge's instruction to a jury; to purchase for credit without making an immediate payment.

CHARGE ACCOUNT: a credit convenience whereby qualified persons and other entities may purchase and receive goods and services for which they agree to pay at a later time.

CHARGE OFF: to treat as a loss; to designate as an expense an amount originally recorded as an asset.

CHARGES FORWARD: the purchaser pays for merchandise and shipping charges only when he or she receives them, or following receipt of goods when a bill arrives.

CHARITABLE DEDUCTION: a deduction from gross income on an income tax return for contributions to causes recognized by the government as charities.

CHARTER: the instrument of incorporation.

CHARTERER: an individual or organization, usually a state agency, which grants a business the right to incorporate and transact business.

CHARTER PARTY: a contract under which a ship is leased.

CHARTIST: one who predicts future price movements of past price charts.

CHATTEL MORTGAGE: a mortgage secured by personal property.

CHATTELS: tangible, personal property other than real property.

CHEAP JACK: an individual who sells merchandise rapidly by unorthodox approaches.

CHEAP MONEY: money that is available at relatively low rates of interest.

CHECK AUTHORIZATION/ VERIFICATION: an inquiry process undertaken to reduce the risk of accepting a fraudulent check or a check written for an amount that exceeds the account balance.

CHECKING COPY: a copy of a publication delivered to an agency or advertiser to verify the inclusion of an advertisement as requested.

CHECKLIST: a series of questions or instructions to be followed in particular circumstances.

CHECKOFF SYSTEM: a system under which union dues are collected from employees by having the employer make deductions directly from wages and remit the amounts to the union.

CHECK REGISTER: a book of original entry in which the details of checks issued are recorded.

CHECK TRADING: selling bank checks to a customer, who is expected to repay the amount of the check plus interest in installments.

CHEQUE: the designation of a check in Canada and other countries where French or English is spoken.

CHOSE IN ACTION: the right to possession rather than possession itself.

CHRONIC UNEMPLOYMENT: unemployment lasting for a minimum of six months.

CHUMMING: artificially inflating the market's volume to attract other orders in some issues that stock exchanges compete in.

CHURNING: in the stock market, creating a large number of transactions for the purpose of giving the impression of an active market.

CIRCULATING CAPITAL: a synonym for working capital.

CIRCULATING CAPITAL GOOD: any capital goods item in use which is consumed by a single use.

CIRCULATION: the number of distributed copies of one issue of a periodical.

CITATION: notification in a legal matter; an oral or written attestation of merit.

CIVIL ACTION: a legal action that is not a criminal action.

CIVIL CORPORATION: an artifical being, created by law for the purpose of engaging in the business purposes stated in its charter, which is granted by the state.

CIVIL LAW: law for civil administration not dealing with felonies.

CIVIL LOANS: loans contracted by a federal, state, or municipal agency.

CLAIM: a demand for payment, reimbursement, or compensation for damages or injury as identified in a contract or under law.

CLAIM JUMPING: an unfair or illegal appropriation of another's claim, particularly a mining or homestead land claim.

CLASS: a category of employees in the schedule of group insurance.

CLASS-ACTION SUIT: a lawsuit in which the plaintiff is a group of all persons.

CLASSICAL ECONOMICS: economic concepts from the late eighteenth century until the 1930s.

CLASSIFICATION: an assortment of items, all of which are substitutional for one another to the customer; insurance.

CLASSIFICATION MERCHANDISING: a system of recordkeeping that assists inventory control and results in categorization of merchandise.

CLASSIFIED ADVERTISING: advertising limited by a publisher as to both position in the publication and maximum size of type permitted.

CLASSIFIED PROPERTY TAX: the description of properties by owners for the purpose of setting assessment with respect to market value and tax rates.

CLASSIFIED STOCK: equity security divided into groups such as Class A and Class B, the typical difference between classes being the right of voting.

CLASSIFIED TAXATION: a tax structure in which real property is categorized by function, with differing tax rates applied to each class.

CLAYTON ACT: an antitrust act passed in 1914 as an amendment to the Sherman Act; the Clayton Act outlawed tying contracts and interlocking directorates, and in other ways redefined restraint of trade.

CLEAN BILL OF LADING: a bill of lading receipted by the carrier for goods received in appropriate condition.

CLEAN HANDS: without guilt.

CLEAN HOUSE: to discharge employees of a former adminstration to make room for one's own appointees; to sell off obsolete merchandise at reduced prices; to discard old records.

CLEAN UP: to take all available profits in a market; to make a substantial and rapid profit.

CLEANUP FUND: a reserve to cover costs of last illness, burial, legal administrative, and miscellaneous expenses.

CLEAR: to replace information in a storage device to zero; free from encumbrance.

CLEARANCE: a sale intended to clear discontinued items from inventory.

CLEARING: the process of making clear or freeing from anything.

CLEARING CHECKS: the return of checks to the bank on which they are drawn for payment.

CLEARINGHOUSE: an organization acting as a medium for the daily settlement of transactions between its members.

CLEARING TITLE: the process of removing clouds on the title of real estate.

CLERICAL: a person who works with business records; describing the work of a clerical employee.

CLOSE: to finish or wind up; to conclude a sale or agreement; to sign legal papers indicating that a property has formally changed ownership.

CLOSE CORPORATION: a corporation whose stock is held by few owners and not traded on a public exchange.

CLOSED ACCOUNT: an account with equal debits and credits.

CLOSED-END: a capital structure of an organization under which shares are transferable but cannot be canceled or redeemed except by resolution of the shareholders or under legislation.

CLOSED-END FUND: an investment company with fixed capital and no provision for redemption of shares at the option of the shareholders.

CLOSED MORTGAGE: a mortgage that cannot be paid off until maturity occurs.

CLOSED SHOP: a place of employment where a worker must be a member of a union in order to be employed and all employees must be hired through the union.

CLOSED STOCK: merchandise sold only in sets.

CLOSED TRADE: a transaction concluded by selling a security that has been paid for previously, or the converting of a short sale.

CLOSED UNION: a labor union that limits its membership by making entrance conditions artificially difficult.

CLOSELY HELD CORPORATION: a corporation in which the shares are held by a small number of shareholders.

CLOSE MONEY: a term applied when changes in prices between successive stock transactions are fractional, or when the last bid-and-asked quotation are hardly different.

CLOSE OUT: an offer by a manufacturer or retailer to clear away his inventory.

CLOSING: the final procedure in which documents are executed and recorded.

CLOSING COSTS: the expenses that are incurred by sellers and buyers in the transfer of real estate ownership.

CLOSING DATE: in publishing and advertising, the last day on which advertisements can be accepted for publication in a magazine or other periodical.

CLOSING ENTRY: an entry made at the end of an accounting period for the purpose of transferring the balances in the revenue and expense accounts to retained earning or similar accounts.

CLOSING PRICE: the price at which the last sale on an organized market is made on a particular day.

CLOSING PURCHASE: a transaction in which a holder liquidates his position by purchasing an option having the same terms as an option previously written.

CLOSING STATEMENT: the statement that lists the financial settlement between a buyer and a seller, outlining the amounts each must pay.

CLOUD ON TITLE: an encumbrance, usually invalid, on real property.

CLUSTERING: the phenomenon of firms selling similar but not identical products that attract rather than repel each other in primary location considerations.

COBOL: an acronym for common business-oriented language; COBOL is a computer procedure-oriented language widely used in coding scientific applications.

CODE: an organized collection of laws or regulations.

CODICIL: a document, executed in the same manner as the will itself, which alters a will.

COEMPTION: purchasing the entire supply of any commodity, usually for purposes of gaining a monopoly.

COERCIVE POWER: influence over others based on fear.

COEXECUTOR: an executor whose responsibility is shared with at least one other person.

COGNITION: what individuals know about themselves and their surroundings.

COGNOVIT NOTE: a note containing a clause authorizing the holder to appear in court without notice to the maker and have judgment entered against the maker.

COINCIDENT INDICATOR: a measure of activity that traditionally moves in the same direction and during the same time period as total economic movement.

COINSURANCE: insurance by more than one insurer, such as partial insurance by an underwriter and the balance by the insured.

COINSURER: one who shares the loss sustained under an insurance policy or policies.

COLD CALL: contacting a potential customer without prior notice in order to make a sale or arrange for an appointment.

COLD CANVASSING: determining potential customers without assistance from others or from references.

COLLABORATE: to work with.

COLLAPSE: a sudden drop in business activity or business prices; failure or ruin of a specific firm.

COLLATE: to combine items from two or more ordered sets into one set having a specified order.

COLLATERAL: securities or other valuable assets pledged to insure an agreement, such as the payment of a loan.

COLLATOR: a device that merges two or more sorted decks of punch cards into a sorted resultant deck.

COLLECTIBLE: anything that can be converted into cash.

COLLECTION AGENCY: an individual or organization in the business of collecting debts for others.

COLLECTION CHARGES: those fees charged for collecting drafts, notes, coupons, and accounts receivable.

COLLECTION CYCLE: the activity taking place between the extension of credit and the receipt of payment.

COLLECTIVE AGREEMENT: a contract between one or more unions and one or more employers.

COLLECTIVE BARGAINING: a method of determining conditions of employment through direct negotiations between the union and the employer.

COLLECTIVE NEGOTIATIONS: a term used in the public sector as an alternative to collective bargaining.

COLLISION INSURANCE: coverage from damage to the insured object caused by collision with any object, stationary or moving.

COLLUSION: an agreement to engage in an unfair or illegal business practice.

COLOR OF TITLE: an appearance of title founded on a written instrument that would, if valid, convey title.

COLUMN INCH: an area of publication advertising space one column wide by an inch in depth.

COMAKER: one who, in addition to the borrower of funds, signs a note and becomes jointly responsible for payment.

COMBINATION ADVERTISING RATE: the cost per unit area for space in a combination of more than one publication; similarly, the cost per time unit for a combination of broadcast media.

COMBINATION POLICY: an insurance policy, or more often two policies printed on one form, providing coverage against several hazards under a single document.

COMFORT LETTER: a letter by which the writer conveys assurance that something is or is not so.

COMMAND ECONOMY: an economic system under which an authoritarian government exercises major control over decisions concerning what and how much to produce.

COMMAND GROUP: a group specified by the formal organization chart.

COMMERCIAL: pertaining to trade; a radio or television advertising announcement.

COMMERCIAL ACCOUNT: in general, a checking account.

COMMERCIAL BANK: a bank, one of whose main functions is acceptance of deposits and creation of credit through short-term loans mainly for business purposes.

COMMERCIAL CREDIT: credit used by manufacturers, retailers, wholesalers, jobbers, and commission agents for the production and distribution of goods.

COMMERCIAL PAPER: although sometimes restricted to short-term promissory notes issued by corporations, the term also applies to checks, drafts, and other negotiable instruments.

COMMERCIAL SET: the four major documents covering a shipment; the invoice, the bill of lading, the certificate of insurance, and the bill of exchange or draft.

COMMISSION: a percentage of a sale price paid to a salesman, broker, or agent.

COMMISSIONAIRE: a broker who arranges for purchases for foreign or out-of-town buyers for a percentage of the purchase price.

COMMITTEE: persons elected or appointed to form a subgroup of a larger body to investigate, make findings, and report these findings with recommendations to the larger body.

COMMITTEE DEED: a deed employed when the property of a child or a person declared incompetent is conveyed.

COMMITTEE, TEMPORARY (ad hoc): a group of people in an organization named to accomplish a specific objective.

COMMODITIES: bulk goods, such as wheat or copper.

COMMODITY PAPER: promissory notes, drafts, and similar documents representing loans secured by bills of lading or warehouse receipts covering commodities.

COMMON AREA: the area owned in common, such a walkways, hallways, etc., by the owners of condominiums.

COMMON CARRIER: a person or company in the business of transporting goods and passengers for anyone who wishes to use the services, in contrast to being under an exclusive contract.

COMMON LAW: an unwritten system of laws which originated in England and has grown out of custom and traditional usage.

COMMON MARKET: a group of countries with a uniform trading agreement involving such subjects as uniform tariffs.

COMMON SHARE: a synonym for common stock.

COMMON STOCK: the shares in a corporation which have no fixed rate of dividends and are the last to secure a share in the property when the corporation is dissolved; the shares have voting power.

COMMUNICATION: the transmission and reception of messages.

COMMUNICATION, horizontal: the exchange of information among peers or among people at the same level in an organization.

COMMUNICATION NETWORK: formed when a small number of people exchange information in a well-defined pattern for the purpose of resolving a specific problem or issue.

COMMUNICATION, vertical: the transmission of information between individuals at various levels in an organization.

COMMUNITY PROPERTY: property owned in common by a husband and wife which was not acquired as separate property.

COMMUNITY RATE OF RETURN: the net value of a project to an economy.

COMMUTED VALUE: the present value of future payments due or receivable, computed on the basis of a given rate of interest.

COMMUTER TAX: any income tax levied by a town or city on people who work there but live elsewhere.

COMPACT: an agreement mutually arrived at by two or more people under which all those involved have both obligations and rights.

COMPANY SEAL: the official seal of a corporation which must be affixed to or imprinted on certain documents.

COMPANY STORE: a store maintained by an employer which sometimes advances supplies to workers on a scrip payment basis.

COMPANY UNION: an employee organization that is dominated or strongly influenced by management.

COMPARATIVE ADVANTAGE: a situation in which an individual, firm, locality, or nation can produce goods or services cheaper than another.

COMPARATIVE ADVERTISING: promotional material in which competitors' products are named.

COMPARATIVE STATEMENT: a form of financial statement presentation in which current-period results and positions are presented with corresponding figures for previous periods.

COMPENSATING BALANCE: money deposited in a bank or other lending institution to induce the institution to make a specific loan or establish a particular line of credit.

COMPENSATING ERRORS: errors that happen to cancel out each other.

COMPENSATION: payment for services rendered or damages suffered.

COMPENSATION AWARD: compensation paid to an injured party for a number of periods, either definite or indefinite, as the nature of the injury requires; payment is something made in installments.

COMPENSATORY FISCAL POLICY: an approach to reverse the direction of the business cycle when it is believed that it is becoming inflationary or deflationary.

COMPETENT: able to meet a standard of performance.

COMPETITION: vying for sales and progress.

COMPETITIVE PRICE: a price determined in the market by the bargaining of a number of buyers and sellers.

COMPILE: to collect, as with data.

COMPILER: a computer program that converts a source program written in a procedure-oriented lanaguage or problem-oriented language into an object code suitable for running on a computer.

COMPLEMENTARY PRODUCTS: items that tend to round out a line of products.

COMPLETED CONTRACT METHOD: a method of accounting which recognizes income only when the goods to be provided or the services to be rendered have actually been provided or rendered.

COMPONENT: the smallest unit of a system which performs a part of the transformation or processing activity.

COMPOSITE DEMAND: the sum of demands for an item or service beginning with any number of needs.

COMPOSITE INVENTORY: data accumulation on customers, including the most pertinent information that can be obtained about them.

COMPOSITE RATE: a special single rate based on a measure of exposure that will reasonably reflect the variations in the insurable hazards covered.

COMPOSITE SUPPLY: an indefinite number and variety of items, each of which is able to satisfy a particular need.

COMPOSITION SETTLMENT: the acceptance by a creditor of an amount smaller than that which he is legally entitled to from a debtor; such acceptance waives the right to the full amount.

COMPOUNDED: indicating the frequency with which interest is computed and added to the principal to arrive at a new actual balance.

COMPOUND INTEREST: interest calculated on interest accumulated as well as on the principal amount of a loan.

COMPREHENSIVE: a layout prepared to resemble a completed advertisement as nearly as possible.

COMPROMISE: any agreement between two or more persons, usually in opposition, to settle their differences on areas of controversy without resort to legal action.

COMPTROLLER: a synonym for controller.

COMPULSORY ARBITRATION: arbitration imposed by law on parties to a dispute.

COMPULSORY INSURANCE: any form of insurance that is required by law.

COMPULSORY RETIREMENT: separation from employment at an age specified by union contract or company policy.

COMPUTER: a machine capable of performing many different kinds of calculations by virtue of its ability to direct calculations from a program stored or wired into its memory.

COMPUTER INPUTS: computer stations that process incoming data; the data itself, as prepared on punch cards or audio tape.

COMPUTER INSTRUCTION: a machine instruction for a specific computer; a set of characters that defines an operation.

COMPUTER NETWORK: a complex consisting of two or more interconnected computing units.

COMPUTER OUTPUTS: the data that emerges from a computer; the computer station that processes the outputs.

COMPUTER PROGRAM: a set of instructions telling the computer what to do.

COMPUTER RUN: the processing of a batch of transactions, sometimes restricted to the performance of one routine or several interconnected routines.

COMPUTER SOFTWARE: the computer programs used to activate and instruct the computer system, in contrast to the actual processing equipment.

COMPUTER TERMINAL: a point at which data can be put into or extracted from a computer system.

CONCEALMENT: the willful withholding of any material fact(s); the suppression of truth to the injury or prejudice of another.

CONCENTRATION RATIO: in a specific industry, the breakdown of total business handled by a specified number of the largest organizations.

CONCEPTUAL SKILL: the perception and ability to see the overall picture.

CONCESSION: the granting of a right.

CONCESSIONAIRE: one who rents the privilege of conducting a specified business within an area enlivened by other enterprises.

CONCILIATION: in labor language, a process that attempts to resolve labor disputes by compromise or voluntary agreement in contrast to arbitration.

CONCILIATION SERVICE: the service of a third party, either government or private, in negotiating and resolving a dispute between two parties, without power to make binding decisions.

CONCRETE PROPOSAL: a proposal with definite provisions which, upon acceptance, can become a contract.

CONCURRENT: running at the same time.

CONCURRENT AUTHORITY: condition under which two or more brokers are given an open listing for property.

CONDEMNATION: refusal by government to license for further use, as an unsafe building; exercise of the right of eminent domain.

CONDITION: a contractual clause, implied or expressed, with the effect of investing or divesting the members of the contract with various rights and duties.

CONDITIONAL DISCHARGE: the release of a bankrupt person from his or her liabilities subject to the fulfillment of specified conditions.

CONDITIONAL SALES AGREEMENT: a contract of sale under which the transfer of title does not take place until specified payments have been made.

CONDITIONAL VALUE: the value that will ensue if a particular event occurs.

CONDITIONING PROCESS: the process of shaping material into a usable item.

CONDITION PRECEDENT: a condition that must be met before a contract becomes binding.

CONDITIONS CONCURRENT: conditions that are mutually dependent and must be remdered by all members of the contract at the same time.

CONDITION SUBSEQUENT: a provision in a contract to release one of the parties, for example, from previous duties and rights if a particular event occurs.

CONDOMINIUM: the term describing individual ownership in real property of a specific unit of a multiunit structure.

CONFERENCE CALL: a conversation among a group of people who utilize telephones linked by a central switching unit.

CONFESSION OF JUDGMENT: a clause in a note or agreement consenting in advance to the entry of judgment upon default without notice of the proceeding.

CONFIDENCE GAME: a swindle in which the dupe is induced to show cash to prove that he is financially able to participate in an illegal scheme to make substantial profits quickly at minimum risk.

CONFIDENTIAL: for the attention of the addressee only; private, not to be repeated to others.

CONFIGURATION: a group of interconnected machines that are programmed to operate as one system.

CONFISCATE: to seize, with or without payment, either for government need or because of legal violation, as in the case of contraband.

CONGLOMERATE: the term used to describe a corporate consolidation in which one company acquires another in a different industry.

CON MAN: a person who creates unreasonable confidence in his honesty and integrity.

CONNECTING CARRIER: a carrier who has a direct connection with another carrier, under which freight or people are moved in a joint-line service.

CONNECTION: a party in an influential position thought to be friendly and willing to assist in introductions or other favors.

CONSENSUS: a general agreement by a number of people.

CONSENT ELECTION: voting by employees in a bargaining unit as to their choice of union (or no union).

CONSERVATOR: a person appointed by a court to manage the affairs of an incompetent or to liquidate a defunct business.

CONSIDERATION: a payment for a service or for merchandise as legally required for a valid contract.

CONSIGNEE: the person to whom articles are shipped.

CONSIGNMENT: goods on which title is conveyed to the consignee only when he resells and pays, with the consignee retaining the right to return the unsold portion of the goods.

CONSIGNOR: the owner of goods sent to a consignee.

CONSOLE: the control keys and special devices unit of a computer.

CONSOLIDATED: the results obtained when the accounts of a parent company and its subsidiary companies are combined as if they operated as a single entity.

CONSOLIDATED FINANCIAL STATEMENTS: the combined financial statements of a parent company and its subsidiaries.

CONSOLIDATION: a combination of two or more organizations into one, to form a new entity.

CONSORTIUM: a group of firms allied for a sharing in a business venture of limited duration, such as floating an issue of securities.

CONSPIRACY: a combination of two or more persons designing by concerted action to accomplish some unlawful purpose, or to accomplish a legitimate purpose by criminal or unlawful means.

CONSTANT-COST INDUSTRY: industry that experiences no increase in prices or in costs of production during expansion, despite new companies entering it.

CONSTANT DOLLARS: dollars of a given base year into which dollars of the year under review are restated for the purpose of eliminating the change in purchasing power.

CONSTRAINTS: the events that reduce the range of options available to a problem solver.

CONSULTANT: a specialist in any field of activity; an organization for the purpose of recommending solutions to a problem.

CONSUMER CREDIT: a credit extended to individuals to enable them to obtain goods and services for their own personal use.

CONSUMER GOODS: commodities whose ultimate use is to contribute directly to the satisfaction of human wants or desires, as distinguished from capital goods.

CONSUMERISM: trend toward consumers becoming more activist.

CONSUMER MARKET: buyers who purchase for personal need or family consumption.

CONSUMER PICKETING: picketing of an establishment to persuade consumers to stop shopping there or to stop buying certain products or services.

CONSUMER PRICE INDEX: a monthly measure, compiled by the government, of changes in the prices of selected goods and services consumed by individuals.

CONSUMER SALE-DISCLOSURE STATEMENT: a form presented by a dealer giving essential details on financing charges relative to a purchase on an installment plan.

CONSUMER'S SURPLUS: a buyer's payment that is lower than the maximum amount he or she would have been willing to pay.

CONSUMPTION: the expenditure of a nation or its individuals on consumer goods and services.

CONSUMPTION FUNCTION: describing how consumption expenditures depend on other variables.

CONTAINERIZATION: placing pieces of freight in a reusable container so that the entire container can be shipped as a single unit.

CONTAINERIZED UNIT: a metal container the size of a truck trailer, loaded and sealed for transport by successive multiple means, such as truck, rail, and ship.

CONTANGO: the cost factors in calculating from one given period to a future point; a basic pricing system in futures trading.

CONTESTABLE CLAUSE: in insurance, the section of the contract stating conditions under which the policy may be contested or voided.

CONTIGUOUS: touching, abutting.

CONTINGENCY: a future event or condition that was not predictable.

CONTINGENCY FUND: amounts set aside for unforeseen expenditures.

CONTINGENT ASSETS: recorded items that may or may not become assets.

CONTINGENT INTEREST: the right to property which depends for vesting or realization on some future uncertain occurrence.

CONTINGENT LIABILITY: a recorded item that may or may not become a liability.

CONTINUITY IN ADVERTISING: the extended utilization of advertising—in particular, repetition of theme, layout, or commercial format.

CONTINUOUS BUDGET: a budget that perpetually adds a month in the future as the month just ended is dropped.

CONTINUOUS PRODUCTION: a production activity that yields a standarized product.

CONTRA: an offsetting entry of equal value.

CONTRACT: an agreement between persons having the legal capacity to bind themselves to do a lawful thing for valuable consideration.

CONTRACT ACCOUNT: an account that offsets in whole or in part another account.

CONTRACT CARRIER: a motor carrier transporting goods for one or more concerns under a contract specifically designed to cover the type of service and special equipment.

CONTRACTION: a decline of economic activity in the business cycle.

CONTRACT OF ADHESION: a contract in which one party has no bargaining basis; an insurance contract is a contract of adhesion since there is no bargaining basis between the insurance company and the insured.

CONTRACT OF SALE: a written document whereby an owner agrees to convey title to a property when the purchaser has completed paying for the property under the terms of the contract.

CONTRACT PURCHASING: a form of purchasing defined in a contract for orders and deliveries, covering a time period, usually one year.

CONTRACT RENT: the rent payment agreed upon.

CONTRACTUAL LIABILITY: liability assumed by contract; an additional coverage for a specific exposure for which the basic liability policy does not provide.

CONTRIBUTED CAPITAL: paid-up capital plus contributed surplus.

CONTRIBUTED SURPLUS: the amount received on the issue of par value shares in excess of the par value; the amount received for no par value shares which has been allocated to surplus.

CONTRIBUTION PROFIT: sales revenue less the variable cost of producing the revenue.

CONTRIBUTORY NEGLIGENCE: the negligence attributed to the person making a claim against an insured party.

CONTRIBUTORY PENSION PLAN: a pension plan under which the costs are shared between the employer and the employee.

35

CONSUMP-
TION •
CONTRIBU-
TORY
PENSION
PLAN

CONTROL ACCOUNT: a general ledger account representing the total of the balances of the accounts in a subsidiary ledger.

CONTROLLED COMPANY: a corporation under the control of another corporation or person.

CONTROLLED ECONOMY: an economy that is regulated and greatly influenced by government.

CONTROLLED INFLATION: an economic situation in which the monetary and fiscal authorities of a nation deliberately create inflationary conditions in order to pull the economy out of a recession or period of deflation into prosperity.

CONTROLLER: an officer of an organization with the technical skills of an accountant, who is charged with the responsibility for administration of financial matters.

CONTROLLING ACCOUNT: a general ledger account that contains a summary of all the information recorded in detail in the related subsidiary ledgers.

CONTROLLING INTEREST: the shares held by a controlling shareholder.

CONTROLLING SHAREHOLDER: a shareholder or group of shareholders owning sufficient shares to elect a majority of the board of directors of a corporation.

CONTROL PANEL: the part of a computer console that contains manual controls.

CONVENIENCE GOODS: consumer goods of low price which consumers wish to purchase with little effort and for which they generally do not "shop around."

CONVENTIONAL LOAN: a mortgage loan, usually granted by a bank or loan association.

CONVENTIONAL MORTGAGE: a mortgage not obtained under a government-insured program.

CONVERSION: the unlawful taking of or possession of goods.

CONVERSION COST: usually the cost of changing any existing resource from one form or function to another.

CONVERTIBLE: capable of being exchanged for the currency of another country; capable of being exchanged for securities of another class.

CONVEY: transfer of title to land from one person to another.

CONVEYER: a mechanism to support and carry moving items in a fixed path.

COOPERATIVE: an organization formed for the benefit of its owners, who are usually either producers or consumers; by cooperating, they acquire profits that would otherwise go to middlemen.

COOPERATIVE ADVERTISING: advertising placed by retailers and paid for at least in part by the manufacturers whose products are advertised.

COOPERATIVE BUILDING: a structure whose tenants are stockholders in the building.

COOPERATIVE EDUCATION: a plan under which college students work part of the year or part of the day as trainees in jobs related to their studies, for which they receive both pay and college credit.

COOPTATION: a strategy employed by an organization to minimize the uncertainty that it faces.

COORDINATE: to organize the efforts of multiple individuals, departments, firms, or other units into the efficient accomplishment of a unified objective.

COPIER: an office machine for making copies.

COPY: the words of an advertisement; commercial art ready for camera.

COPYREADER: in publishing, one who marks and corrects written material.

COPYRIGHT: the exclusive right to produce or reproduce an original literary, dramatic, musical, or artistic work.

COPY TESTING: measuring the effectiveness of an advertising campaign.

CORAM: in the presence of.

CORE MEMORY: in data

processing, a fast random-access memory in which one ferrite core serves as the storage for each bit of information; each bit can be accessed as fast as any other.

CORNER: the buying of a stock or commodity on a scale sufficiently large to give the buyers control over the price of the particular stock or commodity.

CORPORATE IMAGE: the opinion that the public holds of a particular corporation.

CORPORATE STATE: represented by the power of a corporation that is out of control, insensitive to human values, and legalistic.

CORPORATE STOCK: the equity shares of a corporation; these shares may be common, preferred, or classified.

CORPORATION: a business entity of limited liability empowered to do business under state law, or, in the case of corporations of the federal government, under federal law.

CORPORATION DE FACTO: despite a minor failure to comply with the regulations for incorporation, a legal entity that thereafter has exercised corporate powers.

CORPORATION DE JURE: a corporation that was formed by fulfilling the requirements of the law permitting the formation of the corporation.

CORPOREAL: tangible.

CORPUS: a business in bankruptcy or liquidation, or a defunct business.

CORRESPONDENT BANK: a bank that is the depository for another bank.

COSPONSORING: joining together in a mutual effort or activity; sharing by two or more advertisers of the cost of a single broadcast program.

COST: the value given up by an entity in order to receive goods or services.

COST ACCOUNTING: account procedures designed to reveal the profitability of unit operations.

COST APPROACH TO VALUE: a method of estimating the value of real property by deducting depreciation from the cost of replacement and adding the value of the land to the remainder.

COST-BASED PENSION PLAN: a synonym for a money-purchase pension plan.

COST-BENEFIT STUDY OR ANALYSIS: evaluating the benefits to be expected from a project, determining the cost of the project, then making a decision on whether to proceed based on the comparison of the two.

COST IN DISTRIBUTION: costs involved in the movement of goods from the producer to the consumer.

COST, INDIRECT: a cost not particularly identifiable with a specific product, job, or function.

COST OF GOODS MANUFACTURED: all direct material, labor, and overhead transferred from work-in-process inventory to finished-goods inventory.

COST OF LIVING: a misnomer; the proper designation is consumer price index; it shows the relationship of wages to the cost of commodities.

COST-OF-LIVING: an automatic periodic pay increase based on changes in the consumer price index.

COST-OF-LIVING INDEX: popular term for the Consumer Price Index issued monthly by the US Department of Labor, Bureau of Labor Statistics.

COST OF MERCHANDISE SOLD: in accounting, the total cost of the units of merchandise sold during a fiscal period.

COST OF SALES: same as cost of merchandise sold.

COST-PLUS CONTRACT: a contract under which the contractor recovers costs incurred in performance plus an agreed fee.

COST-PLUS PRICING: the practice of adding a percentage of the cost of goods to the cost before the selling price is established.

COST-PUSH INFLATION: the theory that inflation is caused by workers demanding higher wages without an increase in productivity, followed by employers raising prices without an increase in demand.

38

*COST-
VOLUME
PROFIT
ANALYSIS •
CREDIT
INSURANCE*

COST-VOLUME PROFIT ANALYSIS: a method used for measuring the functional relationships between the major aspects of profits and for identifying the profit structure of an organization.

COSURETY: one of a group of surety companies executing a bond.

COUNSEL: a lawyer or firm of lawyers.

COUNTERCHECK: a receipt signed by a depositor when withdrawing funds from his own bank account.

COUNTERCLAIM: a claim entered to offset a prior claim.

COUNTERCYCLICAL POLICY: levelling the ups and downs of the business cycle with budget deficits during depression and surpluses during prosperity.

COUNTERFEIT: imitation or fraudulent money.

COUNTERMAND: to cancel an order that has not yet been carried out.

COUNTEROFFER: circumstance in which one to whom an offer is extended proposes terms different from those set forth in the original offer and thus rejects the original offer.

COUNTERSIGN: to sign one's signature to a document that has already been signed by someone else, often as a guarantee of authenticity.

COUNTERVAILING POWER: describing the balancing out of the influences of two economic groups with monopolistic power.

COUNTRY BANK: a national or state bank not located in a Federal Reserve city.

COUNTRY-CLUB BILLING: a billing system in which the account statement is accompanied by copies of original invoices.

COUPLING UP: the overlap of workers at the time of shift changes.

COUPON BOND: a bond having detachable coupons that are presented to the issuer for payment of interest on specified due dates.

COVENANT: an agreement or promise of legal validity.

COVER: to purchase a quantity of stock or commodities equal to what was previously sold short.

COVERED OPTION: an option in which the seller (or writer) owns the underlying security.

COVERING: buying a stock previously sold short; the act of meeting one's obligation.

CRAFT UNION: a union whose members all possess similar skills.

CRASH: a sudden and disastrous drop in business activity, prices, security values, and so on.

CREAM: the insurance policyholders having the lowest premiums, in part because they are the best risks.

CREAMPUFF SALE: an expression suggesting that real property is easily sold.

CREDIT: a loan; the privilege of buying goods and services after delivery; ability to borrow; the right side of a ledger account—increase of a liability or decrease of an asset.

CREDIT APPLICATION: any form used to secure information relating to consumer credit.

CREDIT AUTHORIZATION/ VERIFICATION: an inquiry process undertaken to reduce the risk of credit fraud or of extending credit in excess of an imposed credit limit.

CREDIT BUREAU: an organization that compiles and supplies information about the reliability of individuals or companies in the payment of their debts.

CREDIT CARD: a card issued by an organization entitling the bearer to credit at its establishments.

CREDIT CONTRACT: a written statement showing how, when, and how much you will pay for goods or services.

CREDIT INSTRUMENT: a written guarantee to pay, which serves the purpose of money in consummating commercial exchanges, although actual money or bank notes are not used.

CREDIT INSURANCE: an insurance company's guarantee to manufacturers, wholesalers, and service organizations that they will be paid for goods shipped or services rendered.

CREDIT INVESTIGATION: an inquiry made by a lender to verify data given in a credit application or to investigate other aspects the creditor believes to be relevant to credit worthiness.

CREDIT LINE: an arrangement with a bank under which the bank agrees, usually informally, to make a loan not to exceed a particular amount when needed by the customer.

CREDIT MEMORANDUM: a special business form which is issued by the seller to the buyer and which contains a record of the credit the seller has granted for returns, allowances, overcharges, and similar items.

CREDITOR: one to whom something is owed.

CREDIT RATING: the appraisal of one's credit standing ability and willingness to pay obligations.

CREDIT REPORT: a confidential report made by an independent individual or organization that has investigated the financial standing, reputation, and record of an applicant for insurance.

CREDIT RISK: the risk assumed for possible nonpayment of credit extended.

CREDIT SALE: a sale in which the individual is given time to pay for the items purchased.

CREDIT SQUEEZE: a restriction by a government on the provision of credit to consumers.

CREDIT TERMS: specification of terms for the payment of a credit obligation.

CREDIT UNION: a savings and loan institution organized on a cooperative basis to provide savings and loan services to and for the benefit of its member owners.

CREEPING INFLATION: a gradual but continuing increase in the general price level by as little as 2.5 percent a year.

CRITICAL INCIDENT: a management-training tool;

participants in a discussion describe events that have presented them with difficulty.

CRITICAL-PATH METHOD: in planning and scheduling, a complex series of operations, the sequence of events that are most critical as to timing.

CROSS-ELASTICITY: describing the impact on the demand for one product of price changes of a related product.

CROSS-FOOTING: the totaling of the footings of figures or of totals of individual columns to produce a grand total.

CROSSING: the function performed by a broker in handling both sides of a transaction.

CROSS-ORDER: in the stock market, an order to a broker to buy and sell the same security.

CROSSOVER ANALYSIS: an approach of cost analysis showing the optimum volume of activity that should be used in alternate means of manufacture.

CROSS-PICKETING: situation when two rival unions picket the same business, each contending they are representatives of the striking employees.

CROSS-RATE: the calculation of the rate of exchange of two foreign currencies by using the rate of exchange of each currency in a third nation's currency.

CRUNCH: an economic squeeze; a crisis created by some financial pressure.

CRYOGENICS: the study and use of materials under conditions of intense cold, such as the temperature of liquid air.

CUL DE SAC: a dead-end street.

CULLING: the mechanical or manual removal of letter-size mail from the nonletter size.

CUM RIGHTS: "with rights;" (Latin) stock sold cum rights is sold with rights of subscription to a current new issue of a corporation.

CUMULATIVE DIVIDEND: a dividend that will ultimately have to be paid, if not paid annually, before any common stock dividend can be paid.

CUMULATIVE MARK-ON: the difference between total delivered cost and total original retail values of merchandise handled within a stated time frame.

CUMULATIVE QUANTITY DISCOUNT: a type of rebate given to a store when the total price of all goods purchased is identified.

CUMULATIVE STOCK: a class of preferred stock on which unpaid dividends continue to accumulate.

CURABLE DEPRECIATION: depreciated property that is still considered to be economically useful.

CURIA: a court of justice.

CURING TITLE: the removal of a claim from a title, to make it marketable.

CURRENT ACCOUNT: a running account.

CURRENT ASSETS: assets readily convertible to cash, such as accounts receivable, merchandise inventories, and cash in banks and on hand.

CURRENT COST: what it might cost today to replace an asset or to require equivalent productive capacity.

CURRENT DOLLARS: a term used to describe the actual prices of goods and services each year.

CURRENT EXIT VALUE: what a company could sell an asset for (or remove liability) in today's market.

CURRENT LIABILITIES: accounts payable and loans payable due in one year or less.

CURRENT OPERATION EXPENDITURES: expenditures for salaries and wages, supplies, material, and contractual services, other than capital outlays.

CURRENT RATIO: the ratio of current assets to current liabilities.

CURRENT VALUE ACCOUNTING: a general term used to describe methods of accounting based on current values rather than historical cost.

CURRENT YIELD: the ratio of the current income from an investment to the purchase price or the current price of the investment.

CURRICULUM VITAE: a résumé of one's qualifications and career.

CURVE: a line connecting points on a graph; slang, an unclear, difficult, or dilemma-type assignment, or devious question.

CUSTODIAN: one whose duty it is to hold, safeguard, and account for property committed to his care.

CUSTOMER: an individual or organization that makes a purchase.

CUSTOMER ORIENTED: describing the effort to comprehend the reasons, desires, and problems of the customer with the intent to use this information in fulfilling the customer's needs.

CUSTOMER'S LEDGER: a ledger that shows accounts receivable of each customer.

CUSTOMS: the taxes imposed by a government on the import or export of items.

CUSTOMS UNION: agreement by two or more trading countries to dissolve trade restrictions such as tariffs and quotas among themselves.

CUTBACK: a reduction of planned production or expenditures.

CUTOFF DATE: a specific day chosen for stopping the flow of cash, goods, or other items for closing or audit reasons.

CUT-THROAT COMPETITION: severe but independent endeavoring by two or more firms for business patronage by the offer of very advantageous terms to the buyer.

CYBERNETICS: comparative studies of computers and the human nervous system.

CYCLE BILLING: matching of alphabetical breakdowns to specific days to assist in customer billing.

CYCLICAL INFLATION: variations in a period when there is a sudden increase in the general price level.

CYCLICAL STOCKS: securities that go up and down in value with the trend of business.

CYCLICAL UNEMPLOYMENT: unemployment connected with fluctuations in business activity, reflected by business cycles.

D

DAIS: a raised platform for speakers and honored guests and hosts.

DAMAGES: indemnification for loss.

DARK HORSE: a rear-rank contender who has possibilities of a late surge forward to win.

DATA: a representation of facts, concepts, or instructions in a formalized manner, suitable for communication.

DATA BANK: an organized file of information.

DATA BASE: a collection of information specific to an operation, business, or enterprise.

DATA CAPTURE: the act of collecting data into a form that can be directly processed by a computer system.

DATA CENTER: a data-processing installation serving users or customers; usually restricted to computerized operations.

DATAMATION: the flow of information by way of a computer.

DATA PROCESSING: the assembly, classification, recording, analysis, and reporting of information by manual, mechanical, or electronic means.

DATA REDUCTION: the process of transforming large masses of data into useful, condensed, or simplified intelligence.

DATING: an extension of credit until a specified date.

DATUM: the singular form of "data."

DAYLIGHT TRADING: making a purchase followed by a sale of a security on the same day, to avoid a holding position in the shares traded overnight or longer.

DAY LOAN: a one-day loan, granted for the purchase of stock, for the broker's convenience.

DAY ORDER: a brokerage order that

expires at the close of the day's trading if it is not possible to execute it on that day.

DAYS OF GRACE: additional days, usually three, allowed beyond the due date of a payment, during which payment can still be made.

DEADBEAT: term commonly used (but not recommended) in credit work, describing a person or persons who are undesireable credit risks.

DEAD LETTER: a letter deposited in the mail that is or becomes undeliverable, or is unmailable and cannot be returned to the sender.

DEADLINE: the time, day, or other period on which something is due.

DEAD PLEDGE: an expression for a paid-on-time mortgage.

DEAD STOCK: merchandise that cannot be sold.

DEAD TIME: time lost by workers for lack of materials, machine breakdown, or other causes beyond their control.

DEAD WEIGHT: weight of a vessel or other carrier without any cargo.

DEAL: a large transaction involving a change in ownership.

DEALER: one who confers quantity utility (breaks lots into smaller quantities for resale) and other utilities upon a good or service.

DEALER IMPRINT: a dealer's name, address, or other identification, put on material created by an advertiser.

DEALER TIE-IN: a manufacturer's advertisement given at a countrywide rate with a list of local dealers to be included in the ad.

DEAR MONEY: the presence of high interest rates when loans are difficult to obtain because of the supply and demand for credit.

DEBASEMENT: the act of reducing the metallic content of a coin below its face value.

DEBENTURE: a long- or intermediate-term fixed obligation of a business.

DEBIT: an entry recording the creation of, or addition to, an asset or an expense, or the reduction of a liability, revenue, or owners' equity.

DEBIT CARD: a cash-machine automator and a check guarantee.

DEBIT MEMORANDUM: a document prepared by a purchaser notifying a seller that the latter's account has been reduced because of an allowance, return, or cancellation.

DEBT: a sum of money owing.

DEBT CAPITAL: funds borrowed to finance the operations of a business.

DEBT CEILING: a level controlled by Congress: the maximum limit on the federal debt.

DEBTEE: a creditor.

DEBT FINANCING: the long-term borrowing of money by a business for the purpose of obtaining working capital or other funds necessary for operational needs.

DEBT LIMIT: a maximum amount of money that a state or local government can borrow.

DEBTOR: one who owes money to another.

DEBTOR IN POSSESSION: a business owner appointed by a referee in bankruptcy to administer the bankupt business in an attempt to reestablish its solvency.

DEBTOR NATION: a country whose citizens, companies, and government owe more to foreign creditors than foreign debtors owe them.

DEBT SERVICE: the amount of principal and interest that falls due within a stated period, such as a year, which must be paid by a debtor.

DEBUG: to search for and correct errors, particularly in digital computer programs or in any complex electronic hardware.

DECEASED ACCOUNT: a bank deposit account in the name of a deceased person.

DECEDENT: a deceased person.

DECENTRALIZATION: the practice of placing authority for decision making at lower levels in a corporate or government structure; the geographical deployment and physical separation of business plants and offices.

DECIBELS: units of measurement of the volume of sound.

DECIMAL: referring to the number system in which units are subdivided in tenths, hundredths, etc. written to the right of a decimal point.

DECISION MAKER: a person, usually a member of a group, who either has authority to make a decision or the ability to influence other members of the group.

DECISION MAKING: the process of resolving differing options into one opinion or course of action so that, when supported by authority, the decision becomes a policy of the organization.

DECK: a collection of computer cards.

DECLARATION: any formal document attesting a fact; in relation to a dividend, the formal act of a corporation creating a liability to pay a dividend.

DECLARATION DATE: the date on which payment of a dividend is authorized by a corporation's board of directors.

DECLARATION OF TRUST: a written agreement that property to which one person holds title actually belongs to another person, for whose benefit the title is maintained.

DECLARATORY JUDGMENT: a court's determination on a question of law, stating the parties' rights without ordering any action.

DECLARED VALUE: the value of merchandise stated by the owner when the goods are delivered to the carrier.

DECLINE STAGE: the period in a product's life cycle between saturation and abandonment.

DECLINING-BALANCE DEPRECIATION: a depreciation method that charges larger amounts of depreciation expense in earlier years and lesser amounts later.

DECODING: the application of a set of unambiguous rules, specifying the way in which data may be restored to a previous representation.

DECREASING TERM INSURANCE: a form of term insurance under which the amount of insurance decreases each year, although the premium remains the same.

DECREE: an order of a court.

DECREE NISI: a decree which is not made absolute until after a specified period.

DECREMENT: a loss in value.

DEDUCTIBLE: capable of being legally subtracted, as certain expenses may be subtracted from income in determining taxable income.

DEDUCTION: an expense subtracted from income on a tax return.

DEED: a legally valid certificate of conveyance of ownership of land.

DEED, GENERAL WARRANTY: a deed that carries an agreement of warranty; the seller will warrant and defend the title against all claims.

DEED OF RELEASE: deed that releases property from the lien of a mortgage.

DEED OF SURRENDER: instrument by which property is identified as an estate for life or an estate for a certain number of years to a person who will receive it in reversion.

DEED OF TRUST: an instrument that conveys or transfers to a trustee the title to property as security for the payment of a debt.

DEED, SPECIAL WARRANTY: a deed in which the seller warrants only claims against himself or his heirs, not against previous owners.

DEEP STOCK: frequently used merchandise kept in large quantities and in many sizes and colors.

DE FACTO: in fact (Latin).

DEFALCATION: a form of embezzlement, usually restricted to absconding with cash.

DEFAMATION: words that attribute disreputable conduct or immoral behavior to the person of whom they are spoken.

DEFAULT: to omit to do that which by law a person is required to do.

DEFEASIBLE: able to be annulled or made void.

DEFECTIVE: referring to merchandise that fails to meet either warranty guarantee, claims made for it, or customary standards for such merchandise.

DEFENDANT: in a criminal suit, the accused; in a civil action, the person or entity sued.

DEFENSIVE INVESTMENT: an investment policy that places its major effort on reducing both the risk of loss and the need for special knowledge, skill, and continuous attention.

DEFERRALS: cash collected before revenue is recognized as being earned, or in which cash is disbursed before an expense is recognized as being incurred.

DEFERRED ANNUITY: an annuity under which payments are not due to begin until some years in the future even though the premium is payable now.

DEFERRED CHARGES: expenditures that are written off over a time period.

DEFERRED COMPENSATION: the postponement of distribution of a portion of current earnings until a later date, usually at retirement.

DEFERRED EXPENSES: in accounting, a nonrecurring charge not currently payable although it involves a service already partially consumed.

DEFERRED INCOME: an amount of income received or receivable but not yet earned.

DEFERRED PAYMENTS: mortgage allowances for postponement of interest payments; delayed payments postponed until a future time.

DEFERRED STOCK: stocks whose dividends are not to be paid until the expiration of a stated date, or until a specified event has taken place.

DEFERRED TAX: a tax liability accrued on income that is reported but not subject to income tax until a later time period.

DEFERRED WAGE INCREASE: a future increase specified in a union contract.

DEFICIT: the opposite of a surplus.

DEFICIT FINANCING: a condition when government expenditures exceed revenues and the difference is made up by borrowing.

DEFICIT SPENDING: the spending of public funds raised by borrowing rather than by taxation.

DEFICIT WEIGHT: the difference between actual shipment weight and the minimum weight when the actual is less than the minimum.

DEFLATION: a direction in the monetary cycle during which goods and services become less costly.

DEFLATIONARY GAP: the amount by which demand falls short of full employment supply, thus lowering the real value of a nation's output.

DEFRAUD: to deprive an individual, by deceit, of some right; to cheat; to withhold improperly that which belongs to another.

DEFRAY: to pay; to carry an expense.

DEFUNCT COMPANY: a firm that has ceased to exist; a dissolved organization.

DEGREE OF FREEDOM: a concept in organizational theory describing a person's exemption or liberation from the control of some other person or power.

DEGRESSIVE TAXATION: a type of progressive taxation, wherein the rates increase as the base amount taxed increases.

DEHIRE: to discharge from a position.

DE JURE: by right (Latin).

DELAYED BROADCAST: a repeat broadcast of a program, often used to compensate for time differentials between station locations of a network.

DELAYED OPENING: the situation created when buy and sell orders accumulate prior to the opening of a stock exchange.

DELEGATE: one chosen to represent many.

DELEGATION: the process by which authority is distributed downward in the organization.

DELINQUENT: in arrears in payment of ordinary debts, loans, and taxes.

DELISTED STOCK: a security that has been removed from the list of those traded on a major stock exchange.

DELIVERY: the transfer of the possession of an item from one person to another.

DELPHI TECHNIQUE: a forecasting approach: at intervals, the organization polls experts who predict long-range technological and market changes that eventually will affect the organization.

DEMAND: the amount of goods or services that will be purchased at various prices at a given time in a market.

DEMAND CURVE: the graphic representation of the quantity of goods demanded in relation to price.

DEMAND DEPOSIT: a deposit on account in a commercial bank on which checks can be drawn and funds taken out without any advance notification.

DEMAND LOAN: a loan that must be repaid whenever the lender requests repayment rather than at a stated time.

DEMAND NOTE: an obligation of the signer payable on the demand of the lender.

DEMAND PRICE: the maximum price a purchaser is willing to pay for a stated quantity of a commodity or service.

DEMAND-PULL INFLATION: a theory holding that inflation is caused by an excess of demand for goods over the economy's ability to supply them.

DEMAND SCHEDULE: a table illustrating the number of units of an item that purchasers would be able and willing to buy at differing prices at a specified time period.

DEMISED PREMISES: quarters formerly occupied.

DEMONETIZATION: the withdrawal of specified currency from circulation; the reduction in the number of government bonds and securities by a commercial bank.

DEMONSTRATOR: a person employed to show machinery and other merchandise in use; an automobile or other device used for demonstration purposes.

DEMOTION: changing of a worker's status; the result is a lower classification, salary, or title.

DEMURRAGE: a charge by a common carrier for loading, unloading, or storage time in excess of agreed limits.

DENOMINATION: the value printed on paper currency or stamped on coinage.

DENOMINATION VALUE: the face value of all currencies, coins, and securities.

DE NOVO: anew; once more; again (Latin).

DEPARTMENTALIZATION: the manner in which an organization is structurally divided.

DEPARTMENT MANAGER: an executive charged with the operation of a selling department of a store.

DEPENDENT COVENANTS: two or more related agreements specifying that the performance of one promise must take place before the performance of other promises.

DEPLETION: the reduction and exhaustion of natural resources.

DEPLETION ALLOWANCE: a tax allowance made to compensate for the reduction in value of the remaining assets as of a mine, oil well, or gas well.

DEPONENT: a person who gives evidence.

DEPOSE: to make a statement under oath.

DEPOSIT: a lodgment of cash or securities with another party, such as depositing money; a synonym for downpayment.

DEPOSITARY RECEIPT: mechanism to allow for the trading of foreign stocks on US stock exchanges when the overseas nation involved will not allow foreign ownership of the stock of domestic firms.

DEPOSIT CERTIFICATE: a document certifying that a deposit of a specific amount has been made with a financial institution for a specified period of time and at a specified rate of interest.

DEPOSIT CREATION MULTIPLIER: the dollars of lending generated by an independent increase of one dollar in bank deposits.

DEPOSIT CURRENCY: checks and other credit items deposited with a bank as the equivalent to cash.

DEPOSIT INSURANCE: the insurance on deposits made to a financial institution, protecting the depositor from loss up to a stated amount should the financial institution fail.

DEPOSITION: a statement made under oath and signed, as for use in a legal trial.

DEPOSIT LOAN: a loan granted by establishing a credit in the deposit account of the borrower.

DEPOSITORY: a place where a deposit is received; one who receives a deposit.

DEPOSIT PREMIUM: the deposit on premiums required by the company on forms of insurance subject to periodic premium adjustment.

DEPOT STORE: a store carrying popular items that customers purchase because of the store's convenient location.

DEPRECIATED COST: original cost less accumulated depreciation.

DEPRECIATION: the decline in book value of an asset due to wear, use, or obsolescence.

DEPRESSED AREA: a community that is not part of the nation's economic growth pattern and has a high level of unemployment.

DEPRESSION: the slowest phase of the business cycle, marked by low prices and high unemployment.

DEPTH INTERVIEW: a method based primarily on the use of open-ended questions, to elicit from the person interviewed natural and lengthy statements about a predetermined subject.

DERELICTION: the intentional abandonment of property.

DERIVATIVE DEPOSIT: a deposit that is created when a person borrows money from a bank.

DERIVED DEMAND: that need for goods or services which has come about as a result of the demand for other goods or services.

DESCRIPTIVE BILLING: a billing system in which an account statement contains sufficient detail to permit the customer to identify the nature, date, and amount of each transaction processed during the statement period.

DETAIL OPERATION SCHEDULE: a production control schedule covering minor details of the items produced.

DETENTION TIME: the period when there is a lack of equipment or space on a store's receiving docks to enable the carrier to unload merchandise, requiring that additional charges be made by the carrier.

DETERMINANT ATTRIBUTES: the product characteristics that help consumers discriminate among products and influence product preferences.

DETERMINISTIC PROPERTIES: characterizing something that does not vary.

DETINUE: a common law action to recover property.

DEVALUATION: the lowering of the value of a nation's currency in relation to the currency of other countries.

DEVELOPING NATION: a nation whose people are beginning to utilize their resources in order to bring about an increase in production of goods and services.

DEVELOPMENT EXPENSE: the cost of developing products, processes, or other commercial activities to make them functional.

DEVISE: to contrive, invent, or bequeath something: a gift of real property by will; to be distinguished from bequest; a will, or clause in a will.

DEVISEE: any person receiving title to real property in accordance with the terms of a will.

DEVISOR: the donor of a gift of real property by will.

DEVOLUTION: the passing of real estate title by hereditary succession.

DEXTERITY TEST: a measure of speed and accuracy in performing simple manual activities.

DEXTROSE: grape sugar.

DIAGONAL EXPANSION: a process whereby a business grows by creating new items that can be produced by using the equipment that is already in use, requiring few additional materials.

DIALECTIC PROCESS OF CHANGE: a concept recognizing that any change introduced by management will create a new situation out of which new problems will develop.

DIARY METHOD: a technique used to determine brand purchase and frequency of buying.

DICTA: rules or arguments given in the written statement of a judge that have no bearing on issues involved and are not critical for their determination.

DIES NON: a day on which no business can be transacted (Latin).

DIE WITHOUT ISSUE: having no children at the date of death.

DIFFERENTIAL: the difference between two quantities, such as railroad rates; a differential rate.

DIFFERENTIAL ADVANTAGE: selling characteristics providing an advantage over competitors.

DIFFERENTIAL COSTS: reflecting the difference in costs between an actual situation and a proposed one.

DIFFERENTIAL OLIGOPOLY: an industry composed of a small number of sellers manufacturing products that are only slightly different.

DIFFERENTIATION: the process by which subunits in an organization develop particular attributes in response to the requirements imposed by their subenvironments.

DIFFUSION THEORY: a theory that tax income is eventually distributed throughout the population by price alterations or other means whereby funds find their way to the government.

DIGESTED SECURITIES: the securities owned by investors who are not expected to sell them soon.

DIGIT: a component of an item of data.

DIGITAL COMPUTER: a computer that handles data in the form of discrete digits.

DILUTION: a the watering down or weakening of something; the reduction in the value of an asset such as a stock.

DIMINISHING-BALANCE METHOD: a method of calculating depreciation in which the periodic charge is computed as a constant percentage of the depreciated cost.

DIMINISHING MARGINAL UTILITY, LAW OF: the consumption of each succeeding unit of a good will yield less satisfaction than the preceding unit.

DIMINISHING RETURNS: dwindling results from repeated use of identical techniques such as marketing promotions.

DIRECT COST: an item of cost that can reasonably be identified with a specific operation or other cost center.

DIRECT EXPENDITURES: payments to employees, suppliers, contractors, beneficiaries, and other final recipients of government payment.

DIRECT FINANCING: raising capital without resorting to underwriting.

DIRECT COSTING: a method of cost accounting in which only direct materials, direct labor, and variable overhead expenses are charged to inventory.

DIRECT INVESTMENTS: investments in foreign corporations where the investors have a controlling interest in the overseas firm.

DIRECTIVE: a policy pronouncement to implement something according to specific instructions to those at a lower echelon in the chain of command.

DIRECT LABOR: cost of wages paid to workers; cost of labor applied directly to a product in processing.

DIRECT LIABILITY: a debtor's obligation arising from money, goods, or services received by him or her from another.

DIRECT MAIL: the advertisements sent directly by mail to the reading audience, such as printed pieces, catalogs, circular letters, postcards, and telegrams.

DIRECT-MAIL LIST: the names and addresses of potential customers, purchased by or given without charge to an organization.

DIRECT MATERIAL: the cost of material forming an integral part of a final product in a manufacturing process.

DIRECT OFFERING: the public offering of a security issued through the issuer's own facilities rather than through investment dealers.

DIRECTOR: any person elected by shareholders to establish company policies.

DIRECTORATE: a corporation's board of directors.

DIRECTORY ADVERTISING: advertising appearing in printed directories.

DIRECT OVERHEAD: overhead costs traceable to a specific part of an operation.

DIRECT PACKAGE: a bundle of letters tied together, all addressed to the same office.

DIRECT SELLING: selling by the manufacturer directly to the user, the retailer, or the final consumer without the intervention of a middleman.

DIRECT TAX: the burden of a tax that cannot be easily shifted or passed on by the person on whom it is levied to another individual.

DISABILITY INCOME: a benefit provided by a specific health insurance contract that indemnifies the insured for loss of time in the event of sickness or accident.

DISAGIO: the charge for exchanging a depreciated foreign currency.

DISBURSEMENT: payment in cash.

DISCHARGE: to sever the employment of an employee; to wipe out by satisfying, as a debt.

DISCIPLINARY LAYOFF: a suspension because of violation of company rules.

DISCLAIMER: a denial.

DISCLOSURE: the divulgence of confidential information.

DISCOUNT: to pay a bill promptly, thus earning an offered cash inducement for so doing; excess of par or stated value of a security over the purchase price; the amount of interest on a loan deducted in advance.

DISCOUNTED CASH FLOW: a method of calculating return on an investment which takes into consideration the changing value of money over time.

DISCOUNTED VALUE: the value at a given date of a future amount, determined by applying compound interest at a given rate to the payment of the future amount.

DISCOUNTING: method by which an institution lends money to a business with a customer's debt obligation to the firm as security on the loan.

DISCOVERY: the disclosure by one party of facts or statements needed by a party seeking those facts in connection with a pending cause or action.

DISCRETION: cautious judgment.

DISCRETIONARY ORDER: an order given to a broker specifying the stock or commodity and the quantity to be bought or sold, but leaving to the judgment of the broker the time and the price of the transaction.

DISCRETIONARY POLICY: monetary policy, purporting to compensate for a business cycle, which leads to a decision by a person or government.

DISCRETIONARY SPENDING POWER: designating money available for consumption after necessities have been purchased.

DISCRIMINATION: an unfair distinction, such as unequal treatment of workers because of race, creed, sex, or union membership or activity.

DISCRIMINATORY DISCHARGE: the firing of an employee for union activity.

DISECONOMIES OF SCALE: increase of costs as a business grows in size.

DISHONOR: to refuse to pay against one's own check or other commercial instrument.

DISINFLATION: the result of a strategy to reduce the general price level by increasing the purchasing power of money.

DISINTERMEDIATION: the taking of money out of interest-bearing time accounts for reinvestment at higher rates for bonds, such as in bonds.

DISINVESTMENT: a negative investment; the disposal of a piece of capital or the failure to maintain a capital good that is being used up.

DISK MEMORY: a random-access memory in which bits of information are stored magnetically on a set of parallel disks.

DISK PACK: a set of magnetic disks designed to be placed in a computer central-processing unit for reading and writing.

DISMISS: to release an employee; to dispose of a case without a trial.

DISPATCH EARNING: a saving in shipping costs arising from rapid unloading at the point of destination.

DISPATCHER: an agent responsible for efficiently routing and sending merchandise off to its destined location.

DISPENSE: distribute; to do without.

DISPERSION: the spread of values in a frequency distribution.

DISPLAY ADVERTISING: advertising in the form of window and interior display.

DISPLAY CONSOLE: a visual display unit of a computer, similar to a television screen.

DISPOSABLE INCOME: an individual's income after taxes.

DISPOSSESS: to put an individual out of his or her property by force.

DISPRODUCT: a damaging item, in particular one that results from negligence on the part of the manufacturer.

DISSEMINATE: to broadcast, as information; to distribute widely, as knowledge.

DISSOLUTION (CORPORATE): termination at the expiration of a charter, by order of the attorney general of the state, by consolidation, or by action of the stockholders.

DISSOLUTION (PARTNERSHIP): termination by the wishes of the partners at a specified time, or by operation of law because of incapacity, death, or bankruptcy of any partner.

DISTRAIN: to seize another's property as security for an obligation.

DISTRESS FOR RENT: the taking of a tenant's personal property in payment of rent on real estate.

DISTRESS SELLING: selling because of necessity.

DISTRIBUTION: marketing; the physical movement and storage of goods in the marketing process; a payment to creditors or stockholders of a portion of the assets of a company in liquidation.

DISTRIBUTION COSTS: a synonym for selling costs, such as advertising, ect.

DIVERSIFICATION: a program of acquiring subsidiaries in industries other than that in which the parent company is engaged.

DIVERSIFIED COMPANY: a corporation engaged in several different lines of business either directly or through subsidiary companies.

DIVEST: to remove a vested right.

DIVESTITURE: the disposal of a subsidiary by sale or spinoff.

DIVIDEND: a payment of a portion of profits to shareholders.

DIVIDEND CHECK: a negotiable instrument in the form of a check drawn on a depository bank of the corporation issuing the dividend.

DIVIDEND-PAYOUT RATIO: the ratio of dividends per share of common stock to earnings per share of common stock.

DIVIDEND RATE: the indicated annual rate of payment to a shareholder based on a company's latest quarterly dividend and recurring extra or special year-end dividends.

DIVISION: an organizational component larger than a department.

DIVISIONALIZATION: the creation of autonomous units in an organization.

DIVISION OF LABOR: breaking a job down into the smallest number of operations without jeopardizing performance.

DOCKING: a pay deduction for breakages, poor work, absenteeism, lateness, and similar causes.

DOCUMENTATION: the support of an argument or thesis with published or written documents to substantiate facts and views.

DOLDRUMS: a state of low business activity.

DOLLAR AVERAGING: purchase of equal dollar amounts of a security as its price falls or rises, either at fixed intervals or a predetermined prices.

DOLLAR DIPLOMACY: foreign diplomacy in the financial interest of the country conducting it or in the financial interest of its nationals.

DOLLAR DRAIN (GAP): the amount by which imports from the United States into a foreign country exceed that nation's exports to the United States.

DOLLAR SHORTAGE: a nation's lack of sufficient money to buy from the United States, caused by a steady favorable balance of payments for the United States.

DOLLY: a low platform mounted on casters or small wheels, designed primarily for moving loads short distances.

DOMESTIC CORPORATION: a corporation within the state where it is chartered; in all other states it is a foreign corporation.

DOMESTICS: the yard goods from which sheets, linens, towels, are cut.

DOMINATION: describing the situation of one who receives objectives by way of direct command.

DOMINION: in transferring property, the separation by the transferor from all power over the property and passing such power to the transferee.

DONATED SURPLUS: in accounting, a capital surplus account that contains a record of the par value of donated stock and of the proceeds from donated stock that has been sold.

DONEE: a person who receives a gift.

DONOR: a person who makes a gift.

DOOMAGE POWER: the power of the government to base a tax assessment on any available data where the taxpayer fails or refuses to furnish a return.

DOOMSDAY STRIKE: a threatened strike that may occur immediately before the beginning of contract negotiations, created to put pressure on management.

DOOR-TO-DOOR SELLING: the process of taking a product or service directly to the potential customers in their homes or offices.

DORMANT ACCOUNT: an account that has had little or no activity for a period of time.

DORMANT COMPANY: an inactive company that continues to comply with legal requirements to continue its existence.

DOUBLE EMPLOYMENT: holding down two jobs at the same time.

DOUBLE ENTRY: bookkeeping method in which each transaction is recorded by means of two or more balancing entries.

DOUBLE INDEMENITY: a clause in an insurance policy providing for payment of twice the face value of the policy under specified conditions.

DOUBLE JEOPARDY: the risk in a second trial for an offense of which one has been acquitted.

DOUBLE-PAGE SPREAD: an advertisement appearing on two facing pages.

DOUBLE SPOTTING: the placing of two broadcast commercials back-to-back with no program material intervening.

DOUBLE TIME: twice the regular rate of pay for working overtime, on Sundays or on holidays.

DOUBLE TRUCK: an advertisement occupying two facing pages in a magazine or newspaper.

DOWER: a wife's right to inherit a portion of the real property held by her husband during their marriage.

DOW JONES AVERAGES: stock price averages computed by Dow Jones & Company, giving the average stock prices by class based on the highest, lowest, opening, and closing stock price averages for representative issues.

DOWNER: a brief work stoppage to draw attention to a particular grievance.

DOWNGRADING: a form of demotion created by a reduction in corporate functions.

DOWNPAYMENT: the cash payment that the purchaser of merchandise sold on an installment-payment plan is required to make at the time of the sale.

DOWNSTAIRS MERGER: a merger of a parent corporation into a subsidiary.

DOWNSTREAM: describing movement of a business activity from a higher to a lower level.

DOWNTIME: a period during which machinery is out of operation for adjustment, repair, or other similar reasons.

DRAFT: an instrument directing a depositary to make payment to a payee or bearer; a written version of a speech, article, or other composition.

DRAWEE: the person against whom a draft is drawn.

DRAWER: any party or company who draws a draft or check upon another party for the payment of funds.

DRAWINGS: withdrawals of cash or merchandise from a business by a sole proprietor or partner.

DRAYAGE: a charge for animal-drawn cartage, and by extension, for any local vehicular transport.

DROMEDARY: a vehicle combining the characteristics of a truck and a truck tractor.

DROP SHIPMENT: merchandise shipped directly from manufacturer to retailer.

DROP SHIPPER: a middleman who secures orders from buyers and sends the orders to manufacturers or other suppliers who ship directly to the buyers.

DRUG: an article in plentiful supply and low demand, said to be a drug on the market.

DRUM MEMORY: a random-access memory in which bits of information are stored magnetically on a cylindrical surface.

DRUMMER: a salesman, particularly a traveling salesmen calling on retailers of soft goods.

DRUM STORAGE: a form of computer storage that uses magnetic recording on a rotating cylinder.

DRY GOODS: specifically, fabrics made from cotton, wool, rayon, silk, and other textile materials; includes ready-to-wear clothing and bed linens.

DUAL BANKING: a condition in which some banks are chartered by the state in which they operate, and others by the federal government.

DUAL DISTRIBUTION: the sale of a product through more than one distributive system.

DUAL MUTUAL FUNDS: funds that divide their portfolios between capital growth investments and income investments.

DUAL SAVINGS PLAN: a plan whereby two separate operations are required to post a savings deposit or a withdrawal to an account.

DUE BILL: a signed instrument acknowledging a debt, negotiable and payable in goods and services.

DUE CARE: the standard of conduct displayed by an ordinary, reasonable, prudent individual.

DUE DATE: the date on which an instrument of debt becomes payable; the maturity date.

DUMMY: one who represents that he is acting for himself but who in reality is acting for another.

DUMMY INVOICE: a statement prepared by a retailer as a temporary replacement for a vendor's invoice.

DUMPING: selling quantities of goods below market prices.

DUN: to press for payment of a debt; to repeatedly demand what one is owed.

DUNNAGE: material other than packaging employed to prevent damage to freight or to support it in shipment.

DUOPOLY: a market structure in which there are only two sellers of a commodity or service.

DUOPSONY: a condition when two buyers are seeking a similar item.

DURABLE GOODS: goods with a normal life expectancy of three years or more, such as automobiles or furniture.

DURESS: compulsion or constraint by force or fear of personal violence, prosecution, or imprisonment which induces a person to do what he does not want to do or to refrain from doing something he has a legal right to do.

DUTCH AUCTION: a form of auction where the auctioneer begins the bidding at a very high price and reduces it until he gets a bid.

DUTY: a customs duty of tax on imports.

DUTY DRAWBACK: a tariff concession allowing a rebate of all or part of the duty on goods imported for processing before being reexported.

DUTY FREE: describing items that are not affected by any customs duty.

DYNAMIC ECONOMY: an economy of growth and change.

DYNAMICS: in economic theory, the consideration of the effect of the time dimension on economic situations.

DYNAMITER: a securities broker who attempts to sell fraudulent or unregistered stocks and bonds over the telephone.

E

EAGER BEAVER: an energetic, imaginative, hardworking person,

EARLY-RETIREMENT BENEFITS: reduced pension received by some employees when they voluntarily leave their company prior to the mandatory-retirement age.

EARMARK: to affix a mark of ownership to any object; such an identifying mark.

EARNED INCOME: the amount received for goods or services delivered and for which no future liability is anticipated.

EARNED RATE: the amount an advertiser pays for media space or time actually used.

EARNED SURPLUS: retained earnings.

EARNEST MONEY: something of value conveyed to a seller by a buyer to bind the bargain.

EARNING POWER: an employee's potential capacity on his or her job to earn wages over a period of time.

EARNINGS: income received for personal services; net profit after taxes of a business.

EARNINGS PER SHARE: a corporation's income for a period divided by the number of shares outstanding at the end of the period which are entitled to full participation in the earnings.

EARNINGS REPORT: a statement issued by a company showing its earnings or losses over a given period.

EASEMENT: the right enjoyed by one owner of real property over the real property of another person, for example, a right-of-way.

EASY MONEY: money that can be borrowed at very low interest rates.

EASY-PAYMENT PLAN: an attractive phrase for an installment method of purchase wherein the full price of the goods or service plus carrying charge may be paid in installments over a period to time.

ECHELON: rank or level of authority in a business organization.

ECONOMETRICS: the study of economic measurements in order to test and develop hypotheses in economic theory.

ECONOMIC COSTS: payments to the owners for the requirements for manufacturing to convince them to supply their resources in a specified activity.

ECONOMIC GOODS: items produced from scarce resources.

ECONOMIC GROWTH: increasing per capita real income over a period of time.

ECONOMIC INDICATORS: classification of economic information, to be used in business-cycle analysis and forecasting.

ECONOMIC PROFIT: the residual profit after explicit and implicit costs have been paid; synonymous with pure profit.

ECONOMICS: the study of the factors that affect the production, distribution, and consumption of wealth and of the use of the earth's resources to satisfy the needs and desires of man.

ECONOMIC SANCTIONS: the provision for securing conformity to a position, decree, or law by economic steps such as boycott, embargo, credit controls, or trade restrictions.

ECONOMIC STRIKE: a work stoppage over money issues and working conditions rather than unfair labor practices.

ECONOMIC VALUE: the value given to an item as a function of its usefulness and its scarcity.

ECONOMIES OF SCALE: the result of production functions showing that an equal percentage increase in all inputs leads output to increase by a larger percentage.

ECONOMY: the financial state of the nation; thrift.

ECONOMY OF SCALE: the condition that exists when the average cost of production declines as output increases.

EDGE CORPORATION: a foreign banking organization structured in compliance with the Federal Reserve Act.

EDIT: to rearrange data or information into a meaningful form; to prepare an author's work for publication.

EDITORIAL: an article stating the opinion of the editor or management of a publication, broadcast facility, or other medium of mass communication.

EDITORIAL CREDIT: identification

of a specific retail operation as a source for a fashion item featured editorially in a consumer magazine or newspaper.

EFFECTIVE DATE: the date on which an agreement or contract goes into effect; the starting date.

EFFECTIVE DEBT: the total debt of a firm.

EFFECTIVE PAR: with preferred stocks, the par value that would ordinarily correspond to a given dividend rate.

EFFECTIVE TAX RATE: the average rate of taxation; total tax payable divided by the income on which the tax was calculated.

EFFICIENCY: highly mechanized, accident-free production, well coordinated, with good marketing, financing, recordkeeping, and management.

EFFICIENCY EXPERT: a specialist who analyzes and reports on doing the correct thing, at the proper time, in the right place, by the appropriate person.

EFFICIENCY VARIANCE: quantity variance, applied to labor.

EFFORT BARGAIN: a collective-bargaining agreement that identifies the quantity of work to be completed for a stated wage payment.

EJECTMENT: an action brought to regain possession of real property from a party wrongfully in possession of it.

ELASTIC DEMAND: a demand that changes in relatively large volume as prices increase or decrease.

ELASTIC SUPPLY: a supply that changes in relatively large volume with a minor change in price.

ELECTRIC EYE: a photoelectric cell, frequently used to open a door when an approaching person blocks a light beam.

ELECTRONIC DATA PROCESSING: the data processing largely performed by electronic devices.

ELECTRONIC FUNDS-TRANSFER SYSTEMS: a loose description of computerized systems that process financial transactions or process information about financial transactions.

ELECTRONICS: the industry based upon the emission, behavior, and effects of electrons.

ELECTROPLATING: deposition of metal on a cathode in an electrolytic cell; usually the cathode is either of metal or graphited to receive a metal deposit.

ELEOMOSYNARY: charitable or nonprofit.

ELEVATION: a front or side view on a set of architectural plans; altitude from sea level; a rise in responsibilities and job title; a promotion.

ELIGIBLE INVESTMENT: any income-producing investment that is considered to be a sound repository for the funds of savings banks and similar institutions.

ELIMINATING ENTRIES: adjustments in the preparation of consolidated financial statements made to prevent duplication due to intercompany transactions.

EMBARGO: a government order stopping the import or export of a particular commodity or commodities.

EMBEZZLEMENT: misappropriation of assets in one's custody and control.

EMBOSS: to raise in relief from a surface.

EMBRYONIC: in the very early stages.

EMERGENCY DISPUTE: a strike or the threat of a strike that would affect the national welfare and/or safety.

EMINENT DOMAIN: the right of governmental bodies to acquire private property necessary for public use for reasonable compensation.

EMOLUMENTS: total payment for work done or services provided.

EMPATHY: the ability to perceive how potential customers feel and what their attitudes, needs, and expectations are.

EMPHYTEUTIC LEASE: a perpetual lease whereby the owner of an uncultivated parcel has granted it to another in perpetuity or for a lengthy period on condition that the leasee will improve the land.

EMPIRICAL: based on experience.

EMPLOYEE PROFIT SHARING: setting aside a previously stated portion of the profits for a calendar period for distribution to employees, frequently in proportion to individual earnings for the period.

EMPLOYEES' ANNUAL REPORT: a report of company activities for a given year, chiefly an explanation and interpretation of the company's financial statement, prepared particularly for employees.

EMPLOYEE STOCK-OWNERSHIP PLAN: one of a number of forms of plans whereby key employees or all employees of a corporation can acquire stock either by grant of rights to purchase or by purchase out of payroll deductions.

EMPLOYER INTERFERENCE: unfair labor practices.

EMPLOYMENT ACCOUNT: credit account arranged for an employee, on which a discount may or may not be given.

EMPLOYMENT AGENCY: a licensed firm that recruits qualified applicants for jobs and finds suitable positions for job seekers.

EMULATE: to strive to equal or excel; when a system accepts the same data, executes the same programs, and achieves the same results as the system imitated.

EN BLOCK: as a unit.

ENCLOSURE: material other than a letter inserted in an envelope.

ENCLOSURE SALE: a sale in which property placed as security for a debt is sold to pay the debt.

ENCROACHMENT: gradual or stealthy inroads upon the rights, possessions, or property of another.

ENCUMBRANCE: a lien against real or personal property.

ENDORSEE: the person to whom a negotiable item payable or endorsed to order is negotiated by endorsement and delivery (also spelled indorsee).

ENDORSEMENT: a signature on the back of a check by the payee acknowledging receipt of, or guaranteeing the face amount.

ENDORSER: one who endorses; the person who transfers his title to an instrument to another by endorsement (also spelled indorser).

ENDOWMENT: a substantial gift or bequest, as to an institution of learning; describing an insurance policy payable as a benefit on a definite date.

ENERVATE: to weaken; to render powerless.

ENFEOFF: to invest with an estate held in fee.

ENGAGE: to hire.

ENGEL'S LAW: the economic concept that the proportion of a family's budget allocated for food goes up as the income goes down.

ENGRAVING: a photomechanically produced metal plate used in printing and as an original for molds to make electrotyped copies.

ENGROSS: to purchase a sufficient quantity of a commodity to secure a monopoly for purposes of reselling at a higher price.

ENHANCEMENT: to increase in value.

ENJOIN: to issue a legal order to forbid or stop an action.

EN ROUTE: on the way.

ENTAIL: to limit or curtail the succession to property by ordinary rules of inheritance.

ENTERPRISE: a business undertaking; a personal quality combining ambition, energy, and hard work.

ENTREPOT TRADE: reexporting imports from a warehouse.

ENTREPRENEUR: a person who, on his own initiative, establishes and operates a business enterprise.

ENTREPRENEURIAL WITHDRAWALS: amounts withdrawn by independent businessmen or farm operators from their business receipts, as personal compensation or otherwise, for nonbusiness purposes.

ENTRUST: to deliver goods or money to another for safekeeping; to grant decision making power over its investment to that party.

ENTRY: an input received from a terminal device attached to a computer; a recording of data in an account or account book.

ENVELOPE: a piece of folded paper that completely encloses a letter.

ENVIRONMENT: the total surrounding conditions of influence and atmosphere.

ENVIRONMENTAL SELLING: displaying items for sale in a setting that simulate a buyer's home.

EQUAL DIGNITY: a reference to mortgages or other legal obligations so that all have equal ranking to prevent one from taking precedence over another.

EQUAL PAY: pay that is the same for all people performing the same work.

EQUATION PRICE: a price attained by the adjusting action of competition in any market at any time, or in a unit of time, such that the demand and supply become equal at that price.

EQUILIBRIUM: economic or physical conditions that tend to maintain themselves in the same situation.

EQUILIBRIUM PRICE: the price that maximizes a firm's profitability; the price of goods determined in the market by the intersection of supply and demand curves.

EQUILIBRIUM QUANTITY: the quantity that maximizes a firm's profitability; the quantity of goods determined in the market by the intersection of supply and demand curves.

EQUIPMENT BOND: a bond secured by mortgage on rolling stock, machinery, or other equipment; equipment trust certificate.

EQUIPMENT LEASING: the renting of expensive equipment to save a substantial and immediate cash outlay.

EQUITABLE CONVERSION: permitting real property to be converted into personal property.

EQUITABLE MORTGAGE: a written statement making certain property security for a debt.

EQUITABLE OWNERSHIP: the estate or interest of a person who has

a beneficial right in property, the legal ownership of which is in another person.

EQUITABLE TITLE: ownership by a person who does not have legal title.

EQUITY: the residual interest of an owner after all relevant debts have been paid.

EQUITY CAPITAL: paid-in capital plus retained earnings.

EQUITY FINANCING: the selling of capital stock by a corporation.

EQUITY OF REDEMPTION: a mortgagor's right to get back his or her property after it has been forfeited for nonpayment of the debt it secured.

EQUITY SECURITIES: any stock issue, common or preferred.

EQUITY TRANSACTION: a transaction resulting in an increase or decrease of net worth or involving the transfer between accounts making up the net worth.

EQUITY TURNOVER: the ratio that measures the relationship between sales and the common stockholders' equity.

ERASE: to obliterate information from a storage medium.

ERGONOMICS: matching of machines and people to increase efficiency.

ERRATIC FLUCTUATIONS: short-term changes that are difficult to measure and predict because they tend to be unexpected.

ERRORS AND OMISSIONS: referring to insurance coverage for liability arising out of errors or omissions in the performance of professional services other than in the medical profession.

ESCALATION CLAUSE: a clause in a contract which permits upward adjustments of price under specified conditions.

ESCAPE CLAUSE: a provision allowing one or more parties to a contract to withdraw therefrom or to modify their performance when stipulated conditions exist.

ESCHEAT: the reversion of property to the state by failure of persons legally entitled to hold the property to lay claim to it.

ESCROW: the state of something being held in trust by a person who is not a party to the matter until such time as certain conditions are met.

ESCROWED SHARES: shares of a corporation which, while still entitled to vote and receive dividends, cannot be bought or sold without special approval.

ESPIONAGE: spying.

ESTABLISHMENT: a business and, particularly, its quarters; the founding of a business.

ESTATE: the right, title, or interest a person has in any property, to be distinguished from the property itself, which is the subject matter of the interest.

ESTATE AT WILL: an estate of indefinite duration; the estate allows the lessee possession as long as both lessor and lessee mutually agree to it.

ESTATE IN REVERSION: the remaining portion of an estate that the grantor retains after certain interests in it have been transferred to another.

ESTATE IN SEVERALTY: an estate held by one person only.

ESTATE PLANNING: the arrangement of a person's affairs to facilitate the passage of his assets to his beneficiaries and to minimize taxes upon death.

ESTATE TAX: a tax on the wealth of a decedent.

ESTIMATED COST SYSTEM: a method of cost accounting in which the costs of production are initially based on estimated costs, with adjustments later for differences between estimated and actual costs.

ESTIMATED REVENUES: the account title used in governmental accounting to set up the budgeted revenues for a period.

ESTOPPEL: a bar to denying a fact because of previous admission of it.

ESTOVERS: the materials or supplies that a tenant is permitted to take from the custody of the landlord in order to make necessary repairs and prevent constructive eviction.

ETHICAL: morally right; pertaining to a pharmaceutical sold only on prescription.

ETHICS, BUSINESS: that branch of moral study concerning those duties a member of a business owes to the public, to the court, and to his associates.

ETHICS, CODE OF: a system of principles or rules guiding the conduct of persons in the same business or profession.

EUROBOND: a bond released by a United States or other non-European company for sale in Europe.

EUROCURRENCY: monies of various nations deposited in European banks that are used in the European financial market; synonymous with Euromoney.

EURODOLLAR: a US dollar held outside the United States, particularly in Europe.

EUROPEAN COMMON MARKET: an economic union for trade purposes, consisting of Italy, the Federal Republic of Germany, Belgium, Luxembourg, France, the Netherlands, Great Britain, and Greece.

EVALUATION: a procedure determining the worth of a business, quality, person, good, service, or almost anything.

EVASION: surreptitious or illegal avoidance.

EVEN LOTS: lots or number of stock shares sold in units of 100 or multiples thereof.

EVICTION: legal expulsion from premises.

EXAMINATION FOR DISCOVERY: the pretrial examination and cross-examination under oath of the parties to an action, enabling both the plaintiff and defendant to assess each other's case.

EXCESS CONDEMNATION: in condemnation proceedings, taking more land or property than is truly required for the government project in question.

EXCESS-COVERAGE CLAUSE: claiming that in the event of a loss, a specific insurance will be considered in excess of any other insurance held against the identical risk.

EXCESS-DEMAND CURVE: reflecting the quantity demanded less the quantity offered at each price.

EXCESS INSURANCE: a policy or bond covering the insured against certain hazards, applying only to loss of damage in excess of a stated amount.

EXCESS LOAN: a bank loan made to one customer that is in excess of the maximum stated by law.

EXCESS OF LOSS REINSURANCE: reinsurance that indemnifies the ceding company for the excess of a stipulated sum or primary retention in the event of loss.

EXCESS-PROFITS TAX: a tax added to the normal tax placed on a business, usually levied on profits above what the law declares as normal.

EXCESS RESERVES: a term used to designate the amount of funds held in reserve by banks in excess of the legal minimum requirements.

EXCESS-SUPPLY CURVE: reflecting the quantity offered less the quantity asked at each price.

EXCHANGE: to barter; to give currency of one country in exchange for that of another; to return for credit or other merchandise; a marketplace, usually for securities or commodities.

EXCHANGE ACQUISITION: a method of filling an order to purchase a block of stock on the floor of an exchange.

EXCHANGE COMMERCIAL: the last advertisement on a program when the time is employed by the alternate series sponsor.

EXCHANGE CURRENT: the current rate of exchange.

EXCHANGE DISTRIBUTION: a method of disposing of large blocks of stock on the floor of an exchange.

EXCHANGE RATE: the ratio at which the money of one country is exchanged for the money of another country.

EXCISE TAX: a tax charged on goods produced or manufactured.

EXCLUSION: any restriction or limitation; a provision of an insurance policy or bond referring to hazards, circumstances, or property not covered by the policy.

EXCLUSION ALLOWANCE: the portion of an annuity payment that can be excluded from taxable income each year.

EXCLUSIVE: goods obtainable from a limited number of stores or dealers; sales of merchandise limited to a single retailer in a given location.

EXCLUSIVE-DEALING CONTRACTS: an agreement that a buyer will make all purchases of a specific item from only one seller and will refrain from carrying competing goods.

EXCLUSIVE DISTRIBUTION: a manufacturer's protection given to a dealer against the location of other dealers in the same area.

EXCLUSIVE LISTING: a contract between the owner of real estate and a broker such that the broker will receive a commission regardless of who makes the sale.

EXCLUSIVE-OUTLET SELLING: a condition under which one retailer or wholesaler in a location has exclusive control over the sale of an article or service.

EXCLUSIVITY: the right acquired by an employee organization to be the sole representative of the bargaining unit.

EXCULPATORY CLAUSE: a clause that relieves the landlord of liability for personal injury to tenants as well as for property damages.

EX-DIVIDEND: a stock's price after deduction of dividend; referring to the quotation on stock on or directly after the record date of the dividend.

EXECUTED CONTRACT: a contract in which performance by both parties has been completed.

EXECUTION: the signing of written documents, making them legally valid.

EXECUTIVE: a person whose position calls for the making of decisions and the exercise of power over others in the conduct of the affairs of a business or government.

EXECUTIVE COMMITTEE: a formal group responsible for the direct operation and management of an organization.

EXECUTIVE COMPENSATION: the total monies paid to an executive, including the regular salary, plus additional payments, but not including warrants or options to purchase stock.

EXECUTIVE SUBSYSTEM: a system of jobs and their definitions devised to accomplish work.

EXECUTIVE TRAINEE: a younger person who works in various units of a business to receive on-the-job training and to acquire familiarity with the entire operation.

EXECUTOR: a person appointed under a will to administer the affairs of the deceased.

EXECUTORY: that which has not yet been executed, as a part of a contract.

EXECUTORY CONTRACT: a contract in which something remains to be done to complete the original agreement.

EXECUTRIX: a woman executor.

EXEMPT COMMODITY: merchandise shipped in interstate commerce to which published rates do not apply.

EXEMPT EMPLOYEES: the employees who are not subject to the rulings of seniority; employees not subject to wage and overtime provisions of the Fair Labor Standards Act.

EXEMPTION: a sum not taxed, such as an exemption from taxable income for the sole support of a dependent; an excuse from duty or service as jury duty.

EXERCISE NOTICE: a notice issued by a clearinghouse that was formed to insure stock deliveries, obligating a customer to send the securities covered by an option against payment of the exercise price.

EXERCISE PRICE: the fixed price at which a stock can be purchased in a call contract or sold in a put contract; synonymous with striking price.

EX GRATIA: voluntary (Latin).

EXHAUST PRICE: in the stock market, the price below which stock bought on margin will be sold unless more security is put up.

EXISTING MORTGAGE: a mortgage that is encumbering a property.

EXODUS: mass emigration, such as the exodus from the cities to the suburbs.

EX OFFICIO: officially; by virtue of an office (Latin).

EX PARTE: on behalf of (Latin).

EXPECTED EXIT VALUE: the nondiscounted amount of cash a company expects to realize from holding a particular asset.

EXPECTED RETURN: the profit that is anticipated from a business venture.

EXPECTED VALUE: a weighted average of all the conditional values of an act.

EXPECTED YIELD: the ratio of expected return over the investment total.

EXPEDITE: to follow up the progress of an order, cajoling and needling others, and suggesting methods for speeding up delivery.

EXPENDABLE FUND: a fund whose assets may be applied by administrative action for general or specific purposes.

EXPENDITURE: the incurring of a liability, the payment of cash, or the transfer of property for the acquisition of a good or service.

EXPENDITURE MULTIPLIER: the amount resulting from an increase in sales because of the induced spending created thereby.

EXPENSE: the cost of acquiring goods or a service.

EXPENSE ACCOUNT: an account carried in the general ledger in which all operating expenses are recorded.

EXPENSE BUDGET: the planned cost of the volume at which it is expected that an activity will be undertaken.

EXPENSE CONSTANT: a flat amount included in some premiums, covering the minimum expense of an insurance transaction.

EXPENSE RATIO: the percentage of

the premium used to pay all operating costs.

EXPENSION: extending or broadening the operation or area of a business; a business-cycle fluctuation characterized by an increase in industrial activity.

EXPERT TESTIMONY: the testimony given by one acknowledged to have special training and knowledge of a particular subject.

EXPERT WITNESS: one who is acknowledged to have special training and knowledge of a particular subject.

EXPIRE: to arrive at the termination period of an agreement, contract, or other instrument.

EXPLICIT INTEREST: the amount of money or goods paid on a loan.

EXPLOITATION: an ingenious, opportunistic, and thorough development of methods to achieve high marketability of a product or service.

EXPORT: to sell and ship to foreign customers; merchandise so sold and shipped.

EXPORT-IMPORT BANK: that governmental agency formed to engage in the general banking business in helping exports and imports of the United States, but not to compete with private banking activities.

EXPOSITION: a show or exhibition of wares and attractions with multiple participants and promotion to attract buyers.

EX POST FACTO: by a subsequent act (Latin).

EXPRESS: a means of transportation of merchandise by truck, rail, or air characterized by faster handling of shipments than by freight; to ship by express.

EXPRESS MAIL: a speedy, reliable, and dependable personal mail service to meet customers' needs.

EXPRESS WARRANTY: a statement by a seller to a buyer that a specific condition exists in the character of goods.

EXPRESSWAY: a limited-access highway for fast automobile and truck travel.

EXPROPRIATION: the right of the state to take private real property for public use, with compensation being given to the owner.

EX-RIGHTS: price after deduction of value or rights declared.

EX-STOCK DIVIDEND: without any stock dividend.

EXTEND: to multiply the unit price by the quantity of units in order to ascertain the total cost on an invoice; to allow a period of time for the payment of a debt.

EXTENDED COVERAGE: in insurance language, coverage beyond the normal, standard policy.

EXTENSION: an allowance to a creditor of additional time in which to pay a debt.

EXTENUATING CIRCUMSTANCES: conditions that may permit an infraction of rules or an illegal act to be judged more leniently.

EXTERNALITY: an economic concept that relates to the effects of a transaction between two parties which affects a third unrelated party.

EXTERNAL STORAGE: storage facilities removable from a computer but holding information in a form acceptable to the machine.

EXTINGUISH: to wipe out, settle, or conclude, as with a debt or obligation.

EXTORTION: the taking of something of value from someone by force, fear of exposure, or threat of force.

EXTRACTIVE INDUSTRY: a business that takes products directly from nature, especially from land or water.

EXTRACTORS: businesses that grow products or take raw materials from nature.

EXTRA DATING: adding days beyond the regular date for invoice payment.

EXTRADITE: to procure the transfer of a person to another jurisdiction to face criminal charges.

EXTRA DIVIDEND: a dividend declared and paid in addition to the regular dividend.

EXTRANEOUS ITEMS: charges for gift wrapping, special mailing, and so on, that must be removed when auditing sales to arrive at true net sales totals.

EXTRAPOLATE: to estimate values in an unknown area by projection of known values.

EYEBALL CONTROL: visual coverage of inventory to determine whether there is sufficient stock on hand to fulfill amounts requested by a wholesaler, retailer, or consumer.

F

FABRICATION: a construction, usually from standardized and preassembled components.

FACED MAIL: mail arranged with addresses and stamps all in the same position.

FACE VALUE: the stated value on the face of an instrument of wealth, as a treasury bill, certificate, check, note, etc.

FACILITATE: to assist.

FACILITATING AGENCY: organization that services other institutions but does not take title to goods.

FACILITY: something that makes easy an action or operation, hence such operating installations as a power plant, factory, depot, fuel, or communication line.

FACSIMILE: a reproduction.

FACSIMILE BROADCASTING: transmission of words or pictures by radio.

FACSIMILE SIGNATURES: signatures on checks, stock certificates, bonds, or other documents which are mechanically imprinted.

FACT-FINDING: the investigation, collection, and making known to a specified organization of the facts regarding a specific situation.

FACTOR: one who finances the transactions of a business.

FACTORAGE: the commission collected by a factor.

FACTOR ANALYSIS: a statistical method for interpreting scores and correlations of scores from a number of tests.

FACTOR HOURS: the sum of all hours worked by one employee operating two or more pieces of equipment simultaneously.

FACTORING: a means of advancing credit, whereby the factor purchases at a discount and without recourse, the accounts receivable of a firm.

FACTORS: ingredients needed for the production of any goods or services; limited agents who buy accounts receivables from small firms at discount.

FACTORS OF PRODUCTION: the "ingredients" used by an enterprise in producing a commodity.

FACTORY OVERHEAD: manufacturing costs excluding direct material and direct labor.

FACTOTUM: a person employed to do many kinds of work.

FACT SHEET: an outline of major product data supplied to copywriters or to broadcast announcers, who use it when ad-libbing.

FACULTATIVE: describing a specific transaction, one risk at a time, with the ceding and acceptance being optional on the part of the ceding company and the reinsurer.

FAIR MARKET VALUE: the amount a willing buyer would pay and a willing seller would accept in an open and unrestricted market.

FAIR PRICE: the price that results in a fair return on funds invested, to claim a reasonable profit.

FAIR RATE OF RETURN: the profit that a public utility can earn to pay interest and dividends and expand facilities, as determined by federal and state law.

FAIR-TRADE ACTS: the laws passed by various states in which retailers are obliged to maintain specified prices on select goods.

FAIR-TRADE AGREEMENT: an agreement between manufacturer and distributor or manufacturer and retailer setting a minimum resale price on the manufacturer's trademarked merchandise.

FALL: decline, as a market price.

FALLBACK: the condition that exists when manual functions or special computer techniques are used when a system errs.

FALL-BACK PAY: a guaranteed minimum pay level.

FALL OUT OF BED: a crash in stock prices, a sharp drop in the market.

FALSE ADVERTISING: advertising that is misleading in a material respect.

FAMILY ALLOWANCE PLAN: a scheme providing every family, rich or poor, with a certain amount of money, based exclusively on the number and age of its children.

FAMILY BRANDS: brands that appear on two or more products of the company.

FARM OUT: to subcontract.

FARM SURPLUS: the farm products purchased by the US government for purposes of keeping agricultural prices stable.

FASCISM: a centralized authoritative form of government with a private economy that is controlled by the government.

FASHION WORLD: the people who work in the garment industry both manufacturing and retail and their efforts from apparel design through store operation.

FAST TRACKING: choosing of certain workers for rapid advancement while the remaining members of the work force are essentially bypassed.

FAT BUDGET ITEMS: merchandise approved by buyers in anticipation that the goods will substantially increase sales potential.

FATIGUE: diminished ability to do work, either mental or physical, as a consequence of previous exertion.

FEASIBILITY STUDY: an investigation before the commencement of a project to determine the probable success thereof.

FEATHERBEDDING: a labor union requirement of employing more personnel for a task than is considered necessary by management.

FEATURE: the components of an item or service yielding a benefit; the more active stocks in the general list.

FED: the Federal Reserve System.

FEDERAL ADVISORY COUNCIL: a committee of the Federal Reserve System that advises the Board of Governors on major developments and activities.

FEDERAL RESERVE BANK: one of a dozen banks created by and operating under the Federal Reserve System.

FEDERAL RESERVE BOARD: the seven-member governing body of the Federal Reserve System.

FEDERAL RESERVE SYSTEM: the title given to the central banking system of the United States as established by the Federal Reserve Act of 1913.

FEDERALS: a name given to items drawn on banks in a large city in which a Federal Reserve bank is located, although the banks do not belong to the city's Clearinghouse Association.

FED WIRE: a communications network linking Federal Reserve banks, branches, and member banks, used both to transfer funds and to transmit information.

FEEDBACK: market information from the field.

FEEDFORWARD: anticipating any errors in a process prior to its being carried out, with the intent to control it more accurately.

FEE SIMPLE: outright ownership of real property without limitations.

FELONY: a serious legal offense; crime.

FENCE: a receiver of stolen items.

FIAT: a decree, directive, or instruction carrying the authority of business or government leadership.

FIAT MONEY: the paper currency of a government not backed by specie or promise of redemption.

FIDELITY BOND: the insurance for an employer for loss sustained by him or her because of any dishonest act by an employee covered by the insurance.

FIDELITY INSURANCE: coverage against loss from embezzlement or theft by employees.

FIDUCIARY: a person or institution entrusted with custody of securities or other valuables, or handling of affairs, in confidence for another.

FIELD EXPERIMENT: the attempt of an investigator to manipulate and control variables in a natural or real setting, rather than in the laboratory.

FIELD MAN: a company employee traveling a certain territory, developing new agencies as well as servicing agencies already representing the company.

FIELD SURVEY: a sampling of opinion or facts among industry members, dealers, or consumers assembled from interviews on the premises of those interviewed.

FIELD WAREHOUSING: an approach for receiving collateral pledged in business loans.

FIFO: an acronym composed of the first letters of the words "first in, first out," denoting adherence to that method of inventory accounting.

FIGURE: to do an arithmetical computation, especially to prepare a bid or estimate; a numeral.

FILE: a storage cabinet for orderly placement and retrieval of letters, documents, and/or data; an orderly collection of papers; on magnetic tape the data between end-of-file marks.

FILE, ACTIVE: a file in which entries are made on a continuous basis.

FILE MAINTENANCE: the activity of keeping a file up to date by adding, changing, or deleting data.

FILE, MASTER: a current, fully updated file into which new entries are entered.

FINAL SALES: the total of net sales to consumers, governments, and foreigners.

FINANCE: to provide capital, either through borrowing or from internally generated funds; the management of monetary affairs.

FINANCE, PUBLIC: a special branch of finance dealing with the provision of means of payment to meet public or government expenditures.

FINANCE COMPANY: a discount house or commercial credit company; at times, also a personal loan company.

FINANCIAL EXPENSE: interest expense on long-term debts.

FINANCIAL INTERMEDIARIES: financial institutions such as commercial banks, insurance companies, and mutual-trust funds that act as an intermediary between lenders (and savers) and borrowers.

FINANCIAL MARKETS: the money and capital markets of the economy.

FINANCIAL POSITION: the status of a company, combining the assets and liabilities as listed on a balance sheet.

FINANCIAL RATIOS: the relationships that exist between various items appearing in balance sheets and income accounts and occasionally other items.

FINANCIAL SOLVENCY: a normal business condition: current assets are above current liabilities.

FINANCIAL STATEMENT: any report summarizing the financial condition or financial results of an organization on any date or for any period.

FINANCIER: an individual who earns his or her living by supplying money for other people's business.

FINDER: a person who locates a buyer or a seller in order to complete a transaction that would probably not take place through ordinary efforts.

FINDER'S FEE: a brokerage fee paid to a third party who brings two principals together.

FINENESS: the closeness of fabric weave; the degree of purity when speaking of gold or silver coin.

FINE SORT: in bookkeeping, the act of sorting posting media in an alphabetical arrangement within a letter of the alphabet.

FINISHED GOODS: goods that have gone through the manufacturing process and have been made ready for sale.

FIRE INSURANCE: a contract providing idemnification for specified loss by fire in return for payment of specified premiums.

FIRE-RETARDANT: capable of retarding the spread of fire, as walls of fire-retardant materials.

FIRE SALE: goods sold at reduced prices because they have been damaged or water-soiled in a fire.

FIRM: strictly speaking, a partnership, although the term is often applied to corporations as well.

FIRM ORDER: a definite order, written or verbal, that cannot be canceled.

FIRST DEED OF TRUST: a deed of trust that is recorded first and is the first lien.

FIRST-GENERATION COMPUTER: a computer utilizing vacuum-tube components.

FIRST LEVEL: the lowest level position in an organization.

FIRST LIEN: a first mortgage.

FIRST-LINE MANAGEMENT: the management level just above the workers.

FIRST MORTGAGE: a mortgage having priority over all other mortgages on a property.

FIRST-MORTGAGE BONDS: bonds secured by a first mortgage on all or part of the property of the issuing organization.

FIRST-PARTY INSURANCE: insurance indemnifying the policyholder against loss or damage to his own property.

FIRST QUARTER: the first three months of the fiscal year of a business or government.

FIRSTS: the top grade of any item.

FISCAL: relating to financial matters.

FISCAL CHARGES: expenses or charges that are normal for a given type of business and must be incurred in order to engage in a given type of business.

FISCAL DRAG: the tendency of a high-employment economy to be restrained from its full growth potential because it is incurring budgetary surpluses.

FISCAL PERIOD: the period for which financial statements are prepared, usually the fiscal year.

FISCAL POLICY: in a general sense, a government's activities concerned with taxes, receipts, debt expenditures, currency, and trust funds.

FISCAL YEAR: the US Treasury year, extending from July 1 to June 30, or any other one-year period selected for accounting and tax purposes.

FIXED ANNUITY: an annuity contract providing payments that remain constant throughout the annuity period.

FIXED ASSET: a tangible long-term asset, such as land, buildings, or equipment, held for use rather than for sale.

FIXED CAPITAL: the investment in capital assets.

FIXED COST: an indirect expense, such as rent, that remains relatively unchanged in total, regardless of the volume of production or activity.

FIXED CHARGES: bond interst, taxes, and other charges that must inescapably be met on fixed dates.

FIXED FEE: payment for services in an amount stipulated prior to the performance of the service.

FIXED INCOME: any constant income that does not fluctuate over a period of time, such as that from bonds, annuities, and preferred stocks.

FIXED LIABILITIES: all liabilities that will not mature within the ensuing fiscal period.

FIXED-PRICE CONTRACT: a contract under which the contractor receives a fixed amount regardless of his costs of completion.

FIXED ROUTING: calling on customers on a regular basis.

FIXTURE: a fixed asset attached to or forming a normal part of a building.

FLAG: a bit of data assigned to a character or word to indicate a boundary or a limit: a character that signals the occurrence of some condition.

FLAGGING AN ACCOUNT: temporarily suspending activity on an account until brought up to date or for other relevant reasons.

FLAG OF CONVENIENCE: the national flag flown by a ship that is registered in a country other than that of its owners.

FLAGSHIP STORE: a downtown or home office store where executive, merchandising, and sales personnel are located.

FLASH REPORT: a preliminary report of estimated earnings issued to top management as soon as possible after the close of an accounting period.

FLAT: without the addition of interest as the price of a defaulted bond.

FLAT CANCELLATION: the cancellation of a policy as of what would have been its effective date, before the company has assumed liability.

FLATCAR: a railroad freight car without top or sides, ideally suited to the transportation of heavy machinery.

FLATION: neither inflation or deflation; a period of economic stability.

FLAT RATE: a special rate quoted for an entire service, although the usual practice would be to charge by the unit.

FLEECE: the taking advantage of a poorly informed individual by a person conversant with security-market conditions.

FLEET POLICY: an insurance contract covering a number of automobiles.

FLEXIBILITY: the quality of nonrigidity, particularly in negotiations or applications.

FLEXIBLE BUDGET: a budget that is established for a range rather than for a single level of activity.

FLEXITIME: a system that allows employees to choose their own starting and finishing times within a broad range of available hours.

FLIER: a handout used to promote an idea, product, or person; a speculative purchase or investment.

FLIGHT OF CAPITAL: movement of capital, which has usually been converted into a liquid asset, from one place to another to avoid loss or to increase gain.

FLIGHT SATURATION: maximum concentration of spot advertising in a relatively short period.

FLIP-FLOP: a circuit or device containing active elements capable of assuming either one of two stable states at a given time.

FLOAT: to get, as to float a loan, i.e., borrow funds; the total of currency in circulation not including bank deposits.

FLOATER POLICY: a policy under whose terms protection follows movable property.

FLOATING ASSET: a current asset.

FLOATING CHARGE: debt security in the form of a general claim on the assets of a corporation without attachment to specific assets.

FLOATING DEBT: current liabilities.

FLOATING EXCHANGE RATE: a technique that allows exchange rates in a particular country to float freely, allowing that country's currency to find its own level in a free market.

FLOATING RATE: a variable interest rate.

FLOOR: in the stock-market, the trading area of services.

FLOOR TRADER: an employee of a member firm of an exchange who trades on the floor of the exchange on behalf of his firm's clients.

FLOORWALKER: person who moves about a store through various selling departments and assists customers in ways not handled by sales personnel.

FLOTSAM: goods from or parts of a shipwrecked vessel which are found floating on the surface of the sea.

FLOW CHART: a graphic presentation of the movement in an operational sequence.

FLOWER BONDS: US government bonds.

FLUCTUATION: the ups and downs of prices.

FLUID SAVINGS: savings that have neither been spent nor invested.

FLURRY: suddenly accelerated pace of trading on an exchange, of brief duration and usually characterized by sharp price movement.

FLUSH PRODUCTION: the sizable production yielded by new oil wells during the first cycle of their life.

FLYING SQUADRON: composed of supervisors who rotate assignments to increase their overall understanding and skills among several departments.

FOLDER: a folded printed piece, not stapled.

FOLIO: a page number. A page in an account book; a page number.

FONT: any source or point of origin.

FOOTING: the act of adding a column of figures or the total so obtained; paying for, as footing the bill, particularly for business entertainment.

FORBIDDEN COMBINATION: a combination of bits or other representations that is not valid according to some criteria.

FORCED BILLING: a means used to secure payments for freight delivery when no bill can be found.

FORCED LOAN: a loan that cannot be collected at maturity and is extended without much possibility of the lender's doing otherwise.

FORCED SALE: the sale or loss of property when one does not wish to dispose of it, as in bankruptcy.

FORCED SAVING: occurs when consumers are prevented from spending a portion of their income on consumption.

FOREBEARANCE: surrendering the right to enforce a valid claim in return for a promise.

FORECAST: to predict market potential, sales volume, and/or prices, often for the purpose of determining sales and production quotas.

FORECLOSE: a legal action, a compulsory auction sale of mortgaged property with proceeds used first to satisfy the claims of the first mortgagee, then junior

mortgagees, with the balance to the owner or equity holder.

FOREGROUND: describing a program of high priority that is used immediately, or when and where needed.

FOREIGN CORPORATION: in law, a corporation doing business in states other than the state (or country) in which it was chartered.

FOREIGN EXCHANGE: a transaction involving the exchange of currency of one country for currency of another.

FOREIGN-EXCHANGE RATE: the price of one currency in terms of another.

FOREIGN INCOME: income earned by Americans from work performed in another country.

FOREIGN INVESTMENT: the purchase of assets from abroad.

FOREIGN TRADE: exporting or importing for a private or government account.

FOREMAN: a workingman who is also in charge of others; a supervisor of others.

FORFEITURE: the automatic loss of cash, property, or rights, as a punishment for failure to comply with legal provisions, or for damages.

FORGERY: fraudulent signing of another's name to deprive him of rights, such as criminally endorsing or signing a check.

FORMAL COMMUNICATION: any communication that follows an organization's prescribed lines of authority.

FORMAL ORGANIZATION: the established organizational structure used to achieve goals and objectives.

FORMAT: an arrangement of data; a predetermined arrangement of characters, page numbers, lines, and so on.

FORM LETTER: an identical letter sent to many people.

FORTRAN: an acronym for formula translation; FORTRAN is a procedure-oriented algebraic language widely used in coding scientific applications for computers.

FORWARD EXCHANGE: a foreign bill of exchange purchased or sold at a stated price that is payable at a given date.

FORWARDING: in an account extending over several pages, carrying the balance from one page to the top of the next page of an account as the first entry on the new page.

FORWARD MARKET: market that deals in futures.

FORWARD PRICES: a proposal for minimizing price uncertainty and encouraging greater stability in farming by utilizing the price system as an adjustment mechanism.

FORWARD STOCK: stock that is brought into the selling department.

FOUL BILL OF LADING: a bill of lading identifying shortage or damages that existed at the time of shipment.

FOURTH-CLASS MAIL: merchandise or book mail, otherwise known as parcel post.

FOURTH MARKET: the buying and selling of unlisted securities directly between investors.

FRACTIONAL CURRENCY: any currency that is smaller than a standard money unit.

FRACTIONAL LOT: less than one hundred shares of stock.

FRACTIONAL SHARES: portions of shares as declared in stock dividends which must become even shares either by sale of the fraction or purchase of a complementary fraction to make a whole share.

FRAME: an area extending across the width of a magnetic or paper tape perpendicular to its movement; a box containing a major portion of a computer.

FRANCHISE: a privilege under a contract, usually exclusive, permitting the sale of a product, use of a trade name, or provision of a particular service within a specified territory.

FRANCHISE CLAUSE: provision that payment shall not be made unless the loss or damage equals or exceeds a specified amount.

FRANCHISED DEALER: a retail dealer who, under terms of a franchise

agreement, carries a supplier's products.

FRANCHISE STORE: independently owned store that sells branded items produced by a franchise holder.

FRANCHISE TAX: the charge made by a governmental unit for the right to exercise a private monopoly such as public utility or bus line.

FRANCO DELIVERY: the full delivery of items to a consignee, with all charges paid, as with a prepaid delivery.

FRANK: the mark or wording on letters indicating free postage granted to certain government bodies and officials.

FRAUD: a deliberate act of deception or manipulation with the intention of cheating another person organization.

FRAUDULENT CONVEYANCE: conveyance of property entered into by a debtor with the objective of defrauding creditors.

FREE ALONGSIDE: with freight, paid to the loading dock.

FREE AND CLEAR: in real estate, property against which there are no encumbrances.

FREE AND OPEN MARKET: a market in which supply and demand are freely expressed in terms of price.

FREE CURRENCY: currency of a country that permits its unrestricted exchange for the currency of any other country.

FREEDOM SHARES: US government savings notes sold from 1967 through the mid-1970s.

FREE ENTERPRISE: the economic system of capitalism.

FREE GOODS: the inclusion of extra merchandise with the purchase of a given quantity, such offered to stimulate sales.

FREEHOLD: tenure of real property; the estate itself; a life interest in it.

FREE LANCE: one whose services are for hire, especially an artist or writer.

FREE LIST: statement prepared by a customs department of items that are not liable to the payment of duties.

FREE MARKET: describing the

unrestricted movement of items in and out of the market, unhampered by the existence of tariffs or other trade barriers.

FREE MATTER: matter sent through the mail free of postage.

FREEPORT: a port free of import and export duties.

FREE RESERVES: Federal Reserve bank term describing the margin by which excess reserves exceed the bank's borrowings.

FREE SURPLUS: that portion of retained earnings which is available for common stock dividends.

FREE TRADE: trade between nations with no customs duties or other restrictions imposed.

FREEZE: to fix and maintain a price or wage at a definite level over a period of time.

FREE ZONE: an enclave or other geographical area free of import and export excise taxes.

FREIGHT ABSORPTION: a term used when a seller does not charge a customer with freight out; the seller is said to have absorbed the freight.

FREIGHT ALLOWED: an agreement whereby a store pays the transportation charges on incoming goods but is permitted to charge back all or part of that cost to the vendor.

FREIGHT EQUALIZATION: a partial allowance on customer-paid freight on goods from a distant location so that the transportation costs will equal those on goods purchased nearer by.

FREIGHT FORWARDER: a private agency that consolidates the small freight shipments of a number of shippers and takes advantage of carload rates.

FREIGHT INWARD: freight paid on shipments received.

FREIGHT OUTWARD: freight paid by a seller on outgoing customer shipments.

FREQUENCY: the number of times an advertisement is delivered within a set time period; the number of cases in a class or other subdivision of a group.

FREQUENCY DISCOUNT: a

reduction in advertising rates based on the number of insertions or broadcasts used in a given time period.

FREQUENCY DISTRIBUTION: statistically, the number of units in each classification of a group.

FRICTIONAL UNEMPLOYMENT: time lost in changing jobs rather than as a result of lack of job opportunities.

FRINGE BENEFIT: compensation for labor in a form other than wages, such as health insurance, pension, or paid vacation.

FRINGE TIME: time slots when there are relatively few in the audience to receive an advertisement.

FRONTAGE: the linear measurement along the front of a parcel of land such as that fronting on a major road, street, or waterway.

FRONT-END LOADING: the practice of taking from the first installment the amounts required to cover administrative and selling costs, interest, risk, and other factors.

FRONT FOOT: the first twelve inches of property frontage on the principal thoroughfare it abuts.

FRONT OFFICE: a popular description for the offices of the major executives within a company.

FROZEN ACCOUNT: an account on which payments have been suspended until a court order or legal process again makes the account available for withdrawal.

FROZEN ASSETS: those assets of a business which are not readily salable, or which cannot be sold immediately without serious loss.

FROZEN PENSION: a pension paid up in full.

FULL-BODIED MONEY: gold; any currency that is worth its face value as a commodity.

FULL-COST PRICING: the practice that includes all appropriate manufacturing costs in determining inventory.

FULL COVERAGE: any form of insurance coverage that provides for payments of losses in full, subject to the limit of the policy, without application of a deductible.

FULL-CREW RULE: regulation stating the minimum number of workers required for a given operation.

FULL DISCLOSURE: the requirement that every company that has securities listed on an exchange must file reports disclosing financial and other data.

FULL LIABILITY: liability not shared with others.

FULL LOT: usually, 100 shares of stock traded on the New York Stock Exchange.

FULL-SERVICE BANK: a commercial bank that is capable of meeting the total financial needs of the banking public.

FULL-SERVICE WHOLESALER: a wholesaler who provides the full line of services, including taking the merchandise title, retaining a sale force, and making credit available to consumers.

FULL SHOWING: the advertising message used on public transportation carriers; refers to a 100 percent display of outdoor advertising.

FUNCTION: performance, operation, duty.

FUNCTIONAL COSTING: classifying costs by allocating them to the various functions performed.

FUNCTIONAL DISCOUNT: a deduction taken to produce differing prices to different customers.

FUNCTIONAL DISTRIBUTION: the payment of wages, rent, interest, and profit to the factors of production, as related to their respective contributions.

FUNCTIONAL INCOME DISTRIBUTION: wages, rents, interests, and profits paid to manufacturers in return for supplying their labor, land, capital, and management talents.

FUNCTIONAL OBSOLESCENCE: created by structural defects that reduce a property's value and/or marketability.

FUNCTION TABLE: two or more sets of data so arranged that an entry in one set selects one or more entries in the remaining sets.

FUND: assets set aside for a specific purpose; a self-balancing accounting entity.

FUNDED DEBT: long-term debt for which a schedule of repayments has been established.

FUNDING: acquiring funds by borrowing; provision made to pay pensions out of a special fund set aside for that purpose.

FUNGIBLE: in law, describing goods or securities; any unit is the equal of any other like unit.

FUNNY MONEY: convertible preferred stocks, convertible bonds, options, and warrants that appear to have characteristics of common stock equity but did not reduce reported earnings per share before 1969.

FURLOUGH: to grant to an employee a leave of absence without pay or, less often, with pay; such leave.

FUTURE ESTATE: an estate developed for the purpose of possession, to be taken at an identified later date or upon the occurrence of a future event.

FUTURES: contracts to purchase or sell commodities for future delivery; such contracts are normally traded on an organized exchange.

FUTURE SUM: the money that a borrower agrees to repay for an obligation.

FUTURE WORTH: the equivalent value at a future date based on time value of money.

G

GAIN: a monetary profit.

GAIN ON DISPOSAL: the sale of a noncurrent asset for more than book value.

GAIN SHARING: an incentive system where wage increments given to employees for increased output become progressively smaller as output increases.

GALLEY PROOF: printer's proof of columnar matter not made into pages, usually submitted for author's alterations.

GALLOPING INFLATION: the rapid and unlimited rise of prices.

GANG PUNCH: to punch all or part of the information from one punched card into succeeding cards.

GAP: hiatus; break in continuity, as the family formations gap during World War II.

GARBAGE: unwanted and meaningless information in computer memory or on tape.

GARNISHEE: a person against whom a garnishment is issued.

GARNISHMENT: a legal proceeding under which a peron's salary or other payment due them is taken for payment of a debt by the debtor.

GATE: the total receipts received from admission to an establishment.

GATEFOLD: an insert that unfolds to a size larger than the two-page size of the magazine into which it is bound.

GENERAL ACCOUNTING OFFICE: independent nonpolitical agency that audits and reviews federal financial transactions and examines the expenditures of appropriations by federal units.

GENERAL ADVERTISING: national or nonlocal newspaper advertising.

GENERAL CONTROL EXPENDITURES: expenditures for the legislative and judicial branches of the government, the office of the chief executive, auxiliary agencies, and staff services.

GENERAL EQUILIBRIUM ANALYSIS: an economic inquiry in which the interaction of all markets is considered.

GENERAL EXPENDITURES: total expenditures less utilities, sales of alcoholic beverages, and insurance-trust expenditures when used in reference to state or local governments separately.

GENERAL EQUILIBRIUM SYSTEM: a model that attempts to define all the relevant market interactions.

GENERAL EXPENSE: administrative expense on a classified income statement.

GENERAL FUND: money that can be utilized.

GENERAL INSURANCE: insurance other than life insurance.

GENERAL JOURNAL: a book of original entry in which transactions for which specialized journals do not exist may be entered.

GENERAL LEDGER: a ledger comprising all assets, liabilities, proprietorship revenue, and expense accounts.

GENERAL LIEN: lien against an individual but not his real property.

GENERALLY ACCEPTED ACCOUNTING PRINCIPLES: the accounting principles that have been given formal recognition or authoritative support in a particular jurisdiction.

GENERAL MORTGAGE: mortgage covering all properties of a debtor and not restricted to one parcel.

GENERAL-MORTGAGE BOND: bond that is secured by a blanket mortgage on the company's property but may be outranked by one or more other mortgages.

GENERAL PARTNERSHIP: a partnership that includes responsibility for the liabilities of the firm up to the full extent of the partner's private fortune.

GENERAL PRICE-LEVEL ACCOUNTING: a method of accounting where assets, liabilities, revenues, and expenses are stated in terms of the purchasing power of money at the date of the current financial statements.

GENERAL-PURPOSE COMPUTER: computer designed to handle a wide variety of problems.

GENERAL REVENUE: total revenue less utilities, sales of alcoholic beverages, and insurance-trust revenue when used in reference to state or local governments separately.

GENERAL STORE: a small retailing operation, not departmentalized, often found in country areas, where a wide variety of items, including food, clothing, and supplies, can be bought.

GENERAL STRIKE: a strike by the majority of workers in all the vital industries of a particular locality or region.

GENTLEMEN'S AGREEMENT: an unsigned, unsecured contract based upon the faith of both parties that each will perform.

GEOGRAPHICAL DIFFERENTIAL: the variation in wage rates for identical work between areas or regions of the country.

GHOST WRITER: one who writes for the avowed authorship of another.

GIFT CAUSA MORTIS: a gift made in the anticipation of death to avoid inheritance taxes for one's heirs.

GIFT CERTIFICATE: a retail merchandising device used by the certificate purchaser to give the recipient a free choice of goods to the dollar amount of the certificate.

GIFT INTER VIVOS: a gift of property given during the donor's life to another living person.

GIFT TAX: a tax to preclude escape from inheritance tax, levied on total gifts above the exemption amount made during a year or during a lifetime to each recipient.

GILT-EDGED SECURITIES: a synonym for blue-chip securities.

GIMMICK: any clever idea or device.

GIVE-UP: term applied when a member of a stock exchange on the floor acts for a second member by executing an order for him or her with a third member.

GLUT: to oversupply.

GNOME: a banker or money expert conducting business in the international finance market.

GOAL: an objective, or something specific to be achieved.

GOAL ORIENTATION: the focus of attention and decision making among members of a subunit in an organization.

GOAL SETTING: establishing steps to meet the objectives of an individual or firm.

GO-BETWEEN: intermediary; special representative; one who may introduce or aid in adjusting a difference between two parties to a transaction.

GODOWN: in the Far East, a commercial-storage warehouse.

GO-GO FUND: an investment purporting to acquire sizable earnings in a short time period, resulting in risky, speculative market activity.

GOING-CONCERN CONCEPT: the concept that a particular business will continue in operation indefinitely.

GOING PUBLIC: the situation when a firm's shares become available on a major exchange, as distinguished from being held by a few shareholders.

GOLDBRICK: one who does as little work as possible while on a payroll; a malingerer; a shirker.

GOLD CLAUSE: a contract term defining a money debt in terms of a US dollar or a specified weight and quality of gold.

GOLD POINTS: the range within which the foreign exchange rates of gold-standard countries will differ.

GOLD STANDARD: the use of gold as a monetary standard to back currency.

GOOD-FAITH BARGAINING: applied to the requirement that both parties to a labor dispute meet and confer at reasonable times, with minds open to persuasion with a view to reaching agreement on new contractual terms.

GOODS AND SERVICES: the result of industrial work, equaling the gross national product for one year; any movable personal property.

GOODWILL: the value of a business in excess of its net assets.

GOSPLAN: the state planning commission of the Soviet Union responsible for general economic planning.

GOVERNMENT BONDS: obligations of the US government, regarded as the highest grade issues in existence.

GOVERNMENT DEPOSITS: the funds of the US government and its agencies.

GOVERNMENT EXPENDITURES: gross expenditure amounts without deduction of any related receipts.

GOVERNMENT INSURANCE: protection of up to $10,000 provided by the US government to individuals who have served, or are serving, in the armed forces.

GOVERNMENT MONOPOLY: a monopoly owned and controlled by a local, state, or federal government.

GOVERNMENT REVENUE: all money received other than from issue of debt, liquidation of investments, and agency- and private-trust transactions.

GOVERNMENT SAVING: tax receipts less government expenditures.

GRACE PERIOD: a formally specified extension of time beyond the due date for payment of obligations or for performing a specific duty.

GRADED TAX: a form of real property tax with rates higher on unimproved land than on improved land so as to encourage improvement.

GRADE LABELING: as authorized by government agencies, the labeling of certain consumer items as specified by standards.

GRADING: the sorting of goods into classes or groups, according to size or quality.

GRADUATED SECURITIES: stocks that have moved from one exchange to another.

GRADUATED TAX: a tax where the rate increases as the amount of property or income of the taxpayer increases.

GRAFT: to accept bribes; bribes.

GRANDFATHER CLAUSE: any condition that ties existing rights or privileges to previous or remote conditions or acts.

GRAND MEAN: the average of a set of averages.

GRANGER: a member of a farm organization called a grange; a railroad that carries a substantial amount of grain; to admit as true; to allow; to give.

GRANT: a clause in a deed reflecting the transfer of title to real property.

GRANTEE: one to whom title to land

is transferred; a recipient of a grant, as a stipend for research.

GRANTER: a person who offers credit.

GRANTOR: an individual who makes a grant; a person who executes a deed giving up title to property.

GRANTS-IN-AID: payments made by one government unit to another for specified purposes.

GRAPEVINE: the informal communications network found in most organizations.

GRAPH: a chart, frequently one with rectangular coordinates displaying statistics as lines or areas.

GRAPHIC ARTS: the industry embracing printing and its allied arts of making and reproducing graphics.

GRAPHIC-DISPLAY PROGRAM: a computer program designed to display information, in graphic or alphanumeric form, on the face of a display tube like a television picture tube.

GRATIS: free of charge (Latin).

GRATUITIES: payments for services not directly charged.

GRATUITOUS COINAGE: a government policy of producing coins from metal without cost to the owner of the metal.

GRAVEYARD SHIFT: the working period from about midnight to about 8 AM.

GRAVURE: the printing process that transfers an image to paper by means of the ink retained in plate depressions.

GRAY KNIGHT: an opportunistic second bidder in a company takeover, not sought out by the target, who attempts to take advantage of the problems between the target and the initial bidder.

GRAY MARKET: transactions made for immediate delivery at a premium over usual prices because of a sudden or unexpected shortage of a commodity.

GREAT SOCIETY: a series of programs of social welfare, developed by President Lyndon B. Johnson.

GREENBACKS: the unconvertible notes issued during the Civil War period which were legal tender for all public and private debts except interest on national debt or import duties.

GREEN HANDS: workers who are new to a job and inexperienced in performing their tasks.

GREENLINING: a response of community citizens who withdraw their accounts from lending institutions that they believe practice redlining.

GREEN POWER: the power of money.

GREEN RIVER ORDINANCE: a municipal law regulating selling from house to house.

GRESHAM'S LAW: bad money drives out good.

GRIEVANCE: a complaint against an employer by one or more employees alleging a breach of a collective agreement.

GRIEVANCE MACHINERY: procedures identified in the collective-bargaining agreement to resolve problems that develop in interpretation and/or application of the contract.

GROSS: 12 dozen, thus, 144; coarse; common.

GROSS DEBT: all long-term credit obligations incurred and outstanding, whether backed by a government's full faith and credit or nonguaranteed, and all interest-bearing, short-term credit obligations.

GROSS INCOME: revenues before the deduction of expenses.

GROSS LEASE: lease according to which the landlord will pay for all repairs, taxes, and other expenses incurred.

GROSS LINE: the amount of insurance a company has on a risk, including the amount it has reinsured.

GROSS MARGIN: the amount that covers operating and financial expenses and provides net income; the dollar difference between the net sales and the net cost of goods sold during a stated time frame.

GROSS NATIONAL DEBT: the total indebtedness of the federal government, including debts owed by one agency to another.

GROSS NATIONAL DISPRODUCT: the total of all social costs or reductions in benefits to the community that result from producing the gross national product.

GROSS NATIONAL EXPENDITURE: the full amount spent by the four sectors of the economy (household, government, business, and foreign) on the nation's output of goods and services.

GROSS NATIONAL PRODUCT (GNP): the total retail market value of all items and services produced in a country during a specified period, usually one year.

GROSS PROFIT: excess of sales over cost of goods sold.

GROSS REVENUE: the total revenues received from selling goods or performing services.

GROSS SALES: the total of all sales before deducting returned sales.

GROSS SAVINGS: the sum of capital consumption (depreciation) and personal and corporate savings.

GROUND LEASE: a lease of vacant land, or a lease of land exclusive of any buildings on it.

GROUPAGE: a service that consolidates small shipments into containers for movement.

GROUP BANKING: a form of banking enterprise whereby a group of existing banks form a holding company that supervises and coordinates the operations of all banks in the group.

GROUP BONUS: a method of wage payment based on the performance of a team on the job.

GROUP DISCOUNT: a special discount for the purchase of large quantities of an item or service.

GROUP DYNAMICS: the study of techniques and procedures for altering the structure and/or behavior of a social group.

GROUP-INCENTIVE PLAN: a plan under which pay is based on total or group output.

GROUPING: in computers, a mass of information having common characteristics that are arranged into related clusters.

GROUP INSURANCE: insurance policies taken out on the lives of a particular group, such as the employees of a corporation.

GROUP SELLING: the presentation for sale of goods or services to two or more people simultaneously.

GROWTH STAGE: the second phase in a product's life cycle, characterized by a rise in sales and profit and the appearance of competitors in the market.

GROWTH STOCK: the shares of a corporation which have excellent prospects for future increase in value.

GUARANTEED ANNUAL WAGE: a contractual obligation for an employer to provide an employee a minimum amount of income during a year.

GUARANTEED DEBT: the obligations of certain semipublic and public corporations that are guaranteed by the federal government as contingent liabilities.

GUARANTEED LETTER OF CREDIT: travelers' letters of credit or commercial letters of credit.

GUARANTEED RATE: the minimum-wage rate guaranteed to an employee who receives incentive pay.

GUARANTEED STOCK: usually, preferred stock on which dividends are guaranteed by another company under much the same circumstances as a bond is guaranteed.

GUARANTEED WORKING WEEK: the result of a labor-management agreement whereby workers will be paid for a full working week even when there is insufficient work for the employees during that week.

GUARANTEES: federal credit aid in which the federal government pledges its financial liability for loans made by private or state or local government institutions.

GUARANTOR: a person who provides a guarantee.

GUARANTY: a written promise by one person (the guarantor) in the event that the principal debtor fails to perform his obligation and provided the guarantor is notified of that fact by the creditor.

GUARDIAN: a person appointed by a court to administer specific affairs of an infant or one judged incompetent.

GUARDIAN AD LITEM: a person appointed by a court to represent and defend a minor or an incompetent in connection with court proceedings.

GUARDIAN DEED: a deed to convey the property of an infant or incompetent.

GUEST WORKER: a foreign worker who is allowed to enter the country for purposes of employment but cannot bring his or her family.

GUILD: organization of skilled craftsmen to provide services for and fulfill the needs of its membership.

H

HABEAS CORPUS: a legal writ requiring the presence of a person before a court or judge, usually employed to bring before a judge a person held in prison to determine the legality of his imprisonment (Latin).

HABENDUM: that clause in a deed which states, "to have and to hold to said grantee, his heirs, successors and assigns, forever" (Latin).

HAIRLINE RULE: a very thin printing rule.

HALLMARK: after the hallmarks of eighteenth century English silversmiths, a trademark or manufacturer's identification.

HALO EFFECT: a "bias" whereby one favorable characteristic influences an overall judgment of an individual.

HALSEY PREMIUM PLAN: an incentive-wage plan under which the employee receives a minimum wage for all work up to the standard output and thereafter compensation for additional output.

HAMMERING THE MARKET: the persistent selling of securities by speculators operating on the short side who believe that prices are inflated and that liquidation is imminent.

HANDBILL: a sheet printed with an advertisement for hand distribution.

HANDCRAFT: a skill used in producing handmade articles of utility.

HANDICRAFT SYSTEM: that stage in the economic development of industry when skilled artisans carried on industries and fashion.

HAND-TO-MOUTH PURCHASING: purchasing that satisfies needs of the moment only, neglecting long-range requirements of the individual or entity.

HARD CASH: metallic currency, as distinguished from paper money.

HARD COPY: printed reports, listings, documents, summaries.

HARD-CORE UNEMPLOYED: a group within the labor-age population which is able and willing to work but remains unemployed.

HARDENING: a firming of prices of stocks or commodities after a period in which prices have declined.

HARD GOODS: durable consumers' goods.

HARDHAT: construction worker.

HARDHEADED: shrewd, practical, purposeful, not easily subject to blandishment.

HARD LOAN: a foreign loan that must be paid in hard money,

HARD MONEY (CURRENCY): currency of a nation having stability in the country and abroad; coins, in contrast to paper currency.

HARDWARE: in computers or rocketry, equipment as contrasted with software and systems.

HATCHWAYS: openings in a vessel's deck permitting access to the cargo holds.

HEAD: a device that reads, writes, records, or erases data on a storage medium; the foremost person.

HEADBOARD: the front-end wall of a container.

HEAD-END BUSINESS: the transportation of property behind the locomotive of a passenger train.

HEAD-HUNTER: slang, an individual or agency involved in finding managers and executives for a client organization.

HEADLINE: those words of an advertisement appearing in largest type; the caption over a story or article.

HEADLINER: a device for printing type characters stored on a disk onto phtographic printing paper.

HEAD-ON POSITION: an outdoor advertising location facing the flow of traffic, as contrasted with being placed on an angle or in a position parallel to the traffic.

HEAD TAX: a tax levied equally on individuals.

HEARSAY: repetition of another's unsupported statement, inadmissible as court evidence; rumor.

HEAVY HAULER: a trucking firm that transports heavy and/or large items, and therefore requires special equipment for loading, unloading, and shipping.

HEAVY INDUSTRY: one involved in manufacturing basic products such as metals or equipment such as machines.

HEAVY MARKET: in stock-market language, the condition when a large number of selling orders are on the market, apparently without sufficient buying orders to balance them off.

HEDGE: to buy or sell futures for the specific purpose of restricting the risk involved in price fluctuations.

HEDGING: a type of economic insurance used by dealers in commodities and securities and other producers to prevent loss due to price fluctuations.

HEDGING CLAUSE: a caution to customers attached to circulars, brochures, advertisements, and so on.

HEIR: inheritor of an estate.

HEREDITAMENT: property that can be inherited.

HETEROGENEOUS: of different classes or kinds.

HEURISTIC: any method used to assist a person in discovering or learning something for himself or herself.

HICCUP: a short-lived drop in the stock market.

HIDDEN AGENDA: matters that are important to an individual attending a meeting but which cannot be raised because the matters are not on the agenda.

HIDDEN AMENITIES: desirable aspects of property which are provided but not always noticed on first inspection.

HIDDEN ASSETS: assets of a firm which are not easily identifiable by examining the balance sheet.

HIDDEN CLAUSE: in a contract, any obscure provision that stipulates requirements that may be against the buyer's interests.

HIDDEN OFFER: a special offer buried in the copy of an advertisement as a test of readership.

HIDDEN TAX: a tax that is included in the price of the product and not stated separately.

HIERARCHY: a specified rank or order of persons or things, thus, a series of persons or things classified by rank or order.

HIERARCHY OF NEEDS: the theoretical model detailing the sequence of accomplishment necessary for personal fulfillment.

HIGGLING: term used when the buyer offers a low price and the seller asks a high price, and a third price is arrived at, through bargaining, to satisfy both parties.

HIGHEST AND BEST USE: the use of property which will bring the greatest economic return.

HIGH FINANCE: utilizing another's funds in a speculative fashion; borrowing to the maximum of one's credit; extremely complicated transactions.

HIGH FLYER: a stock issue characterized by wildly fluctuating prices.

HIGH GRADE: describing an item of superior quality.

HIGH TICKET: having a high price tag.

HIGH TIME: extra pay for a worker employed in places high above ground or deep below ground.

HI-LO-INDEX: a moving average of individual stocks that reach new highs and new lows each day.

HIRE-PURCHASE AGREEMENT: a lease containing a purchase option.

HISTOGRAM: a diagrammatical presentation of statistical data.

HISTORICAL COST: figures based on actual cost.

HOLDBACK: a portion of a payment called for under a contract which is not payable until certain conditions have been fulfilled.

HOLDER OF RECORD: person to whom dividends are declared payable; stockholders owning shares on a specific date.

HOLD-HARMLESS AGREEMENT: a contractual agreement in which the liability of one person for damages is assumed by another.

HOLDING COMPANY: a corporation whose primary purpose is owning shares of one or more other corporations.

HOLDING PERIOD: the period during which an asset is owned.

HOLDING POWER: the ability of a product, program, or entity to retain an audience over a period of time.

HOLDOVER TENANT: a tenant who remains in possession of leased property after the expiration of the lease term.

HOLD THE LINE: as used in price stabilization, the use of many devices to stop price increases.

HOLD TRACK: a railroad track where cars are sitting awaiting disposition instructions.

HOLIDAY PAY: wages for holidays not worked.

HOLOGRAPH: a document written entirely in one's own handwriting, such as a will.

HOME LOAN: a real estate loan for which the security is residential property.

HOMEOWNERS' POLICY: a package of insurance for the homeowner.

HOMESTEAD LAW: a federal law granting homestead lands (such as parcels of 160 acres) to those who settle them.

HOMOGENEOUS: of like kind or class.

HONCHO: a boss, senior executive, or head man.

HONOR: to pay or to accept a draft complying with the terms of credit.

HONORARIUM: an honorary payment, as to a public official for a speech, or for a service freely rendered and upon which custom or propriety suggests that no price be set.

HOOKING: the process of trapping a worker in order to have him spy on the union of his fellow workers: synonymous with roping.

HOOKUP: a network, as of broadcast stations, or more than two telephones connected for a limited period for specific purposes of communication.

HOOPERATING: the percentage of individuals listening to radio stations, ascertained by using the telephone as a coincidental method of data gathering.

HORIZON: the time limit in the future to which a business is projected.

HORIZONTAL EXPANSION: the establishment of facilities to permit a firm to expand its business in the same product line it is producing or selling.

HORIZONTAL MERGER: a combination formed when two or more businesses producing the same goods or service merge.

HORIZONTAL PRICE FIXING: an agreement on prices among competitors at similar levels of distribution.

HORIZONTAL PUBLICATION: a business publication edited for employees in similar job classifications in differing industries.

HORIZONTAL SPECIALIZATION: factors in the division of labor involving specialties.

HOST COMPUTER: the primary or controlling computer in a multiple-computer operation.

HOT CARGO: any goods made or shipped by nonunion labor.

HOT-CARGO PROVISIONS: contract provisions that allow workers to refuse to work or handle "unfair goods."

HOT ITEM: any goods that show quick salability.

HOT MAIL: preferential mail.

HOT MONEY: any money that is received through means either illegal or of questionable legality.

HOUSE AGENCY: an advertising agency that has only one client.

HOUSE BRAND: the branding by a wholesaler with his own name of goods he has purchased from a producer unlabeled.

HOUSEHOLD SAVING: household disposable income less the existing household consumption.

HOUSEKEEPING: operations in a routine that do not directly contribute to the solution of the problem at hand but are made necessary by the method of operation of the computer.

HOUSE OF ISSUE: an investment banking firm engaged in underwriting and distribution of security issues.

HOUSE OF LABOR: the American Federation of Labor—Congress of Industrial Organizations (AFL—CIO).

HOUSE ORGAN: a publication of a business concern containing articles of interest to its employees and customers.

HOUSE-TO-HOUSE SALESMAN: a sales representative who visits homes in an attempt to make direct sales.

HOUSING STARTS: the number of new housing units in residential buildings on which construction has begun.

HUCKSTER: a peddler or petty retailer who will attempt to sell anything mercenary or profit-making.

HUMAN CAPITAL STOCK: the value of future labor earnings.

HUMAN RELATIONS: meeting the human problems encountered by management in dealing with personnel, suppliers, customers, and owners.

HUMAN-RESOURCE ACCOUNTING: the reporting of and emphasis on the relevance of skilled and loyal employees in a firm's earning picture.

HUSH MONEY: the money given to assure the silence of the receiver; a bribe.

HYBRID COMPUTER: a computer for data processing using both analog and digital representations of data.

HYDROELECTRIC: referring to electricity-generating plants powered by descending water.

HYPE: an activity that attempts to encourage consumer interest and sales.

HYPERINFLATION: extreme inflation.

HYPOTHECATE: to pledge as security.

HYPOTHECATED ACCOUNT: an account that is pledged or assigned as collateral for a loan.

HYPOTHECATION: an agreement or contract that permits a bank or a creditor to utilize the collateral pledge to secure a loan, in case the loan is unpaid at maturity; the pledging of securities as collateral.

HYSTERESIS: in economics, a term referring to the nonreversibility of an economic function.

I

IBID.: in the same place (Latin).

ICEBERG PRINCIPLE: 10 percent of the required data is apparent and the other 90 percent not seen.

ICONOSCOPE: an early form of television camera, now used for film transmission.

IDEAL CAPACITY: the absolute maximum number of units that could be produced in a given operating situation, with no allowance for work stoppages or repairs.

IDEM: the same (Latin).

IDENTIFIER: a symbol whose purpose is to identify, indicate, or name a body of data; a key.

IDLE CAPACITY: normal capacity that is not being used.

IDLE MONEY: uninvested available funds; inactive bank deposits.

IDLE TIME: time when an employee is unable to work because of machine malfunction or other factors not within the control of the worker.

ILLEGAL OPERATION: the process resulting when a computer either cannot perform the instruction part or will perform with incorrect and irrelevant results.

ILLEGAL STRIKE: a strike in violation of a contract, one not properly voted by the union membership, not authorized by established union or legal procedures, or one in violation of a court injunction.

ILLIQUID: not easily convertible into cash; not established by any documentary evidence.

ILLTH: consumer items that are harmful to people who consume them and to the general welfare.

ILLUSORY: appearing false.

ILLUSTRATION: a picture for a specific purpose, such as to identify an advertised product or to clarify an idea.

IMAGE: the corporate reputation as established in the public concept by its reported actions, advertising, and other communicated impressions.

IMAGE BUILDING: a public-relations approach to advance, upgrade, or, in general, improve the customer's attitude toward an item, service, organization, or person.

IMAGINEERING: imaginative thinking disciplined to plan new products, business strategy, and the like.

IMMATERIAL: not pertinent; not having a major substantive relation.

IMMUNITY: that which confers the ability to escape from the legal duties or penalties imposed on others.

IMPACT: the way in which an advertisement or a medium affects the audience receiving it.

IMPAIRED CAPITAL: a condition in which the capital of a business is worth less than its stated capital.

IMPAIRMENT: the amount by which stated capital is reduced by dividends and other distributions, and by losses, where liabilities exceed assets by reason of losses.

IMPARTIAL CHAIRMAN: the chairman of a panel acceptable to the parties to negotiations, invested by them with power to mediate disputes between them, and make recommendations for solutions.

IMPASSE: the point in negotiations at which one party has determined that no further progress in reaching agreement can be made.

IMPEACH: to charge a public officer before a competent body with actions warranting his removal from office.

IMPERFECT COMPETITION: the market situation where at least one trader can materially affect the market price of a product.

IMPERFECT MARKET: a market in which the price (or terms of trade) falls as the quantity exchanged increases.

IMPERIAL GALLON: the British or Canadian gallon, equal to 1.29 US gallons.

IMPLICIT COSTS: the costs originating within the business that are the responsibility of the owner.

IMPLICIT RENT: the amount of income from a business which the owner attributes to the land he owns as an estimate of the rent he would have had to pay if he leased it.

IMPLIED CONTRACT: a contract in which the parties speak by their actions rather than by their oral or written words.

IMPLIED EASEMENT: infringement on property that has been left unchallenged over a period of time.

IMPLIED WARRANTY: representation, not in writing, that insurable conditions exist.

IMPORT: to purchase abroad and bring or have transported across domestic borders.

IMPORT DUTY: any tax on items imported.

IMPORT QUOTA: a government limitation on the quantity of a specific type of goods which may be imported within a given period.

IMPOSITION: a demand or tax made by a taxing authority on items such as property.

IMPOST: a tax, particularly used to describe import duties.

IMPOUNDS: to seize or to hold; to place in protective custody by order of a court.

IMPRESARIO: the manager of an opera company or ballet company.

IMPRESSION: in printing, the contact between the form and the paper; effect created upon an employer or customer by one's efforts to please.

IMPREST SYSTEM: a system for handling disbursements under which a specified amount of cash is entrusted to an individual.

IMPRINT: the identification printed on a container during the process of manufacture.

IMPROVEMENT: a plant addition or some other physical betterment of production facilities; the attainment of increased profit.

IMPROVIDENT: failing to provide for the future or doing so inadequately.

IMPULSE PURCHASE: unpremeditated buying of merchandise; bought on sudden decision.

IMPUTED: describing a value estimated when no cash payment is made, in order to establish that value.

IMPUTED INCOME: income not in the form of money, such as free board or lodging, or food produced and consumed by a farmer.

IMPUTED INTEREST: interest that is considered to be a cost even though no actual cash outlay is made.

IMPUTED NEGLIGENCE: negligence not attributed to a person directly, but resulting from the negligence of another who participates with him or her and with whose fault he or she is chargeable.

INACTIVE ACCOUNT: an account that has little or no movement.

INACTIVE STOCK: a stock infrequently traded.

INADMISSIBLE: not to be admitted, such as hearsay evidence in a trial.

INADVISABLE: not recommended, such as flouting the instructions of one's superior.

INALIENABLE: not able to be sold or transferred; synonymous with nonassignable.

IN-AND-OUT: the purchase and sale of the same security within a short period.

IN ARREARS: not paid when due, as unpaid interest due, or a past-due account payable.

INAUGURATE: to initiate or to introduce, such as a new busines procedure.

IN BOND: items shipped by a producer several months before a store's usual selling season and held in the store's warehouse until selling season.

INCENTIVE: a promised or actual reward for improved productivity, quality of product, or safety.

INCENTIVE PAY: a pay system based on the productivity of a worker above a specified level.

INCHOATE: newly begun or incomplete.

INCHOATE INTEREST: a future interest in real estate.

INCOME ACCOUNT: an account in the general ledger of a bank.

INCOME APPROACH TO VALUE: a procedure for property appraisal in which the value on the net amount of income produced by the property is used.

INCOME BOND (DEBENTURE): a bond on which the payment of interest is contingent upon earnings.

INCOME DISTRIBUTION: the way in which personal income is dispensed throughout the various socioeconomic levels in a nation.

INCOME EFFECT: the change in the quantity of an item demanded because a person's purchasing power has been altered.

INCOME PROPERTY: property, usually commercial, industrial, or residential, owned or purchased for a financial return expected.

INCOME STATEMENT: a summary of revenues and expenses of an enterprise for a specified accounting period.

INCOME TAX: a tax on annual earnings and profits of a person, corporation, or other entity.

INCOME VELOCITY OF MONEY: the average number of times each year that a dollar is spent on purchasing the economy's annual flow of final goods and/or services; its gross national product.

INCOMPETENT: inadequate or unwilling to perform satisfactorily in employment; adjudged legally unable to conduct one's own affairs.

INCONTESTABLE: a clause stating that after a certain period the insurance policy may not be disputed except for the nonpayment of the premiums.

INCONVERTIBLE MONEY: irredeemable money; money that may not be converted into the standard; such as US money which is not redeemable in gold.

INCORPORATE: to form a corporation.

INCORPORATION: the legal process of bringing a corporation into existence.

INCORPOREAL: of no material substance; existing with no physical properties.

INCORPOREAL PROPERTY: intangible, personal property.

INCORRUPTIBLE: honest, even when tempted by bribes.

INCREASING-COST INDUSTRY: industry that experiences increases in resource prices or in manufacturing costs as it expands when new firms enter it.

INCREASING RETURNS: a situation in which production is increased even though there has been no increase in the various factors of production, such as land, labor, capital, or management.

INCREMENT: an addition.

INCREMENTAL: describing the additional investment required for a project or additional cash flows resulting from a project.

INCUMBENT: one who holds office.

INCURABLY DEPRECIATED: describing damaged property that is beyond rehabilitation.

INCURRED LOSSES: loss transactions occurring within a fixed period, usually a year.

INDEBTEDNESS: a debt that is owed; any form of liability.

IN DEFAULT: owing interest or principal or both past the due date.

INDEFEASIBLE: incapable of being annulled or rendered void, as an indefeasible title to property.

INDEMNIFY: to pay or reimburse for damages, as under an insurance policy.

INDEMNITY: an option to buy or sell a specific quantity of a stock at a stated price within a given time period; a guarantee against losses; payment for damage.

INDEMNITY BOND: a bond that protects the obligee against losses resulting from the principal's failure to fulfill his obligations.

INDENT: to position the beginning of a line to the right of the left-hand alignment of the lines after it.

INDENTURE: the agreement with lenders filed with the fiscal agent and printed in the prospectus under which certificates of indebtedness or bonds are issued.

INDENTURED SERVANT: one who pays indebtedness by personal services for a stated number of years.

INDEPENDENT BANK: a bank that operates in one locality.

INDEPENDENT CONTRACTOR: one who agrees to perform certain actions for another and is responsible for the results but not subject to direction by the party hiring him.

INDEPENDENT UNION: a union not affiliated with a federation of unions.

INDEX: a number that measures change in a factor, such as cost of living, from one specific time to another specific time.

INDEXING: an increasingly popular form of investing: investments are weighted in line with one of the major stock indices.

INDEX NUMBER: a measurement of relative change arrived at by employing statistical procedures.

INDEX REGISTER: a register containing a quantity that may be used to automatically modify addresses under direction of the control section of the computer.

INDICATOR: a charted index on which a change in direction is taken as indicating a change in an economic trend.

INDICIA: indications or signs.

INDICTMENT: the finding of a grand jury in a criminal case that there is reasonable ground to believe an accused person may be guilty.

INDIFFERENCE SCHEDULE: a table illustrating all combinations of two commodities that are equally satisfactory or yield the same total utility to a recipient at a specified time.

INDIRECT COST: an expense that cannot reasonably be identified with a specific operation or cost center.

INDIRECT DAMAGE: term used to describe a consequential loss.

INDIRECT LABOR: the cost of labor that does not directly affect the composition of a finished product in a manufacturing process.

INDIRECT LIABILITY: liability assumed by a party who endorses the note of a maker for a bank or guarantees a note as guarantor for a maker.

INDIRECT MATERIAL: the cost of material necessary to the production of a product for sale but not forming an actual part of the final product.

INDIRECT OVERHEAD: overhead costs that are not traceable to a specific part of a manufacturing operation.

INDIRECT PRODUCTION: producing an item needed for the manufacture of major goods or services.

INDIRECT TAX: a tax that can be shifted from the original payor to the ultimate consumer of the thing taxed.

INDIVIDUALISM: conducting one's affairs in one's own way; the concept that individual economic freedom should not be restricted by governmental regulation.

INDIVIDUAL-RETIREMENT ACCOUNTS: individual pension accounts available to anyone not covered at work by a qualified pension plan.

INDIVISIBILITY: reflecting a claim that certain production factors cannot be divided into smaller components.

INDORSEE: one to whom an instrument is transferred by indorsement.

INDORSEMENT: transferring title (ownership) or guaranteeing payment by writing one's name on the back of a negotiable instrument where one is not the maker, drawer, or acceptor.

INDORSER: one who has put his name on a negotiable paper in order to transfer title (ownership) from himself to another or to guarantee payment.

INDUCED CONSUMPTION: purchases that are derived from consumers as a result of capital investment.

INDUCED INVESTMENT: the capital investment in such forms as plant and machinery produced as a result of increases in spending by consumers.

INDUCEMENT: an additional consideration to persuade another to make an agreement.

INDUCTIVE METHOD: a form of reasoning that approaches a problem from the particular and arrives at a generalization, emphasizing data gathered from observing the empirical world.

INDUSTRIAL ADVERTISING: advertising goods or services for use in the manufacture or distribution of other goods and services.

INDUSTRIAL BANK: a financial institution originally organized to extend loans to employees.

INDUSTRIAL CONCENTRATION: reflecting the extent to which a large proportion of an industry's sales are produced by a few companies.

INDUSTRIAL DISTRIBUTOR: a full-service wholesaler representing industrial manufacturers and selling to industrial buyers.

INDUSTRIAL ENGINEERING: the applications within engineering to the design, improvement, and installation of integrated systems of workers, materials, and equipment.

INDUSTRIAL GOODS: goods that are destined for use in producing other goods or rendering services.

INDUSTRIALIST: an individual who owns, controls, or plays a critical role in the operation of an industrial organization.

INDUSTRIAL PSYCHOLOGY: the branch of applied psychology concerned with the behavior and motivation of individual workers.

INDUSTRIAL RELATIONS: any activity, event, or interaction between employer and employee.

INDUSTRIAL REVOLUTION: that period starting in the late eighteenth century in which rapid advancements were made in production, largely due to the use of steam and machinery.

INDUSTRIAL STANDARDIZATION: the orderly and systematic formulation, acceptance, usage, and revision of the given requirements to be achieved in order to attain a goal.

INDUSTRIAL UNION: a union of workers in a single industry and its extension to workers in related fields, who may engage in tasks requiring diversified skills.

INELASTIC DEMAND: demand that does not change at a proportionate rate with the rate of change in price.

INELASTIC SUPPLY: supply that does not change at a proportionate rate with the rate of change in price.

INEQUITIES: rates or conditions substantially out of line with those paid or existing for comparable work in a plant, locality, or industry.

INFIRMITY: any known act, or visible omission in detail, in the creation or transfer of title which would invalidate an instrument.

INFLATION: an increase in the price level, creating a decrease in the purchasing power of the monetary unit.

INFLATION ACCOUNTING: the bookkeeping practice that shows the impact of inflation on corporate assets and profits.

INFLATIONARY GAP: the amount by which government and private spending exceeds the amount needed to maintain a stable price level and full employment.

INFLATIONARY SPIRAL: the process in which, in a time of rising prices, employees demand higher wages, which in turn increases costs, leading sellers and producers then to demand still higher prices.

INFORMAL GROUPS: natural groups of employees in the work situation.

INFORMAL INVESTIGATION: the method of seeking information through conversation, observation, and the subsequent analysis of data.

INFORMATION COSTS: the costs, including time, expended in securing data.

INFORMATION RETRIEVAL: the methods and procedures for recovering specific information from stored data.

INFORMATION SCIENCE: the study of how data are processed and transmitted through digital processing equipment.

INFRA: below (Latin).

INFRASTRUCTURE: the basic structure of a nation's economy, including transportation, communications, and other public services, on which the economic activity relies.

INGRESS: the ability to enter property or land.

INHERIT: to acquire the property of a person who dies.

INHERITANCE: that which is willed to an heir.

INHERITANCE TAXES: taxes levied on the estate of a deceased person or on legatees' shares of such estate.

INHERITED AUDIENCE: the segment of a broadcast audience that keeps tuned to a succeeding program.

INITIAL MARK-ON: the difference between the retail value of goods and the delivered cost, when first priced and placed on display.

INJUNCTION: a court order to do or not to do a particular thing.

IN KIND: referring to the replacement of lost or damaged property with material or property of a similar description and quality.

IN LOCO PARENTIS: in the place of a parent (Latin).

INNKEEPER'S LIEN: the right of an innkeeper to keep possession of baggage and property of a guest for unpaid charges.

INNOCENT PURCHASER: an individual who in good faith does not expect any hidden property defects to appear when he has gained title to real property.

INNOVATION: a new concept or approach in the production cycle, frequently involving the use of inventions in a practical task.

IN PERSONAM: a proceeding against a specific persons (Latin).

INPUT: information in a form in which it can be fed into a computer.

INPUT BLOCK: a segment of the internal storage reserved for receiving and/or processing input data.

INPUT DATA: data to be processed.

INQUIRY: a request for information from computer storage.

INQUIRY TEST: a technique of testing advertisements by noting the number of inquiries made from listeners, viewers, or publication readers.

IN RE: in the matter of (Latin).

IN REM: a proceeding (Latin).

INSERTION ORDER: written instructions for an advertisement to be placed in a particular issue of a publication at a stated rate.

INSIDER: a director or senior officer of a corporation, or anyone who may be presumed to have access to inside information concerning the corporation.

INSIDER REPORT: a report of all transactions in the shares of a corporation by those considered to be insiders.

INSIDE UNION: synonymous with company union.

INSOLVENT: unable to meet financial obligations.

INSOLVENCY: the inability of a person or organization to pay its debts as they become due.

INSPECTION: the process of examining units or goods to determine acceptability against a standard and to accumulate information about product quality.

INSTALLATION: an induction, as of officers of a corporation; placement of construction materials or equipment in position.

INSTALLATION TIME: the time spent in installing and testing hardware, software, or both until they are accepted.

INSTALLMENT: a regular payment of a portion of the principal due on a loan or purchase.

INSTALLMENT BUYING: acquiring goods or services with no down payment or a small down payment, to be followed by additional payments at regular intervals.

INSTALLMENT CREDIT: a form of consumer credit involving regular payments.

INSTALLMENT LOAN: a sale in which the price is to be paid by a series of payments over a period of time; synonymous with personal loan.

INSTANT VESTING: the right of employees to change employers within a given industry or area without losing pension rights.

IN STATUS QUO: in the former position (Latin).

INSTITUTIONAL ADVERTISING: advertising intended to promote a favorable opinion of the advertiser rather than any particular product the advertiser may offer for sale.

INSTITUTIONAL INVESTOR: an institution, such as an insurance company, pension fund, or mutual fund, which invests large sums of money in securities.

INSTITUTIONAL OPERATION: a factory or group of plants under one management that performs all processes of production including preparation for sale.

INSTRUMENT: a written legal document.

INSTRUMENTALITIES: agencies of the federal government whose obligations are not the direct obligation of the federal government.

INSTRUMENT OF INCORPORATION: the legal document by which a corporation is created.

INSUFFICIENT FUNDS: a term used when a depositor's balance is inadequate for the bank to pay a check that has been presented.

INSURANCE COMPANY: an organization chartered under state or provincial laws to act as an insurer.

INSURANCE COVERAGE: the total amount contracted to indemnify one for particular losses under stated conditions.

INSURANCE POOR: carrying too much insurance, more than one really needs.

INSURANCE TRUST: an instrument composed wholly or partially of life insurance policy contracts.

INSURED: the person or persons protected under an insurance contract.

INSURED BANK: a bank that is a member of the Federal Deposit Insurance Corporation.

INSURED MAIL: a service whereby postal customers who have paid a special fee may obtain payment for mail that has been lost, rifled, or damaged.

INSURER: the party to the insurance contract who promises to indemnify losses or provide service.

INSURGENT: a member of a group rebelling against authority.

INTANGIBLE ASSET: an asset without substance, such as goodwill, patents, and trademarks.

INTANGIBLE REWARDS: feelings derived from recognition, applause, and so on, having no monetary value.

INTANGIBLE TAX: a state tax levied on all deposits in a bank excluding certain exempted items.

INTEGRATE: to assemble into one, as multiple business departments, or a company and its subsidiary.

INTEGRATED COMMERCIAL: a broadcast commercial that appears or is heard as part of the program's entertainment.

INTEGRATION, FORWARD: expanding the area of operation of a business to include activity near the ultimate user.

INTEGRATION, HORIZONTAL: the absorption by one firm of other firms functioning on the same level of production.

INTEGRATION, VERTICAL: the absorption by one firm of other firms involved in all stages of manufacture, from raw materials to sales of the finished goods.

INTEGRATIONIST MODEL: particularly in public administration, a model defining federal administration as a closed hierarchical system with the President at the top, surrounded by a staff of loyal subordinates committed to his programs.

INTEGRATOR: a worker who is neither line nor staff but has informal power to bring together the efforts of overlapping working units.

INTEGRITY: a quality of honesty and reliability of an individual or of a company.

INTELLIGENCE QUOTIENT (IQ): measure of a person's rate of development up to the age at which he is tested, computed by dividing the test score by the chronological age.

INTENSIVE COVERAGE: the use of frequent, large-scale advertising in a market.

INTENSIVE CULTIVATION: use of large proportions of fertilizer, machinery, labor, and other capital on relatively limited agricultural acreage.

INTENSIVE DISTRIBUTION: the procedure of placing an item in all outlets available.

INTERACTION: the technique of repeating a group of computer instructions; the impact or relationship that exists between a salesperson and his or her potential customer, individual, or firm.

INTERACTION ANALYSIS: method involving observations of groups working on solving a problem, through which a profile of human relationship develops and can be measured.

INTER ALIA: among other things (Latin).

INTERCHANGEABLE PARTS: the first fundamental principle of mass production, credited to Eli Whitney, whereby assemblies no longer have to be made from uniquely fashioned and fitted components.

INTERCHANGE TRACK: a track on which cargo is moved from one railroad to another.

INTERCOM: a unit of intercommunication equipment for exchange of vocal messages over short distances, usually by wireless.

INTERCOMPANY TRANSACTION: a transaction between divisions or wholly owned subsidiaries of a corporation.

INTERCORPORATE STOCKHOLDING: an unlawful condition when a corporation holds stock in other corporations, which interferes with competition.

INTERDICTION: in law, the prohibition of commercial traffic between a country and specified other countries or ports.

INTEREST: a charge made for the use of money.

INTEREST COVERAGE: the frequency with which interest charges are earned.

INTEREST GROUP: a group that forms because of some special topic of concern.

INTEREST INVENTORY: a questionnaire concerning the activities a person likes or in which he or she has an interest.

INTERFACE: a common boundary between automatic data-processing systems or parts of a single system.

INTERGOVERNMENTAL EXPENDITURES: payment to other governments as fiscal aid or as reimbursements for the performance of services for the paying government; synonymous with revenue sharing.

INTERGOVERNMENTAL REVENUE: revenue received from other governments as fiscal aid, shared taxes, and reimbursements for services performed; synonymous with shared revenue.

INTERIM AUDIT: the phases of an audit conducted sometime before the end of the accounting period being reviewed.

INTERIM BOND: a temporary certificate that will be replaced by a permanent bond at a later date.

INTERIM RECEIVER: a court-appointed individual asked to protect a debtor's property until an official receiver is appointed.

INTERINDUSTRY COMPETITION: the competition that develops between companies in different industries.

INTERLEAVE: a procedure for combining parts of one computer program with another program to enable both to be executed simultaneously.

INTERLINE: describing the transfer of equipment carrying freight from one carrier to another.

INTERLOCKING DIRECTORS: directors of or more similar corporations who simultaneously hold office in the corporations.

INTERLOCUTORY DECREE: an intermediate determination made by a judge, subject to later final decision.

INTERMEDIARY: a middleman.

INTERMEDIATE: a range between low and high, beginning and advanced.

INTERMEDIATE CARRIER: a transportation line over which a shipment moves in interline but without touching the origin or destination point.

INTERMEDIATE GOODS: goods that enter into the production of other goods.

INTERMITTENT PROCESS: any process designed to produce a variety of items.

INTERMODAL SHIPMENT: freight shifted from one carrier to another.

INTERNAL AUDIT: an audit of an organization's operations conducted by one or more employees of the organization itself.

INTERNAL AUDITOR: an employee who performs audit functions within an organization.

INTERNAL CHECK: coordinated methods and measures adopted by an organization to check the accuracy and validity of data and to safeguard assets.

INTERNAL CONTROL: the plan of organization and the methods adopted by an organization to safeguard its assets and to ensure the accuracy and reliability of accounting data.

INTERNAL ECONOMIES SCALE: factors that bring about increases or decreases to an organization's long-run average costs or scale of operations resulting from size adjustments.

INTERNAL GENERATION OF FUNDS: the making and retention of profits which then become available for capital expenditures in lieu of borrowed funds.

INTERNAL MEMORY: the internal parts of a data-processing machine capable of retaining data.

INTERNAL REVENUE SERVICE: the federal agency empowered by Congress to administer the rules and regulations of the Department of the Treasury, including the collection of federal income and other taxes.

INTERNAL STORAGE: in computer language, storage within the computer system.

INTERNATIONAL BANK FOR RECONSTRUCTION AND DEVELOPMENT: an organization designed to aid underdeveloped nations; after phasing out activities of reconstruction, primary efforts are made to provide loans for economic development.

INTERNATIONAL MONETARY FUND: an institution through which nations may obtain foreign exchange to meet temporary needs in their balance of international payments and thus avoid nationalistic trade barriers and currency depreciation.

INTERNATIONAL PAYMENTS MECHANISM: the organization of markets whereby the monies of different nations are exchanged.

INTERNATIONAL REPRESENTATIVE: an agent of a national or international union, who may be primarily an organizer, an administrator, or an all-around troubleshooter.

INTERPHONE: equipment for vocal interoffice communication by wire.

INTERPLEADER: a court procedure under which a bank or other stakeholder, in order to be protected from possible double liability, acknowledges its obligation to make payment, or to turn over property, and compels the rival claimants to litigate their respective rights.

INTERPOLATE: to estimate a value between two known values by proportion or other, more accurate means.

INTERPRETER: a computer program that translates and executes each source language statement before translating and executing the next one.

INTERROGATORIES: in law, questions in writing presented to one who is to testify in a case so that he may answer.

INTER SE (OR INTER SESE): among themselves (Latin).

INTERSELLING: assigning sales personnel so that each is able to work in two or more related departments rather than being limited to one.

INTESTATE: not having a valid will.

INTERSTATE CARRIER: a common carrier whose business extends beyond the boundaries of one state.

INTERSTATE COMMERCE: commerce across state lines.

INTERSTATE TRAFFIC: cargo moved from one state to another.

INTERVIEW, EXIT: a conference with an employee before termination of his relationship with the organization to determine reasons for leaving, future plans, and general attitudes toward the job and company.

INTERVIEW, STRUCTURED: an interview in which the asking of definite questions closely controls the subjects discussed.

INTERVIEW, UNSTRUCTURED: an interview in which the interviewer does not determine the format or subject to be discussed, thus leaving the interviewee in major control of the conversation.

INTERVIEWER BIAS: influence resulting from the personal prejudice of the individual conducting the interview.

INTER VIVOS: between living persons (Latin).

IN THE BLACK: showing a profit.

IN THE MONEY: a call option in which the striking price is below the market price of the underlying stock.

IN THE RED: showing a loss.

IN TOTO: completely (Latin).

IN TRANSIT: describing items that have left the consignor's location and are en route to the destination.

INTRASTATE: completely within a state, as a transaction, sale, or shipment.

INTRASTATE CARRIER: a common carrier whose business is conducted entirely within the boundaries of a state.

INTRASTATE COMMERCE: commerce conducted solely within a state's geographic borders.

INTRASTORE TRANSFER: the purchase of goods from one selling department for use by another selling department.

INTRINSIC VALUE: the value possessed by a particular thing considered in itself.

INTROJECTION: lack of objectivity; the tendency of an interviewee, in an interview, to analyze everything in a personal way, either negatively or positively.

INTRUSION: forcefully taking possession of another's real property.

INTUITIVE PRICING: a practice of establishing a price based on the intuition of the responsible party.

INVALIDATE: to nullify, as a permit or license.

INVENTORY: the merchandise on hand at any given time, applicable to raw materials, goods in process, or finished goods; the listing of such merchandise, with valuations.

INVENTORY CERTIFICATE: a letter of representation obtained by an independent auditor from his client, certifying the basis of valuation and the ownership of goods in the inventory.

INVENTORY CONTROL: the control of merchandise on hand by accounting and physical methods; an approach used in emergencies to regulate inventories for the purpose of increased utilization of items and to prevent hoarding.

INVENTORY SHORTAGE (SHRINKAGE): an inventory reduced by theft, internal or external fraud, waste, sabotage, or careless operation.

INVENTORY TURNOVER: the number of times that the investment in merchandise or stock on hand is replaced during a stated period, usually 12 months.

INVERSE DEMAND: condition under which price and volume vary at the same time, and more is sold at a high price than at a lower one.

INVESTED CAPITAL: the amount of capital contributed to a company by its owners.

INVESTIGATION: a search for information necessary for a business decision; an undercover study of a person, as to his character, for employability or to reveal causes of company losses.

INVESTMENT: a purchase of an equity or a certificate of indebtedness in which such factors as safety and yield are of major consideration.

INVESTMENT BANKER: the middleman between the corporation issuing new securities and the public.

INVESTMENT BANKING: the financing of the capital requirements of an enterprise.

INVESTMENT CLUB: a voluntary grouping of people who pool their monies to build up an investment portfolio.

INVESTMENT COMPANY: a company of trust that uses its capital to invest in other companies.

INVESTMENT COUNSELOR: one whose profession is giving advice on investments and managing the investments of others for a fee.

INVESTMENT CREDIT: an income credit on a tax return granted in the form of total write-off of newly purchased fixed assets or write-down at a rate faster than allowed in customarily applied depreciation guidelines.

INVESTMENT PROPERTY: real estate acquired for profit.

INVESTMENT TRUST: a fiduciary primarily engaged in making investments.

INVESTOR: an individual whose principal concerns in the purchase of a security are regular dividend income, safety of the original investment, and if possible, capital appreciation.

INVITATION TO BID: an advertisement issued by one who desires a number of different persons to bid on the job.

INVOICE: a bill of sale.

INVOLUNTARY ALIENATION: forced sale of real estate.

INVOLUNTARY BANKRUPTCY: a bankruptcy brought about by a petition of creditors.

INVOLUNTARY LIEN: a lien on property demanded without the consent of the owner.

INVOLUNTARY UNEMPLOYMENT: a condition under which people who wish to work are unable to locate opportunities at going wage rates for the related skills and experiences that they have to offer.

IOTA: a minute amount of any item.

IOU: an informal written agreement acknowledging a cash debt.

IPSO FACTO: by that very fact (Latin).

IRISH DIVIDEND: a trade term for an assessment imposed on a security instead of a dividend.

IRON LAW OF WAGES: the concept that wages tend to equal what the employee needs to maintain a subsistence level of living.

IRREGULAR ROUTING: a sales call pattern; the sales representative determines the frequency of calls to be made.

IRREGULARS: items having defects that may affect appearance but not wear.

IRREPARABLE HARM: injury or damage that is so constant and universal that no fair or reasonable redress can be achieved in court.

IRREVOCABLE LETTER OF CREDIT: a letter of credit that cannot be canceled until after a stated date without the consent of the person in whose favor it is drawn.

IRREVOCABLE TRUST: a trust that cannot be altered by the person who created the trust.

IRRIGATION: the farming practice of watering crops artificially by means of narrow canals or ditches, or by flooding.

ISLAND DISPLAY: merchandise shown in a store's aisle or open space.

ISLAND POSITION: describing the placement of newspaper advertising copy that is surrounded by editorial matter or page margin.

ISOTOPE: chemical variant of an element; isotopes have diversified uses in industry, sciences, medicine, and archaeology.

ISSUED CAPITAL: proportion of authorized capital stock for which subscriptions have been received and the stock allotted.

ITEM: one member of a group.

ITEMIZE: to list, item by item; to supply details on a bill, voucher, or request for traveling expenses for a business.

ITEMIZED APPROPRIATION: a restriction of an appropriation to be made only for and in the amounts listed.

ITEMIZED DEDUCTIONS: a listing of allowed expenses that are subtracted in arriving at taxable income.

ITEM VALIDITY: the extent to which an item of a test, survey, poll, or other predictive device measures what it is supposed to measure.

ITERATION: the process of repeating a sequence of logical steps for purposes of improving or refining.

ITINERARY: a route list of names and locations of customers to be visited on a trip.

ITINERANT WORKER: a work who is not a permanent member of a community and finds work by moving from opportunity to opportunity.

J

JACKKNIFE: the behavior of a moving tractor that turns sideways to its semitrailer and is dragged out of control.

JAWBONING: an influential individual pressuring someone to submit to specific rules and regulations.

JEOPARDY: danger inherent in being placed on trial for a criminal offense, as in double jeopardy.

JERRY-BUILT: built cheaply, flimsily, and sometimes temporarily.

JETSAM: goods or parts of a ship thrown overboard in order to lighten the vessel.

JETTISON: to throw overboard part of the cargo or any article on board a ship for the purpose of lightening the ship in case of emergency.

JOB: a specific group of tasks prescribed as a unit of work; to purchase or sell merchandise in quantity, not in selected categories.

JOB ACTION: an employee protest, falling short of a strike.

JOB ANALYSIS: a systematic study of the specific tasks required for a particular job, set of conditions, rate of pay, and so on.

JOB ANALYST: the person who makes a job analysis.

JOB BATCH: a succession of job definitions placed in sequence to form a batch.

JOBBER: a wholesaler.

JOB CLASSIFICATION: evaluation of job content and required skills, for the purpose of setting up wage brackets for each classification.

JOB CONTENT: for a given classification, the duties, functions, and responsibilities.

JOB-COST SYSTEM: a method of cost accounting in which costs for distinguishable units are determined by accumulating identifiable costs during the entire production process.

JOB DEPTH: refers to the amount of control an employee can exert to alter or influence his or her job and the surrounding environment.

JOB DESCRIPTION: written summary of the important features and requirements of a job; usually based on a job analysis.

JOB DILUTION: the approach of dividing the tasks of a job into levels of skill.

JOB ENLARGEMENT: a procedure for increasing the scope and responsibilities of a job to increase satisfaction to the employee.

JOB EVALUATION: a systematic rating of job content on factors such as skill, responsibility, and experience.

JOB LOT: a miscellaneous grouping of items of various styles, sizes, colors, and so on, bought at a reduced price by store or individual middleman.

JOB MANAGEMENT: a general term that collectively describes the functions of job scheduling and computer command processing.

JOB ORDER: an order or ticket directing the work to be done on a particular lot of materials.

JOB-ORIENTED TERMINAL: a computer terminal designed for a particular application.

JOB PLACEMENT: the assignment of a person to a job.

JOB PROCESSING: the reading of job-control statements and data from an input stream, the initiating of job steps defined in the statements, and the writing of system output messages.

JOB RANGE: the number of operations a job occupant performs to complete his or her work.

JOB ROTATION: a planned approach to management training which involves the transfer of the trainee through a series of different types of positions.

JOB SATISFACTION: an expression given in terms of the positive or negative aspects of an employee's attitude toward his or her job or some part of it.

JOB SECURITY: usually described in a union contract, a means of protecting a worker's job.

JOB SPECIFICATION: a carefully written description of a specific job with duties and opportunities described.

JOB STANDARDIZATION: clearly defined techniques for work procedures and uniformity.

JOB TICKET: a card with instructions which accompanies a printing assignment through all departments; the progress of the work is noted on the card.

JOINDER: acting jointly with one or more other persons; joining, such a joinder of cause of action.

JOINT ACCOUNT: a bank account that may be drawn upon individually by two or more persons.

JOINT ADVENTURE: two persons entering into a single business for their mutual benefit, as with partners.

JOINT AGREEMENT: the contract between union and management where more than one union or employer is involved.

JOINT AND SEVERAL: parties that may be sued alone or together as being responsible for the actions of each other.

JOINT CONTRACT: two or more people who make a promise to another are joint obligators to the contract and to the other party identified.

JOINT COST: a cost which is common to all the segments in question and which can be assigned only by means of arbitrary allocation.

JOINT DEMAND: demand for two or more items that are usually used together because of necessity or consumer preference.

JOINT LIFE INSURANCE: insurance on two or more persons, the benefits of which are payable on the first death.

JOINTLY AND SEVERALLY: condition under which each person is legally obligated to become individually liable for the payment of a note.

JOINT NOTE: a note signed by two or more persons who have equal liability for payment.

JOINT OWNERSHIP: the interest in property of two or more people.

JOINT PRODUCTION COSTS: the cost to produce goods that are made in a single process and are not identifiable as individual products up to a certain stage of production.

JOINT RETURN: the federal and or state income tax reports for a husband and wife to file their income jointly rather than individually.

JOINT-STOCK COMPANY: a form of business ownership that combines the unlimited liability of the general partnership with corporate features, such as a board of directors, stock transferability and share-owner investors.

JOINT TENANCY: two or more persons, with equal right to possession and equal title, have an undivided interest in a land holding.

JOINTURE: an agreement before marriage providing lands for a wife upon the death of the husband for the life of the wife.

JOINT VENTURE: a business undertaking entered into by two or more parties which is intended to

terminate upon the completion of a specific project.

JOINT WILL: a single will of two or more individuals.

JOURNAL: a book of original entry.

JOURNAL VOUCHER: a document supporting an entry in a general journal.

JOURNALIZE: to record a transaction in an entity's records using the double-entry system.

JOURNEYMAN: a skilled workman.

JUDGMENT: a court award substantiating a money claim and opening the way to its legal enforcement; a judicial ruling; an opinion.

JUDGMENT CREDITOR: an individual who has proved a debt in court or has won an action for the recovery of a debt.

JUDGMENT DEBT: any debt contested in a suit at law and proved to be valid.

JUDGMENT DEBTOR: an individual who has been ordered by the court to make a payment to another.

JUDGMENT NOTE: a note authorizing a creditor to enter a judgment against a debtor in case of nonpayment, without the need for court action.

JUDICIAL SALE: a sale conducted under the authority and supervision of the court.

JUMBLE DISPLAY: a collection of items tossed together in a container or on a table counter.

JUMP: a departure from the normal sequence of executing instructions; synonymous with branch.

JUMP BAIL: to flee, when released on bail until a set time to appear in court, failing to appear, thus forefeiting bail.

JUNIOR EXECUTIVE: one subordinate to an executive, such as an assistant.

JUNIOR ISSUE: an issue whose claim for dividends or interest, or for principal value, comes following that of another issue.

JUNIOR MORTGAGE: a second or

third mortgage that is subordinated to a prior mortgage.

JUNIOR SECURITY: a security having a lower priority of claims on assets than another security.

JUNKET: a journey combining pleasure with business, the expense of which is borne by the employer.

JURAT: an attestation to an affidavit stating its date, before whom it was sworn, and the authority of the attest.

JURISDICTION: the legal power of authority to hear and determine a cause or case.

JURISDICTIONAL DISPUTE: a conflict between rival unions over which should maintain control over a given job or activity and be recognized as the collective-bargaining agent.

JURISDICTIONAL STRIKE: a strike resulting from a jurisdictional dispute.

JURISPRUDENCE: the science, system, practice, and area of law.

JUSTIFICATION: the act of adjusting, arranging, or shifting digits to the left or right, to fit a prescribed pattern.

JUSTIFIED PRICE: a fair-market price that an informed buyer will give for property.

JUSTIFY: to adjust computer characters for line length and regular margins on a page.

JUST TITLE: a title that will be supported against all claims.

K

KAMERALISM: a concept of mercantilism concerned with the production of wealth by the state and how the wealth is used.

KEELAGE: money paid for the use of port or harbor facilities.

KENTLEDGE GOODS: weighty goods, placed low in a ship to increase stability.

KEY: critical, essential; one or more characters in a item of data used to identify it or control its use.

KEYBOARD: a device for the encoding of data by key depression.

KEYBOARD ENTRY: a technique whereby access into the contents of a computer's storage may be initiated at a keyboard.

KEY DRIVEN: term describing any device for translating information into machine-sensible form which rqeuires an operator to depress a key for each character.

KEYED ADVERTISING: advertising so designed that replies can be identified by the medium and issue in which the advertisement appears.

KEY-EXECUTIVE OPTION: a privilege extended to key executives to buy stock in the company from a block set aside by stockholder vote.

KEY INDUSTRY: an industry that holds major importance in the country's economy because of a unique characteristic.

KEYING AN ADVERTISEMENT: placing a code or letter in a coupon or in the advertiser's address so that the specific advertisement producing an inquiry can be noted.

KEY-MAN INSURANCE: life insurance on a key employee, partner, or proprietor; the business is the beneficiary under the policy.

KEYPUNCH: the equipment used to record information in cards or tape by punching holes that represent letters, digits, and other characters.

KEY QUESTION: a question of major importance.

KEYSTONE PRICING: nominal pricing in which the marked price is intended to be higher than the selling price to make the buyer feel he or she is getting a bargain.

KEY WORD: a significant or informative word in a title or document that describes the content of a particular document.

KICKBACK: forcing employees to return a part of their wages; an illegal rebate given secretly by a seller for granting an order.

KILLING: an unusually profitable trade.

KILN: an oven, as used in ceramics, wood seasoning, and lime manufacture.

KILO: prefix meaning one thousand.

KILOGRAM: the basic weight of the metric system, equal to 2.205 pounds.

KILOMETER: 1000 meters, approximately 0.62 of a mile, or about 1093.6 yards.

KILOWAT HOUR: a unit of electric power, equal to 1000 watts, sold throughout the United States at lower prices for large users.

KIMBALL TAGS: prepunched tags affixed to goods, containing size and style data that are utilized in speeding inventory control.

KINESCOPE: motion-picture film made by kinescope; equipment that uses a cathode-ray tube for producing images of the scenes on which it is trained.

KIP: hide of a lamb or sheep.

KITE: to issue checks for amounts exceeding one's bank balance in the expectation of making deposits in time to cover the checks.

KITING: the act of depositing in one bank account a check drawn on another bank account but recording only the deposit on the day of the transfer.

KNOCKED DOWN: disassembled, as for shipment, and capable of ready reassembly.

KURTOSIS: a measure of the concentration or clustering of cases around the mode of a frequency curve.

KRAFT PAPER: strong paper made from wood sulfate pulp, used for wrapping and as linerboard.

L

LABEL: a slip of paper or other material with adhesive back which when affixed to anything identifies it.

LABOR AGREEMENT: an employee contract between the employer and the union which covers the conditions of employment.

LABORATORY: quarters and equipment for experiments and tests.

LABOR DISPUTE: any controversy concerning terms, tenure, or conditions of employment.

LABOR ECONOMICS: a specialty in the field of economics concerned primarily with the relationship between the worker and his or her job.

LABOR EXCHANGE BANK: the aim of exchanging commodities in proportion to their labor content.

LABOR FORCE: the total number of workers willing to work at prevailing wage rates; in the census definition, all persons over 14 years old who are employed or temporarily out of work.

LABOR GRADE: job or job groups in a rate structure, set usually through job classifications and evaluations, or by agreement with a union.

LABOR INTENSIVE: describing the use of additional manpower to increase output or earnings.

LABOR MOBILITY: the ease with which workers change positions and jobs.

LABOR PIRACY: the attempt to attract workers away from a firm by offering higher wages and other beneifts.

LABOR POOL: the established source of trained people from which prospective workers are recruited.

LABOR RELATIONS: a general term to identify all matters arising out of the employer-employee relationship.

LABOR-SAVING EQUIPMENT: any mechanized equipment that reduces the number of workers or the number of working hours.

LABOR SKATE: semihumorous name for a full-time union employee.

LABOR UNION: any organization of employees which has as its purpose the improvement of the condition of its members.

LACHES: an unreasonable delay by a person in claiming something due to him or her.

LADING: the cargo in a vehicle or ship.

LAG: extent of time between two operations, as between completion of a product design and its availability for marketing.

LAGAN: goods sunk at sea with a buoy attached, so that they may be recovered.

LAISSEZ FAIRE: the economic doctrine of noninterference (French).

LAMBS: ignorant or inexperienced speculators in stock.

LAME DUCK: a member of a stock exchange who is unable to meet his debts; an ineffectual or helpless individual.

LAMINATE: to cover a flat surface with an adhering sheet of material, generally plastic.

LAND CERTIFICATE: a legal document indicating proof of ownership of land or property.

LAND CONTRACT: a written agreement for the sale of land.

LAND FREEZE: government limit on the sale or transfer of land.

LAND GRANT: a donation of public land by a governmental agency to be used for the benefit of the public.

LANDLORD: the owner of leased property; the lessor.

LAND-OFFICE BUSINESS: a booming or rushing business.

LAND PATENT: the legal document used by the federal government in conveying the title of land to a citizen or individual.

LAND POOR: term for person who owns land but is short of funds because of taxes or other obligations.

LAND REVENUE: any form of payment derived from ownership of land.

LAND TAX: a tax levied on the ownership of real property; synonymous with ad valorem tax or property tax.

LAND TRUST: title to land held by a trustee in the interest of the beneficiaries of a trust.

LAND WARRANT: a government document given as proof of ownership to anyone buying public land.

LANGUAGE: a defined character set used to form words and symbols; the rules for combining these into useful communications.

LANGUAGE, ARTIFICIAL: a language for the computer designed for ease of communication in a particular area of endeavor.

LANGUAGE, COMMON: the result of a technique that reduces all information to a form that is intelligible to the units of data-processing systems.

LANGUAGE SYMBOLIC: a formalized artificial language (symbolic calculus) designed to avoid the inadequacies of natural languages.

LANGUAGE TRANSLATOR: any assembler, compiler, or other computer routine that accepts statements in one language and produces equivalent statements in another language.

LAPIDARY: a specialist in precious and semiprecious stones, as a diamond cutter or rock hunter.

LAPPING: concealing shortages by a series of entries postponing the receipt of some asset from one accounting period to the next.

LAPSE: to expire before intended renewal, such as a lease or insurance contract.

LAPSING SCHEDULE: a form on which are recorded the costs of fixed assets or the total yearly additions to a group of fixed assets.

LARCENY: theft; stealing.

LAST WILL: the will last executed by an individual; all former wills are revoked by the last one.

LATENT DEFECT: a defect in goods not visible to the naked eye.

LATITUDE: the freedom to make a range of choices.

LAUNCH: to initiate, start, put in motion, as a plan or program.

LAWFUL MONEY: all forms of money that are endowed by federal law with legal tender status for the payment of all debts, both public and private.

LAWSUIT: a civil action in a court of law.

LAYAWAY: goods purchased to be called for at a later date; a deposit is put down and the balance paid when the goods are picked up.

LAY DAYS: agreed-upon number of days that a chartered vessel is permitted to remain in port for loading and unloading without penalty.

LAYOFF: a temporary discharge with intent to rehire as soon as business conditions permit.

LAYOUT: the arrangements of the physical elements of a factory, office, or store; a plan or visualization of an advertisement or newspaper page.

LEADER MERCHANDISING: promoting several items at attractive prices for the purpose of inducing customers into the store.

LEADERSHIP: exercising the qualities of guidance and command in a resourceful and responsible manner in a business, a business association, or in government.

LEADERSHIP TRAINING: training provided by means of workshops, conferences, seminars, and other programs designed to upgrade skills and to offer information of use to those in leadership positions.

LEAD-IN: part of the interaction that permits a sales representative to move toward a summing up or to close with a customer.

LEAD MAN: an employee whose job involves some supervision, planning, and organization of tasks and materials performed by a group.

LEAD TIME: the length of time between ordering something and actually receiving it.

LEAKAGE: the removal of funds from the income stream for repayment of debts previously contracted, or for addition to hoards.

LEARNING CURVE: a graphic representation of the measured changes at successive units of practice.

LEASE: a form of contract transferring the use or occupancy of land, space, structures, or equipment in consideration of a payment, usually in the form of rent.

LEASE-BACK: the situation under which the owner of a property sells it to another on condition that the former owner can lease it back for a specified period of time at a specified rent.

LEASEHOLD: an estate or interest a tenant holds for a number of years in the property he or she is leasing.

LEASEHOLD IMPROVEMENTS: improvements made by a lessee.

LEASEHOLD INSURANCE: insurance that protects a lessee who has subleased property to another person.

LEASEHOLD VALUE: the market value a lease may increase or decrease over what was originally paid.

LEASE INSURANCE: a form of protection for the landlord against a default in rental payments on the lease's remaining time.

LEASE-OPTION AGREEMENT: a lease that gives the lessee the option to purchase the subject property at a particular date for a stipulated price.

LEASE-PURCHASE AGREEMENT: an agreement providing that a portion of a tenant's rent can be applied to the price of purchase.

LEAVE OF ABSENCE: time off from work, usually without loss of seniority, granted with the assumption that the employee will be reinstated.

LEDGER: a financial record book for all control accounts for customers or for suppliers, into which postings are made and from which statements can be compiled.

LEGACY: bequest, something of value left to a person by a decedent.

LEGAL ASSET: any property that can be used for payment of a debt.

LEGAL ENTITY: any individual, partnership, or organization that has the capacity to make a contract or an agreement and an obligation to discharge an indebtedness.

LEGAL INTEREST: the maximum rate of interest permitted by state law.

LEGALITY: compliance with the law.

LEGAL LIST: a list of investments selected by various states in which certain institutions and fiduciaries, such as insurance companies and banks, may invest.

LEGAL MONOPOLY: a privately owned organization that is granted an exclusive right by the government to function in a specified market under their strict control and pricing.

LEGAL RATE OF INTEREST: the rate of interest the law implies in the absence of agreement by the parties on the question of interest.

LEGAL RESERVE: policy reserves maintained by an insurance company to meet future claims and obligations; part of a bank's cash assets that must be retained as protection for depositors.

LEGAL RESIDENCE: where a person lives.

LEGAL SECURITY: a stock or bond that can be bought by a fiduciary and retained for beneficiaries.

LEGAL TENDER: bills and coins legal for payment of purchases.

LEGAL TITLE: the claim of right to property that is recognized by law.

LEGATEE: one to whom a legacy is bequeathed.

LENDER: an individual or institution loaning money with the expectation that the money (or other item) will be returned with interest.

LENDING INSTITUTION: a finance company, bank, loan organization, or other entity that lends money and makes money by advancing funds to others.

LESSEE: one who rents from an owner.

LESSOR: an owner who rents out his property.

LET: to award or assign work to be done or equipment rented from a supplier; synonymous with lease.

LETHAL: deadly, as a lethal weapon or a lethal (gas) chamber.

LETTERHEAD: a sheet of correspondence paper bearing a printed or engraved name and address.

LETTER OF ATTORNEY: a document showing a power of attorney.

LETTER OF CREDIT: a bank document issued on behalf of a buyer on another bank or on itself; it gives a buyer the prestige and the financial backing of the issuing bank.

LETTERS OF ADMINISTRATION: a written court authorization to an administrator authorizing him to administer the affairs of a deceased person.

LETTERS, TESTAMENTARY: a written court authorization to the executor of a will authorizing him to act as executor.

LETTER STOCK: an unregistered stock, usually issued by a new, small firm to avoid the expense of a formal underwriting.

LEVEL-CHARGE PLAN: in investment companies, a plan under which the sales charge is deducted at the same rate as periodic purchases of shares are made.

LEVELING: a procedure in time and motion study used to measure and evaluate an employee's output.

LEVEL OUT: to become stabilized after a climb or dip, as prices.

LEVEL PREMIUM: an unchanging rate for policy premiums.

LEVEL-PREMIUM INSURANCE: insurance in which the annual premium remains the same throughout the period over which premiums are paid.

LEVERAGE: the condition existing when money is borrowed and reinvested or used to produce a return exceeding the cost of borrowing.

LEVY: to impose a tax; an assessment.

LIABILITY: something owed.

LIABILITY, CURRENT: those pecuniary obligations ordinarily intended to be paid in the usual course of business within a relatively short time.

LIABILITY, FIXED: a long-term debt; recurring expenses.

LIABILITY INSURANCE: insurance to pay for injuries or damages to others or to their property.

LIABILITY LEDGER: the record of all outstanding loans made by a bank to every borrower.

LIABILITY LIMITS: the sum or sums up to which an insurance company protects the insured on a particular policy.

LIABLE: subject to a particular risk, expense, or penalty, which is more or less likely to occur or be incurred; obligated by law or equity.

LIAISON: the contact maintained between units, in order to ensure concerted action.

LIBEL: the publication of an untrue defamatory statement regarding another.

LIBERALIZATION: the increase of privileges or rights of compensation, particularly to employees.

LICENSE: a paid certificate of privilege granted by government to a qualified person or firm to carry on a business otherwise not permitted.

LICENSED LENDER: a lending group of people or organizations authorized by license to conduct business in the state in which residence is shown.

LIEN: the right to retain possession of another's property until debts owned to the holder of the property are satisfied.

LIEN AFFIDAVIT: an affidavit either stating that there are no liens against a particular property, or documenting and properly describing any existing liens.

LIFE ANNUITY: an insurance policy providing regular payments to the insured beginning at a stated age.

LIFE ESTATE: a freehold interest in land, the duration of which is confined to the life of one or more persons or contingent upon certain happenings.

LIFE INSURANCE: a contract providing for payment, upon the death of the insured or other maturity, of a sum of money outright or in installments.

LIFE TENANT: a person whose interest in property is limited to the duration of his or her life.

LIFO: an acronym in merchandise inventories, meaning "last in, first out."

LIGHTERAGE: the price paid for loading, transporting, and unloading freight from a ship not lying alongside a dock to a dock, or the reverse.

LIGHT GOLD: gold coins that have been reduced in weight, either by error of the mint or as the result of usage.

LIGHT-PEN TRACKING: the process of tracing the movement of light emitted by a penlike instrument across the screen of a display device.

LIMESTONE: calcium carbonate rock quarried for buildings and for conversion to lime.

LIMITED ACCESS: land or property that is difficult to reach; land made more inaccessible.

LIMITED-COINAGE SYSTEM: the US Mint's program under which the right of the individual to bring bullion for purposes of being coined is limited.

LIMITED COMPANY: a British business corporation, usually abbreviated as "Ltd."

LIMITED-FUNCTION WHOLESALER: a middleman who takes title to the goods he deals in but performs only one or two of the functions of wholesaler.

LIMITED LIABILITY: limited responsibility for debt, as for a corporation.

LIMITED LIFE: a characteristic of a single proprietorship or partnership.

LIMITED-LINE STORES: small retail operations that carry most goods in a narrow line of items.

LIMITED ORDER: an order in which the customer has set restrictions with respect to price.

LIMITED PARTNERSHIP: a partnership in which the liability of one or more of the partners for debts is limited to a stated amount.

LIMITED-PRICE ORDER: an order with directions to buy or sell a stated amount of a security at a specified price or better.

LIMIT OF LIABILITY: the maximum

amount an insurer is bound by the policy to pay in the case of proved losses covered by the terms of the policy.

LINAGE MEASUREMENT: measurement of a newspaper or magazine advertisement in agate lines.

LINE: apparel style; items carried by a merchant; a system or carrier; a chain of command.

LINE AND STAFF: a form of organization characterized by direct-line authority, with staff assistants to those in the higher ranks.

LINEAR: one dimensional.

LINEAR PROGRAMMING: a means for indicating how materials should be combined to produce the highest profits.

LINE AUTHORITY: authority that is exerted downward (i.e., over subordinates) in an organization.

LINE CONTROL: the scheme of operating procedures and control signals by which a telecommunications system is controlled.

LINE MANAGER: a high-level officer having direct responsibility for carrying out a superior's requests and with authority to give orders to subordinates.

LINE OF CREDIT: an agreement between a bank and a customer, wherein the customer borrows and pays interest on the borrowed portion only.

LINE OF DISCOUNT: the maximum credit that a bank will extend to a retailer on the basis of his accounts payable, which the merchant discounts with the bank.

LINE ORGANIZATION: a company structure, where top officials have total and direct authority, and subordinates report to only one supervisor.

LINE PRINTER: a computer device that prints all characters of a line as a unit.

LINE RATE: the price per agate line of newspaper or magazine space.

LINE SHEET: a guide for insurance underwriters, stating the amount of liability the company is willing to assume on various classes of risks.

LINKAGE: a system of links and bars joined together to transmit motion, as a gearshift assembly.

LINOTYPE: a trademarked keyboard machine that casts characters (type) and prints one line at a time.

LIQUID: capable of being readily converted to cash.

LIQUID ASSETS: quick assets.

LIQUIDATE: to convert (assets) into cash; to discharge or pay off an indebtedness; to settle the accounts of, by apportioning assets and debts.

LIQUIDATED DAMAGES: the payment by all parties of an agreed-upon sum of money as damages for breaching their contract.

LIQUIDATING DIVIDEND: the declared dividend in the closing of a firm, to distribute the assets of the organization to properly qualified stockholders.

LIQUIDATION: turning assets into cash; winding up the affairs of a business, as in a receivership.

LIQUIDATION VALUE: the amount an asset might realize upon a forced sale; the amount that would be realized upon the winding-up of a business.

LIQUIDATOR: a person appointed to oversee the winding-up of the affairs of a corporation or other organization.

LIQUIDITY: the convertibility of assets into cash.

LIQUIDITY PREFERENCE: the schedule of the amount of resources valued in terms of money or of wage units an individual wishes to retain in the form of money in different sets of circumstances.

LIQUID RATIO: the ratio of readily available current assets to current liabilities.

LIST BROKER: a commission agent who rents direct-mail lists to advertisers.

LISTED SECURITIES: securities entitled to trading privileges on a stock exchange.

LISTING: an agreement between a real estate agent and a land owner under which the owner pays the agent a commission if he sells the property.

LIST PRICE: the posted, published price, which may at times be reduced by such devices as volume discounts, commissions, discounts for prompt payment, or other rebate.

LITERAL: describing a symbol or a quantity that is itself a piece of data, rather than a reference to data.

LITIGANT: a person engaged in a lawsuit.

LITIGATION: legal action through the courts.

LIVE: telecast at the time of enactment, as sports events.

LIVING TRUST: a trust that becomes operative during the lifetime of the settler, as opposed to a trust under will; the same as a trust inter vivos.

LOAD-FACTOR PRICING: changing the price at various periods for the purpose of maximizing the utilization of manufacturing facilities.

LOAD FUNDS: mutual funds sold by sales representatives.

LOADING: an amount referred to as finance charges, included in a contracted installment price to cover administrative and selling costs and interest.

LOADING CHARGE: a premium charged by open-end investment funds when selling new securities, to cover selling costs.

LOAD POINT: the beginning of the recording area on a reel of magnetic tape.

LOAD UP: to buy a security or commodity to one's financial limit, for purposes of speculation.

LOAN: that which is placed in the possession of another without transfer of title and for later return.

LOAN CROWD: stock-exchange members who will borrow or lend securities to investors who have sold short.

LOAN POLICY: a title-insurance policy prepared by a title-insurance company for a holder of a mortgage.

LOAN RATE: the rate charged for borrowing money at a specific date for a stated period.

LOAN SHARK: a person who lends money at exorbitant rates of interest.

LOAN STOCK: securities that have been loaned to a broker or short seller to fulfill the terms of a short-selling contract by delivering shares.

LOAN-TO-VALUE RATIO: ratio of a property's appraised value in proportion to the amount of the mortgage loan.

LOAN VALUE: the amount a lending organization will lend on property; the amount of money that can be borrowed on a life-insurance policy.

LOBBY: a person or an organization seeking to influence the proceedings of legislative bodies through personal intervention.

LOBBYIST: a person or group of persons trying to affect and influence the proceedings of governmental agencies.

LOCAL BRAND: a brand sponsored by a distributor or manufacturer in a limited area.

LOCAL OPTION: a privilege of local residents to vote as to whether a law or regulation should apply in the area they inhabit, as liquor laws.

LOCAL UNION: also called a local; the organization of members of an international union in a particular plant, region, or locality.

LOCKED IN: an investor who is unwilling to sell his securities on which he has a profit because of the capital-gains tax.

LOCKER STOCKS: a manufacturer's or wholesaler's shipment of additional inventory assortment retained unopened in the store's central warehouse.

LOCKOUT: the action of management in closing a plant and laying off its employees.

LOCKUP: securities that have been withdrawn from circulation and placed in a safe-deposit box as a long-term investment.

LOGARITHMIC: exponential, particularly as logarithmic scales and charts on which statistical data are displayed.

LOGIC, COMPUTER: the sequence of steps necessary to perform a particular function.

LOGO: a distinctive symbol used by an organization to identify itself.

LOGROLLING: supporting another's cause in return for his support of yours.

LOMBARD STREET: the London financial area similiar to Wall Street in New York or LaSalle Street in Chicago.

LONG: signifies ownership of stocks; holding a sizable amount of a security or commodity in anticipation of a scarcity and price rise.

LONGEVITY PAY: salary adjustments based on seniority or length of service.

LONG POSITION: term describing a holder of securities who expects an increase in the price of his or her shares and holds these securities for income.

LONG-RANGE PLANNING: a systematic procedure for directing and controlling future activities of a firm for periods longer than a year.

LONG RATE: the reduced premium rate, when a policy runs longer than one year.

LONGSHOREMAN: dockworker engaged in the handling or movement of freight.

LONG-TERM ASSET: long-term investments, fixed assets, and other assets that are not current assets.

LONG-TERM BOND: a bond of 15 years' or longer maturity.

LONG-TERM CONTRACT: a collective-bargaining agreement negotiated for a period longer than one year.

LONG-TERM DEBT: liabilities that become due more than one year after the signing of the agreement.

LONG-TERM GAIN: profit on a capital asset acquired six months or longer before its sale.

LONG-TERM LIABILITY: an obligation that will not become due within one year.

LOOP: a sequence of computer instructions where the last instruction in the series returns the machine to the first instruction in the series.

LOOPHOLE: an ambiguity or omission in a law which allows the intent of the law to be evaded; sometimes applied to contracts.

LOOP MODIFICATION: alteration of instruction addresses, counters, or data by means of instructions of a loop.

LOSS: any decrease in quantity, quality, or value of property; the excess of the cost of an asset over its price of sale.

LOSS CONSTANT: a flat amount included in some insurance premiums which measures the average provision for losses.

LOSS-CONTROL REPRESENTATIVE: an insurance representative who assists insureds in loss-prevention practices and in obtaining rating and underwriting information.

LOSS EXPECTANCY: an underwriter's estimate of damage that would result from the peril insured against.

LOSS LEADER: a product or service sold at a loss to attract new customers who will buy other products or services that are profitable.

LOSS ON DISPOSAL: the result of a sale of a noncurrent asset for less than the book value or unrecovered cost.

LOSS-PAYABLE CLAUSE: provides for payment to a mortgagee or lienholder in addition to the insured, for any losses to the insured property, according to the extent of that party's interest in the property at the time of the loss.

LOSS-PREVENTION SERVICE: loss-control and inspection work done by insurance companies or independent organizations for prophylaxis of loss.

LOSS RATIO: a percentage arrived at by dividing the amount of the losses by the amount of the insurance premium.

LOSS RESERVE: a part of an insurance firm's assets retained in available form to meet expected claims.

LOT: any group of goods or services making up a single transaction; a parcel of land having measurable boundaries; a quantity of shares.

LOW GRADE: of inferior quality, applied to merchandise, stock, and so on.

LOW-MARGIN RETAILING: discount selling or mass merchandising.

LUCRATIVE TITLE: a title that is obtained by a person who pays less than the true market value of the property; title to property obtained as a gift.

LUG: a part, protruding like an ear, tapped for a bolt to secure the housing or machine of which it is a part.

LUMP-SUM PURCHASE: a group of assets obtained for an indicated figure, without breakdown by individual assets or classes of assets.

LUMP-SUM SETTLEMENT: a single sum of money offered and accepted in payment of a claim; as in accident cases or insurance claims.

LUXURIES: comforts and beauties of life that are in excess of what is needed for normal or standard living.

LUXURY MARKET: people who can afford to buy luxury products, and, in the wholesale sense, the retailers who serve them.

LUXURY TAX: a tax imposed on items not considered essential for daily living.

M

MACH: the ratio of the speed of an object to the speed of sound, which is about 1,087 feet per second at sea level at 0°C.

MACHINE, BUNDLING: a machine used to collate multiples of unit packages.

MACHINE, SCANNING: a machine that facilitates the input of data by reading printed data and converting them into machine language.

MACHINE ADDRESS: the direct, absolute, unindexed address expressed as such or resulting after indexing has been carried out.

MACHINE CODE: an operation code that a machine is designed to recognize.

MACHINE INSTRUCTION: an instruction that a machine can recognize and execute.

MACHINE LANGUAGE: information or data expressed in a code that can be read by a computer or by peripheral equipment without interpretation.

MACHINE-ORIENTED LANGUAGE: computer language that describes programs in terms of the individual computer instructions composing them.

MACHINE TOOL: a stationary power tool used for removing or reshaping metal.

MACROCOSM: the great cosmos of the astronomical universe, hence the national and international economy rather than the problem of the individual business or person.

MACROECONOMICS: that school or phase of economics which concentrates on aggregates such as gross national product.

MADCAP: machine-oriented language for mathematical problems and set operations.

MAGISTRATE: a public officer, usually a judge, with power to issue a warrant for the arrest of a person charged with a public offense.

MAGNETIC CARD: a card with a magnetic surface on which data can be stored by selective magnetization of portions of the flat surface.

MAGNETIC CORE: a configuration of magnetic material that is placed in a spatial relationship to current-carrying conductors and whose magnetic properties are essential to its use.

MAGNETIC DISK: a flat circular plate with a magnetic surface on which data can be stored by selective magnetization of portions of the flat surface.

MAGNETIC DRUM: a storage device in which information is recorded on the magnetic surface.

MAGNETIC INK: an ink containing particles of a magnetic substance whose presence can be detected by magnetic sensors.

MAGNETIC STORAGE: a storage device that utilizes the magnetic properties of materials to store data.

MAGNETIC TAPE: tape coated with magnetic ferric oxide on which can be recorded signals to be played back as sound, computer inputs, or television signals.

MAGNETIC-TAPE MEMORY: a sequential-access memory in which bits are stored on a magnetic tape.

MAILABLE: acceptable for mailing, as within weight and size limits, and otherwise complying with the post office's regulations.

MAILGRAM: a low-cost message transmitted electronically by Western Union and delivered by the US Postal Service.

MAILING: a group of identical pieces placed in the mail at one time.

MAIL ORDER: a form of distribution in which goods are ordered, shipped, and paid for by mail usually as a result of advertising.

MAIL-ORDER ADVERTISING: advertising designed to yield orders directly from prospects by mail.

MAIL-ORDER WHOLESALER: an individual who sells by mail and usually advertises goods and services in a book, known as a catalog.

MAIN FRAME: the major part of the computer, the arithmetic or logic unit; same as central-processing unit.

MAIN STORAGE: the general-purpose storage of a computer.

MAINTENANCE OF MEMBERSHIP: a clause in a labor contract requiring all union members to remain in the union for the term of the current contract, usually under penalty of losing their jobs.

MAINTAINED MARK-ON: the

difference between the cost for delivering goods and the price at which they are sold.

MAJORITY STOCKHOLDERS: those who own more than 50 percent of the voting stock corporation, thus having controlling interest.

MAJOR-MEDICAL INSURANCE: insurance designed to cover medical expenditures above a deductible amount but not in excess of the face value of the policy.

MAKE-GOOD: free republication of an advertisement to make good for an error or other cause of dissatisfaction with its original appearance.

MAKE-OR-BUY DECISION: the decision of whether to produce an item in a given firm or to purchase it elsewhere.

MAKER: any individual, or legal entity who signs a check, or other type of negotiable instrument as a primary responsible party.

MAKE THE CASH: to decide whether the funds on hand, following receipts and payments, balance with the record of sales and payments of obligations.

MAKEUP: newspaper page layout; complete layout of a printed piece with advertising.

MAKEUP TIME: the part of available time used for reruns due to malfundtions or mistakes during a previous operating time.

MAKE-WHOLE: an order made to an employer to pay a worker all wages lost dating from the date of firing, minus what he or she may have earned elsewhere meanwhile.

MAKE-WORK PRACTICES: labor policies that compel, through hiring or extra help, the spreading of available work.

MALA FIDE: in bad faith (Latin).

MALE DIE: that part of a two-part die with raised or protruding features.

MALFEASANCE: criminally dishonest acts in office by a business executive or officeholder.

MALFUNCTION: usually refers to the failure of equipment to operate as designed; the effect of a fault.

MALICIOUS MISCHIEF: vandalism; wanton destruction or ruin of the chattels or property of another.

MALICIOUS PROSECUTION: the tort of bringing a lawsuit in bad faith without reasonable grounds to believe the action will be successful.

MALINGERER: one who feigns illness to avoid work or duty.

MALLEABLE IRON: iron of a particular quality capable of being extended by rolling.

MALONEY ACT: the 1938 amendment to the Securities Exchange Act that requires all brokers dealing in the over-the-counter market to register with the SEC except those dealing exclusively intrastate or in exempt securities.

MALPRACTICE INSURANCE: insurance protecting professional people from claims resulting from negligent performance of professional services.

MALTHUSIAN LAW OF POPULATION: as stated by Malthus, population tends to increase faster than the food supply.

MAMMOTH: a large size of individual units of food packaged in container.

MANAGE: to organize and direct the efforts of others under a coordinated plan for accomplishment of objectives.

MANAGEMENT: the administration and policy makers of a business or other organization.

MANAGEMENT ACCOUNTING: a resource of management that supplies financial information at all levels to be used in the planning and administering of the business.

MANAGEMENT AUDIT: a system for examining, analyzing, and appraising a management's overall performance.

MANAGEMENT BY CRISIS: a leadership style that purports to clear away shortcomings and failures by waiting until things get so bad that people will accept drastic measures.

MANAGEMENT BY EXCEPTION: the practice, by an executive, of focusing attention primarily on significant deviations from expected results.

MANAGEMENT BY OBJECTIVES: a process specifying that superiors and those who report to them will jointly establish objectives over a specified time frame.

MANAGEMENT COMPANY: a firm that manages and sells the shares of open-end investment companies and claims a fee or commission.

MANAGEMENT CONSULTING: analysis of management problems and recommendation of practical solutions by hired consultants.

MANAGEMENT DEVELOPMENT: leadership training for middle- or top-level personnel to upgrade their skills.

MANAGEMENT FEE: the annual charge of an investment company fund's manager, usually based on the value of the assets and for the income handled.

MANAGEMENT GAME: a dynamic training approach utilizing a model of the business world.

MANAGEMENT INFORMATION SYSTEM: a specific data-processing system that is designed to furnish management and supervisory personnel with current information.

MANAGEMENT PREROGATIVES: the rights believed by management to be exclusively theirs and not subject to collective bargaining.

MANAGEMENT RATIO: the ratio of the number of management personnel to 1,000 employees.

MANAGEMENT SCIENCE: the broad field employing information systems, operations research, and decision theory.

MANAGER: an individual responsible for the control or direction of people, a department, or an organization.

MANAGERIAL GRID: a means of measuring a manager's leadership style in terms of concern for production and concern for task.

MANDAMUS: a legal writ ordering the enforcement of a public law or duty.

MANDATE: a court order to an authorized agency or officer to enforce a decree, judgment, or sentence to the court's satisfaction.

MAN-HOUR: the labor of one person for one hour.

MANIFEST: a document listing the contents, value, origin, destination, carrier, and time a cargo is shipped.

MANIPULATION: the illegal practice of buying or selling stock to create the impression of an active market, to affect the price to induce others to buy or sell.

MANIT: an abbreviation for "man-minutes" used in connection with an incentive-wage plan in which the worker is paid a premium for man-minutes of work achieved over the standard output per worker.

MAN-MACHINE MANIPULATION: simulation with models of systems in which human beings participate.

MANNERISMS: peculiarities of speaking or behaving exhibited by an individual when interacting with others.

MANNING TABLE: the number of employees or a listing of positions to be used in a machine's operation, a described task, or a unit within a firm.

MANPOWER: all employees in an organization, from chief executive officer down.

MANUAL: a booklet of instructions on the assembly and takedown of equipment or its operation, or both; hand operated.

MANUAL ENTRY: a hand insertion of data for some units of a computer.

MANUAL OPERATION: processing of data in a system by direct hand techniques.

MANUAL RATING: the determination of an insurance premium rate from a general manual, without reference to the particular conditions of an individual case.

MANUAL SKILL: the ability to use one's hands efficiently in the operation of tools and machinery.

MANUFACTURE: to produce, make, or fabricate something, by hand or using equipment.

MANUFACTURER'S AGENT: an independent, commissioned to sell the entire output of a manufacturer in a specified territory, usually not barred from handling noncompeting lines.

MANUFACTURER's BRAND: a brand sponsored by one or more manufacturers without limitation as to area.

MANUFACTURER'S REPRESENTATIVE: same as manufacturer's agent.

MANUFACTURING: converting raw materials into a completed product by a mechanical, electrical, or chemical process.

MANUFACTURING EXPENSE: the cost of converting raw materials into finished goods exclusive of the cost of raw materials and direct labor; manufacturing overhead.

MANUFACTURING INVENTORY: a general term covering all items of inventory for a manufacturing entity.

MANUFACTURING ORDER: instructions for directing production.

MANUFACTURING OVERHEAD: all the costs of the manufacturing department except raw materials, purchased parts, and direct labor.

MARGIN: that portion of the cost of a security put up by the purchaser who, immediately upon purchase, hypothecates the security with the broker as collateral for the balance.

MARGINAL: an existing situation characterized by the occurrence of the smallest possible increment or decrement in certain variables.

MARGINAL ANALYSIS: analysis of economic information by examining the results of the value added when one variable is increased by a single unit of another variable.

MARGINAL BORROWER: a borrower who will reject an opportunity to borrow if the interest charge is increased.

MARGINAL BUYER: a buyer who will refuse to buy at any given price if the price is increased.

MARGINAL COST: the amount of money one extra unit of production will add to the total cost of production.

MARGINAL FARMERS: farmers who work land that produces only enough to cover the cost of production at given prices.

MARGINAL LABORER: the laborer who produces goods whose value just equals the amount of his wages.

MARGINAL LAND: land that will merely repay the cost of products grown on it and will not yield increased revenue.

MARGINAL LENDER: a lender or investor who will refuse to lend or invest if the rate of interest is lowered.

MARGINAL PRODUCER: a producer who is just able to meet his costs of production with little actual profit.

MARGINAL PRODUCT: the additional product derived by increasing by one further unit a given factor of production.

MARGINAL PROPENSITY TO CONSUME: measure reflected by the percentage of increases in income that is spent for consumption purposes.

MARGINAL PROPENSITY TO INVEST: measure reflected by the percentage of increases in sales that is spent on investment items.

MARGINAL PROPENSITY TO SAVE: measure reflected by the percentage of increases in income that individuals save.

MARGINAL REVENUE: the added revenue a business receives from the sale of one additional unit.

MARGINAL-REVENUE PRODUCT: the added revenue a business receives by the addition of one more unit of a production factor.

MARGINAL SELLER: a seller who refuses to sell if the price is lowered.

MARGINAL TRADING: the purchase of a security or commodity by one who borrows funds for part of the purchase price rather than paying for the entire transaction with his own money.

MARGINAL UTILITY: the increase in satisfaction one receives from adding or consuming one more unit of an item; the value of a commodity.

MARGIN BUYING: the purchasing of securities with the aid of credit extended by the purchaser's broker.

MARGIN CALL: the demand made on a purchaser by his broker for additional sums that may become necessary in order to maintain the required deposit level.

MARGIN OF PROFIT: net profit from operations divided by net sales; the amount of profit remaining after costs have been deducted from income.

MARGIN OF SAFETY: in investment banking, the difference between the total face value of a bond issue and the actual value of property put up as security for the issue.

MARGIN REQUIREMENT: the portion of a total purchase price of securities that must be put up in cash.

MARITIME LAW: the law of the sea.

MARK: a presence of a signal; an impulse that causes a loop to be closed in a neutral circuit; synonymous with flag.

MARKDOWN: a reduction of an originally established selling price; a revaluation of stocks based on a decline in their market quotations.

MARKDOWN CANCELLATION: the increase in the retail price of an item that has been reduced.

MARKET: people possessing the ability and desire to purchase a product or service; a geographical area where they're located.

MARKET ANALYSIS: an aspect of market research involving the measurement of the extent of a market and the determination of its characteristics.

MARKET AREA: that territory within which the purchase or sale of a commodity affects the price generally prevailing for that commodity.

MARKET AUDIT: a method for studying the marketing activities and structure of a business.

105

*MARKET
CHANNEL •
MARKETING
MANAGE-
MENT*

MARKET CHANNEL: a path made in the transfer, direct or indirect, of ownership of a product, as it goes from a manufacturer to industrial or retail customers.

MARKET DEMAND: the total amount of an item that is wanted at a specified price at a specific time.

MARKET EQUILIBRIUM: the balance that occurs when buyers and sellers decide to stop trading at the prevailing prices.

MARKET OFF: an expression indicating that prices on the various stock exchanges were down for the day.

MARKET ORDER: an order to a broker to buy or sell immediately at the best available price.

MARKET-OUT CLAUSE: a clause in some underwriting agreements permitting the underwriter to withdraw if the market becomes unfavorable.

MARKET OUTLINE: a summary of the relative place of a type of brand or item in the total market.

MARKET PENETRATION: extent to which a given establishment, firm, or plant shares or dominates the sales in a given market area.

MARKETPLACE: a general term identifying business and trade activities.

MARKET POTENTIAL: maximum sales potential for all sellers of a product or service over a fixed period.

MARKET PRICE: the price that prevails in a market at a given period of time.

MARKET PROFILE: data about potential customers, who make up the market for a particular item or service.

MARKET RATIO: the power of one good to command another in exchange for itself in a free market.

MARKET REPRESENTATIVE: the executive of a firm's buying office who gives his time and effort to a particular grouping of goods.

MARKET RISK: in finance, the combined effect of financial risk, interest-rate risk, and purchasing-power risk.

MARKET SEALING: the situation in which goods sold in a low-price market cannot be resold in a higher-priced market.

MARKET SEGMENTATION: separating the market into categories for the purpose of impossing different terms (such as prices) on each part of the market.

MARKET SHARE: the percentage of a market controlled by a certain company or product.

MARKET STRATEGY: a marketing approach designed to enable a product to fulfill the objectives set for it by management.

MARKET TARGETS: groups of consumers toward whom the firm decides to direct its marketing effort.

MARKET VALUE: the prevailing price.

MARKETABLE SECURITY: a security that can be easily sold.

MARKETABLE TITLE: title to property that is free of defects.

MARKETING: the sum total of all operations necessary to move a product from the production line into the hands of the consumer.

MARKETING AGREEMENT: a price-fixing or similar arrangement between producers of like products, usually illegal.

MARKETING BOARDS: government organizations with the power to promote, control, and regulate the marketing of natural products, for example, milk or eggs.

MARKETING CONCEPT: a business philosophy composed of the notions that marketing strategy should be developed based on customer needs and desires.

MARKETING COOPERATIVE: an association of producers to market their products jointly, e.g., California Fruit Growers Exchange.

MARKETING-COST ANALYSIS: the examination of the costs incurred from the time items are produced to final delivery and payment.

MARKETING MANAGEMENT: the planning, directing, and controlling of the total market operation.

MARKETING MIX: a term used to describe the four elements of a marketing strategy, distribution strategy, promotional strategy, and pricing strategy.

MARKETING RESEARCH: systematic gathering, recording, and analyzing of data about problems relating to the marketing of goods and services.

MARKING: placing the correct tag on new goods.

MARK-ON: the percentage of cost added to cost to equal the selling price.

MARK SENSING: a technique for reading marks made on a card by special pencil and automatically punching the information into the card.

MARKUP: the percentage of selling price added to cost to equal selling price.

MARRIAGE SETTLEMENT: settling before marriage certain property rights on one or both members of the matrimonial contract.

MASK: a pattern of characters used to control the retention or elimination of portions of another pattern of characters; synonymous with filter.

MASS APPRAISING: appraising of numerous parcels or properties at the same time.

MASS COMMUNICATION: the delivery of quantities of identical messages at the same time by communication firms or media.

MASS MARKETING: the approach used to sell large volumes of items to everyone.

MASS PICKETING: picketing by large numbers for dramatic effect or forcibly to prevent entry of nonstrikers or customers.

MASS PRODUCTION: production of goods in quantity, using machinery, interchangeable parts, and either complete automation or short, repetitive work sequences at each station.

MASTER: one who has achieved the highest level of skill in a trade or craft and employs others as journeymen or apprentices.

MASTER AGREEMENT: a contract covering a number of companies and one or more unions, or an agreement covering several plants of a single employer.

MASTER BUDGET: comprised of all the departmental budgets.

MASTER CARD: a card that contains fixed or indicative information for a group of punched cards.

MASTER LEASE: an original lease.

MASTER POLICY: a policy issued to an insured to cover property at more than one location.

MASTER SCHEDULE: a schedule in production control that applies only to a completed product and its major elements.

MASTER TARIFF: a tariff controlling the use of other tariffs.

MASTHEAD: the name of a publication in the form in which it is displayed at the top of its front page.

MATERIAL: physical equipment and supplies of a business, as distinguished from personnel.

MATERIAL COST: that cost of a product which is due only to the cost of raw material and not such indirect expenses as wages, rent, interest, and management costs.

MATERIAL MANAGEMENT: the material-handling functions as they relate to the physical distribution chain.

MATRIX: any mold used in casting; in mining, the worthless ore body containing the valuable minerals.

MATRIX ORGANIZATION: system in which organizational members have a dual allegiance: to a particular assignment or task and also to their department.

MATS: short term for "matrices," which includes all printing devices serving as dies from which the printing plate is made.

MATTE: a quality of photostats that denotes a dull finish; in smelting, partially concentrated sulfide ores.

MATURE ECONOMY: a nation's economy with a declining rate of population growth and a decrease in the proportion of national income utilized for new capital investment.

MATURITY: the due date of a security or debt.

MATURITY DATE: the date on which a financial obligation becomes due for payment and/or an obligation or contract expires.

MATURITY STATE: the beginning of the demise of a product.

MATURITY VALUE: the money that is to be paid when a financial obligation or other contract becomes due.

MAXIM: a proposition of law needing no proof or argument because of its general acceptance.

MAXIMUM: highest, most; peak, zenith, highest possible, highest to date, as maximum effort, production, sales, or profits.

MCGUIRE ACT: a 1952 amendment of the Miller-Tydings Act extending the legality of resale-price-maintenance agreements.

MEAN: average.

MEAN DEVIATION: same as average deviation.

MEANS TEST: an inquiry into a person's ability to support himself or herself as a criterion for receiving public assistance, unemployment relief, and so on.

MEASURED DAY RATE: a wage system under which the employee's rate of pay is periodically adjusted according to his efficiency in working.

MEASUREMENT GOODS: in transportation, goods whose freight charge is determined by cubic feet rather than weight.

MEASURE OF VALUE: a function of money that gives the standard for identifying the results of production, using the monetary unit as the common denominator.

MECHANICAL-APTITUDE TEST: a test designed to predict how well a person can learn to perform tasks involving the understanding and manipulation of mechanical devices.

MECHANIZATION: the use of machines to replace human effort.

MEDIA: plural of medium; means for

advertising, such as publications, broadcasting stations, and outdoor posters.

MEDIAN: midpoint between maximum and minimum; in a statistical group the value of the middle quantity.

MEDIA ANALYSIS: the study and evaluation of various media approaches for promoting items and services aimed at reaching a wide or specific audience.

MEDIATION: in labor language, a synonym for conciliation.

MEDIATOR: a person, acting as a third party, who attempts to resolve a labor dispute.

MEDIUM: any means for transmitting a message to an intended recipient in a communication network.

MEDIUM OF EXCHANGE: any commodity (commonly, money) which is widely accepted in payment for goods and services and in settlement of debts.

MEETING: conference of two or more people in the daily course of business; a formal scheduled conference as of a business committee.

MEGABIT: a unit of information equal to one million bits or binary digits.

MEGABUCK: a million dollars.

MEGALOPOLIS: an urban continuum of two or more large cities undivided by rural lands.

MELON: unusually large profits that have not been dispersed to eligible persons.

MEMBER BANK: a state or national bank that belongs to the Federal Reserve System.

MEMBER CORPORATION: a securities-brokerage firm, organized as a corporation, whose director is a member of a stock exchange and a holder of voting stock in the corporation.

MEMBER FIRM: a securities-brokerage firm organized as a partnership and having at least one general partner who is a member of a stock exchange.

MEMO POSTING: a systems technique in which item records are posted to a temporary file before permanent master files are updated.

MEMORAN: in computer language, a synonym for storage.

MEMORANDA: notes to aid memory.

MEMORANDUM CHECK: a check drawn by a borrower in favor of his creditor to be used to reduce a loan if a run is not paid at the due time.

MEMORY: a device into which a unit of information can be copied, held, and retrieved at another time.

MEMORY DUMP: a listing of the contents of a storage device, or selected parts of it.

MEMORY UNIT: a component within automated equipment that registers what the equipment should be accomplishing at each step of the operation.

MENIAL: lowly, as the sanitation chores of business.

MENS REA: a knowledge of the wrongfulness of an act (Latin).

MERCANTILE: engaged in trade or commerce.

MERCANTILE AGENCY: an organization that supplies to its subscribers credit data on individuals and firms.

MERCANTILISM: the system of business from about 1550 to 1850 in England in which great emphasis was put on retention of a favorable balance of trade.

MERCHANDISE: purchased articles of business held for sale; to plan or promote the sale of goods.

MERCHANDISE CONTROL: the collection and analysis of data on purchases and sales items, either by unit or dollars.

MERCHANDISE INVENTORY: products held by an entity for resale to customers.

MERCHANDISE MANAGER: an executive responsible for supervising the purchasing, selling, and inventory control activities in a store.

MERCHANDISE MART: a building, usually large, containing showrooms of manufacturers where retailers can examine goods and place orders.

MERCHANDISE TRANSFER: the transfer of goods from one accounting unit of a store to another.

MERCHANDISING: all activities affiliated with the buying and selling of a product.

MERCHANT: an individual who takes title to goods by buying them, for the purpose of resale.

MERCHANT MARINE: a nation's facilities and equipment for carrying on trade and international commerce on the ocean.

MERCHANT WHOLESALER: a middleman who receives title to merchandise purchases for resale to firms that plan to resell the goods.

MERCURIAL: capable of swift rise and fall; volatile, as rapidly fluctuating price quotations or the unbridled temper of a poor executive.

MERGE: to combine two or more into one.

MERGER: a combination of two businesses, usually through purchase of one by the other.

MERIT: to deserve, as a raise in salary or a more important position; worthiness attained through achievement.

MERIT INCREASE: an individual wage increase in recognition of superior performance or service.

MERIT RATING: a system of evaluation in which the past experience of the individual risk is a factor in determining the rate.

MESNE PROFITS: the profits taken by the wrongful possession of land.

MESSAGE: any communication between persons.

METERED MAIL: any class of matter on which the required postage is printed by a meter approved for the purpose by the US Postal Service.

METES AND BOUNDS: a system of describing land in conveyances employing measurements (metes) and boundaries (bounds) which is used in states not employing US surveys.

MICROECONOMICS: the approach

to the study of economics which concentrates attention on individuals or single products or goods.

MICROFILM: 8-millimeter film used for photographic recording and storage of large volumes of documentary material in compact space.

MICROMOTION STUDY: time or motion study.

MICRON: unit of length, one-thousandth of a millimeter or one-millionth of a meter.

MICROPROCESSOR: a tiny electronic circuit chip that contains so-called logic elements needed for computation.

MICROSECOND: one-millionth of a second.

MICROWAVE TOWER: a tower for picking up and relaying the microwaves carrying television signals.

MIDDLEMAN: a person who serves as a link between the producer of goods and the eventual user of the goods.

MIDDLE MANAGEMENT: management personnel who report directly to top management; a level of management responsible for carrying out the directives of top management.

MIDNIGHT SHIFT: the work shift commencing at midnight and usually terminated at 8 AM.

MIGRANT: a worker in or from a foreign country or other agricultural worker who follows the ripening crops.

MIGRATORY WORKER: a worker moving from one region to another to find work, according to the harvest schedule of the different crops.

MILITARY-INDUSTRIAL COMPLEX: the community of interests created between armed services officials and manufacturers of weapons and defense material.

MILKING: management's attempt to squeeze the last remaining profits from the firm.

MILL: a factory or plant; to process on milling machines.

MILLAGE: the factor usually

employed as the rate of taxation in computing taxes.

MILLER-TYDINGS ACT: a 1937 amendment to the Sherman Antitrust Act, which allows resale-price-maintenance agreements.

MIMEOGRAPHING: the reproduction of multiple copies of work typewritten or drawn on a stencil.

MINERAL RIGHTS: the right or title to all or to certain specified minerals in a given tract of land.

MINIMUM SUBSCRIPTION: the figure given in a firm's prospectus identifying the minimum that must be raised for the organization to become operational.

MINIMUM WAGE: the lowest amount of money that may be paid to workers, as prescribed by law.

MINING: extraction of metallic ores and fuels from the ground.

MINISTERIAL DUTY: a duty requiring little judgment or discretion.

MINOR: a person less than 21 years of age; an infant.

MINORITY INTEREST: common shareholders who neither control a corporation nor form part of a group that controls the corporation.

MINORITY INVESTMENT: retaining less than 50 percent of a corporation's voting stock.

MINT: a government factory for the manufacture of coins.

MINTAGE: the charge made by a government for converting bullion into coins.

MINT RATIO: the fixed ratio between the price of gold and silver set by the US Mint under a system of bimetallism.

MINUTE BOOK: a book containing the formal minutes of meetings.

MINUTES: a record of the proceedings of a meeting.

MIRROR PRINCIPLE: a human relations approach suggesting that people will respond in the same fashion as they are treated.

MISDEMEANOR: a criminal offense, less than a felony, not punishable by imprisonment or death.

MISFEASANCE: wrongful or injurious but not necessarily illegal acts of a business executive or officeholder.

MISJOINDER: in law, the improper union of causes of action or of parties in a lawsuit.

MISMANAGEMENT: poor management resulting from lack of knowledge, bad judgment, or serving other interests.

MISREPRESENTATION: the giving of a positive statement or the claim to an alleged fact that is not true, thus leading to a false conclusion.

MISSENT ITEM: an item that has been sent in error to another bank.

MISSIONARY SALES: the activity of personnel from a manufacturer who work closely with various firms and middlemen to increase the product sales.

MISSION BUDGETING: budgeting by social function.

MISTRIAL: a legal trial judged to be of no effect because of an error in the proceedings.

MIXED ECONOMY: an economy having some of the characteristics of free enterprise and some of socialism.

MIXED ESTATE: ground rent for 99 years which is forever renewable.

MIXED PROPERTY: property having characteristics of both personal and real property.

MNEMONIC: tending to assist human memory.

MOCKUP: a full-size, nonoperative dummy or structural model, as of an airplane.

MOD: modifications made in computer programs after they have been written.

MODE: the most frequently occurring item in a statistical group; fashion.

MODEL: a theory used to analyze various forms of behavior.

MODEL STOCK: having the right goods at the right time in the right quantities at the right price.

MODERATOR: chairman of a town meeting, hearing, debate, or seminar.

MODIFICATION: a moderating alteration, limitation, or qualification, as of a proposal or contract.

MODIFIED UNION SHOP: a labor clause requiring new employees to join the union, although existing employees may or may not be members.

MODULE: a particular segment of information or a particular piece of equipment.

MODUS OPERANDI: manner or method of operation (Latin).

MOMENTUM: the tendency of a trend to continue.

MONETARY: pertaining to currency or coinage.

MONETARY LIABILITY: the promise to pay a claim against a specified quantity of money, the amount of which is unaffected by inflation or deflation.

MONETARY POLICY: the policy followed by a government for controlling credit and money supply in the economy.

MONETARY RESERVES: the amount of gold and silver held by the Treasury or monetary authorities to secure the issue of credit money in circulation.

MONETARY STANDARD: the basis upon which a money is issued, that is, the principle that determines the quantity of money.

MONEY: any denomination of coin or paper currency of legal tender that passes freely as a medium of exchange.

MONEY BROKER: one who deals in foreign exchange but often on his own account (and then he is a dealer).

MONEY ILLUSION: condition under which an increase in all prices and incomes by the same proportion produces an increase in consumption, although real incomes remain the same.

MONEY INCOME: income measured in money units.

MONEY MARKET: market for

short-term, high grade, open-market assets.

MONEY ORDER: money instruments purchased at a post office or bank.

MONEY PRICE: the number of money units that must be sacrificed to purchase a particular commodity.

MONEY-PURCHASE PENSION PLAN: a pension plan under which the benefits are determined by the employee's amount of accumulated contributions.

MONEY RATES: interest rates that lenders charge their borrowers.

MONEY SUPPLY: a general term for the total sum of currency circulating in a country.

MONEY WAGES: a term applied to the number of dollars received by employees, as contrasted with what those dollars will purchase.

MONGER: any trader or seller, often used in a derogatory fashion.

MONITOR: any observer, human or machine, installed to record either continuous or sample data about a system.

MONOLITHIC: constituting a single massive unit, as a giant corporation under strong central control, or even completely dominated by one individual.

MONOMER: a chemical compound of simple atomic structure capable of having its atoms linked by polymerization to make other compounds, such as lucite.

MONOPLANE: an airplane with its main wingspread on a single level.

MONOPOLISTIC COMPETITION: an industry where few firms produce and sell products that are different from those of competitors.

MONOPOLY: an industry in which there is only one producer and many customers.

MONOPOLY PRICE: a price set on a good or service within an industry as the result of restricting the supply.

MONOPSONY: a market situation in which there is only one buyer for an item.

MONORAIL: a single rail, sometimes overhead, that serves as the tract for a wheeled vehicle.

MONOTONE: results in the worker showing low interest and boredom.

MONOTYPE: a typecasting machine activated by punched tape which casts single characters; such type characters.

MONTAGE: an assemblage of illustrations into a composite unit, frequently for advertising.

MONUMENT: in real estate, a stone, stake and stones, or other permanent feature of terrain which can be cited as the corner of a piece of property.

MOONLIGHTING: holding a second job or working at a second income-producing occupation.

MOOT CASE: a question whose decision would be premature or useless because it has already been agreed upon or otherwise resolved.

MOOT POINT: a debatable point.

MORALE: an employee's moral or mental condition with respect to job satisfaction.

MORALE STUDY: a technique to measure the level of morale among a group of employees.

MORAL HAZARD: the possibility of loss being caused or aggravated by dishonesty or carelessness of the insured, his or her agents, or employees.

MORAL SUASION: Federal Reserve System pressure exerted on United States banking, unaccompanied by any effort to compel compliance with the suggested action.

MORATORIUM: a period of suspension of legal rights.

MORNING LOAN: an unsecured loan of an unspecified amount to a stockbroker to carry on his business during the day.

MORTALITY TABLE: an actuarial table based on a sample group of the population, giving the percentage of people who live to any given age.

MORTGAGE: a conveyance of property as security for the payment of a debt.

MORTGAGE BANKER: a banker who specializes in mortgage financing.

MORTGAGE BOND: a bond secured by a mortgage.

MORTGAGE BROKER: a person who, for a fee, brings together borrowers and lenders and handles the necessary documentation.

MORTGAGE DEBT: an indebtedness created by a mortgage and secured by the property mortgaged.

MORTGAGEE: the creditor or lender to whom a mortgage is made.

MORTGAGE-INSURANCE POLICY: issued by a title-insurance firm to a mortgage holder, resulting in a title policy.

MORTGAGE LIEN: in a mortgage given as security for a debt, serving as a lien on the property after the mortgage is recorded.

MORTGAGE PREMIUM: an additional mortgage fee when there is a shortage of mortgage money and the legal interest rate is less than the prevailing mortgage-market rate.

MORTGAGOR: the person who borrows money and gives a mortgage.

MOST-FAVORED-NATION CLAUSE: a contract provision which guarantees each party to the contract equal treatment.

MOTHER HUBBARD CLAUSE: a mortgage provision permitting the lender, upon default of the conditions of the mortgage, to foreclose on the overdue mortgage.

MOTION STUDY: the observation and analysis of a person's motions during a repetitive task, with recommendations for accomplishing the same task with fewer or shorter motions.

MOTIVATION: a stimulus that energizes differentially certain responses within a person.

MOTIVATION, UNCONSCIOUS: a motivation inferred from a person's pattern of behavior, of which the individual is not aware.

MOTIVATIONAL NEEDS: psychological forces that affect thinking and behavior.

MOVEMENT: an increase or decrease in the price of a specific stock.

MOVING AVERAGE: a statistical term used to indicate an average calculation made for a series of figures.

MUCKRAKER: an individual who seeks to uncover business corruption or other activities that are unethical or harmful to the well-being of society.

MULTICOMPANY: diverse organizations or a variety of firms under a single management.

MULTIEMPLOYER BARGAINING: the result of a collective-bargaining agreement covering more than one company in a given industry.

MULTIEMPLOYER PENSION PLANS: transferable plans for workers in which more than one employer pools pension contributions in a single fund.

MULTIPLE SALES: the result of selection by customers of multiple rather than single items to purchase.

MULTI-INDUSTRY: the management of firms involved in different activities.

MULTILATERAL: many-sided, as a business agreement among more than two participants.

MULTINATIONAL: term used in reference to a corporation that normally has investments and business activities in a number of countries.

MULTIPACK: a container holding two or more separately packaged items.

MULTIPLE: a synonym for price-earnings ratio.

MULTIPLE ACCESS: describing a system where output or input can be received or released from more than one location.

MULTIPLE BANKING: the offering of all types of banking services to a bank's customers.

MULTIPLE BRANDS: several brand names used by a manufacturer on essentially the same product to open up new market segments.

MULTIPLE LISTING: in real estate language, a listing submitted to all members of a real estate association so that each has an opportunity to sell the property.

MULTIPLE MANAGEMENT: a description of worker participation in a firm's management by assisting in the development and execution of policy.

MULTIPLE PACKAGING: including more than one item in a single container.

MULTIPLE PRICING: a price system in which the same basic product is sold in many different models, each at a different price, in order to take advantage of those customers who buy for prestige reasons.

MULTIPLIER PRINCIPLE: the ratio between the change in income (+) and the change in investment (×).

MULTIPLEX: to carry out two or more functions in a computer essentially simultaneously.

MULTIPROCESSING: term describing a computer system containing two or more central processors.

MULTIPROGRAMMING: term describing a computing system with two or more programs.

MUNICIPAL BOND: the bond of a state or of a municipal corporation.

MUNICIPAL CORPORATION: a political subdivision of the state, which exercises a portion of power under legislative grant from the state.

MUNICIPAL LIEN: a government lien against a property owner to solicit monies for the purpose of making improvements to that and neighboring properties.

MUNICIPALS: a popular word for the securities of a governmental unit.

MUNIFICENT: of compensation, liberal or lavish.

MUNIFUNDS: synonymous with mutual funds.

MUNIMENT OF TITLE: deeds and contracts that prove ownership or title to property.

MURPHY'S LAW: if something can go wrong, eventually it will.

MUTUAL ASSENT: agreement by all parties to a contract to the same thing.

MUTUAL COMPANY: a corporation without capital stock; the profits are distributed among the owner-customers in proportion to the business activity carried out with the corporation.

MUTUAL FUND: a company organized to invest in the securities of other companies.

MUTUAL INSURANCE COMPANIES: companies with no capital stock, owned by policy holders.

MUTUAL SAVINGS BANK: a bank that is owned by the depositors and managed for them by a self-perpetuating board of trustees; it has no capital stock.

MUTUAL WILLS: a common arrangement executed pursuant to an agreement in which the husband and wife leave everything to each other.

N

NADERISM: synonym for consumerism.

NADIR: low point; minimum.

NAMED INSURED: any person or firm or corporation, or any of its members, specifically designated by name as insureds in a policy.

NAMED-PERIL INSURANCE: coverage that specifies the perils that are insured against.

NAME SLUG: an advertiser's signature or logotype.

NANOSECOND: one-billionth of a second.

NARROW GAUGE: the distance between railroad tracks, 2 feet 10 inches, or any other dimension less than standard gauge.

NARROW MARKET: a condition that exists when the demand for a security is so limited that small alterations in supply or demand will create major fluctuations in the market price.

NATIONAL ADVERTISING: the advertising of a manufacturer or wholesaler, as contrasted with that of a retailer or local advertiser.

NATIONAL BANK: a bank whose charter is granted by the federal government, and which is a member of the Federal Reserve System and of the Federal Deposit Insurance Corporation.

NATIONAL BRAND: loosely used to designate a manufacturer's brand that has wide circulation.

NATIONAL DEBT: the total amount owed by a federal government.

NATIONAL INCOME: the aggregate earnings of all factors in current production.

NATIONALIZATION: the acquisition and operation by the government of a previously privately owned and operated business.

NATIONALIZED INDUSTRY: an industry that has been brought under direct government control and ownership.

NATIONAL WEALTH: the combined monetary value of all the material economic products owned by all the people.

NATURAL BUSINESS YEAR: a 12-month period usually selected to end when inventory or business activity is at a low point.

NATURAL CAPITAL: land that is used as a factor of production.

NATURAL DISASTER: a synonym for an act of God.

NATURAL FINANCING: a real estate transaction requiring no outside financing; the selling of properties that do not call for a third party.

NATURAL GAS: underground gas occurring in salt domes as distinguished from gas manufactured above ground, as from coal.

NATURALIZATION: the granting of citizenship to an alien.

NATURAL MONOPOLY: a monopoly due to natural conditions.

NATURAL ORDER: a philosophy under which each individual would do what would provide the greatest return with the least effort.

NATURAL RESOURCES: all materials furnished by nature.

NAVAL STORES: resins, gums, and turpentine, produced from pine trees.

NAVICERT: a wartime document issued by a belligerent nation.

NAVIGABLE: of waterways, having sufficient depth to provide adequate draft for vessels.

NEAR MONEY: highly liquid assets, such as government securities, excluding official currency.

NEEDLE TRADES: apparel-producing industries.

NEGATIVE FILE: an authorized system file containing a simple list of accounts for which credit, check cashing, and other privileges should be denied.

NEGATIVE GOODWILL: the excess of the book value of a business over the amount paid for it.

NEGATIVE INCOME TAX: proposed by some to provide financial aid to individuals with incomes below a certain minimum.

NEGLIGENCE: failure to exercise due and reasonable care, thus a contributory or total cause of an accident.

NEGOTIABLE: capable of transfer of ownership without signature, as a negotiable bond, bearer check, etc.

NEGOTIATED PRICE: the result obtained by a purchaser who persuades a seller to accept a lower price.

NEGOTIATIONS: dealings between two parties or their representatives for the purpose of coming to an agreement.

NEOCLASSICAL ECONOMICS: an economic approach developed between 1870 and 1918, utilizing mathematics in the analysis of data and models.

NEPOTISM: the practice of placing relatives in organizational positions without regard to the claims by others that better qualified people can be found.

NERVE CENTER: a command post of business, government, or military operations, where messages are received and commands sent out.

NESTED: packaged one within another.

NEST EGG: an accumulation of wealth to hatch into more wealth.

NET: that which remains after certain designated deductions have been made from the gross amount.

NET ASSETS: net worth.

NET AVAILS: the funds given to a borrower in the discounting of a note.

NET BOOK VALUE: the portion of the cost of an asset as carried in the records of an organization, reflecting the amount that has not yet been written off.

NET CASH FLOW: the net cash consumed or produced in a period by an activity or product during a unit of time, including all revenue and expenses except noncash items.

NET CHANGE: the change in the price of a security between the closing price on one day and the closing price on the following day on which the stock is traded.

NET COST: the actual cost of something, after all income or other financial gain is subtracted from the gross cost.

NET CURRENT ASSETS: a synonym for working capital.

NET DEBT: the total debt (gross debt) of an obligor less sinking fund accumulations or other provisions for debt retirement.

NET EARNINGS: the amount of the gross income less the operating expenses and any other expenses and before payment of any dividends.

NET ESTATE: the part of an estate remaining after all expenses to manage it have been taken out.

NET INCOME: net profit.

NET LEASE: a lease under which the tenant agrees to pay, in addition to the rent, expenses such as taxes, insurance, maintenance, etc., of the property leased.

NET LONG-TERM DEBT: total long-term debt, less cash and investment assets of sinking funds and other reserve funds specifically held for redemption of long-term debt.

NET LOSS: the excess of expenses and losses during a specified period over revenues and gains in the same time frame.

NET NATIONAL PRODUCT: gross national product minus capital consumption.

NET PRICE: the price paid after all deductions such as discounts, rebates, allowances, and kickbacks.

NET PROFIT: gross profit less operating expenses for a given period.

NET RATE: in insurance, either the premium paid less dividends received, or the premium paid less the expense loading.

NET REALIZABLE VALUE: selling price less costs of disposal.

NET SALES: sales minus discounts, allowances, and returns.

NETWORK: an interconnected group, such as radio or television stations that broadcast the same commercials simultaneously, for a unit fee.

NETWORK ANALOG: the expression and solution of mathematical relationships between variables, using a circuit or circuits to represent these quantities.

NETWORK-LOAD ANALYSIS: a listing of the flow of messages between stations to develop station characteristics by volumes of documents, frequency of processing, and special time requirements.

NET WORTH: excess of assets over liabilities; equity; capital.

NET YIELD: the income of a bond less annual amortization if bought at a premium, but plus annual accumulation if bought at a discount.

NEVER-OUTS: items that should never run out of stock during a season, because of continuous demand.

NEW DEAL: the popular designation for the political policies and administration of President Franklin D. Roosevelt.

NEW ISSUE: a stock or bond being sold by a corporation for the first time.

116

*NEWSPRINT •
NON
CUMULATIVE
QUANTITY
DISCOUNT*

NEWSPRINT: paper made from wood pulp, readily identifiable because it is chiefly used for newspapers.

NEXUS: a relationship used in tax laws to express a connection between a tax and the activities of the individual or group being taxed.

NIELSEN RATING: the percentages of households tuned to a stated radio or television program, as reported by the A. C. Nielsen Company.

NIGHT DIFFERENTIAL: extra, nonovertime pay for time worked between 6 PM and 6 AM.

NITRATE: a salt or ester of nitric acid used in fertilizer.

NIXIE MAIL: letters or packages not easily deliverable because of incorrect, illegible, or insufficient address.

NODE: a state or an event, as represented by means of a point on a diagram.

NO-FAULT INSURANCE: state laws requiring claims payments by the insurance company to the policyholder without regard to fault, and limiting the right of victims to sue.

NOISE: any disturbance tending to interfere with normal computer operation.

NO-LIMIT ORDER: a request to buy or sell a security without any stipulation about price.

NO-LOAD FUNDS: mutual funds that are not sold by a salesman.

NOLO CONTENDERE: a plea of no contest by a defendant in a criminal case, accepting conviction but not admitting guilt.

NOMENCLATURE: the names or system of names used for a class of objects as drugs, machines, parts, etc.

NOMINAL: in bookkeeping, a ledger account that is closed out when the books are balanced.

NOMINAL GROUP TECHNIQUE: a forecasting strategy by which seven to ten experts gather to exchange their ideas and projections.

NOMINAL OWNER: a person who holds title to an asset on behalf of someone else, the latter being the beneficial owner.

NOMINAL PARTNER: an individual who lends his or her name to a business organization but is not a true partner.

NOMINAL PRICE: price quotation on a commodity future for a period in which no actual trading took place.

NOMINAL YIELD: the rate of return specified in a security, calculated on the face or par value.

NOMINATION: the naming or proposing of candidates for office.

NONACCRUAL ASSET: an asset, such as a loan, which has been questioned on bank examination as a "slow" or "doubtful" (of payment) loan.

NONASSESSABLE STOCK: most securities or stock whose owners cannot be assessed in the event of failure or insolvency.

NONASSIGNABLE: a contract whose rights cannot be transferred to another person.

NONCOMMUNIST AFFIDAVIT: an affidavit by union officers declaring that they are not members of the Communist Party.

NONCONFORMING USE: any building or land lawfully occupied or used at the time of the passage of a zoning resolution.

NONCONTRIBUTORY: term describing a group-insurance plan under which the policyholder (employee) pays the entire cost.

NONCONTRIBUTORY-PENSION PLAN: a pension plan funded completely by employer contributions.

NONCOOPERATIVE EQUILIBRIUM: a condition that occurs when each participant in a market tries to improve only his own well-being.

NONCUMULATIVE: a preferred stock on which unpaid dividends do not accrue.

NONCUMULATIVE STOCK: a class of preferred stock in which the right to dividends lapses annually.

NONCUMULATIVE QUANTITY DISCOUNT: a price reduction based on the size of the individual order placed.

NONCURRENCY: the situation that exists when two or more policies provide differing coverages on the same risk.

NONCURRENT: that which is due more than one year after the date of issuance.

NONCURRENT LIABILITIES: claims against the assets of an entity that will become due a year or more in the future.

NONDEGRADABLE POLLUTANTS: impurities that do not disintegrate or dissolve naturally.

NONDURABLE GOODS: items that have a relatively brief lifetime.

NONEXCLUSIVE LISTING: a real estate listing under which the owner may sell the property without using an agent and not be liable to pay a commission.

NONFEASANCE: in law, the failure to perform a duty.

NONINSTALLMENT CREDIT: credit granted, with payment to be made in a lump sum, at a future date.

NONINTEREST-BEARING NOTE: a note whose maker does not have to pay any interest.

NONINVESTMENT PROPERTY: property that will not yield income.

NONMEMBER BANK: United States banks that are not members of the Federal Reserve System.

NONMERCHANTABLE TITLE: an unmarketable title that is legally unsound because it shows property defects.

NONNEGOTIABLE: incapable of transference to another, as a savings account passbook, registered bond, etc.

NONNEGOTIABLE TITLE: a title that cannot be transferred by delivery or by endorsement.

NONOPERATING EXPENSE: an expense of an enterprise not directly connected with the operation for which it was organized, as interest paid.

NONPERFORMANCE: the failure of a contracting party to provide goods or services according to an agreement.

NONPRICE COMPETITION: applied to markets in which a seller maneuvers for influence on the basis of special aspects of the items.

NONPROFIT ORGANIZATION: an organization formed for social, educational, religious, or similar purposes and not intended to be operated for profit.

NONPROGRAMMED DECISION: the finding of a solution to a problem by a creative approach rather than by using a standard routine or program.

NONRECOURSE LOAN: a US agricultural loan on the security of surplus crops for farmers who deliver to the government rather than to the market.

NONRECURRING CHARGE: any cost, expense, or involuntary loss that will not, it is felt, be likely to occur again.

NONRECURRING ITEM: a gain or loss not encountered in the usual transactions of the company, as from the sale of capital assets.

NONREFUND ANNUITY: an annuity that provides income to the recipient only, with no residual payments to a third party.

NONRENEWABLE NATURAL RESOURCES: natural resources that are used up in the process of production.

NON SEQUITUR: illogical inference (Latin).

NONSUIT: a court judgment against the plaintiff when he is unable to prove the case or fails to continue with the trial once it has commenced.

NONTAXABLE INCOME: incomes that are not liable to income tax.

NONZERO-SUM SITUATION: a competitive situation, in which each group benefits.

NO-PAR-VALUE STOCK: stock of a corporation without designated par value.

NO-PASSBOOK SAVINGS: the same as a regular passbook savings account, except that no passbook is used.

NO PROTEST: instructions given by one bank to another collecting bank not to object to items in case of nonpayment.

NO-RAIDING AGREEMENTS: agreements between unions not to persuade workers to leave one union and join another when the first union has established bargaining relationships.

NORM: a pattern of results developed during a considerable experience, leading to an expected level of performance in the future, as norms of production or sales.

NORMAL CAPACITY: the maximum level of operation under normal circumstances.

NORMALCY: business as usual.

NORMAL GOOD: an item whose consumption changes directly with money income, where prices remain constant.

NORMALIZE: to shift the information in a computer word until some character, usually the leftmost, contains a nonzero digit.

NORMAL PRICE: the price to which the market price tends to return following fluctuations up or down.

NORMAL PROFIT: the lowest price that an entrepreneur will accept as compensation for his or her activity.

NORMAL SALE: a transaction that pleases both the seller and buyer of property and in which no unforeseen or abnormal situations surface.

NORMAL TIME: the time needed by an average employee to complete some arbitrarily determined unit of work.

NORMAL VALUE: the price of a property commanded on the open market.

NORMATIVE ECONOMICS: the study of economics which includes the value judgments of the economist.

NO SHOW: nonappearance to pick up a reservation that has not been canceled, as for an airplane ticket.

NO-STRIKE CLAUSE: a contract clause barring a strike during the life of an agreement.

NOSTRO ACCOUNT: "our accounts," an account maintained by a bank with a bank in a foreign country.

NOSTRO OVERDRAFT: part of a bank's statement indicating that it has sold more foreign bills of exchange than it has bought.

NOSTRUM: proprietary drug or medicine, especially a quack medicine.

NOTARIZE: to attest or acknowledge a signature on an affidavit, protest, contract, or other document, as by a notary public.

NOTARY PUBLIC: a person commissioned by a state to administer certain oaths and certify documents, thus authorizing him to take affidavits and depositions.

NOTE: an instrument, such as a promissory note, which is the recognized legal evidence of a debt.

NOTE OF HAND: any promissory note.

NOTE PAYABLE: a liability, evidenced by a formal written promise to pay a specified sum at a fixed future date.

NOTE RECEIVABLE: a promissory note collected by a business from a customer.

NOT-FOR-PROFIT: describing an activity of an organization established with the sole goal of providing service for society.

NOTHINGS: an income tax term describing expenses that are neither deductible or depreciable.

NOTICE OF DEFAULT: recorded notice that a default has occurred under a deed of trust and that the beneficiary intends to proceed with a trustee's sale.

NOTICE SALE: removing a property from open market by declaring that it has been sold.

NOVATION: an agreement to replace an original contract with a new contract.

NUCLEAR REACTOR: a power generator fueled by controlled fission of nuclear fuel.

NUISANCE: any prolonged conduct that creates annoyance, inconvenience, and damage to an individual or property.

NUISANCE TAX: an unpopular excise tax levied in small amounts and paid by the consumer.

NULL: an absence of information; invalid.

NULL HYPOTHESIS: the logical contradiction of the hypothesis that one seeks to test.

NULLIFICATION OF AGREEMENT: setting aside the terms of an agreement.

NUMBER, RANDOM: a digit set constructed in such a sequence that each successive digit is equally likely to be any of n digits to the base n of the number.

NUMBERED ACCOUNT: a bank account that is identified by a number only, with the name of the account holder being kept secret.

NUMERIC: pertaining to numerals or to representation by means of numerals.

NUMERICAL CONTROL: programming equipment by means of coded numbers, stored on magnetic tapes or cards, according to the needs of different items.

NUMERIC CHARACTER: any allowable digit in a machine's number system.

NUNCUPATIVE WILL: a will given orally before witnesses, which is reduced to writing at a later time.

NUPLEX: any nuclear-powered agricultural-industrial complex.

NURSERY FINANCE: institutional loans to profitable organizations that plan to go public shortly.

O

OBITUARY: a death notice appearing in a newspaper or a periodical.

OBJECTION TO TITLE: a weakness in a title for property, requiring adjustment.

OBJECTIVE: a level of production, sales, or profits planned for a coming period; a goal.

OBJECTIVES: the goals or specific aims of the business.

OBJECTIVE VALUE: the price an item can command in terms of other items in the market.

OBJECT PROGRAM: a computer program in the form in which it is executed by the computer; output from an assembler or compiler.

OBLIGATION: in business, any enforceable debt; in law, a duty owed by one person to another.

OBLIGATION BOND: a bond authorized by a mortgagor that is larger than the original mortgage amount.

OBLIGEE: one to whom one has an obligation to discharge, such as a bondholder.

OBLIGOR: one who has an obligation to discharge, such as a corporation that issues bonds.

OBSCENITY: a display of lewdness or filth exceeding the limits acceptable to the society in which it occurs.

OBSCURANTIST: one who seeks to refute the acceptance of another's ideas by tactics such as befogging their meaning in circumlocution.

OBSERVATIONAL METHOD: studies conducted by actually viewing the overt actions of the respondent.

OBSERVED DEPRECIATION: accrued depreciation determined by physical inspection of operating conditions, expressed as a percentage of original cost or replacement cost.

OBSERVER: an employee who attends a meeting of management and union negotiators but does not participate in the discussions or in the voting.

OBSOLESCENCE: being out of date; of little use to society.

OCCUPANCY TAX: a tax levied on the lessee of quarters.

OCCUPATION: a person's trade, business, or vocational choice.

OCCUPATIONAL ACCIDENT: an accident occurring in the course of one's employment and caused by inherent or related hazards.

OCCUPATIONAL ANALYSIS: a descriptive approach for determining the jobs that have common activities, to permit grouping them under a common occupation.

120

OCCUPA-
TIONAL
DISEASE •
ONE-WRITE
SYSTEM

OCCUPATIONAL DISEASE: a pathological condition caused by or resulting from employment.

OCCUPATIONAL HAZARD: a risk of injury or sickness that is inherent in certain occupations.

OCCUPATIONAL HEALTH: a general description of all activities related to protecting and maintaining the health and safety of working people.

OCCUPATIONAL TEST: a test of ability in a given vocation.

OCTANE RATING: the proportion of iso-octane to heptane in a fuel being tested, compared to a standard.

ODD LOT: in stock-market language, less than the usual unit of trading; usually fewer than 100 shares of a particular security.

ODD-LOT DEALER: a member firm of an exchange that buys and sells odd lots of stock.

ODD-LOT ORDERS: any purchase or sale of stock not in 100-share units.

OFF-BOARD: describing over-the-counter transactions in unlisted securities, or a transaction involving listed shares which was not executed on a national securities exchange.

OFFER: an expressed willingness to sell at a stated price.

OFFERING: a term used to indicate an issue of securities or bonds offered for sale to the public.

OFFICIAL EXCHANGE RATE: the rate at which the monetary authority of a nation will exchange its currency for the currency of another nation.

OFF-LINE: equipment or other devices not under the control of the central-processing unit.

OFF-PREMISES CLAUSE: a policy clause providing insurance protection on personal property while it is away from the premises named in the policy.

OFFSET: either of two equivalent entries on both sides of an account; the right accruing to a bank to take possession of any balances that a guarantor or debtor may have in the bank to cover a loan in default.

OFF TIME: term describing a computer that is not scheduled for use, maintenance, alteration, or repair.

OF RECORD: referring to stock ownership as of the date on which the holder becomes entitled to a dividend declared earlier and payable later.

OGIVE: a distribution curve characterized by cumulative frequencies.

OHM: unit of electrical resistance which produces a current of 1 ampere across a drop in potential of 1 volt.

OLIGOPOLY: leadership or rule by a small group of persons.

OLIGOPSONY: a market dominated by a small number of buyers.

OMBUDSMAN: an official whose duty it is to investigate complaints made to him by members of the public against the government.

ON ACCOUNT: describing a payment made toward the settlement of an account; a purchase or sale made on "open account."

ON A SCALE: the customer purchases or sells equal amounts of a stock at prices that are spaced by a constant interval, as the market price rises or drops.

ON CONSIGNMENT: describing items turned over by an owner (consignor) to someone else (the consignee) with the expectation that the items (the consignment) will be sold by the consignee.

ON DEMAND: describing a bill of exchange that is payable on presentation.

ONE-PRICE POLICY: condition under which the price for goods is firm and cannot be negotiated.

ONE-STOP BANKING: provided by a bank whose clients can do all banking business at that bank.

ONE-TIME RATE: a rate based upon a single publication insertion, broadcasting announcement, or other unit purchase.

ONE-WRITE SYSTEM: a system of bookkeeping in which all records are produced during one operation by the use of reproductive paper and special equipment.

ON-LINE: pertaining to equipment or devices under control of the central-processing unit.

ON-LINE, REAL-TIME: describing a system operation in which the input data are given directly from the measuring devices and the computer results are obtained during the progress of the event.

ON MARGIN: describing securities purchased when the buyer has borrowed part of the purchase price from the broker.

ON ORDER: goods paid for but not yet received.

ON-THE-JOB TRAINING: using the actual work site as a proper setting to instruct workers while they are engaging in productive work at the same time.

OP. CIT.: in the work or works cited (Latin).

OPEN ACCOUNT: an unsecured asset; to sell on open account means to extend credit.

OPEN BID: an offer to perform a contract together with the price.

OPEN CREDIT: a credit established by a bank permitting a borrower to make withdrawals up to a stated amount without depositing securities.

OPEN-DOOR POLICY: a policy whereby citizens and goods of foreign nations receive the same treatment as domestic citizens and goods.

OPEN ECONOMY: an economy free of trade restrictions.

OPEN-END: the term describing the capital structure of an organization whose shares or units are not transferable but may be redeemed at the sole option of the shareholder or unit holder.

OPEN-END AGREEMENT: a union contract having no expiration date.

OPEN-END CONTRACT: an agreement whereby a supplier contracts to meet the buyer's requirements for a specific item during a stated period.

OPEN-ENDED: pertaining to a process or system that can be cut back.

OPEN-END FUNDS: mutual funds where new shares of the fund are sold whenever there is a request, with the expectation that the seller will eventually request to buy back the shares, at no additional charge.

OPEN-END MORTGAGE: a mortgage permitting the borrower to reborrow money paid on the principal up to the original amount.

OPEN HEARTH: the principal method of steel production for decades, now being replaced by the oxygen furnace.

OPENING: the first showing of a new season's line of items by a manufacturer or entire industry; an unfilled position in an organization.

OPENING PURCHASE: a transaction in which an investor becomes the holder of a security.

OPEN INTEREST: the number of outstanding contracts in the exchange market, or in a particular class or series.

OPEN LETTER: a letter to influence people, bearing a salutation to an individual but widely circulated, as by publication in the form of an advertisement.

OPEN LISTING: a listing making property available to more than one broker.

OPEN MARKET: a freely competitive market in which buyers and sellers need not be members of a particular exchange or group.

OPEN-MARKET OPERATIONS: operations carried out by the Federal Reserve System, in which it buys, or sells government bonds in the same market other institutional investors use.

OPEN MORTGAGE: a mortgage that can be paid off, without penalty, at any period prior to its maturity.

OPEN ORDER: an order placed with a broker to buy or sell a definite number of shares of a company's stock at a stated price and "good until canceled."

OPEN PRICE: the price at which a day's first transaction in a security takes place.

OPEN PROSPECTUS: a brochure that aims to obtain financial backing and does not clearly identify the use to be made of the investment.

OPEN RATE: the base rate for the minimum quantity sold from which reductions are sometimes obtainable for larger purchases.

OPEN SHOP: the situation in which some employees in a bargaining unit are members of a union and others are not.

OPEN STOCK: in merchandising, the term for goods kept on hand particularly to fill in sets, as in silverware, with individual pieces.

OPEN SYSTEM: an organizational department in which autonomy, interaction, and a relaxed atmosphere are encouraged.

OPEN-TO-BUY: the quantity of goods a store can receive in stock over a stated time without exceeding its planned inventory levels.

OPEN TRADE: any transaction that has not yet been closed.

OPEN UNION: a union that admits any qualified worker on payment of an initiation fee.

OPERAND: any quantity entering into an operation.

OPERATING COMPANY: a company that is actively engaged in the operation of a business, in contrast to a holding company.

OPERATING CYCLE: the time period between the acquisition of raw materials or merchandise and the receipt of cash from their sale.

OPERATING EXPENSE: all expenses incurred in the normal operation of a business or other organization.

OPERATING INCOME: operating profit; the excess of revenues over expenses.

OPERATING LOSSES: losses incurred in the normal operation of a business.

OPERATING RATIO: the total of expenses of operation divided by the total of operating revenues.

OPERATING STATEMENT: income statement.

OPERATING SYSTEM: the computer program used at a computer facility which allocates facilities and schedules jobs, and input and output operations.

OPERATION: any process or action that is part of a series in work; the act specified by a single computer instruction.

OPERATIONAL: in operation; at times referring to a facility that has recently been built and tested and has now come into regular production.

OPERATIONAL AUDIT: an examination of an organization's operating structure, policies, and systems and procedures, to assess their effectiveness and efficiency.

OPERATIONAL CONTROL: the influence by management over the inputs and activities in the daily performances in a firm.

OPERATIONS RESEARCH: the application of scientific methods, techniques, and tools to problems involving the operation of a system.

OPERATIVE: an investigator, detective; a factory worker.

OPERATOR: one who operates a computer, telephone, switchboard, earth-moving machinery, or other mechanical, electrical, or electronically controlled equipment.

OPPORTUNITY COST: a maximum alternative profit that could have been obtained if the productive good, service, or capacity had been applied to some other use.

OPPORTUNITY COST OF CAPITAL: the expected rate of return from effectively employing funds in the company.

OPPOSITE NUMBER: a person in another organization with whom one has dealings and who holds exactly or approximately equal rank.

OPT: to exercise an option.

OPTICAL-CHARACTER RECOGNITION: the machine identification of printed characters through use of light-sensitive devices.

OPTICAL READER: a device that interprets handwritten or

machine-printed symbols into a computing system.

OPTICAL SCANNER: a device that scans optically and usually generates an analog or digital signal.

OPTIMIST: one with a rosy viewpoint and buoyant disposition, to whom the present looks good and the future better.

OPTIMUM: best, usually of a combination of factors, not all of which peak at the same instant.

OPTIMUM CAPACITY: the quantity of output that permits the minimum cost per unit to be incurred.

OPTION: the right to purchase or sell at a future time at a price stipulated at the time of grant or sale of option.

OPTIONAL CONSUMPTION: the buying of items and services not required for daily fulfillment and well-being.

OPTIONAL DIVIDEND: the stockholder has the choice of receiving either a stock dividend or a cash dividend.

OPTIONEE: the holder of an option; a prospective tenant or buyer.

OPTIONER: a property owner; a seller or landlord.

OPTION SPREADING: the simultaneous purchase and sale of options within the same class.

ORDER: a request to deliver, sell, receive, or purchase goods or services; a command or decree; identifying the one to whom payment should be made.

ORDER-GETTING COST: a marketing cost incurred in an effort to attain a desired sales volume and mix.

ORDINAL: describing the adjectival form of numbers, as first, second, third, ninety-ninth.

ORDINANCE: a local law.

ORDINARY CREDITOR: an unsecured creditor.

ORDINARY INCOME: in income-tax filing, reportable income that does not qualify as capital gains.

ORDINARY INTEREST: interest computed on the basis of 360 days to the year—12 months of 30 days each.

ORDINARY LIFE: a type of insurance policy continuing in force throughout the policyholder's lifetime; also referred to as whole life or straight life.

ORDINARY STOCK: a synonym for common stock.

ORDINATE: in graphs, the vertical distance from the horizontal axis.

ORDNANCE: military hardware of firepower.

ORGANIC STRUCTURE: an organization design characterized by a decentralized hierarchy, flexible work procedures, and democratic leadership, with informal and open communications.

ORGANIZATION: a company; the structure and departmentalization of a company; the personnel of a company.

ORGANIZATION, FORMAL: a highly structured organization with little flexibility in the delegation of authority and assignment of tasks and responsibilities.

ORGANIZATION, INFORMAL: a flexibly structured organization, free of rigid rules for activity and authority.

ORGANIZATION EXPENSE: the cost of forming or incorporating an organization.

ORGANIZATION, INFORMAL: a flexibly structured organization, free of rigid rules for activity and authority.

ORGANIZATION EXPENSE: the cost of forming or incorporating an organization.

ORGANIZATIONAL CHART: a graphic presentation of the relationships and interrelationships within an organization, identifying lines of authority and responsibility.

ORGANIZATIONAL CLIMATE: a set of properties of the work environment perceived by employees and assumed to be a major factor in influencing their behavior.

ORGANIZATIONAL DEVELOPMENT: a reeducation by a company's administration to environmental demands.

ORGANIZED LABOR: union labor, collectively or with respect to individual shops.

ORGANIZER: a union employee whose primary task is to recruit nonunion workers for membership in the union.

ORGMAN: short for organization man.

ORIENTATION: knowledgeable adjustment of oneself to fit or to cope with an existing situation; indoctrination of others to that end.

ORIFICE: opening.

ORIGINAL COST: all costs associated with the acquisition of a fixed asset necessary to place it in effective use.

ORIGINAL ENTRY: a first record of any transaction in a set of account books.

ORIGINATION FEE: a charge made for initiating and processing a mortgage loan.

OSCILLATION: fluctuations of a system's output in excess of the allowable variations; inability to make a decision or resolve a conflict.

OTHER EXPENSE: an expense not considered to be one of the regular operating expenses of a business or other organization.

OTHER INCOME: a financial gain derived from unusual resources, not a regular or routine source of income.

OUTBID: to offer a higher price for an item than that offered by other bidders.

OUTCRY MARKET: commodity tradings by private contract that must be shouted out, as on the floor of an exchange, in order for the agreement to be recorded.

OUTDOOR ADVERTISING: advertising signs displayed outdoors.

OUTGO: expenditures.

OUTLAY: that which is laid out or expended; cost.

OUTLET STORE: a manufacturer-owned store that retails merchandise not readily salable in other channels of distribution.

OUTMODED: rendered obsolete, as by the introduction of more modern or efficient machinery or business practices; out of fashion.

OUT-OF-POCKET EXPENSE: an expense incurred on behalf of another for which reimbursement will be sought.

OUT OF STOCK: term describing goods that are not in the store when requested by a customer.

OUT-OF-THE-MONEY: a call option in which the striking price is above the market price of the underlying stock.

OUT-OF-WORK BENEFITS: payments by a union to unemployed members.

OUTPLACE: assisting an employee about to be fired by sending him to an agency specializing in helping people find new employment.

OUTPUT: information produced by a data-processing system; the quantity of goods or services produced.

OUTPUT BLOCK: a segment of the internal storage reserved for output data.

OUTSIDE BROKER: one who is not a member of an exchange but who works through a member.

OUTSIDE DIRECTORS: members of the board of directors of a corporation who are not employed by the firm.

OUTSIDE MARKET: an over-the-counter market, or a market where unlisted securities are handled.

OUTSIDERS: a name applied by employers, usually in counteracting unionization, to union organizers from another town; the general investing public.

OUTSTANDING: unpaid, uncleared, unredeemed, or unfilled, depending upon the noun with which the term is used.

OVERAGE: items additional to those shown on a bill of lading; created by a spending program that exceeds a specified budget target during a specified time period.

OVERALL MARKET CAPABILITY: the quantity of an item or service absorbed in the general market without allowing for the price or market considerations.

OVER-AND-SHORT: an account in which appear minor differences between actual cash receipts and payments, and the covering documents therefor.

OVERAPPLIED OVERHEAD: the excess of amount of overhead cost applied to a product over the amount of overhead cost incurred.

OVERBURDEN: rock and earth overlying a mineral deposit, especially one to be strip mined; to overload, as an employee.

OVERCAPITALIZED: showing unsatisfactorily low sales and earnings in view of the high capital investment.

OVERDRAFT: the situation existing when withdrawals exceed deposits.

OVERDRAW: to write a bank check for an amount exceeding the deposit in the bank on which the check is drawn.

OVERDUE: a payment that has not been made at the time it was due.

OVER-EXTENSION: credit received or extended beyond the debtor's ability to pay.

OVERFLOW: the portion of the result of an operation that exceeds the capacity of the intended unit of storage.

OVERHEAD: expenses incurred to operate a business which cannot conveniently be attributed to individual units of production or service.

OVERHEATING: excessive price or money activity that some economists believe will lead to inflation.

OVERINSURANCE: insurance against property loss or damage that is in excess of the possible amount of damage or loss.

OVERISSUE: the release of stock in excess of the authorized or ordered amount.

OVERLAY: in printing, layers of thin paper spread under the back sheet of a platen or cylinder press to improve the printing quality of impression.

OVER-LINE: an amount of liability larger than the amount an insurance company wishes to underwrite.

OVERLYING MORTGAGE: a junior mortgage subject to the claim of a

senior mortgage, which has a prior claim to the junior mortgage.

OVERMANNING: using more workers in an operation than are required for an efficient activity.

OVER-ON-BILL: additional freight described on the bill of lading.

OVERPRODUCTION: production exceeding demand.

OVERPRODUCTION THEORY: the idea that an excessive expansion of productive capacity occurs whenever demand increases.

OVERPUNCH: to add holes, usually control punches, in a card column that already contains one or more holes.

OVERRIDE: a commission paid to managers which is added to their salary.

OVERRUN: the number of pieces of printed advertising in excess of the specified quantity.

OVERSAVING: condition in which planned saving exceeds planned investment.

OVERSOLD: the situation of a manufacturer who has become obligated to deliver more than he or she is able to supply within the stated period.

OVERSUBSCRIBED: the condition of a new issue of securities when there are applications for more shares than the total number in the issue.

OVER-THE-COUNTER: term for the sale of an unlisted security.

OVERTIME: hours worked in excess of the usual daily or weekly stint; pay for such work.

OVERTRADING: the activity of a firm that even with high profitability cannot pay its own way for lack of working capital and finds itself in a liquidity crisis.

OVER-WITHOUT-BILL: freight without its bill of lading.

OVERWORK: mental and physical thresholds reached after excess hours of work or other working conditions demanded by the job.

OWE: to be obliged to pay something to someone for something received.

OWN BRAND: bearing the name or brand of the store selling the item rather than the name of the producer.

OWNER: a person possessing title to property.

OWNER-OPERATOR: a regular driver who owns equipment and is a subcontractor to a carrier on a long-term basis.

OWNERSHIP: possession of a legal title with the rights to enjoy the benefits derived from any assets accompanying or accruing from such title.

OXYGEN FURNACE: equipment for making steel with the use of oxygen to burn off unwanted impurities.

P

PACERS: fast-working employees, identified by management, who are used to establish the pace of expected work for others.

PACE SETTER: a speedy, skilled employee whose output in a given period sets the basis on which piecework rates are determined for other workers doing similar work.

PACK: to add to the total cost of merchandise charges for items not included or inflated charges, to give an undeserved discount without lowering the actual price.

PACKAGE: the total gains, including fringe benefits, as the result of collective bargaining; a container of goods.

PACKAGE, PRIMARY: a container that directly holds the product of sale.

PACKAGE, PROGRAM: a group of logically related operational program segments.

PACKAGE ENGINEERING: the principles applied to design and use of containers for shipment, regardless of the product enclosed.

PACKAGE MORTGAGE: a home-financing mortgage covering appliances and other household items.

PACKAGE POLICIES: combination insurance policies in which several coverages are included in one contract.

PACKAGING: the preparation of merchandise for shipment and marketing.

PACKER: meat-processing plant.

PACKING LIST: the document which is included with goods shipped, and which includes a description of the type and number of items but generally not the prices.

PAGING: identification of a computer program and data into fixed blocks, to permit transfers between disk and core to take place in storage systems.

PAID-IN CAPITAL: capital acquired from the sale of company stock.

PAID-IN SURPLUS: a synonym for contributed surplus.

PAID-UP CAPITAL: issued capital that has been paid for.

PAID-UP INSURANCE: a policy on which no further premium payments need to be made.

PAID-UP STOCK: any share for which subscribers have paid the full amount of par value into the corporation's treasury.

PALLET: a portable platform for retaining material while in storage or shipment.

PANIC: sudden mass fear, resulting in urgent attempts to convert securities into cash, thus swiftly depressing prices.

PAPER: a loan contract.

PAPER LOCAL: a local union having a charter but no members.

PAPER MONEY: currency on which a value is printed, usually represents bullion held in government vaults.

PAPER PROFIT: an unrealized profit.

PAPER STANDARD: a monetary system, based on paper money, which is not convertible into gold or any other item of intrinsic value.

PAPER TITLE: a written document that appears to convey proof of ownership but may not in fact show proper title.

PAPER TRUNCATION: the act of

terminating the flow of paper in a transaction-processing system.

PAPERBOARD: board made of matted or felted fibrous material.

PAR: the condition existing when the exchangeable value of an instrument is equal to that expressed on its face without consideration of any premium or discount.

PARALLEL COMPUTER: a computer having multiple arithmetic or logic units that are used to accomplish parallel operations or parallel processing.

PARALLEL STANDARDS: a monetary system in which two or more metals are coined but in which there is no exchange ratio between the metals.

PARAMETER: a definable characteristic.

PARAMOUNT TITLE: the foremost title, a title that is superior to all others.

PARASITE: one who lives by the labor of others.

PARCHMENT: originally the dried skin of a sheep or goat, now high-strength, good-quality paper used for important documents.

PARENT COMPANY: a controlling organization that owns or manages business properties.

PARETO OPTIMALITY: distribution of resources that will make at least one person better off and no one else worse off.

PARI DELICTO: fault or blame that is equally shared (Latin).

PAR ITEM: any item that can be collected at its par or face value upon presentation.

PARITY: the relationship of one foreign currency to another as indicated by their exchange value in gold or silver.

PARITY PRINCIPLE: the concept that the amount of authority that rests with an individual should be equal to the employee's responsibility.

PARITY RATIO: a comparison between the prices farmers receive for farm products and the prices they paid for goods and services from 1910 to 1914.

PARKINSON'S LAWS: work invariably expands to fill the time available for its completion, and expenditures climb to reach income.

PAR LIST: a Federal Reserve System list of banks that will remit in full for items that are payable to the system.

PAROCHIAL: narrow in concept or interest, as applying to the problems of a single sales area or single department of a business.

PAR OF EXCHANGE: the market price of money in one national currency that is exchanged at the official rate for a specific amount in another national currency.

PAROL: not written; oral.

PARSIMONY, PRINCIPLE OF: the principle of scientific thinking that the simpler of two hypotheses is to be preferred.

PART-TIME EMPLOYEES: those who work less than a full day or full week.

PARTIAL-EQUILIBRIUM ANALYSIS: one market inquiry that assumes solutions on other markets will not be affected by the market examined.

PARTIAL LOSS: a loss that does not completely destroy or render useless the insured property, or exhaust the insurance applied to it.

PARTIAL MONOPOLY: condition when there are so few sellers of an item or service that each may alter the price and market.

PARTIAL PAYMENT: a payment that is not equal to the full amount owed and is not intended to constitute the full payment.

PARTICIPATING INSURANCE: insurance or reinsurance that contributes proportionately with other insurance on the same risk.

PARTICIPATING STOCK: a class of preferred stock that will carry a dividend not less than that paid on the common stock.

PARTICIPATION LOAN: a loan having two or more banks as creditors.

PARTICULAR AVERAGE: damage or loss less than the total value; partial loss.

PARTICULARS: specific allegations or complaints in a bill of particulars filed in a civil suit.

PARTITION: a division of property held jointly or in common; it may be effected by the consent of the parties or by compulsion of law.

PARTNERSHIP: two or more persons engage in a business with a view to making a profit.

PARTY AT INTEREST: individual or group of individuals having a vested interest in a commercial enterprise.

PAR VALUE: the face value of a security.

PASS: one cycle of processing a body of data.

PASSBOOK: a savings bankbook showing deposits, withdrawals, and balance to the credit of the depositor.

PASSIM: in various places (Latin).

PASSING TITLE: the handing over of title to a new owner.

PASSIVE TRADE BALANCE: an unfavorable balance of trade.

PASSIVE TRUST: one whose trustee has no tasks to perform and merely retains title to the trust property.

PASS THE DIVIDEND: to fail to declare a dividend at a meeting of the Board of Directors called to act upon the declaration of dividends.

PASSWORD: a unique string of characters that a program, computer operator, or user must supply to meet security requirements before gaining access to data.

PAST-DUE ITEM: any note, acceptance, or other time instrument of indebtedness that has not been paid on the due date.

PAST-SERVICE PENSION COST: the pension cost relating to an employee's employment before a pension plan is put into effect.

PAST-SERVICE PENSION LIABILITY: the present value of the cost of unpaid past-service pension benefits.

PATCH: to settle; to bring to an end; to modify a routine in a rough or expedient way.

PATENT: the authority given by a government to a first inventor to enjoy the exclusive benefits from the invention for a particular period, usually 17 years.

PATENT AMBIGUITY: an unclear statement in a written document that becomes clear upon rereading.

PATENT MONOPOLY: an organization holding a monopoly after the government has conferred on it the exclusive right to use or manufacture its own innovation.

PATENT PENDING: the Patent Office's statement that a worldwide search is being conducted to determine whether the invention is new and patentable under the law.

PATERNAL AGGRESSIVE COMPANY: an organization that is aggressively attempting to achieve various objectives and liberally rewards good performance.

PATERNALISM: the actions of a company or a government in providing social-welfare benefits for workers or citizens.

PATERNAL PASSIVE COMPANY: an organization that is not aggressively pursuing various objectives and treats its workers in a protective manner.

PATRON: a regular customer, as of a store; a benefactor, as of an institution; a supporter, as of a person of promising talent.

PATRONAGE DIVIDEND: a distribution to customers based on the volume of business done with each customer over a period of time.

PATRONAGE MOTIVES: reasons customers shop in a particular retail outlet.

PATRONIZE: to frequent a store; to be a regular customer.

PAUPER: an individual totally dependent on public funds for subsistence.

PAVILION: a large public building, sometimes of light construction, sometimes temporary, and sometimes either.

PAWN: the pledge to pay a debt; an

individual who is easily manipulated by another.

PAWNBROKER: a person who is licensed to lend money upon the security of valuable goods left with him until the loan is repaid.

PAY-AS-YOU-GO: the principle of operation without borrowings.

PAYBACK PERIOD: the estimated period of time over which the cash flow from an investment or project will equal its original cost.

PAYEE: the legal entity who is named in an instrument as the recipient of the amount shown on the instrument.

PAYER: the party primarily responsible for the payment of the amount owed, as evidenced by a given negotiable instrument.

PAYLOAD: that part of the weight of a loaded vehicle which is to be delivered.

PAYMENT IN KIND: payment in the form of goods or services rather than money.

PAYMENTS DEFICIT: the excess of the value of a nation's imports over its exports.

PAYMENTS SURPLUS: the excess of the value of a nation's exports over its imports.

PAYMENTS SYSTEM: an approach (involving people, machines, and procedures) used to transfer value from one party to another.

PAYOFF: money given for an unethical or illegal service; the result of a decision problem transformed to represent its true utility to the decision maker.

PAYOLA: bribery.

PAYROLL: the wages or salary earned by a firm's employees for a certain period of time.

PAYROLL DEDUCTIONS: sums withheld from an employee's gross pay.

PAYROLL TAX: used to finance an employer's contribution to the social security program; a tax levied on a company's payroll.

PEAK: an exceptionally busy period in a business.

PEAK CAPACITY: the sum of employee productivity, working at the fastest speed with no regard for efficiency; the primary consideration is output rather than quality.

PEAK LOAD: the highest demand rate encountered, as for electric power.

PEAK SEASON: the period of days or months in which an item is in greatest customer demand.

PECULATION: the embezzlement of funds or goods, especially public funds or goods, by an individual in whose care they have been entrusted.

PECUNIARY EXCHANGE: any trade using money.

PEDDLER: a person who travels and sells small quantities of merchandise.

PEGGING: the manipulation of the price of something so that it remains stationary or within very narrow ranges.

PEG POINT: the pay rate for a major task that becomes the base from which rates of pay for other related tasks are derived.

PENALTY: stipulated loss incurred for failure to meet contractual obligations.

PENALTY CLAUSE: a provision in a contract requiring one party to pay a sum of money to the other if the contract is not kept.

PENDENTE LITE: pending during the progress of a suit at law.

PENDING: unfinished, not yet decided.

PENETRATION PRICING: an approach in which the price of an item is set low in order to enter the market quickly.

PENNY STOCKS: low-priced shares, usually speculative, normally applied to stock selling at less than a dollar per share.

PENSION: a benefit paid to a retired employee.

PENSION FUND: the cash, investments, and other assets set aside for the payment of pensions.

PENSION PLAN: the arrangement under which pensions are paid.

PENSION POOL: an employers group who create a common pension fund for employees transferring accrued pension rights.

PEON: term used to describe a common laborer or a person who performs work that is primarily unskilled.

PEONAGE: forced labor performance in payment of a debt as controlled by either law or contract.

PEOPLE'S CAPITALISM: system in which the full range of the income levels in the population of a community is represented in the ownership of the business.

PEPPERCORN RENT: a small nominal rent.

PER ANNUM: yearly (Latin).

PER CAPITA: for each person (Latin).

PER CAPITA TAX: a tax based on the result of dividing stated sums of money by a specified number of people to show the amount to be paid by each person.

PERCEIVED RISK: the hazards the customer believes to be related to the buying of a specific item.

PERCENTAGE: a ratio between any real number and 100, used for expressing interest rates, statistical comparisons, etc.; a share; a commission.

PERCENTAGE-OF-COMPLETION METHOD: an accounting method under which income is recognized proportionately to the degree of completion of a contract.

PERCENTILE: one of the 99 point scores that divide a ranked distribution into groups or parts, each of which contains one-hundredth of the scores or persons.

PER CONTRA ITEM: a balance in one account that is offset by a balance from another account.

PER CURIAM: a full court's decision when no opinion is given (Latin).

PER DIEM: for each day (Latin).

PER EXCHANGE RATE: the free market price of one country's money in terms of the currency of another.

PERFECT COMPETITION: the market situation where no one trader can materially affect the market for a product.

PERFECT (PURE) MONOPOLY: one person or organization having total control over the manufacture and marketing of an item.

PERFECT TITLE: a title that is not open to dispute or challenge because it is complete in every detail, and has no legal defects.

PERFORATED TAPE: paper tape punched with holes that provide signals, as used in teletypewriters, computers, etc.

PERFORMANCE APPRAISAL: a methodical review of an employee's performance on the job to evaluate the effectiveness or adequacy of the person's work.

PERFORMANCE BOND: a bond posted to ensure completion.

PERFORMANCE BUDGETING: categorizing budget accounts and measuring product cost.

PERFORMANCE REPORT: a comparison at actual results against those anticipated in a stated budget.

PERIL: the cause of a loss insured against in a policy.

PERIOD COSTS: costs charged off as expenses in the period in which they are incurred rather than included in inventory.

PERIODIC STOCK CONTROL: unit control system in which stock is identified and recorded periodically, and sales for intervening time slots are calculated.

PERIODIC TENANCY: month-to-month tenancy without a written lease; also called a tenancy at will.

PERIOD OF DIGESTION: a time immediately following the release of a new security, during which sales are made to regular investment customers.

PERIPHERAL EQUIPMENT: any of the units of computer equipment, distinct from the central-processing unit, that provide the system with outside communication.

PERISHABLE GOODS: items that are subject to rapid decay unless given proper storage.

PERJURY: willful utterance of a false statement under oath.

PERMANENT-DISABILITY BENEFITS: periodic compensations, usually weekly, for a disability that renders any employment impossible.

PERMANENT FINANCING: a long-term mortgage, amortized over 15, 20, or more years at a fixed rate of interest.

PERMIT MAIL: mail with a printed indicia in lieu of stamps, indicating that postage has been paid by the sender under the permit number shown.

PERPETUAL INVENTORY: a method of keeping stock records in which daily entries provide current information on inventories.

PERPETUAL-INVENTORY CONTROL: a unit control system whereby orders, receipts, and sales are identified as they occur and inventory is computed.

PERPETUITY: duration without limitation as to time.

PER SE: by itself.

PERSEVERANCE: the tendency to continue with an activity despite difficulties.

PERSONAL-CARE ITEMS: hair dryers, electric shavers, toothbrushes, facial cosmetics, and so on.

PERSONAL CHECK: a check drawn by an individual on a personal account.

PERSONAL-CONSUMPTION EXPENDITURES: the funds spent by households for consumer items.

PERSONAL DATA SHEET: a questionnaire eliciting any facts of any description concerning an individual.

PERSONAL DISTRIBUTION OF INCOME: the distribution of natural income among individuals or households.

PERSONAL FINANCE COMPANY: a business that lends small sums of money to people, usually for personal needs at relatively high interest rates.

PERSONAL INCOME: the income of individuals.

PERSONAL-INJURY

PROTECTION: the name usually given to no-fault automobile coverage.

PERSONAL INSTALLMENT LOAN: funds, borrowed by an individual for personal needs, which are repaid in regular monthly installments over a specified period.

PERSONAL LOAN: a type of loan generally obtained by individual borrowers in small amounts.

PERSONAL PROPERTY: the rights, powers, and privileges a person has in movable things, both corporeal (as furniture and jewelry) and incorporeal (as stocks and bonds).

PERSONAL SAVING: the difference between disposable personal income and personal consumption expenditures.

PERSONAL SELLING: a promotion method involving interpersonal communication between individuals.

PERSONAL SPACE: the physical area surrounding an employee assigned to him for use in carrying out his work.

PERSONNEL: employees; people.

PERSONNEL ADMINISTRATION: a well-planned, properly executed, and efficiently evaluated approach to manpower recruitment, screening, usage, and development.

PERSONNEL DEPARTMENT: the department of an organization responsible for recruitment, hiring, testing, training, counseling, and promoting of employees.

PERSONNEL PSYCHOLOGY: a subdivision of applied psychology that treats an individual's psychological qualities in relation to his or her job.

PER STIRPES: for each child.

PERSUASION: influencing an individual or group to work for a desired objective.

PERT: program evaluation and review technique.

PETER PRINCIPLE: theory that in a hierarchy, every employee tends to rise to his or her level of incompetence.

PETITION IN BANKRUPTCY: the form used for declaring voluntary bankruptcy.

PETIT LARCENY: larceny involving small amounts, as under $25.

PETRODOLLARS: huge sums of money from oil-producing nations other than the United States or Great Britain.

PHANTOM FREIGHT: freight charges paid by the purchaser which were never absorbed by the seller.

PHANTOM STOCK: used in executive compensation programs; the executive is granted a number of shares of the company.

PHANTOM-STOCK PLAN: a bonus under which an employee is paid a cash amount determined by the rise in value of the employer's stock over a period of time.

PHILANTHROPY: the giving and administration of gifts, endowments, and bequests and trusts primarily devoted to charitable distribution.

PHILLIPS CURVE: a statistical technique whereby the relationship between inflation and unemployment is plotted in curvilinear form.

PHOTOENGRAVING: a letterpress plate made by printing a photographic negative on sensitized metal and etching the metal.

PHOTOSTAT: means of low-cost, rapid reproduction permitting enlargement or reduction.

PHYSICAL DISTRIBUTION: movement of merchandise from manufacturer to consumer.

PHYSICAL HAZARD: characteristics of an insurance risk (e.g., material, structure, or operational).

PHYSICAL INVENTORY: an inventory taken by actual count of merchandise rather than from existing records.

PICA: a measure used in printing equal to one-sixth of an inch.

PICKET: a person stationed outside business premises during a protest or strike to discourage others from entering.

PICKETING: publicizing the existence of a labor dispute by patrolling near the concern involved in the dispute.

PICTOGRAPH: a statistical chart or graph using pictorial symbols instead of bars; one of the symbols so used.

PIE CHART: a circular chart divided into sectors, each representing a proportionate share of the whole.

PIECE RATE: the amount of money received for each unit of output.

PIECE WORK: work performed for which payment is made on the basis of units completed.

PIG: a quantity of iron that has been poured molten into a rough, bar-shaped mold, cooled, and made available for further working.

PIGGYBACK: rail transport of truck trailers or containerized units.

PIGOU EFFECT: a lowering of the overall price level creates higher consumption of times and services.

PILFERAGE: theft of small items from stocks in stores, factories, warehouses, or transit facilities.

PILOT PLANT: a manufacturing plant where trial production runs are made on a new product to gain experience, to eliminate bugs or difficulties, and to evaluate its desirability.

PINCH: a bind or tight situation; a sudden, unanticipated rise in prices.

PINK TEA PICKETING: picketing by a small group of peaceful demonstrators.

PIONEERING STAGE: the first stage in the product life cycle.

PIPELINE: a large-diameter pipe for transmission of oil, gas, etc. over long distances.

PIT: a circular area in the middle of the floor of a stock exchange.

PLACE LAND: the land on both sides of railroad tracks, owned by the railroad.

PLACEMENT: the assigning of a worker to a job for which he is fitted; negotiating for the sale of a new securities issue, or the arranging of a long-term loan.

PLACEMENT TEST: test that enables an individual to be assigned to the appropriate level of class or instruction.

PLACE UTILITY: the additional value in having a product where it is utilized or consumed.

PLAGIARISM: the purloining or use in whole or in part of the previously issued, published, or displayed work of another as if it were one's own.

PLAINTIFF: one who sues in a court of law.

PLANHOLDER: a pension-plan shareholder.

PLANNED ECONOMY: system in which the government plays a major influence in deciding what to manufacture, in what quantity, and often for whom.

PLANNED OBSOLESCENCE: consciously making an item out of fashion by bringing out new products that are promoted as being superior.

PLANNED PRESENTATION: a preplanned, organized statement in which major selling points are memorized for word-by-word presentation.

PLANNING: organizational method that requires the establishment of a predetermined course of action, beginning with a statement of goals.

PLANT: an operating manufacturing complex, (facilities and manpower) the structures maintained by an outdoor advertising company.

PLANTATION: a landed area planted with a crop, such as cotton, trees, or coffee.

PLEA: a defendant's answer of guilty or not guilty to charges; a legal request, as to have a case dismissed, postponed, or transferred.

PLEDGE: to hypothecate; collateral.

PLENARY SESSION: a session of a conference which all delegates attend.

PLOT: in computers and statistics, to draw or diagram.

PLOW BACK: reinvest in the future of the business, usually by setting aside a portion of earnings for addition to earned surplus rather than for declaration of dividends.

PLUG: to work hard and steadily.

PLUGBOARD: a perforated board into which plugs are manually inserted to control the operation of computer equipment.

PLUNGER: an individual speculator who takes great risks, resulting in substantial profits or losses.

PLUTOCRACY: a form of government controlled by the wealthy.

PODIUM: a dais for an individual, as a speaker.

POINT: a unit, such as a dollar in the price per share of a stock or other units of price customary in specific trades; a unit of scoring.

POINT OF IDEAL PROPORTION: in a production process, the place where the most profitable relative amounts of the forces of production are used.

POINT OF INDIFFERENCE: in production, the place where the cost of an added increment of land, labor, capital, or management merely equals the money return of the additional item made because of that increase.

POINT OF ORIGIN: the location at which goods are received for transportation.

POINT-OF-PURCHASE ADVERTISING: interior store displays and literature distributed at retail counters; window displays.

POINT-TO-POINT LINE: a line that connects a single remote station to the computer.

POLICY: a plan of action; a way of doing things; a written agreement about insurance.

POLICY ANALYSIS: the application of systematic research approaches, taken from the social and behavioral sciences.

POLICYHOLDER: the person insured or the one having control of the policy; usually, but not necessarily the insured.

POLICYHOLDERS' SURPLUS: the sum remaining in the policy after all liabilities have been deducted from all assets.

POLICY LOAN: funds borrowed from a life-insurance organization, usually at low interest rates, using as security the cash value of the holder's policy.

POLICY REGISTER: a record maintained by an insurance company for noting the issuance of (thus accounting for) all its policies.

134

*POLICY
VALUE ·
POST–
MORTEM
DUMP*

POLICY VALUE: the amount of money available to the insured upon the maturity of the policy.

POLL TAX: a tax applied equally to every individual required to pay it regardless of personal income or assets.

POLLUTION: adulteration, particularly of water or air.

POLYGRAPH: the lie detector, a machine for measuring pulse, blood pressure, and respiration of applicants and suspects under questioning.

POOL: a combination of resources, or funds for some purpose or benefit.

POP ADVERTISING: promotional material at the point of purchase; interior displays and printed material left at store counters; window displays.

POPULATION STUDIES: tabulations and conclusions drawn from surveys of people's vital and financial data and sometimes opinions.

PORK-CHOPPER: any full-time union employee.

PORT: an entrance to or exit from a network; the left side of a ship, barge, or airplane; anywhere a ship goes, where federal customs officials are able to inspect cargo and levy duties.

PORTABLE PENSIONS: pension plans that increase the mobility of employees by allowing them to transfer earned pension credits from one employer to another.

PORTABILITY: a characteristic of valuables allowing them to be carried easily (e.g., diamonds or stamps are more portable than bullion).

PORTAL-TO-PORTAL PAY: pay for time traveling in getting to and from the job.

PORT AUTHORITY: a government commission established to administer shipping traffic movement and loading and unloading activities.

PORTFOLIO: the aggregate security holdings of an individual or entity.

PORT OF ENTRY: any seaport, airport, or place where custom duties are collected.

POSITION: an individual's stake in the market; a job; an employment situation.

POSITIONING: the projection of an item so that it has a desired image, to make it attractive to a part of the market for that type of merchandise.

POSITIVE ECONOMICS: the study of economics that does not depend on the value judgments of the economist.

POSITIVE FILE: an authorization system file that contains a variety of data on every account holder.

POSSESSION: the condition of being in physical control of property, legally or illegally.

POST: to transfer an amount from a book of original entry to a ledger or from a source document to a book of original entry.

POSTAGE-DUE MAIL: mail on which additional postage is collectible on delivery to the addressee.

POSTAGE METER: a device approved and regulated by the US Post Office Department which meters and postmarks mail.

POST-AUDIT: vertification of the record of transactions that have already occurred.

POSTDATE: a document or check that is dated some time in the future.

POSTDATED CHECK: a check dated prematurely, thus cannot be cashed.

POSTER: an advertising medium; promotional copy, often illustrated, printed on large sheets of paper and pasted on boards or panels.

POSTING: the process of transferring journal entries to the ledger.

POSTMARK: an impression on letters and packages showing the time, date, and post office or sectional center of origin.

POSTMORTEM: a routine that locates a mistake in coding by printing information on tape, concerning the contents of certain registers and storage locations at the time the routine stopped, an analysis of an operation after its completion.

POSTMORTEM DUMP: a static dump, used for debugging purposes, performed at the end of a machine run.

POTENTIAL DEMAND: demand that can be expected to become effective at a future date (e.g., when purchasing power is increased).

POTENTIALLY DILUTIVE: see dilution.

POUND STERLING: the basic currency of Great Britain.

POVERTY: the absence of most of the comforts of life and an undersupply of the necessities.

POWDER METALLURGY: an industrial process of making metal objects, usually parts, from powdered metals sintered under high pressure.

POWER OF ALIENATION: the power to assign, transfer, or otherwise dispose of property.

POWER OF APPOINTMENT: the equivalent of total ownership of a trust, since the individual having this power can identify the ultimate recipients of the trust's assets.

POWER OF ATTORNEY: a signed document empowering one person to act legally for another.

POWER OF SALE: a clause included in a mortgage giving the holder or trustee the right to seize and sell the pledged property upon default.

POWER PLANT: a source of power, as an electricity-generating station, or even a motor.

PRACTICAL CAPACITY: the maximum level at which a plant or department can economically operate most efficiently.

PREAPPROACH: the step in the sales process of finding critical data about a potential customer prior to contract.

PREAUDIT: the examination of a creditor's invoices, payrolls, claims, and expected reimbursements before actual payment; the verification of sales transactions before delivery.

PREAUTHORIZED PAYMENT: a service that enables a debtor to request funds to be transferred from the customer's deposit account to the account of a creditor.

PRECANCELED STAMPS: stamps canceled by printing across the face before they are sold to large mailers,

thus avoiding the need for cancellation at the time of mailing.

PRECAUTIONARY MOTIVE: rationale used by firms and consumers in retaining a portion of their assets in cash, to ensure their ability to easily satisfy unexpected demands.

PRECIPITATOR: a tall stack in which the tiny solid particles in rising gases are trapped by electrostatic attraction.

PRECLUSIVE BUYING: the purchase of goods and services to prevent someone else from buying them.

PREDATORY PRICE-CUTTING: the selling of merchandise or a service below cost so as to drive your competition out of business.

PREDECESSOR: previous incumbent.

PREEMPTIVE RIGHTS: rights of present stockholders to be the first to purchase a proportionate amount of additional shares offered for sale.

PREFABRICATED: a wall or other unit fabricated prior to erection or installation on a building or structure foundation.

PREFERENCE ITEM: a consumer's choice for a particular item even when similar items are less costly.

PREFERENTIAL MAIL: all US mail receiving special handling.

PREFERENTIAL REHIRING: a contract provision for the reemployment of workers on the basis of seniority, after layoffs.

PREFERENTIAL SHOP: a form of union security in which both union and nonunion members may be in a company's employ, in which the union represents union employees.

PREFERRED CREDITOR: a person who is entitled to full satisfaction of his claim against the estate of a bankrupt before other unsecured creditors receive anything.

PREFERRED DEBT: a debt that takes precedence over others; a first mortgage.

PREFERRED POSITION: any advertisement position for which the advertiser pays a premium when specifically requested.

PREFERRED STOCK: stock redeemable in liquidation prior to repayment of any common stock liquidating dividends, and also entitled to dividends before they may be declared on the common stock.

PREFERRED STOCK, CALLABLE: stock that can be called in for payment at a stated price.

PREFERRED STOCK, CUMULATIVE: stock having a provision that must be paid up before dividends may be paid on the company's common stock.

PREFERRED STOCK, PARTICIPATING: a preferred stock entitled to its dividends on a specified basis upon payment of dividends on the common stock.

PREJUDICE: a mental bias tending toward some preconceived judgment or opinion, thus affecting one's attitude toward work or employees.

PRELIMINARY: introductory, preparatory, prior.

PRELIMINARY EXPENSES: expenses incurred in the establishment of an organization.

PREMISES: a parcel of land and all improvements on it.

PREMIUM: the amount by which the selling price of a security exceeds its par value.

PREMIUM AUDIT: an examination by a representative of the insurer of the insured's records related to the policies or coverages under consideration.

PREMIUM FINANCE: a facility that allows an insured to finance his or her payment over a specified period within the term of the policy.

PREMIUM PAY: a wage rate higher than straight time, payable for overtime work, work on holidays or scheduled days off, or for work on evening shifts.

PREMIUM STOCK: a stock that receives a premium fee when it is borrowed for trading, as in short selling.

PRENUPTIAL AGREEMENT: a contract made before marriage; each future spouse forfeits any interest in the other's estate.

PREPACKAGING: packaging of fresh foods in consumer units for self-service sales; packaged by the manufacturer.

PREPAID EXPENSE: incurred expense that is expected to yield benefits only in subsequent accounting periods.

PREPAY: to pay before or in advance of receipt of goods or services.

PREPAYMENT: a privilege extended to installment borrowers to enable them to reduce interest costs by payment of installments prior to due date.

PREPAYMENT CLAUSE: the privilege of repaying part or all of a loan in advance of date or dates stated in a contract.

PREPAYMENT PENALTY: a penalty placed on a mortgagor for paying the mortgage before its due date.

PREPOSTERIOR EVALUATION: a judgment made before an event about the conditions anticipated after the event.

PREREFUNDING: refunding in which securities eligible for conversion mature in no more than one year.

PRERETAILING: assignment by the retailer of retail prices to goods at the time an order is made, thus allowing the determination of retail values of items on order.

PREROGATIVES: the rights, powers, privileges of an individual that others do not possess.

PRESCRIPTION: a title to property or means of obtaining title based on uninterrupted possession.

PRESCRIPTIVE DECISION MAKING: emphasis is placed on what ought to happen, rather than what is happening.

PRESENTATION: a selling solicitation usually made with the aid of graphic materials.

PRESENT VALUE: the discounted value, assuming a given rate of interest over a given period of time.

PRESS KIT: prepared information given to journalists at a press conference.

PRESS TIME: the time at which publication presses are ready to print.

PRESTIGE CARD: a plastic identification card issued by savings and loan associations to their customers to be used in electronic funds-transfer systems.

PRESTIGE PRICING: the approach of increasing the price of an item to establish a quality image of the product or the seller.

PRESUMPTION: an assumed fact.

PRESUMPTIVE TITLE: possession of property that leads others to presume ownership, where in fact ownership may not exist.

PRETEST: a test given to determine an individual's performance in some area in advance of training, education, or other condition expected to improve performance.

PREWRAP: to wrap or package merchandise before it is placed on the floor for sale.

PRICE: the amount of money the seller receives for goods or services at the factory or place of business.

PRICE CONTROL: regulation of the prices of goods and services with the intent to reduce increases in the cost of living.

PRICE CUTTING: offering goods or services for sale at a price below that recognized as typical or appropriate by buyers and sellers.

PRICE DISCRETION: right of decision of a sales representative to alter the price of an item for purposes of making a sale.

PRICE DISCRIMINATION: the practice of charging differing prices for the same quality and quantity of merchandise to different buyers.

PRICED OUT OF THE MARKET: a market situation in which the price asked for a product has eliminated many potential buyers.

PRICE-EARNINGS RATIO: the market price of a share of common stock of a corporation divided by the annual earnings per share for the preceeding period.

PRICE ELASTICITY: term describing a reduction in sales when the price of an item is raised.

PRICE FIXING: setting, by the manufacturer, of the retail price of his trademarked brand; collusive setting of prices on competitive products.

PRICE INDEX: a statistical device for showing the percentage change in the price of a thing or a group of things from the base period, which is assigned the value of one hundred.

PRICE LEADER: an item of merchandise priced abnormally low for the purpose of attracting customers.

PRICE LEADERSHIP: a situation in which a major producer of a product establishes a price and other producers in the same field adopt that price as their own.

PRICE LEVEL: a relative position in the scale of prices as determined by a comparison of process costs (of labor, materials, capital, etc.) at the current time and at some time in the past with prices in the past.

PRICE LIMIT: the maximum change in the price of a commodity from the previous closing price, permitted in a single day's session.

PRICE LINING: placing several items of varying costs together and selling them all at the same price.

PRICE LOCO: the price at the place where a purchase occurs.

PRICE RIGIDITY: a long-term lack of concern for prices of raw or produced items in relation to the inflationary aspects of a depression or recession.

PRICE SPREADING: the simultaneous purchase and sale of options in the same class with the same expiration date but with different striking prices.

PRICE STABILIZATION: keeping prices at a stated level.

PRICE SUPPORT: a subsidy offered to specific growers, producers, or distributors, in accordance with governmental regulations to keep market prices from dropping below a certain minimum level.

PRICE WAR: a systematic reduction in the price of a commodity or service by two or more competing firms.

PRIMA FACIE: on first sight (Latin).

PRIMARY DATA: information collected by any researcher from the original source.

PRIMARY DEPOSITS: cash deposits in a bank.

PRIMARY DISTRIBUTION: the original sale of any issue of a corporation's securities.

PRIMARY INSURANCE: coverage up to a specified amount or against specific perils.

PRIMARY RESERVES: those assets of a bank, consisting of cash and balances on deposit with other banks, which are immediately available for the payment of liabilities.

PRIME COST: cost of direct materials and direct labor incurred in manufacturing.

PRIME MAKER: the party (or parties) signing a negotiable instrument and becoming the original party responsible for its ultimate payment.

PRIME RATE: the interest rate charged by banks to its preferential borrowers; the lowest rate of interest available to borrowers.

PRIMOGENITURE: the principle under which the oldest male child inherits all.

PRINCIPAL: a person who employs another person (called the agent) to act on his behalf with a third person; a sum on which interest is earned or paid.

PRINCIPAL SUM: the amount specified under an accident policy, such as the death benefit.

PRINTER: a device that writes output data from a system on paper or another medium.

PRINTOUT: printed pages produced by a computer's printer.

PRIOR LIEN: a mortgage that ranks ahead of another.

PRIOR-PREFERRED (STOCK): a preferred issue ranking ahead of another preferred issue of the same company.

PRIVATE BANK: a bank chartered by the state in which it operates, subject to state laws and regulations, and subject to examinations by the state banking authorities.

PRIVATE BRAND: a middleman that owns a brand name or trademark.

PRIVATE CARRIER: a transportation line that is not a common carrier.

PRIVATE COST: the cost of a specific item to an individual.

PRIVATE ENTERPRISE: a business owned and operated by people taking risks and motivated by the wish to make a profit.

PRIVATE LENDER: an individual who lends money from institutional funds.

PRIVATE PROPERTY: all land not owned by the government.

PRIVATE RATE OF RETURN: the financial rate of return anticipated by businessmen prior to investing their monies.

PRIVATE SECTOR: the sector of an economy that consists of individuals, corporations, firms, and other institutions that are not under government control.

PRIVILEGED ISSUE: a preferred stock or bond having a conversion or participating right, or having a stock purchase warrant on it.

PRIVITY: condition under which heirs, executors, and certain others succeed to the same rights of a contract as the original party.

PROACTIVE INHIBITION: an existing barrier resulting from a worker's previous experience.

PROBABILITY: the likelihood of the occurrence of an event.

PROBABILITY SAMPLING: a sampling technique in which each unit of the population has an equal chance of appearing in the sample.

PROBATE: to prove a will in court.

PROBATIONARY EMPLOYEE: a worker for whom permanent employment with a firm is contingent on his performance during a trial period.

PROBLEM-ORIENTED LANGUAGE: a computer language in which programs are described in terms of available inputs and required outputs.

PROCEDURE: going through all

customary steps in a repetitive business operation.

PROCEEDING: step taken in an action at law.

PROCEEDS: a very general term used to designate the total amount realized or perceived in any transaction.

PROCESS EFFECTS: the increase in consumer spending and private investment as a result of the spending on public works projects.

PROCESS INSPECTION: inspection at intervals, during or between production operations.

PROCESS INTERVENTION: any effort to alter the attitudes of members of an organization to promote the more successful accomplishment of goals.

PROCESSOR: any device able to carry out operations on data.

PROCURATION: the authority given to another to sign instruments and act on behalf of the person giving the procuration.

PROCUREMENT: the purchase of goods, for resale to a store's customers.

PRODUCE EXCHANGE: a spot market for such items as perishable agricultural products; a market in which future agricultural contracts are bought and sold.

PRODUCER: an individual who manufactures goods and services.

PRODUCER GOODS: items intended to be used and worn out in the course of producing other items in the future.

PRODUCT: goods and services made available to consumers.

PRODUCT ASSORTMENT: brands and types of items in a product class available to consumers.

PRODUCT CLASS: a group of items treated as natural substitutes and/or complements by most consumers.

PRODUCT DEVELOPMENT: the generation of new ideas for new or improved goods to be added to or to replace existing items.

PRODUCT DIFFERENTIATION: a marketing approach based on the creation and promotion of differences among similar items.

PRODUCTION: the creation of something capable of satisfying a need.

PRODUCTION CAPACITY: with available equipment, the maximum quantity of units that can be made in a stated period.

PRODUCTION CONTROL: the planning, routing, scheduling, dispatching, and inspection of operations of a given item being manufactured.

PRODUCTION COSTS: factory costs plus administrative expenses.

PRODUCTION DEPARTMENT: the people responsible for the conversion of copy and artwork into printed advertising material.

PRODUCTION FIT: the compatibility of a new product with established manufacturing equipment and processes.

PRODUCTION FUNCTION: use of the technical data that show the output of which specific input routines are capable.

PRODUCTION SHARING: condition under which a product is manufactured in one country, assembled in another, and marketed in a third.

PRODUCTION WORKERS: the employees engaged directly in manufacturing or operating processes.

PRODUCTIVE EFFICIENCY: point at which there is no possibility of increasing the yield of one item without decreasing the yield of another item.

PRODUCTIVITY: a measurement of the efficiency of production.

PRODUCTIVITY FACTOR: a union contract provision calling for periodic pay increases to compensate for continued increases in man-hour output by workers.

PRODUCT LIABILITY: liability imposed for damages caused by goods or products manufactured, sold, or distributed by the insured.

PRODUCT LIFE CYCLE: the six stages of market acceptance of any goods: pioneering, growth, maturity, saturation, decline, and abandonment.

PRODUCT LINE: the assortment of items presented by a firm or a group of items closely related.

PRODUCT MANAGER: an executive responsible for marketing approaches, such as promotion, pricing distribution, and establishing product characteristics.

PRODUCT MARKETS: markets in which firms sell the outputs that they produce.

PRODUCT MIX: the composite of items offered for sale by one company.

PRODUCT OBSOLESCENCE: loss of value or function due to replacement by an improved model or method.

PRODUCT PLANNING: the process leading to the identification of goals and procedures, as well as the precise nature of the merchandise to be marketed.

PRODUCT RELIABILITY: the probability of a product's performing a stated function, under specific conditions, for a specified period, without failure.

PROFESSION: an occupation that usually requires schooling to enable the professional person to render a service to society.

PROFESSIONAL MAGAZINE: a business magazine edited for and oriented to members of a profession, such as architects, doctors, lawyers, etc.

PROFILE ANALYSIS: a method for appraising individual uniqueness and characteristics, consisting of a search for patterns of behavior displayed by an individual.

PROFIT: the excess of income over expenditures during a period.

PROFITABILITY: the ability of a business to earn a profit and the extent of the profit it can earn.

PROFIT AND LOSS STATEMENT: a financial statement for a stated period showing sales, expenses, gross and net profit, and other details.

PROFIT CENTER: a unit of a business that is accountable for specific revenues and expenses.

PROFITEER: a person who takes advantage of a shortage of goods.

PROFIT MARGIN: the ratio of sales less all operating expenses, divided by the number of sales.

PROFIT SHARING: a plan under which an employer makes bonuses available to employees, either currently or on a deferred basis, based on the profit of the business.

PROFIT SQUEEZE: profit shrinkage resulting from stable prices and increasing costs.

PROFITS TAX: a tax on business profits, excluding income taxes.

PROFIT-TAKING: the process of converting paper profits into cash by selling the securities.

PROGRAM: a detailed sequence of instructions a computer performs in order to solve a problem.

PROGRAM BUDGETING: a long-range approach to budgetary decision-making that relates future expenditures to broadly defined objectives of the organization.

PROGRAMMER: a person who designs, writes, and tests computer programs.

PROGRAM MERCHANDISING: describing the combination of efforts of a retailer and a key source together to make merchandising and promotion plans for a store.

PROGRAMMING: in television, fitting programs and commercial announcements into time slots; in data processing, converting a problem into a series of steps for a computer.

PROGRESSIVE TAX: a tax in which the average amount payable increases with the size of the tax base.

PROHIBITED RISK: a line that an insurance company will not insure under any condition.

PROJECT: resources and activities used to achieve a specific set of objectives within a specified time schedule.

PROJECTIVE TECHNIQUE: observing a person's behavior to determine how he acts in situations that do not demand a particular response.

PROLETARIAT: the working class.

PROLIFERATION: diversified burgeoning growth.

PROMISSORY NOTE: an unconditional written promise to pay a certain sum of money, at a fixed place on demand or at a fixed or determinable future date.

PROMOTER: an individual who brings together those forming a business venture and those interested in backing the enterprise.

PROMOTION: stimulating the demand for goods by advertising or other events to attract attention; advancement to a position of higher rank.

PROMOTIONAL ALLOWANCE: payments given to a middleman by a manufacturer to pay for the middleman's promotion of goods.

PROMOTIONAL FIT: the compatibility of a new product with existing advertising approaches.

PROMOTIONAL MIX: the promotional efforts in the attempt to communicate with customers to sell a product.

PROOFREAD: to compare proof with original manuscript and correct all errors, both those in the original and those caused by not following text.

PROPERTY: the exclusive right or interest of a person in his or her belongings.

PROPERTY, INTANGIBLE: property that cannot be touched or that has no physical structure.

PROPERTY, PERSONAL: chattels, things in possession; everything owned except real estate.

PROPERTY, PUBLIC: real and personal property held by the government for eventual use or benefit of its population.

PROPERTY, REAL: land, including what is naturally growing on it, and any improvements made to the land, including structures.

PROPERTY, TANGIBLE: property that has a physical structure; items in possession.

PROPORTIONAL LAW: indicates the relationship between factors of production and the results of production.

PROPORTIONAL TAX: a tax whose percentage rate stays constant as the tax base increases.

PROPOSAL: a suggestion for an extension of time or a reduction in the amount of debt put forward to creditors by a debtor.

PROPRIETARY ACCOUNTS: accounts that show actual financial such as information as actual assets, liabilities, revenues, and expenditures.

PROPRIETARY COMPANY: the parent or holding company.

PROPRIETOR: sole owner.

PROPRIETORSHIP CERTIFICATE: a certificate filed with a bank showing the ownership of a privately owned business enterprise.

PRO RATA: in proportion (Latin).

PRORATE: to assign or assess proportionately, such as shares of stock in an oversubscribed offering in proportion to the number of shares bid for.

PROSECUTE: to institute or pursue a criminal proceeding or a suit for recovery of assets of which the plaintiff states he has been criminally deprived.

PROSPECT: a potential customer.

PROSPECTUS: a complex document issued by a corporation or promoter giving specific information about investment opportunities.

PROSPERITY: economic condition of high earnings, full employment, satisfactory prices and profits, high growth rate for industrial output, and high gross national product.

PRO TANTO: to that extent (Latin).

PROTECTIONISTS: people who favor high tariffs and other import restrictions to enable domestic items to compete more favorably with foreign items.

PROTECTIVE TARIFF: a type of tariff originally high enough to encourage infant native industries, now high enough to protect against foreign dumping.

PRO TEM: temporarily (Latin).

PROTOCOL: a formal code of etiquette.

PROTOTYPE: a working model or production model of a machine, goods, or even plan or idea, to be developed into a better later model.

PROVED RESERVES: amount of mineral deposits known to exist because exploratory sampling and assaying have given reliable indications of their extent and mineral content.

PROXIMATE CAUSE: the cause that leads to other causes; the factor responsible for any harm.

PROXIMATE DAMAGES: damages that are direct, immediate, and the result of negligence or wrong, and which might have been expected.

PROXY: a person with authority in writing to vote in the place of another; the instrument of proxy itself.

PROXY BATTLE: a contest between two or more factions in a corporation in which each faction seeks to gain control of enough proxies to enable it to win in a vote.

PROXY STATEMENT: printed information to be given to potential holders of securities traded on a national exchange, supplying minimum descriptions of the stock.

PRUDENT MAN: the rule of investing funds as would a prudent man, as legally required of banks, executors, trustees, and other fiduciaries.

PSYCHIC INCOME: a nonmonetary income regarded by an individual as desirable to fulfill his or her needs, wants, and psychological demands.

PSYCHOMETRIC: describing any quantitative measurement of an individual's psychological traits or assets.

PSYCHOMETRICIAN: a person skilled in administering and interpreting mental tests.

PSYCHOMETRICS: the study of mental testing.

PSYCHOMOTOR TESTS: tests of the motor skills of an individual in relation to his or her concomitant sensory and motor activities.

PUBLIC ADMINISTRATION: the use of individuals in federal, state, or local government agencies and the management of such groups.

PUBLIC ASSISTANCE: government assistance to the aged, the permanently and totally disabled, and families with dependent children.

PUBLICATION: anything published of which multiple copies are made and distributed or posted for public viewing, such as a newspaper.

PUBLIC CARRIER: individual or company offering to transport people or merchandise for a fee.

PUBLIC CONSUMPTION MONOPOLY: a governmental monopoly created to regulate the consumption of specific items that are considered harmful.

PUBLIC EMPLOYEE: usually, a worker who is employed by a federal, state, county, or municipal government.

PUBLIC INTEREST: a moral imperative resting on the assumption that there exists some collective overriding community or national good, and that this good should be served.

PUBLICITY: the communication of information usually favorable about a company or its products, through a medium without charge to the company.

PUBLIC MEMBER: the member of a tripartite fact-finding or other group who is not directly connected with the union or the employer.

PUBLIC POLICY: an official position in regard to a national concern or public interest which may lead to legislation and other changes in activity.

PUBLIC CORPORATION: a corporation whose shares are available to the public.

PUBLIC DEBT: that total or subtotal of the debt of any or all governments—federal, state, or local.

PUBLIC DOMAIN: embracing creative works not protected by copyright; embracing inventions unprotected by patent laws; government-owned property for public enjoyment, as national parks.

PUBLIC RELATIONS: good performance of a corporation, union, government, or other organization in the public interest to enhance its reputation in the public's eyes.

PUBLIC REVENUE: income received by a governmental agency.

PUBLIC SALE: a sale of property at a public auction.

PUBLIC SECTOR: the sector of an economy consisting of all government-owned institutions.

PUBLIC-SERVICE ADVERTISING: advertising not related to the marketing of products, but to social-betterment goals.

PUBLIC UTILITY: privately owned corporations engaged in supplying electricity, gas, telephone, water, and other services to the public.

PUBLIC WELFARE: economic assistance given to those in the population who are near or below the poverty level of subsistence.

PUBLIC WORKS: governmental agencies who provide public improvements, such as roads, parks, sewers, and other physical structures.

PUBLISH: to issue a regularly printed publication; to give public notification.

PUBLISHER'S REPRESENTATIVE: an independent organization or person that sells advertising space for a publication.

PUFFERY: exaggerated, misleading claims.

PULL: influential sponsorship.

PULL DATE: the date stamped on perishable products after which the items should not be sold.

PUMP PRIMING: a government making a once-and-for-all autonomous expenditure in an effort to create a self-sustaining increase in economic activity.

PUNCH: a perforation, as in a computer punched card or tape.

PUNCH CARD: a 3 × 7 inch card for punching and printing in a key punch machine for use as a unit of computer input.

PUNCHED TAPE: a tape on which a pattern of holes or cuts is used to represent data.

PUNCTUALITY: personal arrival in time to meet a commitment or appointment.

PUNT: slang, shares that will rarely turn out to be profitable.

PURCHASE ALLOWANCE: a lowering of the price of an item when the merchandise as requested does not meet the expectations as identified on the invoice.

PURCHASE CONTRACT: an agreement between a buyer and a seller, itemizing items and services that are bought and sold, respectively.

PURCHASE DISCOUNT: a reduction in the price of an order that has been paid promptly.

PURCHASE MONEY: monies paid to obtain ownership of property.

PURCHASE-MONEY MORTGAGE: a mortgage secured by property being sold and conveyed to the seller by the buyer at the time of sale in lieu of that part of the payment for the property stated on the mortgage.

PURCHASE ORDER: a form used to order goods or services.

PURCHASER: a buyer; a person who obtains title to or an interest in property by the act of purchase.

PURCHASING AGENT: a broker not on the staff of a company who acts as its agent in purchasing; sometimes the title of the head of the company's department of purchasing.

PURCHASING POWER: the value of money measured by the items it can buy.

PURCHASING POWER OF THE DOLLAR: ratio indicating what a dollar can buy now in comparison to what a dollar would buy at a different time chosen as a standard.

PURE COMPETITION: the market situation in which no one trader can materially affect the market price of a product.

PURE INTEREST: the price paid for the use of capital, not to include monies for risk and all other costs incurred because of the loan.

PURE-MARKET ECONOMY: a competitive economic system of numerous buyers and sellers, where prices are determined by the free interaction of supply and demand.

PURE PREMIUM: premium arrived at by dividing losses by exposure, and to which no loading has been added for commissions, taxes, and expenses.

PURE PUBLIC ITEM: an item consumed in equal amount by all people, even though the item may have different value to these people.

PURE RISKS: the dangers and hazards involved in accident, fire, health, weather, or other potential perils to people.

PURPOSIVE SAMPLE: a small number of observations or subjects chosen from a larger population on a basis of some given characteristic.

PUSH MONEY: commission for retail clerks who are successful in selling specified goods; a type of incentive system.

PUT: a transferable option to sell a given number of shares of a particular stock at a stated price during a particular period of time.

PUTS: an option contract that entitles the holder to sell a number of shares of the underlying stock at a stated price on or before a fixed expiration date.

PUTS AND CALLS: options that give the right to buy or sell a fixed amount of certain stock at a specified price within a specified time.

PYRAMID: to purchase increasing lots of stock on a rising market by hypothecating the securities previously purchased as collateral.

PYRAMIDING: employing profits of open or unliquidated positions to add to the holder's original position.

PYRAMID RATIO: a tool used in the analysis of management and income ratio by the relationship of profits and capital.

PYRAMID SELLING: a method of selling under which a central organization recruits a small number of regional organizers, who in turn recruit a number of subdistributors, who in turn recruit salesmen, who end up selling the goods.

Q

QUADRANT: a quarter of area; in graphs; circles; charts; a quarter part.

QUALIFIED ACCEPTANCE: a counter offer to another's original offer.

QUALIFIED ENDORSEMENT: an endorsement that releases an endorser from all responsibility in the event of nonpayment or nonacceptance of an instrument.

QUALIFIED PROSPECT: a potential customer who is able to buy a product and has the authority to make a decision to purchase.

QUALIFYING SHARE: a share of a corporation held by an individual in order to qualify as a director.

QUALITATIVE FACTOR: a factor that is of significance but cannot be measured precisely and easily.

QUALITY CONTROL: product inspections, machine improvement, assembly-line adjustment, and amelioration of working conditions.

QUALITY MARKET: a market for whom the quality is more important than the price.

QUALITY OF ESTATE: the form in which an estate is to be owned, including type of possession and time.

QUANTITATIVE ANALYSIS: examination that seeks to quantify the information relevant to a decision and to determine a mathematical solution for the decision.

QUANTITATIVE FACTOR: a factor that affects the making of a decision and can be measured numerically.

QUANTITY DISCOUNT: a percentage reduction for purchasing a stated quantity.

QUANTITY THEORY OF MONEY: the belief that prices are related directly to the quantity of money in circulation.

QUANTITY VARIANCE: the standard price for a given resource, multiplied by the difference between the actual quantity used and the total standard quantity allowed for the units of goods produced.

QUARTERLY: a quarter of a year; every three months.

QUARTER STOCK: stock with a par value of $25 for each share.

QUASI-CONTRACT: an obligation similar to a contract, but imposed by law so as to prevent injustice.

QUASI-CORPORATION: a political subdivision such as an unincorporated town that operates in the manner of an incorporated municipality.

QUASI-PUBLIC CORPORATION: an incorporated organization that is privately operated but in which some general interest of the public is evident.

QUESTIONNAIRE: a set of questions seeking objective data or subjective opinion on a given subject.

QUEUE: a line or group of items or people in a system waiting for service.

QUICK ASSETS: assets readily convertible into cash, including cash on hand and in banks, and accounts receivable.

QUICK-FREEZE: a method of food-processing in which rapid lowering of temperature causes the formation of ice crystals too small to rupture cell walls on thawing.

QUICK RATIO: the ratio between existing liabilities and quick assets; shows a firm's ability to pay off its liabilities.

QUICK RATION: the ratio of the total cash, accounts receivable, and marketable securities to current liabilities.

QUID PRO QUO: something for something (Latin).

QUIESCING: a process of bringing a device or a system to a halt by rejection of new requests for work.

QUIET ENJOYMENT: uninterrupted use and possession.

QUIETING TITLE: removing a cloud from a title by a proper action in court.

QUIET-TITLE SUIT: a legal action to remove a defect or any questionable claim against the title to property.

QUITCLAIM: a release.

QUITCLAIM DEED: a deed by which the owner of real estate conveys to another title or interest, but which makes no representation that the property is free from encumbrances.

QUIT RENT: the last rental payment made by a tenant before leaving the property.

QUITTANCE: discharge from a debt.

QUORUM: the number of persons who must legally be present at a meeting in order to effectively transact business.

QUOTA: an assigned quantity or share, as of a sales objective.

QUOTA RULE: a union regulation establishing the number of workers who are to be hired for a particular job within the union's jurisdiction.

QUOTA SAMPLING: a sampling technique in which interviewers look for specific numbers of candidates with special characteristics.

QUOTA-SHARE REINSURANCE: an agreement by which the reinsurer accepts a stated percentage of a risk written by an insurance company.

QUOTATION: the citation or publishing of current prices of securities or commodities; a price on merchandise stated in response to an inquiry.

QUOTE: to name current prices.

QUOTED PRICE: the stated price of a security or commodity.

R

RACK: term used to describe the "rack department," which sorts, distributes, and proves items in the commercial operations of the bank.

RACKET: any shady, dishonest, or illegal method of exploitation for money.

RACKETEERING: the practice of unethical and extortionate use of power or violence to obtain an advantage.

RACK JOBBER: a wholesaler serving retail stores, who offers a complete service in the merchandising and inventory of certain items.

RACK MERCHANDISING: retail display of merchandise on racks or in similar ways convenient for self-service.

RACK RENT: a very high contract rent for a property which equals or exceeds the economic rent of the property.

RADIAL TRANSFER: a procedure for the transfer of data between peripheral equipment and the internal memory of the machine.

RADIATION SELLING: utilizing a specific sale as a starting point for other, future related sales based on the first sale as the example of need.

RADIO RATE: the charge for a unit of commercial broadcasting time made by a radio station or network.

RAG BUSINESS: the sentimental name given to the fashion-apparel industry.

RAID: a deliberate attempt to depress the market price of a stock; one union's attempt to enroll members from another union.

RAILS: railroad companies; per share prices of railroad company stocks as quoted on stock exchanges.

RAISE: an increase in salary, price, or rental rate.

RAISED CHECK: one on which the amount has been fraudulently increased.

RALLY: to recover from a decline, as stock prices.

RANDOM: haphazard, by chance; in sampling, referring to the equal chance for selection of every unit in the universe.

RANDOM ACCESS: the ability to extract information from computer storage without the necessity of searching through the stored information to obtain the data.

RANDOM NUMBERS: a series of numbers obtained by chance.

RANDOM PROCESSING: the arbitrary treatment of data without respect to its location in external storage.

RANDOM SAMPLE: a sample in which all the elements have been drawn according to the laws of chance.

RANGE: between specified limits, as between 18 and 65 years of age.

RANK: to arrange in an ascending or descending series according to importance; a title or position in an organization; the rating from high to low.

RANK-AND-FILE: the body of workers, as distinguished from management.

RAPPORT: the relationship, accord, and balance between two people.

RATABLE: proportionate, such as ratable distribution of wealth.

RATE: to categorize and rank in terms of special qualities or properties; the cost of a unit of insurance; a charge, fee, or price.

RATE CARD: standard charges for advertising.

RATE CUTTING: a unilateral wage rate reduction by an employer in the absence of changes in job content.

RATE DISCRIMINATION: charging different prices for almost identical services.

RATEHOLDER: an advertisement of the smallest size acceptable to the publisher to earn a frequency discount.

RATE OF EXCHANGE: the ratio at which foreign currency exchanges for a domestic currency.

RATE OF INFLATION: the average percentage rate of increase of the price of money, weighted and stated in annual terms.

RATE OF INTEREST: the charge for borrowing money.

RATE SETTING: the establishment of rates by agreement between labor and management or by an employer alone.

RATE VARIANCE: the difference between actual wages paid and the standard wage rate, multiplied by the total actual hours of direct labor used.

RATE WAR: a negative form of competition; sellers drop their prices below their costs for purposes of putting the competition out of business.

RATIFY: to confirm or approve.

RATING: classification according to credit standing; a standard of television circulation; comparative grading of success.

RATING BUREAUS: organizations that develop suggested rates for a substantial proportion of the fire-insurance business.

RATIO: a comparison of two numerical values of the same classification, particularly the ratio of assets to liabilities.

RATIONAL BUYING MOTIVES: all costs of money, use, labor, and profit that affect a purchaser.

RATIONALIZATION: any approach that has the potential to increase efficiency or output.

RATIONING: a technique for limiting the purchase or usage of an item when the quantity demanded of the item exceeds the quantity available.

RAW DATA: data that have not been processed or reduced.

RAW LAND: land that has not been subdivided into lots, and does not have water, sewers, streets, utilities, or other improvements.

RAW MATERIAL: material acquired for the purpose of being changed in form or consumed in a manufacturing process.

RAW-MATERIALS INVENTORY: the items purchased by a manufacturing firm to be used in production.

RE: in the matter of (Latin).

REACTION: a drop in securities prices following a sustained period of increasing prices.

REACTION TIME: tests that measure the speed of an individual's response to a stimulus.

READER: a device that converts information in one form of storage to information in another form of storage.

READ-ONLY: a type of access to data that allows them to be read but not modified.

READ-PROCESS-WRITE: to read in one block of data, while simultaneously processing the preceding block and writing out the results of the previously processed block.

READ-WRITE HEAD: a small electromagnet used for reading, recording, or erasing polarized spots on a magnetic surface.

READY CONDITION: the status of a task that is to be analyzed by the central-processing unit.

READY FOR CAMERA: commercial art completely assembled with lettering, type, borders, etc., ready for photographing for plate-making purposes.

REAL EARNINGS: earnings adjusted to exclude the effects of price change.

REAL ESTATE: immovable property, such as land and buildings.

REAL ESTATE INVESTMENT TRUST: an investment company that specializes in mortgages and/or in real estate property.

REAL ESTATE MARKET: the purchasing and selling of real property which establishes a supply-and-demand situation, resulting in the creation of market values and prices.

REAL INCOME: the sum total of the purchasing power of a nation or individual.

REAL INTEREST RATE: the rate at which a person earns future purchasing power on monetary assets.

REAL INVESTMENT: an expenditure that establishes a new capital asset, thus creating a new capital formation.

REALIZATION: conversion into cash, as by sale, particularly of fixed assets or property.

REAL MONEY: money containing one or more metals having intrinsic value.

REAL PRICE: the price of goods and services measured by the quantity of manpower needed to earn sufficient money to purchase the goods or services.

REAL PROPERTY: land, buildings, and other improvements to property that may legally be classified as real, in contrast to personal.

REAL TIME: the actual time during which a physical process transpires.

REALTOR: a real estate agent who is a member of a real estate board.

REALTY: the contracted form of "real property."

REAL VALUE OF MONEY: the price of money measured in terms of goods.

REAL WAGES: the current purchasing power of wages, in terms of goods, as compared with a previous base period.

REAM: 500 sheets of paper; to machine an existing hole in metal to a larger diameter.

REAPPORTIONMENT: the allocation of operating costs between the service and production departments in proportion to the relative benefits received.

REAPPRAISAL: term applied when property is appraised a second time.

REASONABLE: moderate, as a reasonable price; responsible, as reasonable care; fair, as a reasonable person.

REASONABLE VALUE: value placed on property that parallels the existing market value.

REASSESSMENT: the result of a change in the assessed value of property or reappraisal of property.

REBATE: the return of part of a payment for goods or services, in contrast to a discount, which is deducted in advance.

REBATING: the illegal and unethical practice of selling a policy at less than the legal rate, or allowing the insured a refund of the premium.

REBUTTABLE PRESUMPTION: a presumption that is not conclusive; it may be contradicted by evidence.

RECALL: the return to work of laid-off workers; the return of a distributed product for purposes of adjustment, repair, or other necessary work.

RECAPITALIZATION: altering the capital structure of a firm by increasing or decreasing its capital stock.

RECAPITULATION: a concise summary.

RECAPTURE CLAUSE: a clause in a commercial lease giving the landlord the right to terminate the lease if certain conditions are not met.

RECASTING A MORTGAGE: reconstructing an existing mortgage by increasing its amount, interest rate, or time period.

RECEIPT: a document acknowledging the delivery and acceptance of goods or documents signed or initialed by the recipient.

RECEIVABLES: accounts receivable, notes receivable, accrued income receivable, etc.

RECEIVER: a person appointed by a court or a creditor to take charge of property pending the final decision of the matter either in the courts or by payment in full.

RECEIVERSHIP: bankruptcy.

RECEIVING: the process by which a computer obtains a message from a line.

RECEIVING APRON: a statement used in the receiving department of a store; it contains all pertinent data concerning an incoming shipment.

RECEPTIONIST: a person employed to greet and announce visitors or clients, often doubling as a switchboard operator or typist.

RECESSION: that portion of the business cycle marked by decline of employment, inventories, rate of capital investment, savings, and prices.

RECIPROCAL DEMAND: the situation created when one person offers what another person desires, and vice versa.

RECIPROCAL LAW: state laws providing for equal privileges to all alien insurers, as accorded domestic insurers in alien states.

RECIPROCAL TRADE AGREEMENT: a mutual adjustment of customs duties by negotiation between two governments.

RECIPROCITY: a form of tariff agreement under which nations agree to extend to each other any reduction in import tariffs made by one of them.

RECLAMATION: treatment of lands to increase usefulness, as reclamation of swampland; salvaging and processing of waste materials.

RECOGNITION: an acceptance or acknowledgment, such as an employer agreeing to have a collective-bargaining agent for his employees.

RECOMMENDATION: a favorable opinion; a suggestion or advice.

RECOMPENSE: to compensate for services performed or damages suffered; monetary compensation; pay.

RECONCILIATION: comparing and bringing into agreement a depositor's bank statement with his own record of transactions.

RECONDITIONING PROPERTY: improving a property's value by repairing it or making changes to enhance it.

RECONSIGNMENT: any alteration, including a route change, made in a consignment before the items have arrived at their billed destination.

RECONVERSION: following a war, the shift of a nation's economy from war efforts to a focus on peacetime needs and goals.

RECONVEYANCE: a conveyance to the landowner of the title held by a trustee under a deed of trust.

RECOOPERAGE: the repair of damaged containers.

RECORD: on magnetic tape, the data between inter-record gaps.

RECORD, UNIT: a single card containing one complete record.

RECORDATION: the public acknowledgment in written form that a lien exists against a specific property that is identified in a mortgage.

RECORD DATE: the date on which a person must be registered on the books of a corporation as a shareholder in order to receive benefits.

RECOUP: to cover an outlay through sale, use, or charge to profit and loss; to realize.

RECOURSE: the right to require payment by a guarantor or endorser of a note or other instrument of indebtedness when the maker fails to meet the obligation.

RECOVERABLE ERROR: an error that allows continued execution of a computer program.

RECOVERY: an increase in business activity after a recession.

RECRUITMENT: the policies and practices of a firm in seeking, attracting, evaluating, and hiring new personnel.

RECURSIVE: pertaining to a process in which each step makes use of the results of earlier steps.

RECYCLING: for the purpose of reducing pollution, saving money, and/or conserving resources, the conversion of waste products to usable material.

REDEEMABLE RENT: payments of rent that can be recovered.

REDEEMABLE STOCK: a class of capital stock which can be redeemed at the option of the corporation.

REDEMISE: to renew a lease.

REDEMPTION: the liquidation of an indebtedness, on or before maturity; purchasing back.

REDEMPTION FUND: a fund created for the purpose of retiring an obligation.

REDEMPTION PERIOD: the time allowed by law during which the owner may redeem his property.

REDEMPTION PRICE: the price at which a bond may be redeemed before maturity; the amount a company must pay to call in certain types of preferred stock.

REDEPLOYMENT: the reassignment and accompanying training of employees, resulting from changing technology, equipment, or business decisions requiring new skills.

RED HERRING: slang, a prospectus for a new issue or secondary offering of securities; the raising of an extraneous issue to divert attention.

REDISCOUNT: the resale of a promissory note or bill of exchange by one who has bought such a document; the seller must pay a charge in advance.

REDISCOUNT RATE: the rate set by the Federal Reserve Bank for discounting a second time monies offered by their district member banks.

REDISTRIBUTION OF INCOME: a government policy under which large incomes are reduced through progressive taxation of income and wealth.

RED LABEL: a shipping label indicating flammable contents.

RED LEAD: a red pigment used in paint for preserving iron and steel.

REDLINING: the difficulty of obtaining loans and insurance from certain lending institutions.

REDRAFT: a draft on the drawer of a protested bill of exchange for the amount of the bill plus charges and costs.

RED TAPE: regulations and restrictions resulting in the requirement of complicated procedures for getting things done.

REDUCTION: decrease in price; any decrease; a deoxidation process in smelting by which ores are reduced to metals.

REDUNDANCY CHECK: an automatic or programmed check based on the systematic insertion of components or characters used especially for checking purposes.

REEFER: a refrigerated container.

REEL: a mounting for a roll of computer tape.

REEMPLOYMENT: bringing a laid-off employee back to work.

REENTRY: a landlord's right to reacquire lease property if terms in the lease are not satisfied.

REEXPORT: to export already imported items without duty charges, in basically similar form, to a third country.

REFEREE IN BANKRUPTCY: an officer of a US District Court who controls the actions of a receiver or a debtor in possession.

REFERENCE CYCLE: the sequence of expanding and contracting in the general business activity.

REFERENDUM: a vote by the rank-and-file members of a union.

REFERENT POWER: the influence exerted on a subordinate who identifies with his or her superior's style and personality.

REFERRAL LEADS: names of potential customers given to a sales representative by individuals, usually satisfied customers.

REFERRAL RISKS: risks beyond the underwriting authority of an office, which must be referred to a supervisory office for a decision on acceptance.

REFINANCE: to extend existing financing or to acquire new monies; to revise a payment timetable, and, frequently, to modify interest charges on the obligation.

REFINANCED LOAN: a loan that has had an addition to the principal balance.

REFLATION: upon recovering from a depression or a recession, the period during which prices are returned to the level they had attained during a period of prosperity.

REFORMATION: an action to correct a mistake in a deed or other document.

REFUNDABLE INTEREST: the unearned portion of interest previously charged that will be returned to the debtor if the indebtedness is liquidated prior to maturity.

REFUND CHECK: a check or other instrument of currency that is a repayment of money for any reason.

REFUNDING: redemption of an obligation by new borrowing.

REFUNDING MORTGAGEE: refinancing a mortgage with monies derived from a new loan.

REFUSAL TO SELL: the right of a seller to choose the dealers that will handle his or her merchandise.

REGIONAL DIFFERENTIAL: among broad geographical subdivisions, the difference in prevailing wages for equal work.

REGIONAL DISTRIBUTION: marketing channels that are established for product sales or magazine circulations by regions.

REGIONAL STORE: a branch store

usually located far from the central store, which functions under the name of the parent store.

REGISTER: the making of a permanent record of events; a device capable of storing a specified amount of data

REGISTERED BOND: a bond that is entered on the books of the issuing company in the name of the owner.

REGISTERED CHECK: the title given to a check used in parts of the United States in lieu of cashier's checks or bank drafts.

REGISTERED MAIL: mail recorded in a US Post Office at its mailing and at each successive point of transmission, to guarantee special care in delivery.

REGISTERED REPRESENTATIVE (TRADER): a full-time employee of a stock exchange member organization, who acts as a broker for customers.

REGISTRAR: the person responsible for the maintenance of a corporation's shareholders' and bondholders' records.

REGISTRATION: process required for securities before a public offering may be made of new securities or of outstanding securities by controlling stockholders.

REGISTRY: a listing by a country of ships that fly its flag and are under the regulation of its maritime law.

REGRESSION, MULTIPLE: an analysis program for determining the mathematical relationships and relative significances of boundaries for a particular problem.

REGRESSION ANALYSIS: a method for predicting the values of a quantitative variable from scores of a correlated variable.

REGRESSION EQUATION: a formula for computing the most probable value of one variable, y, from the known value of another variable, x.

REGRESSION LINE: the curve or line that depicts the relationship between two variables.

REGRESSIVE SUPPLY: the market situation in which quantity offered increases as price decreases; farm production tends to do this.

REGRESSIVE TAX: a tax whose average rate declines as the tax base increases.

REGS: regulations.

REGULAR DATING: the terms of a sale under which the period for discount and the date on which payment is due are determined from the date of the invoice.

REGULAR DIVIDEND: a dividend that has been declared at an interval and in an amount customary for the company.

REGULATED INVESTMENT COMPANY: an investment company that can avoid income tax on its ordinary income and capital gains by conforming to statutory rules.

REGULATION: a governmental decree, directive, or rule exercising control over industry practices.

REGULATION Q: the Federal Reserve Board's interest limits on what covered commercial banks pay to their depositors on time deposits.

REHYPOTHECATE: to pledge a second time.

REINSTATE: to place again in a position, as to reinstate a person in a position of responsibility or trust from which he had been suspended, or to reinstate a lapsed insurance policy.

REINSURANCE: the act of an insurance company in farming out part of a large risk to one or more other companies in order to lessen its own risk.

REINSURANCE BROKER: an organization that places reinsurance through a reinsurance underwriter.

REINVEST: to use the proceeds from dividends and sales of securities to purchase the same or other securities.

REINVESTMENT PRIVILEGE: the automatic investment in additional shares from dividends of holdings in a mutual fund.

RELATIONSHIP BY OBJECTIVE: a group-dynamics approach, used primarily in labor-management relations.

RELATIVE ADDRESS: a number used in the address part of a computer instruction to specify a required location.

152

*RELATIVE-
INCOME
CONCEPT •*

*REPEAT
DEMAND*

RELATIVE-INCOME CONCEPT: the hypothesis that spending is a function of a family's relative place in the income distribution of similar family units.

RELEASE: to free, as from obligations; a legal instrument renouncing a claim to possession.

RELEASE CLAUSE: a clause in a mortgage permitting payment of a part of the debt in order that a proportionate part of the property can be freed.

RELEASE OF MORTGAGE: dropping a claim against property established by a mortgage.

RELET: to lease property again after a lease has been terminated or broken.

RELIABILITY: the probability that a device will function without failure over a specified period or until a given amount of usage, accuracy and dependability.

RELIABILITY ENGINEERING: a structural technique for achieving maximum product reliability.

RELOCATE: to move a routine from one portion of storage to another and to adjust the necessary address references; to move from one geographic area to another.

REMAND: the action of an appellate court in sending a cause back to the lower court that sought the appeal, accompanied by the instructions of the higher court.

REMARGINING: placing added margin against a loan.

REMEDIAL LOANS: loans made to consumers in amounts up to some relatively low maximum, such as $600.

REMEMBRANCE ADVERTISING: business gifts of nominal value, frequently imprinted with the donor's name and serving to remind the donee of the donor.

REMISE: to give or grant back; to discharge or release; synonymous with quitclaim.

REMITTANCE: transmittal of money, checks, etc., especially in payment for value received; the money or its equal so sent.

REMONETIZATION: the reinstatement of a coin as standard money after it has been demonetized.

REMOTE ACCESS: communication with a data-processing facility by one or more stations that are distant from that facility.

REMOTE DELIVERY: path of sending goods from a central warehouse to customers via area delivery stations located in the suburbs, or by truck.

REMUNERATIONS: wages and other financial benefits received from employment.

RENEGOTIATE: to seek to pay a lower price for delivered goods or completed services than originally agreed.

RENEWABLE NATURAL RESOURCES: natural resources that maintain their productivity over time.

RENEWABLE TERM INSURANCE: life insurance issued with an option to renew the policy without medical examination for additional five-year periods.

RENEWAL: extending the maturity of an existing loan obligation, or other document of relationship.

RENEWAL CERTIFICATE: document by which an insurance policy is sometimes renewed rather than writing out a new policy.

RENT: income received from leasing real estate.

RENTIER: a person living on income received from fixed investments.

RENT ROLL: all rents receivable from an estate.

RENUNCIATION: giving up a right or claim, without any reservation, or without naming the person who is to assume the title.

REOPENER CLAUSE: a provision calling for the reopening of a current contract at a specified time for negotiations on stated subjects.

REORGANIZATION: the altering of a firm's capital structure, often resulting from a merger, which affects the rights and responsibilities of the owners.

REPATRIATION: the transfer of capital from foreign countries back to one's home country.

REPEAT DEMAND: the demand

created for items that are frequently requested and bought.

REPERTORY GRID: a marketing technique ascertaining the characteristics of product similarities and differences under varied use contexts.

REPETITION INSTRUCTION: an instruction to a computer that causes one or more instructions to be executed an indicated number of times.

REPLACEMENT COST: cost in today's market for new equipment to replace existing equipment, regardless of the age of the existing equipment.

REPLACEMENT-COST INSURANCE: insurance providing for replacement of damaged property without deduction for depreciation.

REPLACEMENT-COST STANDARD: the cost of replacing equipment with new equipment for tasks identical to those performed by worn or obsolete equipment.

REPLACEMENT DEMAND: capital goods or consumer items that are in demand because of depreciation or obsolescence.

REPLEVIN: a legal action to recover goods wrongfully taken, in situations where damages are not satisfactory.

REPLICATION: the repetition of methods by which evidence is gathered.

REPORT: to render an account of a happening; to appear as instructed at a particular place or before a stated person.

REPORT GENERATION: a technique for producing complete machine reports from information that describes the input file and the format and content of the output report.

REPORTING FORM: an insurance policy designed for use when values of the insured property fluctuate during the policy term.

REPORTING PAY: the minimum wage that is guaranteed under union contract if an employee who is scheduled to work is given nothing to do.

REPOSITORY: a depository.

REPOSSESSION: the physical reacquisition of an asset sold on the installment plan for failure on the part of the debtor to meet an installment on time.

REPRESENTATION: acting for an employer or as agent for a principal, frequently as a salesman on the premises of a buyer.

REPRESENTATION ELECTION: a vote to determine whether a majority of the workers in an established unit want to be represented by a given union.

REPRESENTATIVE MONEY: paper money secured by monetary metal deposited in the treasury of a country; funds that are backed in full by a commodity.

REPRESSIVE TAX: a tax that discourages production; its effect is to lower potential taxable income.

REPRODUCER: a device used for duplicating cards and card data or for punching cards in any format.

REPRODUCTION: any printing or duplicating process that makes facsimilies from an original.

REPROGRAPHICS: all the processes, techniques, and equipment used in the multiple copying or reproduction of documents.

REPUDIATION: the intentional and willful refusal to pay a debt in whole or in part.

REPURCHASE AGREEMENT: an agreement between the seller and buyer that the seller will buy back property.

REPUTATION: the opinion in which a company is held, upon which depends its public approval, acceptance of its products, credit standing, etc.

REPUTED OWNER: an individual appearing to be a property owner, although in fact the property belongs to another person.

REQUIRED RESERVES: liquid assets that state-chartered banks must hold in accordance with regulations of state banking agencies and Federal Reserve officials.

REQUIRED RETURN: the lowest return or profit needed to justify an investment.

REQUIREMENT: a qualification, standard; need.

REQUISITION: to make an authorized request formally, as by interoffice form, to a purchase or supply department.

RERUN: a repeat of a machine run, usually because of a correction, an interruption, or a false start.

RESALE: sale of goods purchased for that purpose.

RESALE-PRICE MAINTENANCE: a supplier's control over the selling price of his goods during distribution by means of contractual arrangement.

RESCIND: to void or cancel a contract or a term thereof, as if the object of the rescision had never existed.

RESCISSION: making void or annulling.

RESCUE DUMP: recording on magnetic tape of the entire memory information.

RESEARCH AND DEVELOPMENT: applying the findings of science and technology to create a firm's products or services.

RESERVATION PRICE: the highest offered price at which a seller will continue to hold back from selling.

RESERVE: an amount appropriated for accounting purposes from retained earnings or other surplus for a specific or general purpose.

RESERVE BID: in an auction, a price below which the auctioneer is not permitted to sell an item.

RESERVE FOR BAD DEBTS: same as allowance for bad debts.

RESERVE REQUIREMENT: the percentage of a bank's checking and savings accounts that must be kept in the bank or as deposits at the local Federal Reserve District Bank.

RESERVE-STOCK CONTROL: a technique for earmarking appropriate stock for the maintenance of business until new merchandise is purchased.

RESHIPPER: a shipping container in which empty containers, intended to be used again, are received.

RESIDENT BUYER: any person or firm located in a market area who aids retailers in making market contacts and assists in their purchasing.

RESIDUAL: a fee paid to an individual for repeated broadcast or transmission of a performance in which he or she originally participated.

RESIDUAL ERROR: the difference between the expected result from theory and an optimum result derived from experiment.

RESIDUARY: participating in the residue, as a residuary legatee in a will.

RESIDUARY BEQUEST: the part of a will that gives instruction for the disposal of any portion of an estate remaining after payment of debts and other obligations.

RESIDUARY DEVISEE: a recipient by will of any real property after all other claimants to the estate have received payment.

RESIDUARY ESTATE: what remains of an estate after all bequests and devises have been executed according to the will.

RESIDUARY LEGACY: personal property of an estate remaining after all claims to the estate have been properly disposed of.

RESIDUE: in the language of wills, the property of a deceased after all expenses of administration and all specific bequests have been paid.

RESIGNATION: a step taken by an employee to terminate a relationship with an employer.

RESIN: a stock sap secretion of pines and other conifers having wide chemical application in plastics and paints.

RES IPSA LOQUITUR: the thing speaks for itself (Latin).

RES JUDICATA: a case already settled (Latin).

RESOLUTION: a document expressing the will or resolve of a body of people and carrying the authority of that body.

RESOURCE: raw materials, as minerals, timber, etc.; a retailer's supplier of a particular class of merchandise; wealth.

RESPONDENT: defendant in a suit in equity; the side opposite the appellant in an appeal from the judgment of a court of law.

RESPONDENTIA: under conditions of hypothecation, the security offered against a loan.

RESPONSE TIME: the interval between the submission of an item of work to a computing system and the return of results.

RESPONSIBILITY: a duty or obligation that is performed reliably and creditably.

RESPONSIBILITY ACCOUNTING: a system under which someone is held responsible for each activity occurring in a particular area of a firm's activity.

RESTING ORDER: an order that can remain open or good until canceled.

RESTITUTION: the enforced payment of money, or its equivalent, to its rightful owner as established by law.

RESTORATION PREMIUM: the premium charged to restore a policy or bond to its original value after payment of a loss.

REST PERIOD: a brief paid interruption of the working schedule.

RESTRAINING ORDER: a court order in aid of a suit to maintain the status quo until all parties can be heard from.

RESTRAINT OF TRADE: an action deemed by authority to interfere with the rights of others, such as a demand to refuse to handle competitive products.

RESTRICTED SHARES: common stock released under an arrangement whereby they do not rank for dividends until some event has taken place.

RESTRICTED SURPLUS: part of retained surplus not available for common-stock dividends.

RESTRICTION: a limiting clause in a contract, resolution, regulation, or law.

RESTRICTIVE COVENANTS: written agreements limiting the use of property.

RESTRICTIVE LICENSE: an agreement under which an owner of a patented item allows a licensee to sell his patented goods under certain conditions.

RÉSUMÉ: an outline of one's business aspirations, business history, education, skills, and job qualifications, used as an aid by a person seeking employment.

RETAILER: a merchant whose primary activity is to sell directly to consumers.

RETAILING: store operation, buying, pricing, storage, display, advertising, selling, delivery, and financing of merchandise sold to consumers.

RETAIL METHOD OF INVENTORY: an accounting technique for recording all inventory inputs at their retail values; purchased items are recorded at cost.

RETAIL OUTLET: any store that sells directly to the customer.

RETAIL PRICE: the price at which goods are identified for sale or are sold.

RETAIL-PRICE MAINTENANCE: allowing a manufacturer, under protection of state law, to set retail prices for his products.

RETAIL SALESPERSON: an individual who works inside a store, where customers come to him.

RETAINED EARNINGS: the accumulated balance of profits less losses of a corporation, as adjusted for dividends.

RETAINED RISK: a stated risk or property that is covered by an insurance firm on its own account, after some of the coverage has been reinsured.

RETAINER: an advance fee paid to a lawyer by a client for the right to use his services, but not for the services.

RETALIATORY DUTY: a differential duty designed to penalize foreign nations for alleged discriminatory commerce activity or to force them to making trade concessions.

RETENTION: the amount of liability retained by the company on a given risk.

RETIREMENT FUND: monies set aside by an organization for its employees to receive income from it when they retire.

RETIREMENT INCOME: a stipulated amount of income starting at selected retirement age.

RETIREMENT PLAN: a plan under which a person may draw pension payments from a company after his retirement from it.

RETIRING A BILL: paying a bill of exchange on its due date or beforehand, at a discount.

RETREAT: to draw back; a private, resort-type meeting place for executives and company guests supported by company funds.

RETROACTIVE: affecting previous transactions.

RETROACTIVE PAY: a delayed wage payment for work done when employees were being paid at a lower rate for the same work.

RETROACTIVE RESTORATION: a provision in a policy or bond whereby, after payment of a loss, the original amount of coverage is automatically restored.

RETROCESSION: condition whereby a reinsuring organization cedes (i.e., reinsures) a portion of a reinsurance transaction.

RETURN: a statement of financial and related information required by government tax agencies.

RETURN ITEM: a negotiable instrument, principally a check, that has been sent by one bank to another for collection and payment and is returned unpaid to the sending bank.

RETURN ON INVESTMENT: annual interest rate; yield per annum; the sum of interest plus repayment of principal per annum.

RETURN ON NET WORTH: the ratio of an organization's net profit following taxes to its net worth, providing a measure of the rate of return on the shareholders' investment.

RETURN ON TOTAL ASSETS: the ratio of an organization's net profit following taxes to its total assets.

RETURN PREMIUM: the amount due the insured if a policy is reduced in rate, reduced in amount, or canceled.

RETURNS AND ALLOWANCES: the accounting record of merchandise returned by customers or reduced in price to them, appearing as deductions from sales.

RETURNS TO VENDOR: goods sent to the vendor by a store for a wide variety of reasons.

REVALUATION: the restoration of the value of a depreciated national currency that has previously been devalued.

REVENUE: income.

REVENUE FREIGHT: a local or interline shipment from which earnings go to the carrier on the basis of tariff rates.

REVENUE SHARING: the return by a larger unit of government, with greater taxing powers, of a part of its revenue to a smaller component of government.

REVENUE STAMPS: adhesive stamps issued by the federal or state government, which must be purchased and affixed.

REVENUE TARIFFS: duties placed on imports with the goal of increasing revenues rather than protecting domestic industries.

REVENUE WAYBILL: a written description showing a shipment's charges and goods.

REVERSE SPLIT: the issuance of one share of new stock in exchange for more than one of old.

REVERSE TAKEOVER: a term usually applied to a situation in which ownership of a larger company is acquired by a smaller company.

REVERSION: the return of an estate to the grantor after a particular interest.

REVOCATION: nullification or cancellation or withdrawal, such as revocation of an offer to sell or an offer to buy a parcel of property.

REVOLVING CREDIT: an arrangement that permits a purchaser to charge purchases against an account every month, provided the balance does not exceed a predetermined credit limit.

REVOLVING FUND: a fund from which monies are continuously expended, refunded, and again expended.

REVOLVING LOAN: a loan that is automatically renewed (upon maturity) without additional negotiation.

REWARD POWER: perception of a subordinate that to comply with the wishes of his superior will result in monetary or psychological rewards.

RICARDIAN THEORY OF RENT: theory that differences in rent result from differences in the productivity of land.

RIDER: something added to a contract.

RIG: any combination of truck, tractor, and semitrailer, or truck and full trailer.

RIGGED MARKET: the situation that exists when purchases and sales are manipulated to distort a normal supply and demand price.

RIGHT OF ACTION: the right to enforce a claim in court.

RIGHT OF POSSESSION: a right that one has to real property even when the person is not in physical possession of it.

RIGHT OF REDEMPTION: the right to free a property from foreclosure by paying off all debts.

RIGHT OF RESCISSION: the privilege to cancel a contract under certain circumstances within three business days, without penalty and with full refund.

RIGHT OF SURVIVORSHIP: the right establishing a surviving joint owner as holder of the title to the property jointly owned.

RIGHT-OF-WAY: the right of one person to pass over another's land.

RIGHTS: opportunity extended by a company that wants to raise more funds by issuing additional securities, for its stockholders to buy, ahead of others, the new securities in proportion to the number of shares each owns.

RIGHTS ISSUE: the issue by a corporation to its existing shareholders of the right to purchase new shares in the same proportion as those which they already own.

RIGHT-TO-WORK LAWS: state laws outlawing the union shop.

RINGING OUT: in the commodities market, the practice of periodically settling outstanding future contracts before they mature.

RIPARIAN: term describing an individual if water flows over his or her land or if water flows along the border of the property.

RIPARIAN RIGHTS: rights of owners of land bordering on a river, lake, or tidewater to or in its banks, bed, or waters.

RISK: any chance of loss; the insured, or the peril insured against.

RISK CAPITAL: equity capital.

RISK-EXPERIENCE PROGRAM: the procedure of keeping a listing of premiums and losses on larger risks, for the underwriter's reference.

RISK MANAGEMENT: an approach of management concerned with the preservation of the assets and earning power of a business against risks of accidental loss.

RIVAL UNIONISM: competition between two or more unions for members and recognition in a company and/or industry.

ROBINSON-PATMAN ACT (1936): federal law that outlaws price discrimination between purchasers of like quality and quantities of products, where such discrimination injures competition or tends to create a monopoly.

ROCK BOTTOM: absolutely lowest level.

ROCKET: to rise with astounding speed, as a rocket.

ROLE: behavior patterns expected from people in differing economic, social, or other status positions.

ROLE PERCEPTION: having different opinions, attitudes, or expectations of the roles associated with a given status position in an organization.

ROLE PLAYING: a technique permitting individuals to experience an issue or case through a trainer's dramatization, often with the participants as actors.

ROLLBACK: a reduction of advanced prices to a former lower level.

ROLLER: a cylindrical device of many applications in machinery.

ROLLER BEARING: a low-friction bearing consisting of an outer cage, and inner journal, and an intermediate race holding a number of rollers.

ROLLER CONVEYOR: a conveyor used for gravity feed or for turns between belt conveyors, as on production lines and in loading and unloading operations.

ROLLING STOCK: a term applied to railroad engines and cars.

ROPING: the machinations of management "spies," who bring a worker among them and offer a bribe in return for information about the activities of a union.

RORO SHIP: a freighter that transports loaded trucks or other vehicles that enter at one port and disembark at another.

ROSTRUM: speaker's stand, platform, dais.

ROTATING SHIFT: changing of crews, usually to distribute day and night work on an equal basis.

ROUNDABOUT PROCESS: one that utilizes less direct but more efficient means of production, although investment in equipment must be made to initiate the modification.

ROUNDING ERROR: an error, usually slight enough to be insignificant, resulting from rounding off numbers.

ROUND LOT: a lot of 100 shares of stock; in a few high-priced stocks in small supply, a lot of 10 shares.

ROUNDOFF: to delete the least significant digit or digits of a numeral and adjust the part retained in accordance with some rule.

ROUND SUM: a number, the last digit or digits of which have been rounded off.

ROUND TURN: the completion of an order to purchase a future contract and, later, selling it.

ROUTE: to choose a particular method, carrier, or routing for sending a shipment; to remove, as to route dead metal.

ROUTINE: a set of coded computer instructions arranged in sequence that carry out some well-defined function; the opening of a broadcast program.

ROYALTY: a payment made for the right to use another person's property for purposes of gain.

RUBBER CHECK: a check that bounces; one rejected by the maker's bank for reasons such as insufficient funds, no account, etc.

RUBRICATED ACCOUNT: any earmarked account.

RUCKER PLAN: a group incentive program utilizing day-to-day employee participation and broad coverage to determine where cost reductions can be made and to improve company profits.

RULE OFF: to underscore the last entry in a journal or the last posting in a ledger account for the purpose of indicating a total and preventing any further entry or posting above the line.

RUN: an action of a large number of people; a work assignment; a single, continuous performance of a computer program or routine.

RUNAWAY: the condition in which part of a system undergoes a sudden or undesirable and often destructive increase in activity.

RUNAWAY INFLATION: synonymous with galloping inflation.

RUNAWAY SHOP: a company or plant that moves its facilities to another state to avoid existing state labor laws, or a union contract that it has agreed on.

RUN BOOK: all material needed to execute a computer application, including problem statements, coding, and operating instructions.

RUNNER: a merchandising term for a best-selling item, especially one that is continually kept in stock because of its heavy sales volume.

RUNNING COSTS: direct or indirect costs created from maintaining an operation.

RUNNING DAYS: consecutive days, including Sundays, as distinguished from working days, excluding Sundays.

RUNOFF ELECTION: a procedure used when no single union receives a first-poll majority in the representation election and a second election is called.

RUN ON A BANK: a mass withdrawal of deposits from a bank by depositors who no longer have confidence that the bank has sufficient funds to pay off all depositers.

S

SABOTAGE: malicious destruction or damage to property, as of an employer in a dispute, or as inflicted on military installations by foreign agents.

SACRIFICE: to make a sale at a loss for purposes of raising cash, with the awareness that one's profit will be lowered.

SAFE-DEPOSIT BOX: a rented depository for valuables, etc., in a bank vault.

SAFETY FACTOR: a contributing component to safety; a degree in either index of safety.

SAFETY STOCK: a minimum inventory that provides a cushion against reasonably expected maximum demand and against variations in lead time.

SAG: a minimal drop or price weakness of shares, usually resulting from a weak demand for the securities.

SAGACITY: natural intelligence, business acumen, keen understanding, good judgment.

SALABILITY: attractiveness to buyers, marketability.

SALARY: compensation received by an employee for services rendered during a specified period.

SALARY REVIEW: the examination of an employee's wage rate in terms of his or her performance and cost of living or other economic factors.

SALARY STANDARDIZATION: the process of integrating the rates of pay to the duties and responsibilities performed by employees.

SALE: transfer of title to goods or property or the agreement to perform a service in return for payment of cash or the promise to pay.

SALE AND LEASE-BACK: the sale of an asset with the vendor immediately renting the asset from the purchaser for long-term use.

SALES: the sum of the income received when goods and services are sold; synonymous with total net sales.

SALES AGENT: a middleman who undertakes to sell the entire output of items of a business that he or she represents.

SALES ALLOWANCE: a lowering of the price on an item when merchandise delivered is not exactly what was ordered by a buyer.

SALES ANALYSIS: an aspect of market research involving the systematic study and comparison of sales information.

SALES ANCHORS: concepts and statements used by sales representatives when attempting to overcome customer resistance.

SALES APTITUDE: a capability to achieve success in the sales field.

SALES BRANCH: a producer's outlet that maintains inventory and delivers to buyers from that stock.

SALES FINANCE COMPANY: a financial organization that purchases installment contracts from dealers and finances dealers' inventories.

SALES FORCE: canvassers and sales representatives who contact potential purchasers of goods and attempt to persuade them that they should buy items being sold.

SALES FORECAST: a dollar or unit sales estimate made for a specified period in a marketing campaign.

SALES JOURNAL: a book of original entry in which sales are recorded.

SALES MANAGER: an executive responsible for planning, directing, and controlling the activities of sales personnel.

SALESMANSHIP: the art of selling goods or services by creating a demand for a particular item or need and realizing an actual order.

SALES MANUAL: a book describing the product, merchandise, or service to be sold, and suggested approaches in selling to a customer.

SALES MIX: a combination of the quantities of a variety of company products leading to a firm's total sales.

SALES OFFICE: a facility for taking orders and handling adjustments which serves as a contact point for suppliers and customers.

SALES PITCH: a strong statement aimed at persuading a potential customer to buy the salesman's product or service.

SALES PLAN: a merchandise budget that contains a detailed projection of sales for a given period, specifying what is needed to achieve this goal.

SALES PRESENTATION: the total selling process of describing to a potential customer the product or service, including the attempt to place an order.

SALES PROMOTION: that portion of marketing embracing display, selling schemes, publicity-winning ploys, and special advertising.

SALES QUOTA: a goal projected in sales of a product.

SALES TAX: an excise tax levied on the sale of goods, sometimes also of services.

SALES TRAINEE: a recently hired sales representative engaged in learning the basic concepts of selling.

SALVAGE: equipment or property no longer utilized for its initial purpose; damaged property taken over by an insurance firm following payments of a claim.

SALVAGE VALUE: scrap value.

SAMPLE: to introduce a product to prospective buyers by letting them try it, thus promoting its sale.

SAMPLING: choosing a representative portion of a population to characterize a larger population.

SAMPLING ERROR: situation when the sample used is not representative of the population it was designed to represent.

SANCTION: a penalty for the breach of a rule of law; a coercive measure to force another country to cease violation of a treaty or international agreement.

SANCTUM: a private retreat thought safe from unwanted intrusion.

SANDWICH MAN: a person who carries two advertising display boards, attached to shoulder straps, one in front and one in back, forming a sandwich.

SARTORIAL: of clothes, tailored.

SATELLITE PROCESSOR: a processor that is under the control of another processing piece of equipment and performs subsidiary operations.

SATISFACTION: a criterion of effectiveness referring to an organization's ability to gratify the needs of its employees.

SATISFACTORY: meeting requirements or standards.

SATISFIERS: the activities in a job which bring satisfaction to the worker.

SATURATION: a phase in the life cycle of a product when an item is no longer able to be sold because most consumers have already purchased it.

SATURATION CAMPAIGN: the intensive use of radio or television advertising to promote or sell a product in a market.

SAVING: the amount of existing income that is not spent on consumption.

SAVINGS ACCOUNT: money deposited in a bank, usually in small amounts periodically over a long period, and not subject to withdrawal by check.

SAVINGS-AND-LOAN ASSSOCIATION: an association chartered as a corporation, owned by stockholders, to accept deposits and invest them.

SAVINGS BANK: a mutual bank, owned by depositors and managed by trustees, chartered to accept deposits and to invest them in mortgages on real property and other legal risks, after legal reserves are met.

SAVINGS BOND: a bond issued by the US Treasury for the encouragement of thrift and the financing of wars.

SAVINGS CERTIFICATE: a debt security issued by banks in denominations of ten.

SAVINGS RATE: a ratio showing the portion of income saved to income earned.

SAY'S LAW: a classical economic statement that overproduction is not possible since demand is created from supply.

SCAB: a strikebreaker.

SCALAR PRINCIPLE: a principle of organization that states that authority and responsibility should flow in a continuous line from the highest person in an organization to the lowest.

SCALE: a listing of comparative values, as hour wage rates for specific types of employment.

SCALE ORDER: an order to buy (or sell) a security, specifying the total amount to be bought (or sold) and the amount to be bought (or sold) at specified price variations.

SCALING: trading in securities by placing orders for purchase or sale at intervals of price instead of giving the order in full at the market or at a stated price.

SCALPER: a speculator in amusement tickets who charges a very high differential over the face value.

SCAN: the examination of stored information for a specific purpose, as for arrangement or content in the computer.

SCARCE CURRENCY: the demand for a particular country's currency which decreases the available supply at the usual rates of exchange.

SCARCITY: a condition of high demand and low supply.

SCARCITY VALUE: an increase in value caused by a demand for an item whose supply cannot be increased.

SCARE BUYING: purchase of quantities in excess of current needs to build up inventories against feared reduction of supply.

SCATTER-SITE HOUSING: federally sponsored public housing for low-income persons, usually found in ghetto areas.

SCAVENGER SALE: property taken over by the state as the result of nonpayment of taxes.

SCHEDULE: a list of ads, by stated media, giving dates of appearance, space, time, and so on; a systematic plan for future operations over a given period.

SCHEDULED MAINTENANCE: maintenance carried out in accordance with an established plan.

SCEHDULED PRODUCTION: the rate of activity assigned for the production of a given item in a specified period.

SCHEDULE OF INSURANCE: list of individual items covered under one policy.

SCHEDULE VARIANCE: the difference between actual production and scheduled production.

SCHEDULING: the organization and control of the time needed to carry out a sales effort.

SCHLOCK (SHLOCK): cheap or inferior item or service.

SCIENTER: awareness by a defrauding party of the falsity of a representation.

SCIENTIFIC TARIFF: a duty to cover foreign and domestic manufacturing costs.

SCINTILLA OF EVIDENCE: a small amount of evidence that assists in the proof of an allegation.

SCOOP: to beat out a rival; a considerable profit following a transaction that is likely to involve advance notice over, or exclusion of, competitors.

SCRAMBLED MERCHANDISING: an approach by retail outlets: maintaining types of goods not normally found in the store that engages in scrambling.

SCRAP: to sell, junk, or otherwise dispose of capital goods or inventories that have become obsolete; the materials so disposed of.

SCRAP VALUE: the salvage value of an item that is going to be junked or destroyed.

SCRATCH DAILY REPORT: a copy of the daily report completed by the underwriter for use by the policywriter in preparing the policy.

SCRATCH ENDORSEMENT: a copy of an endorsement completed by the underwriter for use by the policywriter in incorporating the endorsement into the policy.

SCRIP: a certificate that is exchangeable for stock or cash before a specified date, after which it may well have no value.

SCRIP DIVIDEND: a type of scrip issued as a dividend by a corporation to its stockholders.

SCRIPT: short for manuscript; a document; a form of writing.

SCRIVENER'S ERROR: a typographical error introduced when reducing an oral agreement to writing or when an agreement is typed or printed in final form.

SCRUPLES: ethical standards of honor often present in management in times of prosperity.

SEAL: a physical impression made on a document to attest to a signature or to add to its formality.

SEALING: reducing or enlarging an illustration or ad; concealed bids that are simultaneously revealed.

SEAPORT: a tidewater port with harbor and dock facilities for vessels.

SEARCH: the examination of records for evidence of encumbrances; the process of recruiting executive talent for a specific organization.

SEARCH CYCLE: normally, the location of an item and its comparison with others in the course of a computer search.

SEASONAL DISCOUNT: a price reduction given for purchases made off season.

SEASONAL EMPLOYEE: a worker employed for limited periods of activity.

SEASONAL FLUCTUATIONS: regular and predictable shifts in business activity created by changes in the season.

SEASONALLY ADJUSTED: a seasonal variation in rate that is expressed as if the same level of performance as that for the reported period will continue for the entire year.

SEASONAL UNEMPLOYMENT: joblessness due to seasonality of the work.

SEASONED ISSUES: securities from well-established corporations that have been favorably known to the investment population over time, including good and bad periods.

SEASONED MORTGAGE: periodic payments of a mortgage that are made over a long span based on the borrower's payment structure.

SEASONED SECURITY: a security possessing a fine performance record in the paying of dividends or interest and sells at a relatively stable price.

SEAT: membership in a stock exchange.

SEAT ON THE EXCHANGE: a traditional figure of speech designating a membership on an exchange.

SECONDARY DATA: information not received by a user from its original source, coming instead from references gathered earlier.

SECONDARY DISTRIBUTION: the redistribution to the public of a significant number of shares of the corporation which had previously been distributed to the public.

SECONDARY OFFERING: the off-the-floor marketing of a large block of shares of stock owned by the selling stockholders and not by the company treasury.

SECONDARY RENTAL: a lease determined in part by the landlord's costs; as the landlord's costs increase, proportionate rent increases are demanded.

SECONDARY RESERVES: assets other than primary reserves retained by banks and capable of being rapidly converted into cash.

SECONDARY STRIKE: a strike called against an employer doing business with another company whose workers are on strike.

SECOND-CLASS MAIL: a class of mail of low postal rate and fast service for qualified newspapers and magazines.

SECOND-GENERATION COMPUTER: a computer utilizing solid-state components.

SECOND HALF: the second six months of a fiscal or calendar year.

SECONDHAND: not new; merchandise offered for sale which has already been used.

SECOND LIEN: a lien that ranks following the first lien and is to be fulfilled next.

SECOND MORTGAGE: a mortgage secured by the equity in property remaining after the first mortgage.

SECONDS: goods bearing defects that have possible effects on wearability and appearance.

SECOND SALE: achieved by building on a customer's receptive mood following an initial purchase, an additional sale to the same person.

SECRET: classified, secret or top secret information accessible only to those who have security clearance to it.

SECRETARY: a corporate officer; head of a government department; an assistant to an executive; a person skilled in stenography, typing, and filing.

SECRET PARTNER: an active partner in an organization whose capacity as a partner is not known to the public.

SECRET RESERVES: the accounting term applied to reserves kept by a company but not disclosed in its financial statements.

SECTION WORK: the breakup of a complete production process into progressive sets of repetitive operations, each set handled by a different section of workers.

SECTOR: a division of an economy which has characteristics allowing it to be studied in isolation from the rest of the economy.

SECULAR EMPLOYMENT: unemployment resulting from changes in the economic sytem whose long-run effect is a decline in employment.

SECULAR INFLATION: the most serious economic problem of the late 1960s and the 1970s, primarily a long-term social phenomenon.

SECULAR TREND: a tendency of values in a time series to move upward or downward over a number of years.

SECURED CREDITOR: a person who has a claim against a debtor who has pledged his assets to the creditor; a creditor who has a lien.

SECURED DEBT: any debt for which some form of acceptable collateral has been pledged.

SECURED LOAN: loans that are made certain of payment by the pledging of valuable property to be forfeited in case of default.

SECURITIES: any documents that identify legal ownership of a physical commodity or legal claims to another's wealth.

SECURITIES ACT OF 1933: a federal law requiring companies desiring to sell new stock issues to disclose relevant financial information to the general public.

SECURITIES COMPANY: an organization that relies for its income on other firms' securities, which it retains for investment.

SECURITIES EXCHANGE ACT OF 1934: federal law creating the Securities and Exchange Commission (SEC) to regulate the national stock exchange.

SECURITIES TRADING: selling or buying of securities through recognized channels.

SECURITY: a share certificate, bond, debenture, or other document evidencing debt or ownership; property pledged to secure performance of a contract or payment of a debt.

SECURITY AGREEMENT: the agreement between the seller and buyer that the seller shall have an interest in the goods.

SECURITY CAPITAL: low-risk capital.

SECURITY CLEARANCE: a certification by the US government that the individual to whom it is awarded has access to classified documents.

SECURITY EMPLOYEE: the degree to which an employee can rely on a job with no chance of layoffs or arbitrary dismissal.

SECURITY EXCHANGE: a place where stocks and bonds are bought, sold, and traded.

SEED MONEY: funds set aside to commence an activity.

SEGMENT: any division of an organization, authorized to operate within established limitations, under substantial controls by its own management.

SEGREGATION: separating from an operating or holding firm one or more of its subsidiaries or operating divisions.

SEIGNIORAGE: government profit on coinage resulting from the difference between the value stamped on the coins and the lower value of the metal in the coins.

SEISIN (SEIZIN): taking legal possession of real estate.

SEIZURE: the act of taking possession of property.

SELECTION: the process of deciding from a number of job applicants the one individual to be offered a position and/or advancement.

SELECTIVE DISTRIBUTION: choosing retail outlets that will be permitted to receive one's merchandise for sale.

SELECTOR: a device for directing electrical input pulses onto one or two output lines, depending on the presence of a predetermined accompanying control pulse.

SELF-ACTUALIZATION: the desired result of a process of individual development of capacities and talents, and the evolution of self-realization.

SELF-ADAPTING: term for the ability of a system to change its performance characteristics in response to the environment.

SELF-CONCEPT THEORY: the notion that an individual's purchasing behavior is influenced by how the person perceives himself and how he wishes to be perceived by others.

SELF-EMPLOYED: the gainfully occupied part of the work force whose members work for themselves.

SELF-INSURANCE: the assumption by the insured of a risk that might otherwise have been covered by insurance.

SELF-LIQUIDATING: term describing a debt that is amortized or paid off in stated installments, or a premium offered free with the purchase of goods.

SELF-LIQUIDATING LOAN: a short-term commercial loan, usually supported by a lien on a given product or on sale of the product or commodities.

SELF-MAILER: a direct-mail piece that can be sent through the mail without using an envelope or wrap.

SELF-SELECTION SELLING: a merchandising approach allowing customers to make their choices without the initial assistance of sales help.

SELF-SERVICE: term describing a sales outlet or store where the customer chooses, removes and carries.

SELL-AND-LEASE-BACK AGREEMENT: an arrangement whereby a business owning and occupying improved real estate sells it to an investor and takes back a long-term lease on the property, and usually an option to buy it.

SELLER'S LIEN: the seller's privilege of holding onto certain items until the buyer has delivered payment.

SELLERS' MARKET: condition when demand exceeds supply.

SELLER'S-SEVEN SALE: an agreed-upon delay of several or more days for the delivery of a security.

SELLER'S SURPLUS: the difference between the price a seller actually receives and the lowest price that he or she would accept.

SELLING: the process of assisting and/or persuading a potential customer to buy merchandise or services.

SELLING COSTS: marketing costs designed to attract a potential buyer to an item or service.

SELLING GROUP: syndicated dealers of an underwriting company that operates in the public sale of an issue of securities.

SELLING PRICE: the cash price that a customer must pay for purchased items.

SELLING SHORT: a technique employed with the expectation of a drop in the market price of the security.

SELLOUT: an offering that is rapidly sold, as an oversubscribed offering of securities.

SEMIMONTHLY: appearing twice a month, as a magazine.

SEMISKILLED LABOR: a worker's level of performance between skilled and unskilled, often applied to workers who have had some training and perform routine tasks.

SENIORITY: having a greater length of service than another; a greater right to job tenure arising from this situation.

SENIOR DEBT: debt that has a higher priority of claims than other debts.

SENIOR SECURITY: a security that has a higher priortiy of claims than other securities.

SENSITIVE MARKET: characterized by fluctuations determined by the announcement of favorable or unfavorable news.

SENSITIVITY TRAINING: a form of education experience, conducted in small "classes," stressing the emotional dynamics of self-development training.

SENSOR: a device capable of converting measurable information into meaningful data for a computer.

SENTINEE: a symbol or mark to indicate the occurrence of a unit of information.

SEPARATE PROPERTY: property that is owned individually and is not jointly held.

SEPARATION: the permanent termination of employment, initiated by either the employee or the employer.

SEPARATION RATE: the average number of persons dropped from a payroll per 100 employees.

SEQUENCE: an arrangement of items according to a specified set of rules.

SEQUENTIAL COMPUTER: a computer in which events occur in time sequence, with little or no simultaneity or overlap of events.

SEQUESTER: set aside, as to place funds in a special account.

SEQUESTERED ACCOUNT: an account that has been impounded under due process of law.

SEQUESTRATION: legal appropriation of property by a third party until there is a settlement of a stated dispute.

SERIAL BOND: an issue of bonds redeemable in periodical installments.

SERIAL COMPUTER: a computer having a single unit that performs arithmetic and logic functions.

SERIAL TRANSFER: a system of data transfer in which elements of information are transferred in succession over a single line.

SERIATIM: one after another as resolutions voted upon separately instead of by single balloting.

SERVICE BUSINESS: business that does things for you, rather than sells you goods.

SERVICE CHARGE: a charge by a financial institution against an individual or organization for services rendered.

SERVICE EXCESS: a special program for large risks wherein claims within a large deductible or self-insured retention are serviced by the insurer for a fee.

SERVICE LIFE: the anticipated time of usefulness of an asset.

SERVICES: work performed for another; human effort transformed into things other than goods.

SETBACK: term specifying the distance a new structure must be set away from a street or from the lot boundaries; a reversal or partial loss in an activity.

SETTLEMENT: liquidation of a debt.

SETTLEMENT OPTIONS: provisions in a life policy or annuity contract for alternative methods of settlement in place of lump-sum payments.

SETTLER: one who creates a trust.

SETUP: the time or costs needed before production of an item can commence.

SEVERALTY: property owned by one person only.

SEVERANCE PAY: a payment made to an employee whose empoyment is prematurely terminated through no fault of his own.

SEVERANCE TAXES: taxes imposed on removal from land or water of natural products.

SEX DIFFERENTIAL: differences in rates for work of comparable quality and quantity, based on the worker's sex, now forbidden by federal law.

SHADING: giving a small reduction in a price or terms of a sale.

SHAKEDOWN: extortion; obtaining money by threatening exposure or damage if it is not paid.

SHAKE-OUT: any shift in activity that forces speculators to sell their shares; a trend or shift in an industry that forces weaker members toward bankruptcy.

SHAKEUP: widespread reassignments of jobs within an organization, possibly including some dismissals.

SHARE: a unit of stock naming the holder and indicating ownership in a corporation.

SHARE DRAFT: an order to pay to a third party by a credit-union member against funds on deposit with the credit union and cleared through a commercial bank.

SHARED REVENUE: payments to the states and localities of a portion of the proceeds from the sale of certain federal property, products, and services.

SHARED TIME: the condition under which more than one customer shares access to a computer system.

SHAREHOLDER (OR STOCKHOLDER): the owner of a stock certificate; a part owner of the corporation.

SHAREHOLDER OF RECORD: a shareholder in whose name shares are registered in the share register of a corporation.

SHAREHOLDERS' EQUITY: the excess of assets over liabilities of a corporation.

SHARE LOAN: a simple-interest loan secured by funds on deposits at a credit union or a savings-and-loan institution.

SHARE OF AUDIENCE: the percentage of radio or television sets in use or households watching a particular program.

SHARE OF THE MARKET: the ratio or percentage of an advertiser's sales to the total industry sales, based on an actual or potential standard.

SHARES OUTSTANDING: the share issued by a corporation, excluding treasury stock.

SHARE-THE-WORK: the retaining of jobs by shortening the work week for the entire employee group, instead of laying off some of the workers.

SHARK REPELLENT: a state statute that demands strict notification and disclosure of tender offers for companies incorporated or transacting business within its boundaries.

SHAVE: a charge that is higher than the accepted rate; the additional charge (premium) made for the right to extend the delivery time on a security.

SHELL FIRM: an organization that is incorporated, but does not function or produce any goods or services.

SHERIFF'S DEED: an instrument drawn under order of court to convey title to property sold to satisfy a judgment at law.

SHERIFF'S SALE: a court mandated sale of real or personal property made by a sheriff or other like ministerial officer.

SHIFT: the part of a 24-hour work day comprising a working schedule; to move information to the right or left in the arithmetic registers.

SHIFT DIFFERENTIAL: additional pay for working more than one shift, or other than the day shift.

SHIFTING TAX: a tax whose burden is transferred from the original taxpayer to another.

SHIFT PREMIUM: extra compensation given to a shift worker for the inconvenience of altering his daily working hours.

SHILL: a confederate who poses as a customer to induce others to buy.

SHILLY-SHALLY: to favor, first, one decision, and then the opposite.

SHINPLASTER: originally a small-sized civil war fractional-dollar paper currency; currency certificates of very small value.

SHIPMENT: the delivery and transport of items by a carrier; a collection of items that are transported as a unit.

SHOCK LOSS: a loss larger than expected.

SHOP CHAIRMAN: the principal union spokesman in a work place; usually a worker also, selected by his or her co-workers.

SHOP COMMITTEE: a group of union members named to speak for the whole on grievances, negotiations, and other labor-management issues.

SHOPLIFTER: one who steals merchandise from retail stores while posing as a prospective customer.

SHOPLIFTING: thievery of a store's items by a customer.

SHOP MERCHANDISING: establishing certain locations in a store for serving buyers with special interests.

SHOPPING GOODS: typically, medium-ticket items that a consumer prices in more than one store prior to purchase.

SHOP STEWARD: a union official who represents a specific group of members and the union in grievance matters and other employment conditions.

SHORT BILL: a bill of exchange that is payable upon request, at sight, or within a brief period.

SHORT COVERING: buying a stock to return stock previously borrowed to make delivery on a short sale.

SHORTCUT FORECLOSURE: a method of foreclosure in which a power-of-sale clause in the mortgage allows the lender to sell a property if it goes into default.

SHORTER WORK WEEK: any working schedule less than the equivalent of five working days.

SHORT-FALL: spending, usually in a governmental agency, which falls sharply below projections, thus contributing to an economic sluggishness.

SHORT INTEREST: the total short sales of a single issue or of entire market of stocks at a specific time.

SHORT MERCHANDISE: goods bought in small quantities, or to complete an assortment; purchased goods that were not included in a shipment.

SHORT OF DESTINATION: prior to reaching the final port, warehouse or destination.

SHORT OF EXCHANGE: the position of a foreign-exchange trader who has sold more foreign bills than the quantity of bills he has in his possession.

SHORT POSITION: stocks sold short and not covered as of a particular date.

SHORT PURCHASE: buying a stock to cover an earlier short sale of the same stock.

SHORT RATE: the higher rate an advertiser pays when he or she fails to use the space or time contracted for.

SHORT-RATE CANCELLATION: the charge required for insurance or bonds taken for less than one year.

SHORT RUN: a one-time job; a minimal printing production.

SHORT SALE: a sale of borrowed stock to be returned at a later date when the stock is bought back.

SHORT SELLING: selling a stock and purchasing it at a lower price to receive a profit.

SHORT-TERM DEBT: an obligation that is usually due within the year.

SHORT-TERM FUNDS: money borrowed for periods of 30 days up to one year.

SHOTGUN APPROACH: disorganized approach to selling or advertising, aimed at reaching a large number of potential customers.

SHRINK WRAPPING: a plastic coating applied over a package; when subjected to heat, the coating conforms to the shape of the package.

SHUTDOWN: a temporary stoppage of production.

SICK LEAVE: contractually provided conditions under which employees are paid during illness.

SICK PAY: compensation given an employee because of illness, accident, or some other incapacity.

SIDELINE STORES: stores whose primary interest is other than retailing, as with a wholesaler who also sells to the consumer, as an accommodation.

SIGHT BILL OF EXCHANGE: any bill of exchange that becomes due and payable when presented by the holder to the party on whom it is drawn.

SIGHT DRAFT: a bill of exchange payable three days after presentation.

SIGNAL: the output of a circuit, used for control and/or timing of various computer operations.

SIGNATURE: one's own name, handwritten.

SIGNIFICANT PLACES: the number of decimal places to which accuracy is required in a computation.

SIGNING OFFICER: an officer of an organization authorized to sign documents on behalf of the organization.

SIGNOFF: the closing instruction to the computer, which terminates communication with the system.

SIGNON: the opening instruction to the computer, which begins communications with the system.

SILENT PARTNER: a partner who provides money to a partnership but takes no active part in its management or operation.

SILK-SCREEN PROCESS: a stencil process in which paint is forced through prepared screens of silk.

SILO: a cylindrical vat for storing fodder and converting it to ensilage; any cylindrical structure used to store bulk commodities.

SILVER CERTIFICATE: a government banknote stated on the face to be redeemable in silver species, replaced in 1965 by Federal Reserve banknotes without such guarantee.

SIMPLE INTEREST: interest calculated on a principal sum and not on any interest that has been earned by that sum.

SIMPLIFICATION: making simpler by means such as elimination of steps or mechanization of processes.

SIMULATION: a serious imitation of a real-life performance for demonstration or instruction.

SIMULATOR PROGRAM: a program that represents certain features of the behavior of a physical or abstract system.

SIMULCAST: to broadcast simultaneously on radio and television.

SIMULTANEOUS PROCESSING: the performance of two or more data-processing tasks at the same instant of time.

SIMULTANEOUS TRANSMISSION: sending more than one signal over a wire at one time.

SINECURE: a position of limited or nonexistent responsibility demanding little or no labor or service.

SINGLE-ADDRESS MESSAGE: a message that is to be delivered to only one destination.

SINGLE ENTRY: an outmoded accounting system for keeping simple records.

SINGLE-LINE STORE: a store that carries a wide variety of one type of goods.

SINGLE-PAYMENT LOAN: a loan whose entire principal is due on one maturity date.

SINGLE PROPRIETORSHIP: ownership of a business by one person.

SINGLE RATE: a wage rate, identical for all employees working in the same job or classification.

SINGLE STANDARD: the use of gold only as currency backing.

SINGLE STEP: pertaining to a method of operating a computer in which each operation is performed in response to a single manual act.

SINGULAR PROPERTY TITLE: property title granted to only one person.

SINKING FUND: a pool of cash and investments earmarked to provide resources for the redemption of debt or capital stock.

SITDOWN STRIKE: a strike in which workers remain on the premises of their employer but do not work.

SITE: location, as of a building, cellar hole, battlefield.

SITE AUDIT: an audit conducted on the premises of the organization under examination.

SIT IN FOR: render substitute performance for.

SIT-IN STRIKE: a sitdown strike, particularly one of long duration, involving barricaded entrances and ingenious methods of food delivery.

SITUATION: employment, position.

SITUATIONAL-DESIGN THEORY: the point of view according to which there is no single best way to design an organization.

SITUS: location.

SITUS PICKETING: picketing a subcontractor at a construction site, an illegal practice.

SIZING: the application of size; determining the size range and relative quantities in which to make or stock retail items.

SKID: a pallet; an inclined slide for some unloading operations.

SKILLED LABOR: personnel who, as a result of training and experience, can capably perform labor of a specialized type, such as plumbing and electrical.

SKIM-THE-CREAM PRICING: the pricing technique of establishing price at the upper limit of the range.

SKIP: customers who move from a known address without paying.

SKIP TRACER: one engaged in the collection of accounts assigned to tracing the whereabouts of persons who have failed to pay their obligations.

SKY LEASE: a lease of a property's air rights.

SLANDER: defamation through words; often restricted to written words.

SLAVE COMPUTER: a backup system consisting of a second computer that performs the same steps of the same programs executed by the master computer.

SLEEPER: an item that has not realized its potential and needs an impetus to cause it to be successful.

SLIDE: a persistent downward movement of prices.

SLIDE FASTENER: zipper.

SLIDING SCALE: a scale of fees, prices, or wages, in which the amount per unit varies with the change of one or more factors, as the total volume.

SLIPPAGE: lost time.

SLOGAN: a short, memorable, word or phrase, used in a company's publicity so much that by itself it identifies and recalls the company's name in favorable context.

SLOW ASSET: an asset that can be converted into cash, near its book value, usually after a lengthy passage of time.

SLOWDOWN: lessening of work effort by concerted agreement among employees, to force management concessions.

SLUMP: in stock-market language, a sudden drop in prices or a lessening of business activity.

170

SMALL
BUSINESS
ADMINISTRA-
TION •
SORT

SMALL BUSINESS ADMINISTRATION: a federal agency established solely to advise and assist the nation's small businesses.

SMART MONEY: experienced and professional security traders who exploit inside information to make profits at the expense of other investors.

SMELTER: a mill for the reduction of ores to ingots.

SMUGGLING: removing from or putting in goods or persons without permission.

SNAP DECISION: a decision arrived at quickly without apparent survey of factors or due consideration of them.

SNAP STRIKE: a stoppage of work by employees without authorization of the union.

SOCIAL ACCOUNTING: the identification, classification, measurement, and reporting of the social costs and benefits of human activity in and of an organization.

SOCIAL BENEFIT: the value to a society resulting from a specific act or action.

SOCIAL COST: the price paid by citizens for the side effects of economic performance (pollution, destruction of forests, etc.).

SOCIAL-INFRASTRUCTURE EXPENDITURES: expenditures for public projects established for the good of the community.

SOCIALISM: the political and economic system in which the government owns and operates production facilities.

SOCIAL SECURITY: the Federal Old Age Benefits Law of 1936 and subsequent liberalizations of it; payments under these laws.

SOCIOGRAM: describing the preferences people have in being with others.

SOCIOMETRY: the technique of attempting to match individuals to tasks based on their preferences for co-workers.

SOFT CURRENCY: the funds of a country that are controlled by exchange procedures, thereby having limited convertibility into gold and other currencies.

SOFT GOODS: ready-to-wear clothing, piece goods, linens, towels, and small fashion accessories.

SOFT LOAN: a loan whose terms of repayment are generous, at times holding a low rate of interest.

SOFT MONEY: paper currency, as contrasted with coinage.

SOFT SELL: a selling technique that is convincing, subtle, and indirect.

SOFTWARE: basic programs on cards, tape, or other inputs to be stored in a computer; wiring plans to facilitate adaptations of large groups of problems for computer solution.

SOIL BANK: a farm program established by the government to pay farmers for removing land from cultivation.

SOLDIER: to do as little work as possible on the job; goldbrick.

SOLDIERING: the act of loafing on the job, or otherwise reducing productivity.

SOLE OWNER: the only person holding the title to a specific property or business.

SOLE PROPRIETORSHIP: an unincorporated business owned by one person.

SOLICITOR: lawyer who handles commercial and family financial affairs, particularly in England, where, he is not permitted to plead in court.

SOLID-STATE COMPUTER: a computer that uses solid state, or semiconductor, components; a second-generation computer.

SOLVENCY: the ability to pay debts as they become due.

SOLVENT: financially able to pay one's debts.

SONIC BARRIER: the speed of sound, mach 1.

SOPHISTICATED HARDWARE: highly complex electronic devices, such as third-generation computers, missile-guidance systems, etc.

SORT: to segregate items into groups according to some definite rules; a programmer routine that orders data.

SORTER: a device that sorts punched cards in alphabetical or numerical order by selected card columns.

SOUND VALUE: a term used to indicate the value of property for fire-insurance purposes.

SOURCE DOCUMENT: an original record of a transaction.

SOURCE PROGRAM: a computer program in the form in which it is prepared by the computer input to assembler, or compiler.

SOVEREIGN: an individual holding supreme power, usually in a nation.

SPACE: a site intended for the storage of data; the area or medium in which an advertisement is placed.

SPACE BUYER: an advertising agency or executive who assists in the planning of printed campaigns and chooses and purchases space in media.

SPACE RESERVATION: a reservation for newspaper space, guaranteeing appearance in the paper but on no specific page; also, guaranteed seating, without specific place.

SPAN OF CONTROL: in management, the maximum number of subordinates or functions that can be handled effectively.

SPECIAL DELIVERY: a postal service of early delivery by special messenger of first-class mail on which a special-delivery fee is paid.

SPECIAL DISTRICTS: independent governmental units created to provide a single or limited function, and having the power to tax, impose service charges, or incur debt therefor.

SPECIAL HANDLING: a postal service for expediting early delivery of parcel-post packages.

SPECIAL-INTEREST ACCOUNT: the term used by commercial banks to describe a savings account.

SPECIALIST: a member of a stock exchange who specializes in the shares of a limited number of companies.

SPECIALIZATION: reducing an operation or task into separate simplified individual activities.

SPECIAL OFFERING: a large block of stock that becomes available for sale, requiring special handling because of its size and the market.

SPECIAL-PURPOSE COMPUTER: a computer that is designed to handle a restricted class of problem.

SPECIAL-PURPOSE FUNDS: mutual funds that invest exclusively in securities from one industry.

SPECIALTY MERCHANDISE: consumer goods having special features for which buyers are willing to make a major purchasing effort.

SPECIALTY SHOP: a store that retails a single broad category of merchandise, such as ladies' ready-to-wear and accessories.

SPECIALTY STORES: retail outlets that maintain a large selection in a limited line of merchandise.

SPECIAL-WARRANTY DEED: a deed in which the grantor defends property title against demands made by grantees, heirs, and other claimants; no other liability is assumed by the grantor.

SPECIE: metal coins.

SPECIFICATION: stated requirement, as for an item on which bids are sought.

SPECIFIC DUTY: an import duty on a definite quantity of a specific type of merchandise without regard to its value.

SPECIFIC INSURANCE: coverage that applies to separate and specifically named objects or locations.

SPECIFIC PERFORMANCE: a legal action to compel performance under a contract when damages for breach of contract would be unsatisfactory.

SPECIFIC SUBSIDY: the per-unit subsidy on a commodity.

SPECIFIC TAX: the per-unit tax on a commodity.

SPECTACULAR: a large, prominently placed advertising bulletin with lighting and attractive motion of special effects.

172

SPECULA-
TION •
STABILIZA-
TION
POLICY

SPECULATION: purchase and sale of securities and commodities for the purpose of gain on the transactions rather than on dividends and interest earned.

SPECULATIVE PURCHASING: buying items when prices appear lowest, with the expectation that there will be a future price increase, making possible a profit.

SPECULATOR: an investor who deals in risk and uncertainty.

SPEEDUP: a management-directed attempt to increase production without any increase in pay.

SPENDABLE EARNINGS: net earnings after deductions for taxes.

SPILLOVERS: external benefits or costs of efforts for which there is no compensation.

SPINOFF: a dividend issued as shares of stock in a subsidiary to stockholders of the parent company proportional to their holdings in the parent company.

SPIRAL: the upward course of prices and wages, thought of as an inflationary spiral.

SPIRAL BINDING: the insertion of a helical wire as the backbone of a group of uniformly sized pages to form a booklet or book.

SPLIT: a stock dividend that increases the number and decreases the value of each share so that the total value of a holding remains unchanged.

SPLIT-INVESTMENT COMPANY: a closed-end investment firm issuing two types of capital stock.

SPLIT LOAD: cargo in a single shipping unit having more than one terminal destination.

SPLIT RUN: two or more ads of equal size with the identical position in different copies of the same publication issue.

SPLIT SHIFT: the daily working time of an employee that is divided into two or more working periods, to meet peak needs.

SPLITUP: the issuance of two or more stock shares replacing each outstanding share, used for financial and tax purposes.

SPONSOR: an advertiser who pays for the broadcasting time during which a program appears, or shares the cost with other cosponsors, and in return airs his own commercial message.

SPOOLING: the reading and writing of input and output streams on auxiliary-storage devices in a format convenient for later processing or output.

SPOT: time purchased for commercial announcements on individual stations rather than on networks; for immediate delivery.

SPOT ADVERTISING: a campaign wherein advertisers choose specific stations to be used.

SPOT ANNOUNCEMENT: a brief commercial, usually one minute long or less, inserted between portions of a radio or television program.

SPOT CASH: cash immediately available as for a purchase.

SPOT DELIVERY: immediate delivery.

SPOT MARKET: a market where commodities are sold for cash and quickly delivered.

SPOT PRICE: the price of a commodity available for immediate sale and delivery, the commodity being referred to as a spot commodity.

SPOT PUNCH: a device for punching one hole at a time on a computer card.

SPOUSE: one's wife or husband.

SPREAD: two facing pages in a newspaper or magazine.

SPREAD SHEET: a worksheet providing a two-way analysis or recapitulation of accounting data; sometimes used as a basis for postings and regarded as a journal.

SQUATTER'S RIGHT: the right to the common law occupancy of land, for long and undisturbed use, but without legal title.

STABILIZATION: the control of prices by making purchases and sales, as when a new or secondary issue of securities is floated.

STABILIZATION POLICY: the efforts of government to use fiscal and monetary means to eliminate inflation, unemployment, or both.

STABLE MONEY: currency that remains constant in terms of the items and services it can purchase.

STACKER: a freight handler who loads a vehicle.

STAGFLATION: inflation coexisting with economic stagnation.

STAGING: the temporary construction needed for erecting building walls; the elements required to perform a dramatic production.

STAGNATION: the situation in which per capita real income is constant or declining.

STALE-DATED CHECK: a check that has not been presented to the bank for payment within a reasonable time, generally six months.

STAMP TAX: a tax on legal documents, certificates, and papers which requires that revenue stamps be affixed to indicate payment of the tax.

STANDARD AND POOR'S CORPORATION: a leader in the field of financial services which provides corporate as well as financial information.

STANDARD COSTING: a method of cost accounting, achieving cost control through analysis of variances between actual and standard conditions.

STANDARD ERROR: a measure or an estimate of the sampling errors affecting a statistic.

STANDARD GRADE: a grade sanctioned by government or common usage.

STANDARDIZATION: limitation of sizes, qualities; setting standards.

STANDARD OF LIVING: the level of material affluence of a nation as measured by per capita output.

STANDARD PROGRAM: a computer program that meets certain criteria, such as being written in a standard machine language and bringing forth an approved solution to a problem.

STANDING LOAN: a loan requiring payments of interest only, the principal being paid in full upon maturity.

STANDING ORDER: an authority given by a customer's authority for the bank to regularly pay funds, usually a fixed dollar amount, from his demand-deposit account.

STANDSTILL AGREEMENT: an arrangement between a debtor and a creditor under which new limits and conditions for the loan are set.

STAPLE STOCK: goods on hand that are in continuous demand.

STARBOARD: the right side of a ship, barge, or airplane.

STARE DECISIS: to abide by authorities or cases already decided (Latin).

STATE BANK: a bank that is chartered by and organized according to the laws of the state in which it is located.

STATED CAPITAL: the sum of capital amounts contributed by stockholders.

STATE DISABILITY PLAN: a plan of some states, involving short-term insurance, to replace income lost by eligible persons employed in that state.

STATED VALUE: new stock divided by the number of shares issued; stated capital per share.

STATEMENT: a financial report of assets, liabilities, and capital; if in a set, the other is of income, profit, and loss.

STATEMENT ENCLOSURES: a printed advertisement, enclosed in the same envelope in which a statement is mailed.

STATIC ANALYSIS: the determination of an equilibrium at a single point in time without considering the impact of the passage of time.

STATIC DUMP: a dump that is performed at a particular point in time with respect to a machine run, frequently at the end of a run.

STATIC INVENTORY PROBLEM: the tendency to lose value, of items bought for a specific selling season due to seasonal market changes.

STATIC MODEL: a concept for studying economic events without reference to time, without relation to preceding or succeeding events.

STATION: one of the input or output points of a system; a worker's assigned post or place of activity.

STATION BREAK: giving the call letters or identification of a radio or television station.

STATION OPTION TIME: time over which a network affiliate station has priority on first sales.

STATISM: any indication of increased government intervention in a nation's economic activity.

STATISTIC: a value computed from a sample; often misused in the plural as a synonym for figures or numbers.

STATISTICAL ACCOUNTING: the application of probability theory and statistical sampling approaches to the evolution of accounting information.

STATISTICS: the mathematics of gathering data and the approaches used in describing and analyzing numerical information.

STATUS: an individual's relative social or power position in a group.

STATUS CONSENSUS: the agreement of group members about the relative status of members of the group.

STATUS QUO: the existing state of affairs.

STATUS SYMBOL: an item purchased in the hope of communicating one's desired or real status to others.

STATUTE: a law passed by the legislative body of a state.

STATUTE OF LIMITATIONS: a law that makes debts incurred for purchases of goods or services uncollectible if not paid within the stated period, six years in most states.

STATUTORY AUDIT: an audit carried out to comply with the provision of a statute.

STATUTORY LAW: written laws.

STEEL PRODUCTION CAPACITY: the ratio of steel production to theoretical production capacity.

STENCIL: a flat sheet of brass, silk, mimeograph stencil paper, or other substance in which perforations permit passage of paint, ink, or dye to form an image on paper or cloth.

STENOGRAPHY: the skills of rapid writing in phonetic symbols or characters, then typing the transcript.

STENOTYPE: phonogrammic notes on the machine of the same name; the machine.

STEP: one operation in a computer routine.

STEPPED COSTS: costs that climb by increments with increased volumes of activity.

STEPUP: an automatic wage increase based on length of service.

STEREOPHONIC: reproducing sound from two different sources so that the human ear can blend them into one sound.

STEREOTYPES: preconceived notions, often based on superficial characteristics, which often distort communication between people.

STERLING: denoting the silversmiths' standard of 0.925 fine for silver jewelry and tableware bearing the mark Sterling.

STEROID: a drug group widely used in correcting chronic physical conditions.

STEWARDSHIP: financial management of purchases, finances, funds, etc; term or period of such management.

STICKER: an employee who is unwilling to accept an offer for promotion.

STIMULATE THE ECONOMY: a deliberate governmental move to increase employment and otherwise move the country to a higher level of prosperity.

STIPEND: a synonym for salary.

STIPULATION: a limitation of action included in an agreement.

STOCK: supply of goods and merchandise in store for sale; shares of ownership in a corporation which pay dividends, or share in the profits.

STOCK AHEAD: to maintain sufficient quantities of goods in inventory to cover an anticipated surge in future demand for the items.

STOCKBROKER: a company or individual engaged in buying and selling securities for others.

STOCK CERTIFICATE: written evidence of the ownership of one or more shares of the capital stock of a corporation.

STOCK DIVIDEND: a dividend paid by the issue of additional shares of capital stock.

STOCK EXCHANGE: a federally regulated exchange for the trading of stocks.

STOCKHOLDER: a synonym for shareholder.

STOCKHOLDER OF RECORD: a stockholder whose name is registered on the books of the issuing corporation.

STOCK-IN-TRADE: business activity usually carried on; quantity of securities held.

STOCK JOBBING: irresponsible or dishonest manipulation of the price of securities.

STOCK MARKET: a stock exchange; an over-the-counter market.

STOCK OPTION: the right to purchase shares of a corporation's capital stock under fixed conditions concerning number of shares, price, and time.

STOCKPILE: to build up inventories; an inventory exceeding current needs.

STOCKPILING: government purchases of various agricultural commodities and raw materials for storage, to support the prices of these products.

STOCK POWER: a power-of-attorney permitting a person other than the owner of stock to legally transfer the title of ownership to a third party.

STOCK-PURCHASE PLAN: a company plan for the purchase of stock by employees, at terms usually below the market price.

STOCK-SALES RATIO: the inventory retail value at the beginning of a given month, divided by sales for that month.

STOCK SHORTAGE: occurs when the dollar value of the real inventory in stock is less than that shown on the inventory books.

STOCK SPLIT: the issuance of new shares of stock for old, greater in number, frequently in a ratio of two-to-one.

STOCK SPLITDOWN: the reverse of a stock split; the total number of shares outstanding is lowered without reducing the total value of the issue.

STOCK TRANSFER: the act of canceling a stock certificate, issuing a new certificate, and recording the change in ownership on the records of a corporation's stock-transfer book.

STOCK-TRANSFER TAX: the federal and/or state tax on sale or transfer and, in some cases, loan of stock.

STONEWALLING: obstruction or delay of parliamentary proceedings by filibuster or lengthy debate.

STOOLPIGEON: a worker paid by an employer to report to management on union activities; a company spy.

STOOP LABOR: agricultural work requiring constant bending and kneeling.

STOP-LIMIT ORDER: a stop order that becomes a limit order after the specified stop price has been reached.

STOP LOSS: a guarantee from one company to another that losses over and above an agreed-upon amount will be paid by the reinsuring company.

STOP-LOSS ORDER: an order to a stock broker to sell on the next sale after a price drops to a specified level.

STOPPAGE-IN-TRANSIT: under certain conditions, the shipper's right to halt delivery of a shipment that is already in transit, when payment has not been made.

STOP PAYMENT: instructions given to a bank by the drawer of a check not to honor it.

STOP PRICE: the price at which a customer's stop order to his broker becomes a market order.

STORAGE: the holding of goods for future use; any device that can store data.

STORAGE CAPACITY: the amount of data that can be contained in a storage device.

STORE: to transfer information to a device from which it can be recalled later; any place where merchandise, can be purchased.

STOWAGE: cargo properly stored.

STRADDLE: an option allowing the trader to buy or sell securities at an agreed-upon price within a given period.

STRAIGHT BILL OF LADING: a bill of lading which states a specific person to whom the goods should be delivered and which is not negotiable.

STRAIGHT INVESTMENT: a preferred stock or bond, limited in interest or dividend rate, which is bought because of its income return.

STRAIGHT LEASE: a lease describing regular rental payments; also referred to as a flat lease.

STRAIGHT LETTER OF CREDIT: an irrevocable letter of credit that has been confirmed.

STRAIGHT-LIFE INSURANCE: life insurance for a level amount, which matures at death and on which premiums are payable for the lifetime of the insured.

STRAIGHT-LINE DEPRECIATION: a method of depreciation calculation in which the periodic expense is computed by dividing the depreciation by the estimated number of periods of useful life.

STRAIGHT LOAN: a loan to an individual or other legal entity.

STRAIGHT TIME: the wage rate paid for hours worked during the normal period prescribed by the union contract or by law.

STRAP: an option on two calls and one put.

STRATEGIC-RESOURCE MONOPOLY: an organization having a monopoly by virtue of controlling a vital input to a production process.

STRATEGY: guides for making directional decisions that influence an organization's long-run performance.

STRAW: untrue, valueless, or financially irresponsible; a "straw bid" is one whose maker is unable to fulfill the requirements for acquisition.

STRAW BOSS: a group leader or assistant foreman, often one who has no formal title or permanent status.

STRAW MAN: a person who purchases property for another without identifying the valid buyer.

STREET BROKER: an over-the-counter broker, as distinguished from a broker who is a member of an exchange.

STREET CERTIFICATE: a stock certificate registered in the name of an investment dealer rather than in the name of the individual owner.

STREET NAME: the name of a broker on securities owned by a customer and hypothecated to or left for safekeeping with the broker.

STRETCH-OUT: management term for malingering; an increase in work without comparable pay increases.

STRIKE: a concerted and sustained refusal by working men to perform some or all of the services for which they were hired.

STRIKE AUTHORIZATION: a strike vote that invests a designated group with the right to call a strike without further consultation with the union membership.

STRIKE BENEFITS: payments by the union to members on strike, in the form of a flat sum or graduated according to family needs.

STRIKEBREAKER: a person who replaces workers who are on strike.

STRIKE FUND: taken from union dues, funds held by the union covering the costs of approved programs.

STRIKE NOTICE: a formal notice to an employer or to a state labor-management relations agency that a union has rejected the company's latest offer.

STRIKE PAY: monies paid by the union to members of a union to compensate for income loss during a strike.

STRIKE VOTE: a vote to decide whether to empower union leadership to call a strike.

STRING: a set of characters in ascending or descending sequence, according to a key contained in the records of the computer.

STRINGENCY: a money-market condition of hard-to-obtain credit, accompanied by an increase in the rates of interest.

STRONGARM: to use force illegally, assault.

STRONG MARKET: a greater demand for purchasing than there is for selling.

STRUCK WORK: goods produced by strikebreakers, or goods produced by a firm not on strike for the use or relief of a struck company.

STRUCTURAL INFLATION: condition in which increasing prices are caused by an uneven upward demand or cost pressures in a key industry.

STRUCTURAL INTERVENTION: changing the structure of an organization so that people can develop new approaches for dealing with others on the job.

STRUCTURAL PRINCIPLES: principles that assist a manager in designing the formal task and authority relationships in the organization.

STUB: one's own record of a check one has drawn.

STUDY: to investigate, test, conduct a research.

STUFFER: a small piece of advertising literature used as an envelope enclosure or placed, contrary to postal regulations, in a consumer's mail box.

STUFFING: loading cargo or goods into a container or envelope.

STUMPAGE: the right to cut timber on another's land.

SUBCONTRACT: to relet a part or all of a contract.

SUBDIVIDE: to sell portions of a tract of land, as part-acre plots for homes.

SUBENVIRONMENT: characteristics of people and their tasks that affect the performance of employees in their work and relationship with each other.

SUBJECT BID: a bid that is negotiable, rather than firm.

SUBJECTIVE: of or affected by the feelings or temperament of the subject rather than of the object thought of.

SUBJECT-TO-SALE: a stipulation that provides for the automatic withdrawal of the offer if the property is sold before the party has accepted the offer.

SUBLEASE: an agreement under which a tenant transfers part of his rights under a lease to another person.

SUBLIMINAL: below the threshhold of awareness.

SUBLIMINAL ADVERTISING: the delivery of a message below a receiver's awareness level, to be registered subconsciously.

SUBMARGINAL: yielding less than enough to cover the cost of production.

SUBMITTAL NOTICE: a broker's notification to a property owner stating that the owner's property has been offered for sale.

SUBMORTGAGE: the result of a pledge by a lender of a mortgage in his or her possession as collateral to obtain a loan for himself or herself.

SUBORDINATE: one who reports to another of higher rank.

SUBORDINATE DEBT: debt that has a lower priority of claims than other debts.

SUBORDINATED DEBENTURE: a debenture bond stated to be junior to other specified securities.

SUBORDINATED INTEREST: an interest in property that is inferior to another interest.

SUBORNATION: illegally inducing a witness to commit perjury.

SUBPOENA: the legal process under which the appearance of a person or documents in court is required.

SUBPOENA DUCES TECUM: a writ that orders a witness to bring certain documents to court (Latin).

SUBPROGRAM: a section of a large program that can be compiled independently.

SUBROGATION: the substitution of one person for another.

SUBROUTINE: a computer routine that can be part of another routine.

SUBSCRIBER: one who agrees in writing to purchase a certain offering.

SUBSCRIPTION: a signature to an agreement to buy something, such as a stock; the agreement itself.

SUBSET: any group of items contained in a larger grouping of items.

SUBSIDIARY: a self-contained business acquired by another company and administered under its direction.

SUBSIDIARY COMPANY: a corporation in which another corporation owns a majority of the voting shares.

SUBSIDIARY LEDGER: a ledger in which individual accounts of the same type are kept with the aggregate of the accounts being maintained in the control account in the general ledger.

SUBSIDY: a grant in aid, frequently programmed into installments.

SUBSISTENCE: a lower standard of living including no luxuries, and few, if any, comforts.

SUBSISTENCE THEORY OF WAGES: an economic theory claiming that wages per employee tend to equal what the worker needs to maintain himself and his family.

SUBSONIC: describing velocities approaching but below mach 1.

SUBSTANDARD: below acceptable standards but superior to rejects, as seconds or irregulars.

SUBSTANDARD RATE: the wage rate below established plant or occupational minimum, federal or state minimum laws, or prevailing levels.

SUBSTANTIATE: to prove, as to provide original bills to substantiate claimed expenses.

SUBSTANTIVE LAW: relating to the essential legal principles.

SUBSTITUTION LAW: the economic statement that if one product or service can be a replacement for another, the prices of the two must be quite close to each other.

SUBSYSTEM: a secondary or subordinate system usually capable of operating independently of or asynchronously with a controlling system.

SUBTENANT: a tenant who leases premises from another tenant; a sublessee.

SUBVENTION: a grant in aid from a governmental or other public agency for purposes of public benefit.

SUCCESSFUL: profitable, with increasing sales: affluent, enjoying high income and status symbols of modern society; achieving one's ethical, esthetic, personal goals.

SUCCESSION: following another in an office, estate, and so on.

SUCCESSION TAX: a tax on the privilege of receiving property, either by descent or by will.

SUCCESSOR: one who follows in office.

SUE: to prosecute a civil case in court.

SUGGESTION SYSTEM: a system in which employees, or customers, are encouraged to suggest improvements with incentives of awards for acceptable ideas.

SUGGESTIVE SELLING: the strategy of suggesting to a potential purchaser that he might have an additional need, related to what has already been purchased.

SUI GENERIS: of its own peculiar kind (Latin).

SUIT: any proceeding at law for the purpose of obtaining a legal decision.

SULFA DRUGS: a group of drugs effective in reducing body infection, used, at times, by medical prescription in the treatment of illness.

SUMMATION: a totaling, as of figures; a review of evidence and recommendations of conclusions to be drawn from it as by a trial lawyer to a jury.

SUMMONS: a citation to a defendant to appear in court.

SUM-OF-THE-YEARS'-DIGITS METHOD: a method of calculating depreciation in which the depreciation base is allocated to individual years on a reducing basis.

SUMPTUARY LAWS: laws that attempt to minimize the consumption of items believed to be harmful to individuals or society in general.

SUNK COST: a cost that has already been incurred and is now irrelevant to the decision-making process.

SUNSET RULING: an approach for the phasing out of ineffective governmental programs; once a program is found to be unproductive, it is not renewed.

SUPERCARGO: an officer on a freighter responsible for matters relating to the cargo.

SUPERINTENDENT: one in charge of a building or other premise or of a department.

SUPERIOR: one of higher rank or office than another; of higher standing, better quality.

SUPERMARKET: a very large retail store selling food and associated products principally by display and checkout.

SUPERSONICS: the realm of materials performance, machine operation, and human behavior at speeds greater than mach 1; the study of and use of sound waves at frequencies beyond the range of the human ear.

SUPERVISION: close surveillance of the work of others with authority and responsibility to direct it.

SUPPLEMENTAL AIR CARRIER: air carriers permitted to render passenger and freight charter services to supplement the scheduled service of the other approved air carriers.

SUPPLEMENTARY UNEMPLOYMENT BENEFITS: a company provision for benefits to laid-off workers, in addition to unemployment insurance.

SUPPLY: the amount of goods that sellers are ready to sell at each specified price in a given market at a given time; also called supply schedule.

SUPPLY CURVE: a graphic representation of the quantity of output supplied as a function of price.

SUPPLY PRICE: the lowest price needed to produce a specified output.

SUPPORTING THE MARKET: placing purchasing orders at or somewhat below the prevailing market level for the purpose of maintaining and balancing existing prices and to encourage a price rise.

SUPRA: above (Latin).

SUPRAMARGINAL: yielding more than the cost of production.

SURCHARGE: a charge imposed on top of an existing charge.

SURETY: a person who agrees to satisfy the obligation of another.

SURETY BOND: an agreement providing for monetary compensation in the event of failure to perform specified acts within a stated period.

SURPLUS: the excess of assets over the aggregate of liabilities and capital of a corporation.

SURRENDER OF LEASE: a mutual agreement between landlord and tenant to terminate all aspects of a lease before its normal expiration date.

SURRENDER VALUE: the amount of money the insurance company will pay to the policyholder upon surrender of his life insurance policy before death.

SURROGATE: a substitute.

SURTAX: a tax added on an item that is already taxed; usually a percentage of the existing tax.

SURVEILLANCE: guarding, watching over.

SURVEY: to conduct a study, tabulate and analyze results, and make a report; such a study and report.

SURVIVING ENTITY: in a merger or its like, the company that continues the business of the combined interests.

SUSPENDED TRADING: a binding stock-exchange decision to cease trading, resulting from an unusual occurrence.

SUSPENSE ACCOUNT: an account to which an entry is posted until its ultimate disposition is decided upon.

SUSPENSION: disciplinary layoff of a worker without pay; termination of a business; a temporary closing of a bank.

SUSTAINING PROGRAM: an unsponsored television or radio program, regularly aired, used in a time slot available for sale to an advertiser.

SWAP: to exchange or barter; to write the main storage aspects of a job into auxiliary storage and read the image of another job into main storage.

SWAP FUND: a fund into which many investors put their own investments and receive a share in the pooled investment portfolio.

SWAP NETWORK: a series of short-term reciprocal credit lines between foreign banks under which the Federal Reserve System exchanges dollars for their foreign currencies.

SWEATSHOP: a factory with unsatisfactory labor conditions, such as fatiguing tasks or long hours.

SWEETEN: to make more palatable or attractive, as to sweeten a deal by offering more incentives to the other party to the negotiations.

SWEETHEART AGREEMENT: a secret deal with management by a corrupt union agent for an inferior contract.

SWINDLE: to acquire money, goods, or property from another by imposture or deceit.

SWINDLING: the selling of worthless shares through misrepresentation.

SWINGS: up-and-down price movements in the stock market.

SWING SHIFT: the shift between day and night shifts, from about 4 PM to about midnight.

SWITCH: to sell one security and buy another for approximately the same amount of money as realized at practically the same time.

SWITCHBOARD: a panel or panels for measuring, monitoring, switching, connecting, and controlling electrical currents.

SWITCHING: selling one security and buying another.

SWITCHING CUSTOMERS: bringing a sales specialist when the salesperson originally serving a customer is unable to close a sale.

SWITCH ORDER: an order for the purchase (sale) of one stock and the sale (purchase) of another stock at a stipulated price difference.

SWITCH SELLING: an unethical practice of using high-pressure tactics to sell an item more expensive than one advertised at a lower price.

SYMBOL: a pictorial representation, as a trademark.

SYMBOLIC CODING: any coding system in which symbols other than machine addresses are used.

SYMMETRICAL: equally balanced about an axis or plane.

SYMPATHETIC STRIKE: a strike called to support the strike of another union and which may be unmotivated by a grievance of its own.

SYNDICALISM: an economic concept: workers exert control over the industries that employ them.

SYNDICATE: investors participating usually equally, in a joint venture, and, at the conclusion of it, disbanding.

SYNERGY: the condition under which combined activity is more effective than the total of the independent activities.

SYNTHESIZE: to manufacture a raw material by a chemical process in which more complex molecules are developed from simpler ones.

SYSTEM: a collection of objects or events conforming to a plan; the plan itself.

SYSTEMATIC: methodical, organized, regular.

SYSTEMATIC ERROR: the result of a relatively predictable tendency toward error when making a judgment.

SYSTEM-INPUT DEVICE: a device specified as a source of an input stream.

SYSTEM-OUTPUT DEVICE: a device assigned to identify output data for a series of jobs.

SYSTEM PROGRAMMER: a programmer who plans, generates, maintains, extends, and controls the use of an operating system.

SYSTEMS ANALYSIS: the analysis of any business activity to determine precisely what must be accomplished and how to accomplish it.

SYSTEMS DESIGN: the formulation and graphic outlining of input, files, procedures, and output in order to display the necessary connection processes and procedures.

SYSTEMS FLOW CHART: a visual representation of the system through which information provided by the source documents is changed into final documents.

SYSTEMS MANAGEMENT: designing and operating a business as a system, including consideration of the human element and the firm's goals.

SYSTEMS RESEARCH: the study of the daily operations of an organization purporting to upgrade efficiency and lower costs.

SYSTEMS SELLING: the merchandising of a group of items that have some functional relationship to one another as a package.

SYSTEMS THEORY: an analysis that stresses the necessity for maintaining the basic elements of input-process-output.

T

TABLE: a statement of factual information, usually assembled for reference purposes.

TABULAR MATTER: statistical matter listed in rows and columns, particularly in printing.

TABULATING EQUIPMENT: machines and equipment that use punched cards; synonymous with electronic accounting machines.

TABULATING MACHINE: a typing machine with automatic columnar adjustment.

TABULATOR: a device that prints data from punched cards and can do some arithmetic on the card data; tabulating mechanism on a typewriter.

T-ACCOUNT: the simplified form of a ledger account used in demonstrating accounting problems.

TACIT: designating rules that are accepted to be law by reason of custom, tradition, and mores.

TACIT AGREEMENT: unspoken accord or assent, at times arising from failure to disagree with, or abiding by, a unilaterally imposed condition.

TACKING: a process of adding a junior claim to a senior one in order to create some gain.

TACTIC: an approach used to attain certain goals that relate directly to the overall objectives of an organization.

TAFT-HARTLEY ACT: federal statute that amends the National Labor Relation Act to regulate some union activities.

TAG: an addition to a commercial broadcast.

TAG SORT: a sort in which addresses of records, not the records themselves, are moved during the comparison procedure.

TAKE: any profit from a business activity, usually one of a suspicious nature; to lay hold of, seize, or have in possession.

TAKE A BATH: to have a substantial financial loss.

TAKE-HOME PAY: salary or wages after all deductions.

TAKE-OUT LOAN: the long-term financing of a real estate project after completion of construction.

TAKEOVER BID: a bid to purchase shares of a corporation with a view to gaining control of the corporation.

TAKEOVER TIME: the time required in marketing for a superior new product to go from 10 to 90 percent displacement of an inferior older product.

TAKE STOCK: to make an inventory of items on hand.

TAKING INVENTORY: the procedure of counting all inventory on hand at a time set aside for this purpose.

TALISMAN: a juror summoned to fill out a jury when the regular panel is exhausted.

TALON: a special coupon; part of a debt instrument remaining on an unmatured bond after the interest coupons that were formerly attached have been presented.

TAMPERPROOF CONTAINER: a container designed so that it cannot be opened and resealed without leaving evidence of tampering.

TANDEM INCREASE: a pay increase given to certain groups in a factory as the result of a raise negotiated by the production workers.

TANGIBLE ASSET: an asset having physical existence, as distinguished from goodwill, trademarks, etc.

TANGIBLE NET WORTH: the net worth of a business excluding such assets as goodwill and patents.

TANGIBLE PERSONAL PROPERTY: physical things; such as goods and products.

TANK CAR: a railcar used for transporting liquids in bulk.

TANKTAINER: a tank constructed into the standard container frame and used to ship liquids.

TAPE DRIVE: a device on which one mounts a magnetic tape for reading and writing.

TAPE-TO-CARD: term describing equipment or methods that transmit data from either magnetic tape or punched tape to punched cards.

TARE: a deduction or allowance made for the weight of a container or packaging material.

TARGET CUSTOMERS: the people who are the objects of a store's total efforts to attract business.

TARGET LANGUAGE: the machine language to which a statement or source document is translated.

TARGET PRICING: a technique of establishing prices to reach a profit objective.

TARGET RISK: a risk of large value or limits; a severe hazard that is difficult to insure or have reinsured.

TARIFF: a rate of price schedule, most frequently of import duties.

TARIFF RATE: the charge rate or schedule established by the rating organization having jurisdiction over a given class and territory.

TARIFF WAR: a form of competition between nations, as shown by tariff discrimination of various forms.

TASK FORCE: a small group organized to attain a specific objective.

TASK GROUP: a group of employees working as a unit to complete a project or task.

TASK MANAGEMENT: the functions of the control program that regulate the use by tasks of the central-processing unit and other resources, except by input/output devices.

TAX: an assessment or levy required to be paid for the support of government.

TAX ABATEMENT: the reduction of a tax because the tax was improperly levied or because of a legislative directive.

TAXABLE INCOME: the amount of income remaining after all permitted deductions and exemptions have been subtracted; subject to taxation.

TAXABLE VALUE: an assessed value utilized for taxing property, items, or income.

TAX-AND-BOARD: charges included in premiums for state or local taxes and for the support of the various rating offices, bureaus, and boards.

TAX-ANTICIPATION NOTE: any short-term, interest-bearing obligation purchased by businesses with monies reserved to pay taxes.

TAX ASSESSOR: a public official who places an official valuation on wealth or property rights for the government.

TAX AVOIDANCE: the minimizing of one's liability for tax by legal means.

TAX BASE: the measure on which the amount of a tax liability is determined.

TAX BURDEN: the amount of tax actually paid by a taxpayer.

TAX COLLECTOR: an elected or appointed government official who is responsible for the collection of those taxes within his area of responsibility.

TAX DEED: a deed issued to the buyer of property that is sold because of nonpayment of taxes.

TAX DODGE: an activity that constitutes an illegal attempt to avoid paying taxes.

TAX EVASION: the minimizing of one's liability for tax by illegal means.

TAX EXEMPTION: a right, secured by law, permitting freedom from a charge of taxes.

TAX EXILE (EXPATRIATE): an individual choosing to leave his country rather than pay taxes.

TAX FORECLOSURE: seizure of property because of unpaid taxes, by the duly authorized officials of the public authority empowered to tax.

TAX HAVEN: a political jurisdiction that levies little or no income or death taxes.

TAX IMPACT: the immediate obligation of a tax, or the immediate effect of the tax.

TAX INCIDENCE: in general, the final resting place of a tax after all shifting has occurred.

TAX LEASE: a long-term lease issued to the buyer of tax-delinquent property when the law prevents an outright sale.

TAX LIEN: a lien by the government against real property for failure to pay taxes.

TAX LIMIT: a legislative decision that limits the tax ceiling that can be imposed by an appropriate authority.

TAXPAYER: any person who pays taxes.

TAX POLICY: the policy whereby a government structures the tax rates.

TAX RATE: the amount of tax applied per unit of tax base, expressed as a percentage.

TAX ROLL: a governmental unit list of all land, the names of the owners, the assessed value, and the amount of taxes.

TAX SALE: a public sale of property at auction by a governmental authority after a period of nonpayment of tax.

TAX SEARCH: a determination by searching official records to determine whether there are any unpaid property taxes.

TAX SHARING: the situation in which one governmental unit levies and collects a tax whose proceeds are then shared with other units.

TAX SHELTER: a situation in which deductions for tax purposes are created without a corresponding decrease in cash flow.

TAX SHIELD: the amount of depreciation charged against income, thus protecting that amount from tax.

TAX TITLE: title to property acquired by purchasing land that was sold as the result of unpaid taxes.

TEAMSTER: originally a driver of horses, hence a driver of a vehicle, hence any member of the Teamsters Union, regardless of occupation.

TEAR SHEET: a page torn from a newspaper or magazine, proving that an ordered advertisement actually appeared.

TEASER: an ad that purports to increase curiosity by holding back the name of the advertiser or the product, but pledging additional data in future statements.

TECHNICAL EFFICIENCY: the condition achieved when there is no way to use less of one input without using more of another input to yield the same level of output.

TECHNICAL POSITION: a term applied to the various internal factors affecting the market.

TECHNOLOGICAL: term pertaining to applications of science.

TECHNOLOGICAL ASSESSMENT: a technique for evaluating the impact of technological change on society.

TECHNOLOGICAL FORECASTING: determining or predicting changes in technology and their organizational and societal implications.

TECHNOLOGICAL UNEMPLOYMENT: unemployment resulting from the introduction of new methods of production and/or operations.

TECHNOLOGY: an industrial science; applied scientific knowledge utilized in the resolution of practical issues and problems, and in the evolution of new products and new processes of manufacture.

TELEMETER: to transmit digital or analog metering data by communication facilities.

TELEPHONE-ANSWERING SERVICE: a service whereby a subscriber's incoming calls are personally or electronically recorded.

TELETYPE: a method for long-distance transmission by wire of typewritten messages.

TELEVISION: a method of transmitting images and sound, live or from tape or film, to a fluorescent screen scanned by a cathode-ray tube.

TELEX: a Teletype system.

TELLER: a bank employee who pays and receives money; one who counts ballots, as at stockholders' meetings.

TELLER'S CHECK: a check drawn by a bank on another bank and signed by a teller or tellers of the drawer bank.

TEMPLATE: a pattern of thin board, etc., used as a guide.

TEMPORARY-DISABILITY BENEFITS: the weekly benefits payable to employees for nonoccupational accidents and sickness.

TEMPORARY INJUNCTION: a court order restraining conduct until a hearing can be had on whether the injunction should be made permanent.

TEMPORARY STORAGE: an area of working storage not reserved for a single use but used by numerous sections of a program at differing times.

TEMPORIZE: to defer decision, delay, even to yield on minor issues of a larger agreement in order to gain time for meeting the major issue.

TENANCY: the occupation or holding of the land, quarters, or property of another; tenure of such property; period of such tenure.

TENANCY AT SUFFERANCE: condition under which a tenant continues to occupy the premises after the termination of his or her tenancy.

TENANCY AT WILL: condition under which a tenant resides on property legally but has no lease.

TENANCY BY THE ENTIRETY: an estate jointly owned by the husband and wife; the survivor receives the total estate—this agreement cannot be broken without the consent of both spouses.

TENANCY IN COMMON: the holding of property by two or more persons so that each has an undivided interest that passes as such, at death, to the heirs or devisees of the deceased and not to the survivor.

TENANT: one who holds or has the use of real property that is owned by another.

TENDER: an offer to purchase under definite conditions, including those of price and time.

TENEMENT: popularly, an old, run-down apartment structure; originally, any property held by one person for another.

TENNESSEE VALLEY AUTHORITY (TVA): the federal government agency that produces and distributes electricity, provides flood control, recreation areas, and other services in connection with the Tennessee River system.

TENOR: in finance, the period of time between inception and maturity of an obligation.

TENURE: the right to continue to hold a position; tenancy.

TERM: the prescribed time a person has to make installment or other payments, as identified in a loan or credit contract.

TERMINAL MARKET: a market that deals in futures.

TERMINAL POSITIONS: jobs in an organization that do not offer any possibilities for advancement.

TERM INSURANCE: insurance that runs for a stated period of time.

TERM LOAN: a long-term loan running up to 10 years.

TERM MORTGAGE: a mortgage with a fixed time period, usually less than five years, in which only interest is paid.

TERM POLICY: a fire or casualty policy written for more than one year.

TERMS: the details, specifications, and conditions of a loan.

TERMS OF SALE: a vendor's given time to pay an invoice, identifying discounts offered and other conditions of the sale.

TERMS OF TRADE: the number of units of items that must be surrendered for one unit of goods obtained, by a group or nation, that is a party to a transaction.

TERRITORY SCREENING: examining a list of buyers or potential customers to determine the priorities of sales visits in terms of time, opportunity, and profitability.

TESTAMENT: a will.

TESTAMENTARY TRUST: a trust established through a will.

TESTATE: having completed and left an acceptable will.

TESTATOR: one who makes a will.

TEST CASE: a case in a court of law, the outcome of which may serve as a precedent in other similar cases.

TESTIFY: to declare under oath in court or before another legal body.

TESTIMONIAL: a statement in praise of a product or service made by a satisfied user and publicized by the company by advertising or promotion.

TESTIMONY: statements by a witness under oath in a legal proceeding.

TEST MARKETING: the trial distribution of a new product in a small market to determine its likely acceptance in the total market.

TEXTILE: a woven fabric.

THEME: the major idea of an advertising campaign.

THERMOFAX: a photochemical method of readily making multiple office copies from an original.

THERMOPLASTIC: term referring to a group of plastic compounds, rigid at normal temperatures, capable of repeatedly becoming plastic upon reapplication of heat.

THERMOSETTING: term referring to a group of plastic compounds, which are fused by heat into a permanently rigid form.

THIN CORPORATION: a corporation owing a large number of debts relative to its equity position.

THIN MARKET: a market in which there are comparatively few bids to buy or offers to sell, or both.

THINK TANK: an organization purporting to examine issues of society, science, technology, and business.

THIRD-CLASS MAIL: circulars or printed advertising matter of less than 24 pages.

THIRD-GENERATION COMPUTERS: a term used to announce computers in the post-1964 era which use basic building blocks containing several circuits.

THIRD MARKET: listed stocks not traded on a securities exchange; over-the-counter trading in listed securities.

THIRD MORTGAGE: a mortgage that is junior to both the first and second mortgages.

THIRD PARTY: one who is related to a negotiation, transaction, or controversy between two parties but allied with neither.

THIRD-PARTY TRANSACTION: a three-way business activity involving a buyer, a seller, and a source of consumer credit.

THIRDS: goods of extremely poor quality; lower in grade than seconds.

THRESHOLD COMPANIES: companies on the threshold of corporate maturity run intuitively by a handful of entrepreneurs.

THRIFT ACCOUNT: synonymous with savings account or special-interest account.

THROUGH BILL OF LADING: a bill of lading covering items moving from the point of origin to a final location.

THROUGHPUT: the total volume of work performed by a computing system over a given period.

THROWAWAY: a printed advertising handbill, inexpensive and expected by the advertiser to be thrown away by the recipient immediately after reading.

TICKER: the instrument that prints prices and volume of security transactions within minutes of each trade on any listed exchange.

TICKLER: a file or record of maturing obligations or other items of interest maintained in such a manner as to call attention to each item at the proper time.

TICKLER FILE: a follow-up folder in which correspondence, memoranda, etc. are filed by future dates and reviewed on the respective dates.

TIDELAND: shore land under water at high tide.

TIDELANDS OIL: proved deposits of petroleum in the earth strata below the seas within territorial limits.

TIDEWATER: the stale and brackish waters of oceans, seas, and estuaries that rise and fall with the tide.

TIED LOAN: a foreign loan limiting the borrower to spending the proceeds only in the nation making the loan.

TIE-IN SALE: a sale of merchandise the buyer rarely wants tied in with other merchandise the seller wishes to sell.

TIGHT MONEY: high-interest rates demanded in the borrowing of money; synonymous with tight credit.

TIGHT SHIP: a well-coordinated organization with strict regulations and purposeful administration.

TILL FORBID: an instruction to a publication to repeat an advertisement in every issue until countermanded or "until forbidden."

TILL MONEY: funds kept at a front desk or register, as distinguished from monies held in a bank.

TIME, ACCESS: the interval of time between the instant at which information is called for from storage and the instant at which delivery is terminated.

TIME, READ: the time needed to identify data or an instruction word in a storage section and transfer it to an arithmetic unit where the required computations are performed.

TIME-AND-A-HALF PAY: compensation at the rate of one and one-half times the worker's regular pay.

TIME-AND-MOTION STUDY: a study of the operations performed on a given job and the timing of each operation.

TIME BARGAIN: struck when a seller and a purchaser of securities consent to exchange a specific stock at a stated price at a stated future time.

TIME BUYER: an executive in an advertising agency who asists in the planning of media campaigns and choses and buys radio and television time.

TIME DEPOSIT: funds deposited under agreement which bear interest from the date of deposit, when such funds remain on deposit for at least 30 days.

TIME DISCOUNT: reduction in advertising rate determined by the frequency of appearance of an ad.

TIME LOAN: a loan made for a specified period.

TIME ORDER: an order that becomes a market or limited-price order at a specified time.

TIME-SHARING: a method of using a computing system that allows a number of users to execute programs on the same hardware.

TIME-SHARING PRIORITY: a ranking within the group of tasks associated with a single user, used to determine their precedence for the allocation of system resources.

TIME STANDARD: the period an average employee needs to complete a task or job under normal conditions of work.

TIME STUDY: a procedure by which the actual elapsed time for performing an operation or elements thereof is measured and recorded.

TIPS: supposedly "inside" information on corporation affairs.

TITLE: evidence of ownership of anything of value.

TITLE DEFECT: a fact or circumstance that challenges property ownership.

TITLE GUARANTY: a guarantee of clear title to property.

TITLE-GUARANTY COMPANY: a business firm created to examine real estate files to determine the legal status of the property, to find any evidence of encumbrances, faults, and other title defects.

TITLE INSURANCE: an insurance contract from a title-guaranty company presented to owners of property, indemnifying them against having a defective or unsalable title during property ownership.

TOKENISM: the gesture of hiring a few minority group members in an attempt to satisfy affirmative-action requirements or the demands of pressure groups.

TOKEN MONEY: coins circulating at a value above the metal in the coin, such as cents, nickels, and dimes in the United States.

TOLERANCE: the acceptable limits of deviation from a norm.

TOLL: originally, a tax for permission to produce something; presently, a charge for permission to utilize a public facility or service.

TONNAGE: the number of tons of cargo handled.

TOP CREDIT: ready credit.

TOP DRAWER: classified with the elite, as a person of the highest level of competence, performance, or rank.

TOP OUT: to reach a peak and retreat from it, as a market prices.

TORT: a wrongful act committed by a person against another person or his or her property.

TORTFEASOR: a person committing a tort.

TOTAL COST: the sum of a firm's total fixed costs and total variable costs.

TOTAL DEBT: all long-term obligations of the government and its agencies and all interest-bearing short-term credit obligations.

TOTAL FIXED COSTS: the costs that do not change with an organization's output.

TOTAL LOSS: items that have been so badly damaged that they are not considered to be worth repairing.

TOTAL REVENUE: total receipts of a company.

TOTAL VARIABLE COSTS: costs that change directly with the firm's

output, increasing as output rises over the total range of production.

TOUR OF DUTY: hours an employee is scheduled to work.

TRACE: to ascertain whether an item has been disposed of in accordance with source indications.

TRACER: a request to trace a shipment; an official form used in locating delayed or undelivered mail.

TRACK: the portion of a moving storage medium that is accessible to a given reading head position.

TRACTOR: a vehicle built primarily to pull other vehicles.

TRADE ADVERTISING: advertising directed at wholesalers or retailers.

TRADE ASSOCIATION: a nonprofit organization that purports to serve the common interest of its membership.

TRADE DEFICIT: a negative trade balance.

TRADE DISCOUNT: a discount extended to those within an industry, but denied to others.

TRADE-IN: the surrender of an old product for a new one, accompanied by additional payment to make up for depreciation of the traded item.

TRADEMARK: a distinctive mark, or word identifying a product or company and protected by registration with the US Patent Office.

TRADE NAME: the name under which an organization conducts business, or by which the business or its goods and services are identified.

TRADEOFFS: the exchange of one benefit or value at the sacrifice of another.

TRADER: anyone who is engaged in trade or commerce; one who buys and sells for his own account for short-term profit.

TRADE REFERENCE: a person or firm to which a seller is referred for credit data on a potential customer.

TRADE UNION: workers organized into a voluntary association to further their mutual interests with respect to wages, hours, and working conditiongs.

TRADING DIFFERENCE: a difference of a fraction of a point in the charged price for securities bought and sold in an odd lot of transaction.

TRADING DOWN: attempting to increase the market of a store or item with an established reputation by lowering price or quality, or changing promotional strategy to appeal to a larger potential market.

TRADING POST: one of many trading locations on the floor of stock exchanges at which stocks assigned to that location are bought and sold.

TRADING STAMP: a promotional device; a stamp given to customers, worth a small percentage of the total amount paid for purchases.

TRADING UP: the attempt to improve the image of a store or item by increasing prices or quality, or altering advertisement approaches, usually appealing to a market in a higher socioeconomic level.

TRADITIO: delivery and transfer of possession of property by an owner.

TRAFFIC: to trade; total flow within a period.

TRAFFIC DEPARTMENT: the department that schedules the work responsibilities of other units in an agency and has primary responsibility for ensuring that deadlines are met.

TRAINEE: one who receives on-the-job training for his or her own position or an advanced position in a business organization.

TRAINING, BLITZ: rapid training, which attempts to bring personnel to the highest skill level possible under such pressure conditions.

TRAINING, COLD-STORAGE: a form of training offered to prepare employees for positions that they may fill at some future date; synonymous with reserve training.

TRAINING, VESTIBULE: training provided in an area removed from the factory floor, where similar equipment is available.

TRAIT THEORY OF LEADERSHIP: the identification of physical, mental, and personality characteristics believed to be linked to successful leadership.

TRANSACTION: any agreement between two or more parties, establishing a legal obligation.

TRANSACTION FILE: a file containing relatively transient data to be processed in combination with a master file.

TRANSACTIONS MOTIVE: the holding, by consumers and businessmen, of some of their assets in liquid form to make possible participation in day-to-day spending activities.

TRANSACTIONS TAX: a tax on turnover; a sales tax on both retail and wholesale sales.

TRANSCRIBER: specific equipment associated with a computer for the purpose of transferring the input or output data from a record of information to the computer medium and language.

TRANSCRIPTION: a sound recording for audio braodcast; a recording from a recording; typing from stenographic or stenotype notes.

TRANSFER: to move information from one storage device to another or from one part of memory to another; the shifting of an employee from one job to another within the same organization.

TRANSFERABILITY: the ability to transfer ownership or title.

TRANSFER AGENT: the one designated to keep record of stocks and bonds of a corporation.

TRANSFER CLAUSE: a clause in a lease which terminates the agreement if and when the tenant changes employment.

TRANSFER COSTS: the costs that a department accepts for items supplied by other departments.

TRANSFER OF TITLE: the change of property title from one person to another.

TRANSFER PAYMENT: in government statistics, money transactions between people, government, and business for which no services are made.

TRANSFER PRICE: the price charged by one segment of an organization for a product or service it supplies to another part of the same firm.

TRANSFER TAX: a tax on the transfer of securities.

TRANSIENT RATE: the advertising rate of a newspaper for noncontract advertising not subject to either frequency or volume discounts; the daily rate of hotel accommodations.

TRANSIT ADVERTISING: advertising in and on buses, railway cars, ferries, terminals, and other transit facilities.

TRANSITION CARD: in the loading of a deck of program cards, the card that causes the termination of loading, then initiates the execution of the program.

TRANSLATOR: a routine for changing information from one representation or language to another.

TRANSMIT: to move or communicate; to send data from one location and to receive the data at another location.

TRANSOM ORDER: an order that comes in unexpectedly, without direct solicitation, as if over the transom.

TRANSPLACEMENT: an error caused by moving all digits to the right or left of the proper columns without changing the order of the digits.

TRANSPORTATION: the movement of vehicular or marine traffic from one place to another.

TRANSPOSITION: an error caused by interchanging of digits.

TRANSSHIPPING: the transfer of items from one carrier to another; the shipment of merchandise beyond the usual selling area.

TRAPPING: a unique feature of some computers, enabling an unscheduled jump (transfer) to be made to a predetermined location in response to a machine condition.

TRAVELER'S CHECKS: special checks supplied by banks and other companies at small cost for the use of travelers.

TRAVELER'S LETTER OF CREDIT: a letter of credit issued by a bank to a customer preparing for an extended trip.

TRAVELING SALES REPRESENTATIVE: a salesperson who travels considerably to obtain orders.

TRAVEL TIME: the period required to report from a designated point to the place of work, compensated for at negotiated rates of pay.

TREASURESHIP: the functions of management holding responsibility for the custody and investment of money, the granting of credit, and collection of accounts.

TREASURY BILLS: noncoupon obligations, sold at discount through competitive bidding, generally having original maturities of three months and one year.

TREASURY BOND: a US government long-term security, sold to the public and having a maturity longer than five years.

TREASURY CERTIFICATES: a US government short-term security, sold to the public and maturing in one year.

TREASURY NOTE: a US government long-term security, sold to the public and having a maturity of one to five years.

TREASURY SHARES: authorized but unused shares.

TREASURY STOCK: issued stock that has been reacquired by the corporation from stockholders.

TREATY: a reinsurance contract between companies.

TRESPASS: the wrongful entry of one person onto another's property.

TRIAL: a proceeding by authorized officials to examine evidence for the purpose of determining an issue; in the adoption process of a consumer, the period when a product is first used.

TRIAL-AND-ERROR PRICING: selling an item at varying prices in differing locations, then assessing the response to each of the prices.

TRIAL BALANCE: a list of all account balances in a ledger, prepared to determine whether the ledger is in balance.

TRIANGULAR TRADE: trade between three countries, in which an attempt is made to create a favorable balance for each.

TRICKLE-DOWN: the process by which federal funds flowing into the national economy stimulate growth through being distributed into organizations.

TRIGGER-PRICE SYSTEM: a federal system for identifying cut-rate steel "dumped" in the United States.

TRIPLE DAMAGES: a civil penalty award to a successful plaintiff in certain suits, usually legal actions brought under federal antitrust laws, such as collusion to fix prices.

TROUBLESHOOT: the activity of an individual engaged in locating and eliminating the source of trouble in a task or operation.

TROUGH: the lowest point of economic activity.

TROY WEIGHT: a system of weights for gold and silver (12 ounces equals 1 troy pound).

TRUCK JOBBER: a middleman who delivers at the time of sale.

TRUNCATE: to terminate a computational process in accordance with a given rule (see also paper truncation).

TRUNK LINE: a through or main line, as on a railroad or a telephone system.

TRUNK SHOW: the display of a vendor's total line of merchandise before an audience gathered for the purpose of inspecting the wares.

TRUST: an arrangement by which an individual or a corporation as trustee holds the title to property for the benefit of one or more persons.

TRUST, CORPORATE: the name applied to the division of a bank handling the trust and agency business of corporations.

TRUST AGREEMENT: an agreement between an employer and a trustee used in connection with a pension plan.

TRUST COMPANY: an institution, usually state supervised, which engages in the trust business, and usually in all commercial banking activities.

TRUSTEE: a person who holds title to property for the benefit of another.

TRUSTEE IN BANKRUPTCY: a person appointed by a court to administer the estate of a bankrupt and ultimately distribute the available assets to creditors.

TRUSTEESHIP: suspension, by an international union, of the officers of a local union, with the international taking over control and administration of the local.

TRUST ESTATE: an estate held in trust by one individual for the welfare of another.

TRUST FUND: the assets held by a trustee for a beneficiary.

TRUST INDENTURE: an instrument in writing that contains a description of the trust agreement.

TRUSTOR: an individual who establishes a trust.

TRUTH TABLE: a table that describes a logic function by listing all possible combinations of input values and indicating, for each combination, the true output values.

TURN: a description of the full cycle in the buying and selling of a security or a commodity.

TURNAROUND: movement by a freight carrier where the driver returns to his point of origin following the unloading and reloading of cargo.

TURNAROUND TIME: the elapsed time between submission of a job to a computing center and the return of results.

TURNKEY: in real estate language, the condition under which property is ready for occupancy; in computers, a computer that is ready to use upon purchase, with little more than the push of a button.

TURNOVER: the number of times a stock of merchandise is replaced in one year; annual sales divided by merchandise inventory; rate of turnover.

TURNOVER RATIO: a measure of capital activity or another factor of business.

TURNOVER TAX: a form of sales tax employed in the Soviet Union.

TURNPIKES: improved roads for the use of which a toll is commonly charged.

TURNTABLE: a device for reversing the direction of a unidirectional vehicle in a small radius; the table of a record player.

TURN THE CORNER: to pass from a period of losses to one of gains.

TWISTING: convincing an insured to surrender his life insurance for its cash value and replace it with new life insurance.

TWO-DOLLAR BROKERS: members on the floor of the exchange who execute orders for other brokers having more business at that time than they can handle themselves.

TYCOON: a person who has accumulated great wealth in industry or commerce.

TYING CONTRACT: a contract in which the seller forces the buyer to purchase a secondary relatively undesirable product.

TYPEFACE: designs for the capital and lower-case alphabets, numerals, and punctuation of a font, all harmonious with each other and workable in text.

TYPIST: proficient production by a skilled typewriter operator.

U

UBIQUITOUS: worldwide; everywhere present.

ULTIMATE CONSUMER: the individual who actually uses the bought merchandise.

ULTIMO: the month prior to the existing one.

UMBRELLA LIABILITY: a form of insurance protection against losses in excess of amounts covered by other liability-insurance policies.

UMPIRE: an individual called in to decide a controversy; synonymous with arbitrator.

UNAFFILIATED UNION: a local or national union that is not affiliated with the parent labor organization.

UNAMORTIZED BOND DISCOUNT: the portion of the original bond discount which has not been charged off against earnings.

UNAPPROPRIATED PROFITS: the portion of a firm's profit which has not been paid out in dividends or allocated for any special purpose.

UNAUTHORIZED STRIKE: a strike that does not have the authorization of the union.

UNBALANCED GROWTH: capital investment that grows at different rates in different areas of an economy.

UNCALLED CAPITAL: the portion of the issued share capital of a corporation which has not yet been called.

UNCERTAINTY: noninsurable business risk: the unpredictability of the outcome of much of business activity.

UNCERTAINTY THEORY: theory that profit arises from uncertainties due to innovations, changes in taste, price fluctuations, and the vagaries of competition.

UNCLAIMED BALANCES: the balances of the accounts for funds on deposit that have remained inactive for a period designated by the bank.

UNCOLLECTED FUNDS: a portion of a deposit balance that has not yet been collected by the depository bank.

UNCOLLECTIBLE ACCOUNTS: amounts owed by credit customers who do not pay their bills.

UNDERAPPLIED OVERHEAD: the excess of factory overhead incurred over factory overhead applied.

UNDERCAPITALIZED: a business with insufficient ownership funds for the scale of operations it is carrying on.

UNDERCHARGE: to charge less than the legal amount.

UNDERCLASS: a term describing people on the lowest economic level.

UNDERDEVELOPED COUNTRY: a nation in which per capita real income is proportionately low when contrasted with industrialized nations.

192

*UNDER-
DEVELOPED
NATION •
UNFAIR
LABOR
PRACTICES*

UNDERDEVELOPED NATION: a country in which the per capita income is relatively low in comparison to that of industrial nations.

UNDEREMPLOYED: a term describing an individual working on a job of a lower level than that for which he has training or experience.

UNDERINSURANCE: insurance for less than the value of the goods or the amount of the risk.

UNDERLEASE: a tenant's lease of property to a third party; a sublease.

UNDERLYING COMPANY: a term usually limited to a subsidiary that owns franchises or other rights that are not transferable but are essential to the operation of the economic unit.

UNDERLYING MORTGAGE: a mortgage senior to a larger one.

UNDER PROTEST: these words are used by the payor to deny any implication that he is waiving whatever rights he may have, while being compelled to make a payment.

UNDERSELLING: selling at a price lower than that listed by a competitor.

UNDER-THE-COUNTER: dealing in an unethical manner.

UNDERWRITING: the assumption of a risk, as in insurance and investment; assuming all or part of the risk in exchange for a premium payment.

UNDIGESTED SECURITIES: securities that are issued beyond the need for or ability of the public to absorb them.

UNDISTRIBUTED PROFITS: those profits retained by business and not paid out as dividends.

UNDIVIDED INTEREST: an interest by two or more people in the same property without identification of the parts of the property which belong to the respective parties.

UNDIVIDED RIGHT: the right of one person in property owned jointly by several persons.

UNEARNED DISCOUNT: in accounting, interest in the form of a discount already collected but not yet earned.

UNEARNED INCOME: in accounting, income received in advance of the accounting period to which it is allocable.

UNEARNED INCREMENT: increase in value of real estate due to no effort on the part of the owner, often due to increase in population.

UNEARNED PREMIUM: the portion of the original premium which has not yet been "earned" by the company because the policy has not expired.

UNEMPLOYABLE: a person who is unable to find work, because he is too sick, too young, too old, too lazy, or is a criminal.

UNEMPLOYMENT: a condition of not being employed.

UNEMPLOYMENT COMPENSATION: system of insuring workers against hardship during periods of unemployment.

UNEMPLOYMENT INSURANCE: insurance premiums collected by the state and federal governments from which unemployment compensation is paid.

UNEMPLOYMENT STATISTICS: census information compiled from monthly sampling surveys on the employment of citizens classified by such things as age, marital status, and size of family.

UNENCUMBERED PROPERTY: real estate free and clear of any mortgages, liens, or debts of any type.

UNEXPIRED COST: any asset.

UNFAIR COMPETITION: a seller trying to obtain a larger share of the market by adopting any device that unfairly takes advantage of a competing firm, such as false advertising.

UNFAIR GOODS: products or items not produced by members of a union.

UNFAIR-LABOR-PRACTICE STRIKE: a strike provoked by the employer, considered to be an unfair labor practice under federal and state labor laws.

UNFAIR LABOR PRACTICES: illegal antiunion behavior or illegal union behavior, as determined by the National Labor Relations Board.

UNFAIR LIST: a list of firms considered to be unfair to labor, distributed by unions to reduce patronage or otherwise exert pressure.

UNFAIR PRACTICES ACT: a state regulation establishing minimum resale prices.

UNFUNDED PENSION PLAN: a pension plan under which no pension fund has been set up.

UNIFORM BILL OF LADING: a shipping form acceptable to all carriers.

UNIFORM CASH FLOWS: cash flows that are the same for every year.

UNIFORM COMMERCIAL CODE: a comprehensive commercial law that has been adopted in all states except Louisiana which covers the law of sales.

UNIFORM DELIVERED PRICE: a pricing method where all the products are sold at the same delivery price in a stated area without regard for delivery costs.

UNIFORMED SERVICES: public employees, such as police, fire, and sanitation workers.

UNILATERAL CONTRACT: a contract in which complete performance is given by one party at the time of contract in return for a promise by the other party.

UNILATERAL STRATEGY: an organizational development approach that precludes participation by employees.

UNIMPROVED LAND: in real estate language, usually used to indicate land without buildings or undeveloped or raw land.

UNINSURABLE TITLE: property that a title-insurance company will not insure.

UNINSURED-MOTORIST PROTECTION: coverage for the policyholder and members of his family in the event of an accident involving a driver who carries no liability insurance.

UNION: a worker's organization, having as its major objective the representation of the members in bargaining with employers.

UNION RATE: the minimum hourly wage rate, accepted by a union for a specific type of activity and employed in negotiations.

UNION RECOGNITION: the acceptance by an employer of a union as the collective-bargaining representative of his or her workers.

UNION-SECURITY CLAUSES: negotiated contract clauses that protect the institutional life of the union.

UNION SHOP: condition under which employees in a bargaining unit must join and remain in the union.

UNISSUED STOCK: part of the authorized capital stock of a corporation that is not issued or outstanding.

UNIT: single thing or measure; a homogeneous kind or class.

UNIT-BENEFIT PENSION PLAN: a synonym for benefit-based pension plan.

UNIT BILLING: a list of all purchases by a customer prepared on a single statement.

UNIT CONTROL: an approach for listing the quantity of goods bought, sold in stock, and on order, with additional breakdowns as needed.

UNIT COST: the cost of producing or distributing one unit of a processed item.

UNITIZE: to combine a number of freight pieces into one large one by any means of assembling into a unit.

UNITIZED LOAD: a load in which all the containers are bound together in one or more units.

UNIT-LABOR COST: the cost of an employee needed to produce one unit of output; determined by dividing compensation by output.

UNIT OF TRAFFIC: the average tons of cargo hauled per mile.

UNIT PRICING: the quotation of prices given in terms of a standard measurement.

UNIT RECORD: a (punched) card containing one complete record.

UNIT TECHNOLOGY: the approach of a company that spends a large amount of capital on labor relative to the investment in machinery.

UNITY OF COMMAND: a concept that a subordinate must be responsible to only one superior.

UNIVERSAL-DESIGN THEORY: the approach according to which there is "one best way" to design an organization.

UNIVERSE: in statistics, the entire body of possible data.

UNLIMITED ACCOUNTS: large or reputable businesses that are eligible for any amount of credit.

UNLIMITED LIABILITY: concept that the owner is completely liable for all debits of the business even though these debits may be greater than the amount he originally invested.

UNLISTED STOCK: a stock not listed on a recognized stock exchange.

UNLOADING: selling merchandise at a relatively low price; synonymous with dumping; the sale of stocks and commodities to avoid a loss.

UNPAID BALANCE: difference between the purchase price and the down payment or the value of a trade-in.

UNPAID DIVIDEND: a dividend declared but not yet distributed.

UNPROFITABLE: showing a loss.

UNREALIZED PROFITS: paper profits that are not made actual until the firm's securities have been sold.

UNSECURED: not backed by hypothecated collateral, as a loan.

UNSECURED DEBT: a debt for which no collateral has been pledged.

UNSECURED LOAN: a loan made by a bank based on credit information about the borrower; the loan is not secured by collateral.

UNSKILLED: possessing no specialized craft skill, such as carpentry.

UNSTABLE MARKET: a market in which forces of disequilibrium are reinforced so that movements away from equilibrium are not reversible.

UNSTUFFING: unloading cargo from a container.

UNWRITTEN LAW: the body of English common law preceding written jurisprudence.

UPDATE: to modify a master file with current information, according to a specified procedure.

UPGRADING: a well-defined program for training and advancement of qualified workers in an organization; offering of superior goods and greater assortment to customers.

UPKEEP: the cost of maintaining property or machinery in sound, workable condition.

UPSCALE: the households and people who are of well-above-average income and education.

UPSET PRICE: the lowest price at which a seller is willing to sell.

UPSWING: a sharp rise in prices from fairly constant levels or in reversal of a decline.

UP TICK: a transaction made at a price higher than the preceding transaction.

UPTIME: time during which a computer is available for productive work.

UPTREND: an overall upward movement of prices, albeit with fluctuations, over a considerable period.

UPTURN: a rise in prices in reversal of a decline.

URBAN: metropolitan; city.

URBANIZATION: the movement of people from small communities to larger communities.

URBAN RENEWAL: the planned rehabilitation of run-down central areas of a city or community.

USANCE: employment; interest or income; the period allowed for payment of a foreign obligation.

USELESS QUALITY: describing goods created with quality, dependability, and/or performance superior to that demanded by the public.

USER: anyone who requires the services of a system of product, or who employs a service.

USER CALLS: callbacks a sales representative makes on a customer who has already made a purchase from him or her or from the organization.

USER CHARGE: a levy paid by a user of a public transportation system; a time set by custom for the payment of a bill of exchange.

USE TAX: tax imposed in several states on products bought in another state to avoid a local sales tax.

USUFRUCT: the right to the interest earned on property but not to the property itself.

USUFRUCTUARY RIGHT: a right to appropriate use and pleasure from property owned by another.

USURIOUS: describing a contract made for a loan of money at a rate of interest in excess of that authorized by statute.

USURY: interest charged at a rate higher than that permitted by law.

UTILITY: the ability of a material, good, or service to satisfy human wants or desires; colloquial term for "public utility."

UTILITY PROGRAM: a computer program designed to perform an everyday task.

UTTER: to put out or pass off; to "utter a check" is to give it to another in payment of an obligation.

UTTERING: using a forged document with the knowledge that it is forged.

V

VACANCY FACTOR: unrented space calculated over a fixed time period.

VACATION PAY: compensation received for a specified vacation period.

VACILLATION: indecisive wavering and mind-changing.

VACUUM FORMING: a type of equipment on which large plastic forms can be made, as clothes baskets.

VACUUMIZE: to remove air from a filled container prior to closing.

VACUUM PACKING: a type of equipment capable of canning foods

and other products under extreme low pressures.

VALID: that which is sufficient to satisfy the requirement of the law; a fact.

VALIDATE: to render useful, as in the case of affixing a visa to a passport.

VALIDATION: proof or confirmation.

VALIDITY: proof or confirmation, the quality of being truthful and/or factual.

VALIDITY CHECK: an appraisal that a code group is actually a character of the particular code in use.

VALLEY: a V-shape formed by the projection of an indicator on a chart.

VALORIZATION: governmental action leading to the establishment of a price or value for an item or service.

VALUABLE CONSIDERATION: a legal term meaning any consideration sufficient to support a contract.

VALUATION: synonymous with appraising; the fixing of value to anything.

VALUATION RESERVES: reserves established to provide for a drop in the existing value of the assets to which they pertain.

VALUE: the utility of a good weighted by its price.

VALUE ADDED: that part of the value of produced goods developed in a company.

VALUE-ADDED TAX: a tax levied at each stage in the production and distribution chain of a product based on the increased value; ad valorem tax.

VALUE ANALYSIS: a purchasing strategy of asking the buyer's engineers to project the cost of goods in an attempt to keep vendor's prices low.

VALUE APPROACH: including ethical and value judgments in the decision-making process to effect change in the organization.

VALUE DATE: the date on which a bank deposit becomes effective.

VALUED POLICY: a policy providing for the payment of a stipulated amount in the event of a total loss of the insured property.

VALUE ENGINEERING: the systematic use of tools that identify the required function, establish its value, and provide the function at the lowest overall cost.

VALUE IN USE: the value of goods to the individual using them.

VALUE JUDGMENT: a decision utilizing basic issues of fairness, justice, or morality.

VAN CONTAINER: a standard trailer used to carry general cargo.

VANNING: loading a container.

VARIABLE: any quantity that is not constant, varies, or allows the assumption of different values.

VARIABLE ANNUITY: an annuity contract providing lifetime retirement payments that vary in amount with the results of investment in a separate account portfolio.

VARIABLE, DEPENDENT: a variable whose changes are treated as being consequent upon changes in one or more other variables, referred to as independent variables.

VARIABLE, INDEPENDENT: variable whose changes are regarded as not dependent on any other variables.

VARIABLE COSTS: those expenses of a business or industry which vary with the amount of business done or the volume of goods produced.

VARIABLE ERROR: an error of judgment that varies uniformly in either direction from the norm.

VARIABLE INTEREST RATE: an interest rate that moves up and down as the prevailing prime rate of interest fluctuates.

VARIABLE-LIFE INSURANCE: a type of policy in which the death benefit is based on the performance of the stocks in the insurer's portfolio.

VARIANCE: any disagreement between two sets of figures or facts; the measure of dispersion within a distribution of events.

VARIETY STORE: a retail operation that carries limited quantities of apparel and accessories for the family as well as other goods with prices set somewhat lower than in retail stores.

VAULT: a large room or rooms in a bank or financial institution where the cash on hand is stored and safe-deposit boxes are located.

VEIL-OF-MONEY THEORY: theory that money is neutral and does not reflect a nation's true economic condition.

VELOCITY OF CIRCULATION: the rate at which the money supply is spent for a stated time period, usually one year.

VELVET: slang, an unearned income or profit.

VEND: any offer to sell something.

VENDEE: the party who purchases or agrees to purchase property owned by another.

VENDING MACHINE: a coin-operated machine for the sale of merchandise.

VENDOR: a manufacturer, wholesaler, or importer from whom goods are purchased.

VENDOR CHARGEBACKS: the return of goods to a vendor accompanied by an adjusted invoice.

VENDOR RELIABILITY: the capability of the seller to meet the conditions of the contract.

VENDOR'S LIEN: an unpaid seller's right to take possession of property until the purchase price has been recovered.

VENDUE: a public auction.

VENT FOR SURPLUS: the hypothesis that economic progress spreads from developing industrial locations to less-developed locations by means of the increasing demand for goods.

VENTURE: a business undertaking involving potential risk.

VENTURE CAPITAL: funds available from the issue of new stock; reinvested monies from stockholders.

VENTURE-CAPITAL FUNDS: mutual funds invested in securities of firms that are unknown and often not yet registered with the SEC.

VENUE: the geographical legal jurisdiction in which an action or prosecution is brought for trial.

197

VERBAL •
VOICE-
INPUT
COMPUTER
SYSTEM

VERBAL: unwritten, as a verbal agreement.

VERBATIM: word for word (Latin).

VERDICT: finding of a jury; decision of a judge.

VERIFAX: an office copier.

VERIFIER: a device to check the correctness of cards punched by a key punch machine.

VERIFY: to investigate the truth; to confirm.

VERTEX: top; apex; peak.

VERTICALLY COMBINED (INTEGRATED): term describing a business firm that performs all the various stages of production of a single finished item.

VERTICAL PROMOTION: a form of advancement that increases employee opportunities, provides for additional training, increases responsibility, and usually is accompanied by additional pay.

VERTICAL SPECIALIZATION: factors in the division of labor involving degrees of power, influence, and decision-making.

VERTICAL STRAIN: the competition that exists between differing hierarchical levels in a company.

VEST: to obtain absolute ownership.

VESTED ESTATE: an interest in property holding present and future rights, but with the existing interest capable of being transferred.

VESTIBULE TRAINING: training of production workers with machines in a simulated environment.

VESTING: passing title to another.

VEST-POCKET: an expression of control, for example, a politician having a candidate in his vest-pocket.

VETERAN BENEFITS: hospitalization, educational support, bonus, pension, or other federally enacted benefits for war veterans.

VIA: by way of (Latin).

VIABILITY: the ability to meet financial obligations.

VICARIOUS LIABILITY: the principle that an employer is legally responsible for the actions of his employees while on the job.

VIDE: see; used to direct a reader to another item (Latin).

VIDEO: the visual signals of television.

VIDEOTAPE: magnetic iron-oxide tape used for recording television programs for delayed telecasting or private viewing.

VIE: strive for superiority and quest.

VIGNETTE: a display that simulates a product in actual use.

VIOLATION: transgression.

VIREMENT: the power to transfer items from one account to another.

VIRTUAL MACHINE: a functional simulation of a computer and its associated devices.

VIS-À-VIS: face to face.

VISCOSITY: the quality of inertia evidenced by fluids in opposing motion, far higher for a heavy grease than for a light oil.

VISIBLE TRADE: that portion of commerce between nations that is shown by records of transactions involving the exchange of tangible items.

VITALIST THEORY: to plan in terms of the total economic system and then integrate the full system relative to its individual smaller parts.

VITAL STATISTICS: statistical information about births, deaths, and population.

VITAMIN: food constituents necessary to health—isolated, prepared, packaged, and sold as diet supplements.

VITICULTURE: the growing of grapes; viniculture.

VOCABULARY: a list of operations or instructions, available to a computer programmer, to use in writing the program for a given problem on a specific computer.

VOCATION: a person's business, profession, or occupation.

VOCATIONAL: pertaining to craft skills and their study, as vocational training, vocational guidance.

VOICE-INPUT COMPUTER SYSTEM: computers that have been programmed to respond to spoken instructions.

VOID: having no force or effect.

VOIDABLE: capable of being either confirmed or being void.

VOIDABLE CONTRACT: an agreement that can be rescinded by either of the parties in the event of fraud, incompetence, or other sufficient cause.

VOLATILE: characterized by extreme, rapid, random fluctuations, as the prices of some securities or the tempers of some executives.

VOLATILE MEMORY: a storage medium in which information is destroyed when power is removed from the system.

VOLUME: a quantity, bulk, or amount; storage that is accessible to a single read/write mechanism.

VOLUME DISCOUNT: a reduction in the selling price of goods or services in consideration of large purchases over a particular period of time.

VOLUME TEST: the processing of a volume of actual data; to check for program malfunctions.

VOLUNTARY ALIENATION: transfer of title when the property assumes a new owner.

VOLUNTARY ARBITRATION: arbitration agreed to by the parties to a dispute without statutory compulsion.

VOLUNTARY BANKRUPTCY: bankruptcy in which the petitioner is the bankrupt.

VOLUNTARY CHAIN: a wholesaling organization established by independent retailers or wholesalers to gather increased purchasing power.

VOLUNTARY CONVEYANCE OR DEED: the instrument of transfer of an owner's title to property to the lien holder.

VOLUNTARY TRUST: established by a deed of transfer of certain property made voluntarily by an individual or other legal entity to a trustee for a specified purpose.

VOLUNTEER: one who offers his services at times without pay for a mission or task, often perilous or unattractive, which he is not obligated or assigned to perform.

VOSTRO ACCOUNT: "your account," term used by a depository bank to describe an account maintained with it by a bank in a foreign country.

VOTING BY PROXY: having another person cast one's vote.

VOTING RIGHT (STOCK): the stockholder's right to vote his or her stock in the affairs of the company.

VOTING STOCK: stock that gives the right to the holder to vote at corporate meetings.

VOTING TRUST: an agreement among shareholders of a corporation whereby their votes are to be cast by a trustee in the interest of the entire group.

VOUCHER CHECK: a form of check to which is attached another form termed a voucher.

VOUCHER-WRITTEN PROOF: proof that money has been paid or received; a document that establishes the accuracy of books of account.

W

WAGE: compensation of employees receiving a stated sum per piece, hour, day, or any other unit or period.

WAGE-AND-HOUR LAWS: laws regulating minimum wages and maximum hours for employees.

WAGE AND SALARY ADMINISTRATION: a well-defined approach for establishing wages and salaries according to an organization's rules and policies.

WAGE BRACKET (RANGE): the range of salary payment for a specific occupation.

WAGE CEILING: the top wage payable per hour to a given class of workmen.

WAGE CONTROL: during national crises, centralized control and stabilization of wages.

WAGE FLOOR: a minimum wage established in contract, below which an employee cannot be hired, or the legal minimum defined by the Fair

Labor Standards Act or other state labor laws.

WAGE FREEZE: a limit, usually imposed by a government, on salary increases.

WAGE INCENTIVE: additional wages offered for higher production, individual or group, above set norms.

WAGE RATE: the amount of pay for a given period.

WAGE SCALE: a wage-rate structure covering all employees in a department, division, plant, or office.

WAGE STABILIZATION: a governmental program to keep wages for a particular industry or location from rapidly increasing beyond existing levels.

WAGE STOP: a concept of not permitting an unemployed worker from receiving more public monies than he or she would earn while working.

WAGNER ACT (1935): federal legislation that made collective bargaining legal and required employers to bargain with the elected representatives of their employees.

WAITING PERIOD: a time specified in certain policies or contracts which must pass before payment will begin; the time between filing a claim and receiving the benefits.

WAIT ORDER: a request to a medium to hold an advertisement, not releasing it until a certain date in the future.

WAIT STATE: the condition of a specific task that is dependent on one or more events before it can enter the ready condition.

WAIVER: relinquishment of a right, privilege, or claim; the written instrument to do so.

WAIVER CLAUSE: in insurance, a policy provision that either the insurer or the insured may act as he thinks needed to minimize the loss without prejudice to any rights under the policy.

WAIVER OF PREMIUM: a provision that under certain conditions an insurance policy is kept in full force by the insurance company without the payment of premiums.

WAIVER OF PROTEST: a statement, signed by the endorser of a note, indicating that he or she will remain liable even if not notified that the note has not been paid when due.

WALKING DELEGATE: a union official who regularly visits members at their places of employment to verify and enforce observance of contracts, and at times to represent the union in negotiations with employers.

WALKOUT: similar to a strike, except that in a walkout the workers leave work that they have already begun.

WALL STREET: the geographic area of New York City recognized as the business and financial center of the United States.

WANT AD: a classified advertisement in any subdivision of the classified-advertising section.

WANT SLIP: submitted written statements to buyers by salespersons indicating items that have been requested by customers and are not in stock.

WARD: an infant, an incompetent, or other person whose interests are administered by a guardian; a political district.

WAREHOUSE: a structure where goods are stored prior to distribution.

WAREHOUSE, BULK: a warehouse for the tank storage of liquids and open, dry products.

WAREHOUSE, COMMODITY: a warehouse storing commodity goods.

WAREHOUSE, PRIVATE: a warehouse operated by an owner, which hold his goods.

WAREHOUSE, PUBLIC: a warehouse that is rented out by the owner as a facility for the storing of goods.

WAREHOUSE RECEIPT: a negotiable instrument acknowledging receipt of merchandise.

WAREHOUSE, STATE BONDED: a public warehouse under government supervision, which has been licensed by a state prior to operation.

WAREHOUSE STOCK: goods held in quantity in a warehouse for reasons of economy.

WARES: items or commodities that are offered for sale.

WAR-PROFITS TAX: a tax on profits arising from war efforts; a distinction exists between this and excess-profits taxation, which reaches high profits from all causes.

WARRANT: a privilege of future purchase of a share of stock at a price currently determined.

WARRANTY: essentially a guarantee that a thing sold will be suitable for the purpose for which the purchaser intends to use it.

WARRANTY DEED: a deed containing a warranty.

WAR THEORY: theory that wars, causing economic prosperity, are followed by postwar depression.

WASH SALE: a sale that is immediately counterbalanced by a purchase, with the result that the sale was a fiction.

WASTAGE: wear of property or machinery; loss because of usage, deterioration, and so on.

WASTE CIRCULATION: advertising in a location where there is no distribution for the advertised product.

WASTE MATERIALS: junk.

WASTING ASSETS: natural resources subject to depletion, such as timber or mineral deposits.

WASTING TRUST: a trust of property that is gradually being consumed.

WATCH FILING: a procedure by which losses on small risks are referred to the underwriter for his or her attention.

WATERED STOCK: stock issued for overvalued property or services.

WATERLOGGED: a ship's condition of staying afloat only by the buoyancy of the cargo.

WATERMARK: a translucency in paper in the form of a symbol, design, or lettering.

WATER POLLUTION: the presence in river, shore, or lake waters of untreated sewage or wastes that destroy marine life and render the water unfit for human consumption.

WATER RIGHT: the right to make use of the water bordering on or underneath an owner's land.

WATER TABLE: the upper level of underground water in an area.

WAVELENGTH: the distance between two peaks of a wave, such as sound, light, or radio waves.

WAYBILL: a document issued with a freight shipment setting forth the merchandise, route, and charges.

WAY STATION: a stop along a route, especially in railroading.

WEAKEST LINK THEORY: principle that the least durable component in a product will control its useful life.

WEAK MARKET: a situation characterized by a greater demand for selling than there is for purchasing.

WEALTH: ordinarily, anything useful and owned by human beings.

WEALTH TAX: an annual tax on a person's assets above a stated minimum, even those assets that do not yield any income.

WEAR AND TEAR: the loss in value of a property caused by its normal and reasonable use.

WEIGHT, GROSS: the weight of a complete package, ready for shipment, including the item, the inner and outer container, and any packaging materials.

WEIGHT, NET: the weight of the item alone, excluding the packaging material or containers.

WEIGHT, TARE: the weight of the container or packaging materials.

WEIGHT BREAKS: the levels at which the charges per 100 pounds decrease as the shipment increases in weight.

WEIGHTED AVERAGE: an average in which weights are assigned to the items to be averaged; the sum of the weighted items is divided by the sum of the weights.

WELFARE ECONOMICS: a branch of economic theory dealing with the evolution of principles for maximizing social welfare.

WELFARE STATE: a democratic

state with comprehensive social services.

WELFARE STATISM: a major characteristic of government where most of the social-welfare activities are undertaken for its citizens.

WELLHEAD TAX: a government proposal to tax domestic oil as it leaves the well.

WETBACK: a Mexican agricultural laborer who enters this country illegally to obtain employment, usually at substandard pay.

WET GOODS: liquids.

WET LEASE: a contractual aircraft-leasing agreement whereby the lessor leases the craft and the personnel, fuel, and provisioning necessary to operate the plane.

WHARFAGE: a charge levied against a vessel resting at a wharf.

WHEEL: to effect a transaction or contract through nebulous implied promises, blandishments, hints at influence, and undisclosed power and inducements outside the contract.

WHEELER-LEA ACT (1938): federal law that amended the Federal Trade Commission Act to further outlaw "unfair or deceptive acts or practices" in commerce.

WHEEL OF RETAILING: the theory that new forms of retailing, when entering the market, first emphasize lower prices, but as time passes, the prices rise.

WHEN ISSUED: a basis for trading in securities not yet issued because they are in the process of a stock split, etc.

WHITE-COLLAR WORKERS: the term applied to office and professional personnel, in contrast to production and maintenance workers.

WHITE ELEPHANT: a possession, at times received as a gift, of apparent high value, but costly to maintain, unprofitable to own, and hard to sell.

WHITE KNIGHT: a friendly "suitor" brought in to put down another bidder in order to encourage a successful company takeover by another firm.

WHITE LIST: a list of employees considered satisfactory by employers because they do not agitate on labor questions.

WHITE PAPER: a government publication containing a statement of some policy it expects to enact into law.

WHITE SPACE: unprinted area in an advertisement.

WHOLE COVERAGE: any type of insurance that provides for payment from all losses without any deductions.

WHOLE-LIFE INSURANCE: life insurance in which the insured pays a flat premium as long as he lives.

WHOLESALE: relating to the level of marketing between manufacturing retailing.

WHOLESALE PRICE INDEX: a measure showing the average change in the price of about 2,200 commodities at the primary market level compared to the average level in selected base years.

WHOLESALER: an individual who buys and sells goods to retailers and other users.

WHOLESALING: selling merchandise to firms that purchase for reasons other than consumption, usually to resell the items for profit.

WIDE OPENING: a securities situation characterized by a considerable difference in the bid and asked prices at the beginning of the market day.

WILDCAT BANK: one of the unsound banks chartered by the states during the hectic banking years between 1816 and 1863.

WILDCAT STRIKE: an illegal strike in which workers walk off the job without their union's authorization.

WILL: a written, signed instrument for disposing of a person's properties and possessions after his death.

WINDFALL: an unexpected gain.

WINDING UP: the process of liquidating a company or partnership.

WINDOW DRESSING: lawful manipulation designed to show something in its most favorable lights.

202

WINDOW
ENVELOPE •
WORKMEN'S
COMPEN-
SATION

WINDOW ENVELOPE: an envelope with a transparent window showing the addressee's name and address, eliminating the need for double addressing.

WIRE HOUSE: a member firm of an exchange maintaining a communications network linking its own branch offices to offices of correspondent firms or similar such combinations.

WIRE TRANSFER: an order to pay money transmitted by telegraph or cable to secure immediate transfer.

WITH ALL FAULTS: without a guarantee, usually in real estate transactions; of the absence of imperfections; as is.

WITHHOLDING TAX: a tax deducted at source.

WITHOUT PREJUDICE: a term used to describe a statement given on the understanding that it cannot be construed as an admission of liability, nor can it be admitted in evidence.

WITHOUT RECOURSE: a phrase indicating that the holder of a document has no recourse to the person from whom he obtained it.

WITH RECOURSE: a term used in endorsing a negotiable instrument where the endorser of a note continues to be responsible should the obligation not be paid.

WITNESS: one who testifies at a trial or hearing; one who sees the signing of a document and affixes his own name to it as a witness; one who observes.

WOLF: an experienced and crafty speculator.

WOOD ENGRAVING: an engraving on wood made by removing the nonprinting areas of the block with a knife or other cutting tool.

WORD: a unit of data or a set of characters of any length that occupies only one storage location.

WORD LENGTH: a measure of the size of a word, usually specified in units such as characters or binary digits.

WORD PROCESSING: the dissemination of all written material in an office.

WORD TIME: the time interval between the appearance of corresponding parts of successive words in a storage device that provides serial access to storage locations.

WORKAHOLIC: an individual desiring to work constantly.

WORKFARE: a recently introduced concept authorizing state and local officials to require welfare recipients to perform work assigned to them as a condition of getting welfare checks.

WORKING CAPITAL: the excess of current assets over current liabilities, representing capital immediately available for the continued operation of a business.

WORKING CAPITAL RATIO: a synonym for current ratio.

WORKING CONTROL: theoretically, ownership of 51 percent of a company's voting stock, necessary to exercise control; in practice, effective control at times can be exerted through ownership of less than 50 percent of the stock.

WORKING PAPERS: a document authorizing an adolescent to enter gainful employment.

WORKING POOR: marginal employees whose skills and jobs do not provide them with an income above the poverty index.

WORKING STORAGE: a portion of a computer's internal storage reserved for specific functions such as input and output areas.

WORK-IN-PROCESS INVENTORY: includes all products that have begun the manufacturing process but have not been completed.

WORK-IN-PROGRESS: partly finished goods or contracts that are in the process of manufacture or completion at a designated time.

WORK LOAD: a quantitative measure of the amount of performed work, measured by the hour or by day.

WORKMEN'S COMPENSATION: state laws under which workers or their relatives receive compensation for work-incurred illness, injury, or fatality.

WORK ORDER: the written authorization for the performance of requested tasks.

WORK RULES: usually part of a union contract, rules regulating on-the-job working conditions.

WORK SHARING: the distribution of work evenly among employees to prevent layoffs during periods of slack.

WORK SIMPLIFICATION: a reorganization of methods, equipment, resources, and working conditions to minimize worker fatigue and increase efficiency.

WORK STOPPAGES: strikes or lockouts involving six workers or more and extending to a full work shift or longer.

WORKWEEK: the scheduled number of working hours for the week or any seven-day period of work.

WORLD BANK: name by which the International Bank for Reconstruction and Development is known.

WORLDWIDE COVERAGE: insurance coverage of all goods throughout the world.

WORTH: the total value of something, including an investment in a business.

WRAPAROUND MORTGAGE: a second mortgage with a face value equal to the amount it covers and the balance due under the first mortgage.

WRECKER: a demolition contractor; a demolition worker; a tow truck for rescuing disabled autos.

WRIT: a court order.

WRIT OF ENTRY: a legal action to regain possession of property once a party has been removed from the premises.

WRITE: to record data in a storage device or a data medium; to insure or to underwrite; at times, to sell insurance.

WRITE-DOWN: an accounting adjustment to reduce considerably but not wholly the undepreciated value of an asset.

WRITEOFF: an accounting adjustment to reduce to zero the undepreciated value of an asset.

WRITER: the seller of an option contract.

WRITEUP: an increase in net worth achieved through accounting procedures as an upward revaluation of property or inventories; a printed article having publicity value.

WRITTEN-DOWN VALUE: an accounting term for the valuation or cost of any asset minus the written-off depreciation.

X

XEROX: an office copier that deposits inks by electrostatic attraction of particles; a copy so made.

X-MARK SIGNATURE: when a person is unable to sign his name because of illiteracy or injury; provision may be made for him to "sign" with an "X."

X-OFF: transmitter off.

X-ON: transmitter on.

X-RAY: waves of frequencies higher than visible light projected from a machine through a solid onto photographic film, producing images of the interior of the solid.

XYLENE: a petrochemical solvent.

Y

YANKEE BOND MARKET: issues floated in the United States, in dollars, by foreign governments and corporations.

YARD: a place where railway cars or locomotives are stored and made ready for use.

YARD HORSE (MULE): a tractor used for transporting trailers in a terminal yard.

YARDSTICK RATES: rates of one business used as a criterion for the basic regulation of rates charged by other companies.

YEAR-END AUDIT: the phases of an audit conducted at and after the end of the accounting period being reviewed.

YEAR-END DIVIDEND: an extra dividend paid at the end of the fiscal year in addition to the regular dividend.

YELLOW-DOG CONTRACT: a labor contract so favorable to management that any union man who would sign it is nothing but a yellow dog.

YIELD: the return on a security based on its current earnings.

YIELD TO MATURITY: the rate of return on an investment when it is retained until maturity, given as a percentage.

"YOU" ATTITUDE: the approach in a business letter when the letter is written from the point of view of the reader in order to help motivate the reader to do what the writer desires.

YOUTH MARKET: people under 25 years of age, who are often interested in goods and services that are different, unusual, or suggest new values.

YO-YO STOCKS: highly volatile securities that are high-priced specialty issues that fluctuate greatly in price.

Z

ZENITH: highest point.

ZERO-BALANCE ACCOUNT: a practice, currently illegal, involving the establishment by commercial banks of a demand-deposit account and a savings account for the same customer.

ZERO-BASE BUDGETING: a system of budgeting under which all expenditures are revaluated every time a new budget is prepared.

ZERO DEFECTS: describing an approach to reward employees who make no mistakes and waste no resources while discharging their function over a given period.

ZERO PROOF: a mechanical method of posting records in a manner serving to prove that the previous balance on each line of posting was made accurately.

ZERO-SUM SITUATION: a competitive situation in which resources are fixed so that when one group succeeds, the other group must fail.

ZERO SUPPRESSION: the elimination of nonsignificant zeros in a numeral.

ZINC ENGRAVING: a photoengraving etched on zinc.

ZIP CODE: the US postal code.

ZIPPER CLAUSE: a standard clause in a negotiated contract, representing an attempt to preclude any discussion of employment conditions during the life of the agreement.

ZONE: a designated, identified area.

ZONE PRICING: a pricing system under which the seller divides the market into a number of zones, quoting different prices in different zones.

ZONING: ordinances or laws passed by cities and towns restricting certain sections of land in their use, e.g., residential, business, industrial, etc.

Abbreviations and Acronyms

A-1: first class or first quality

AA: Alcoholics Anonymous, American Airlines, Inc., Associate in Arts

AAA: American Automobile Association, American Accounting Association

AAAA: American Association of Advertising Agencies

AAD: Association of American Dentists

AALA: Associate in Arts in Liberal Arts

AAMC: American Association of Marriage Counselors

AAMCH: American Association for Maternal and Child Health

AAP: Academy of American Poets, Association of American Publishers

AAR: Association of American Railroads

AASR: Ancient Accepted Scottish Rite (Masonic)

AAU: Amateur Athletic Union

AAUP: American Association of University Professors

AAUW: American Association of University Women

AAVS: American Anti-Vivisection Society

AB: Alberta

ABA: American Bankers Association, American Bar Association

ABC: Alcoholic Beverage Control (Board), American Broadcasting Company

ABLA: American Business Law Association

ABM: antiballistic missile, Associate in Business Management

ABP: Associated Business Publications

ABS: absent, American Board of Surgery

ABWA: American Business Women's Association

AC: Air Corps, alternating current

ACC: annual capital charge

ACE: AMEX Commodities Exchange

ACLD: Association for Children with Learning Disabilities

ACLU: American Civil Liberties Union

ACM: Association for Computing Machinery

ACR: American College of Radiology

ACS: American Cancer Society

ACT: Australian Capital Territory, American Conservatory Theatre

AD: anno Domini (in the year of our Lord)

ADA: Americans for Democratic Action

ADB: Asian Development Bank

ADC: Aid to Dependent Children, Air Defense Command

ADCC: Associated Day Care Centers

ADL: Anti-Defamation League of B'nai B'rith

ADP: Automatic Data Processing

AEA: Actors' Equity Association

AEC: Atomic Energy Commission

AEF: American Expeditionary Force

AEP: adult education program

AF: Air Force, audio frequency, Air France

AFA: Armed Forces Act, Air Force Academy

AFB: Air Force Base

AFC: American Football Conference

AFDB: African Development Bank

AFDC: Aid to Families with Dependent Children

AFDCS: American First Day Cover Society

AFL: American Federation of Labor

AFL-CIO: American Federation of Labor and Congress of Industrial Organizations

AFT: American Federation of Teachers

AGMA: American Guild of Musical Artists

AHES: American Humane Education Society

AHF: American Heritage Foundation

AHQ: army headquarters

AHS: American Humane Society

AIA: American Inventors Association

AICPA: American Institute of Certified Public Accountants

AID: Agency for International Development

AIDA: Associated Independent Dairies of America

AIGA: American Institute of Graphic Arts

AIM: American Institute of Management

AIR: Action for Industrial Recycling (an organization)

AK: Alaska

AL: Alabama

ALA: American Library Association, Authors League of America

ALD: American Library Directory

ALGOL: algorithmic language (used in computer programming)

ALSS: Association of Lutheran Secondary Schools

ALTA: Alberta, Airline Traffic Association

AM: amplitude modulation (radio); America

AMA: American Medical Association, American Management Association

AMCROSS: American Red Cross

AMEX: American Stock Exchange

AMIH: Association for Middle-Income Housing

AMS: American Montessori Society

AMVETS: American Veterans of World War II

ANG: American Newspaper Guild

ANS: American Numismatic Society

AOA: American Optometric Association

AOB: alcohol on breath (police term)

AP: author's proof, additional premium, Associated Press

APB: Accounting Principles Board

APF: American Psychological Foundation

APH: Association of Private Hospitals

APhA: American Pharmaceutical Association

APHB: American Printing House for the Blind

APO: Army Post Office

APS: American Peace Society

APSA: American Psychologists for Social Action

APT: programming language

APTA: American Physical Therapy Association

AR: Arkansas

ARA: American Railway Association

ARAMCO: Arabian-American Oil Company

ARC: American Red Cross

ARF: Advertising Research Foundation, American Retail Federation

ARIA: Adult Reading Improvement Association

ARS: Agricultural Research Service, American Radium Society

ART: Advanced Research and Technology

AS: Academy of Science; Apprentice Seaman

ASA: Acoustical Society of America, Actuarial Society of America, American Society of Anesthesiologists

ASAP: as soon as possible

ASC: American Safety Council

ASCAP: American Society of Composers, Authors, and Publishers

ASCE: American Society of Civil Engineers

ASCU: Association of State Colleges and Universities

ASE: American Society of Engineers

ASIM: American Society of Internal Medicine

ASMA: American Society of Music Arrangers

ASME: American Society of Magazine Editors

ASO: American Society of Orthodontists

ASPA: American Society for Public Administration

ASQDE: American Society of Questioned Document Examiners

AST: Association for Student Teaching, Atlantic standard time

ASTA: American Society of Travel Agents, Inc.

ASTHMA: A Society to Help the Morale of Asthmatics

ASXT: American Society of X-Ray Technicians

ATCMU: Associated Third-Class Mail Users

ATESL: Association of Teachers of English as a Second Language

ATPI: American Textbook Publishers Institute

ATST: Atlantic standard time

AT&T: American Telephone and Telegraph Company

ATUC: African Trade Union Confederation

AV: audiovisual

AVS: Anti-Vivisection Society

AVTP: Adult Vocational Training Program (HEW)

AWOL: absent without official leave (military term)

AYD: American Youth for Democracy

AZ: Arizona

AZC: American Zionist Council

AZF: American Zionist Federation

BA: Bachelor of Arts, bill of sale

BAC: Business Advisory Council

BBA: Bachelor of Business Administration

BBB: Better Business Bureau

BBC: British Broadcasting Corporation

BC: Before Christ, bill of collection, British Columbia

BCA: Boys' Clubs of America

BCS: Bachelor of Commercial Science

BCSE: Board of US Civil Service Examiners

BD: Bachelor of Divinity, bank draft, bills discounted, brought down

BE: bill of exchange, bill of entry

B of E: Board of Education

BERA: Business Education Research Associated

BF: brought forward

BFI: Business Forms Institute

BH: bill of health

BHE: Bureau of Higher Education (Office of Education)

BIM: British Institute of Management

B/L: bill of lading

BLS: Bachelor of Library Science, Bureau of Labor Statistics

BMOC: big man on campus (slang)

BMR: Basal Metalbolic Rate

BMT: Basic Motion Time

BO: body odor, branch office, buyer's option

BOD: biochemical oxygen demand

BOM: beginning of the month

BOMC: Book-of-the-Month Club

BOY: beginning of the year

BP: bills payable, blood pressure, British Pharmacopoeia

BPOE: Benevolent and Protective Order of Elks

BPW: Business and Professional Women's Foundation

BR: bills receivable

BROS: brothers

BS: Bureau of Standards, Bachelor of Science, balance sheet, bill of sale

BSA: Boy Scouts of America

BSMCP: Blue Shield Medical Care Plans

BSO: Boston Symphony Orchestra

BTU: British thermal units

BU: Boston University

BVM: Beata Virgo Maria (Blessed Virgin Mary)

BVS: Bureau of Vital Statistics

BWI: British West Indies

BX: base exchange

BYO: bring your own (party invitation notation referring to liquor)

BYPU: Baptist Young People's Union

C: Celsius (centigrade) temperature scale, Congress, circa (about)

CA: California, chartered accountant, chief accountant, chronological age, capital account, credit account, current account, commercial agent, circa (about)

CAA: Civil Aeronautics Authority

CAB: Civil Aeronautics Board

CACM: Central American Common Market

CAF: cost assurance and freight

CALTECH: California Institute of Technology

CAP: Civil Air Patrol

CARA: Chinese American Restaurant Association

CARE: Cooperative for American Relief Everywhere

CARIFTA: Caribbean Free Trade Association

CASE: Council for Advancement of Secondary Education

CAT: clear air turbulence (aviation weather term)

CATV: Community Antenna Television

CAUSE: College and University System Exchange

CBA: cost-benefit analysis

CBB: Catholic Big Brothers

CBC: Canadian Broadcasting Corporation

CBD: cash before delivery

CBI: Confederation British Industry, Cumulative Book Index

CBS: Columbia Broadcasting System

CC: cubic centimeter(s), Chamber of Commerce

CCC: Civilian Conservation Corps

CCHD: Committee to Combat Huntington's Disease

CCIA: Consumer Credit Insurance Association

CCR: Commission on Civil Rights

CCSB: Credit Card Service Bureau (of America)

CCTV: Closed Circuit Television

CCU; Cardiac Care Unit

CD: Congressional District, certificate of deposit, Consular Declaration, commercial dock

CE: chemical engineer, civil engineer

CED: Committee for Economic Development

CEEB: College Entrance Examination Board

CETA: Comprehensive Employment and Training Act (1975)

CEU: Christian Endeavor Union

CF: carry forward

CFC: Consolidated Freight Classification

C&F: cost and freight

CFG: Camp Fire Girls

CFI: cost, freight, and insurance

CFM: cubic feet per minute

CFS: cubic feet per second

CG: Coast Guard, Commanding General, Consul General

CGA: Certified General Accountant

CGM: centigram(s)

CH: clearinghouse, courthouse, customhouse

CIA: Central Intelligence Agency

CIF: cost, insurance, and freight

CIO: Congress of Industrial Organizations

CKA: Catholic Knights of America

CLU: Chartered Life Underwriter

CMV: current market value

CN: credit note, consignment note, circular note

CNO: Chief of Naval Operations

CNS: central nervous system

CO: cash order, certificate or origin, commanding officer, Colorado

COB: close of business (with date)

COBOL: common business-oriented language (used in computer programming)

COD: cash on delivery, collect on delivery

COED: Concise Oxford English Dictionary

COL: column

CONUS: continental United States

COPE: Committee on Parenthood Education

COPES: Conceptually Oriented Program in Elementary Science

CORE: Congress of Racial Equality

COS: cash on shipment, chief of staff

COT: checkout time

CPA: Certified Public Accountant, critical path analysis

CPFF: cost plus fixed fee (business and trade term)

CPM: cost per thousand (advertising term)

CPO: Chief Petty Officer

CPP: critical path planning

CPPC: cost plus a percentage of cost

CPS: Certified Professional Secretary (National Secretaries Association)

CPU: central processor unit

CQ: charge of quarters, call to quarters

CR: class rate, current rate, company's risk, carrier's risk

CRC: Civil Rights Commission

CREF: cross reference

CRS: Child Rearing Study

CS: chief of staff, Civil Service, Christian Science

CSA: Confederate States of America

CSB: Civil Service Board

CSC: Civil Service Commission

CSF: Civil Service Forum

CSR: Certified Shorthand Reporter

CST: central standard time

CSU: cash surrender value

CT: central time, Connecticut

CTC: cold-type composition

CTCLS: Court of Claims

CTS: Contract termination settlement

CTST: cassette tape/selectric typewriter

CUNA: Credit Union National Association

CW: clockwise, commercial weight

CWO: cash with order.

CWPM: correct words per minute (typewriting, etc.)

CWS: Child Welfare Service

CWT: hundred weight

CYO: Catholic Youth Organization

3-D: three-dimensional (pictures or films)

DA: district attorney, deposit account, documents against acceptance, discharge afloat

DAR: Daughters of the American Revolution

DART: data analysis recording tape

DAT: Differential Aptitude Test (psychology)

D&B: Dun & Bradstreet, Inc.

DBA: doing business as

DC: direct current, District of Columbia

DCA: Digital Computers Association

DCnL: Doctor of Canon Law

DD: Doctor of Divinity (honorary)

DDC: Dewey Decimal Classification

DDS: Doctor of Dental Surgery, Doctor of Dental Science

DDT: dichlorodiphenyltrichloroethane

DE: dictating equipment, distributive education

DECAL: decalcomania

DEP: depart(ure)

DEPT: department

DEW: Distant Early Warning (military term)

DF: damage free

DFA: division freight agent

DFC: Distinguished Flying Cross

DFM: Distinguished Flying Medal

DID: data input display (data processing)

DIV: division(al)

DJ: disc jockey

DJI: Dow-Jones Index

DJS: Doctor of Juridicial Science

DK: don't know

DKL: dekaliter

DL: day letter, deciliter

D. Lit(t): Doctor of Literature or Letters

DLO: Dead Letter Office (US Postal Service)

DM: Doctor of Music

DMD: Doctor of Dental Medicine

DMV: Department of Motor Vehicles

DMZ: demilitarized zone

D. Mus.: Doctor of Music

DN: debit note

DNB: Dictionary of National Biography

DO: Doctor of Osteopathy, ditto

D/O: delivery order

DOA: dead on arrival (medicine)

DOT: Dictionary of Occupational Titles

DOZ: dozen

DP: documents against payment, data processing, dew point

DPC: data processing control

DPI: disposable personal income

DQC: data quality control

DS: days after sight, Doctor of Science

D.Sc.: Doctor of Science

DSC: Distinguished Service Cross, Doctor of Surgical Chiropody

DSM: Distinguished Service Medal

DSO: Distinguished Service Order (British), district sales office

DST: daylight saving time

DTs: delirium tremens

DV: Deo volente (God willing)

DVM: doctor of Veterinary Medicine

DW: dead weight, dock warrant

DWD: driving while drunk (police term)

E: east, Eastern

E & OE: errors and omissions excepted

EAL: Eastern Air Lines, Inc.

EBS: Emergency Broadcast System

EBSR: Eye Bank For Sight Restoration

ECC: Employee's Compensation Commission

ECG: electrocardiogram (medicine)

ECM: European Common Market

ECS: Educational Career Services (an organization)

ECT: estimated completion time

ED: edition, extra duty

Ed.D.: Doctor of Education

EDD: estimated delivery date

EDF: European Development Fund

EDP: electronic data processing

EDPRESS: Educational Press Association of America

EDT: eastern daylight time

EE: electrical engineer

EEC: European Economic Community (Common Market)

EEG: electroencephalogram; electroencephalograph

EEOC: Equal Employment Opportunity Commission

EET: Education Equivalency Test

EEF: English for foreigners

EFL: English as a foreign language

EHME: Employee Health Maintenance Examination

EKG: electrocardiogram, electrocardiograph (medicine)

ELS: extra-long staple (cotton)

EM: engineer of mines

EMA: Employment Management Association

EMCEE: master of ceremonies (slang)

EMMA: Eye-Movement Measuring Apparatus

EMP: end-of-month payment

ENRT: en route

EOA: effective on or about

EOD: every other day (advertising)

EOM: end of month

EOY: end of year

EQ: educational quotient (psychology)

E/R: en route

ERA: earned run average

ERB: Educational Records Bureau

ERCA: Educational Research Council of America

ERDA: Energy Research and Development Administration

ERICR: Eleanor Roosevelt Institute for Cancer Research

ERT: Educational Requirements Test

ES: electrostatic

ESCRU: Episcopal Society for Cultural and Racial Unity

ESL: English as a second language

ESOL: English to Speakers of Other Languages (program)

ESP: extrasensory perception

ESQ: esquire

EST: eastern standard time

ETA: estimated time of arrival

et al.: et alii (and others)

ETD: estimated time of departure

ETLT: equal to or less than

ETR: estimated time of repair

ETS: Educational Testing Service

EWC: electric water cooler

EXAM: examination

EXIM: Export-Import Bank

F: Fahrenheit

FA: free alongside

FAA: Federal Aviation Agency

FAAAS: Fellow of the American Association for the Advancement of Science

FABB: Filene's (Boston) Automatic Bargain Basement

FABX: fire alarm box

FACS: Fellow of the American College of Surgeons

FACT: factor analysis chart technique

FAGS: Fellow of the American Geographical Society

FAIA: Fellow of the American Institute of Architects

FAM: foreign air mail

FAO: Food and Agriculture Organization

FAQ: fair average quality

FAS: free alongside, Foreign Agricultural Service

FAT: fixed-asset transfer

FATS: Fight to Advertise the Truth about Saturates

FAX: facsimile

FB: freight bill

FBI: Federal Bureau of Investigation

FBL: form block line

FC: file copy

FCA: Fellow of the Institute of Chartered Accountants

FCC: Federal Communications Commission

FCDN: Ferrocarril de Nacozari (AAR code)

FCE: Foundation for Character Education

FCIS: Fellow of the Institute of Chartered Secretaries and Administrators

FCPO: First-Class Post Office

FDA: Food and Drug Administration (of HEW)

FDIC: Federal Deposit Insurance

FDR: Franklin Delano Roosevelt

FEA: Foreign Economic Administration

FEAST: Food Education and Service Training

FEP: fair employment practice

FEPC: Fair Employment Practices Commission

FET: federal excise tax

F&F: furniture and fixtures

FHA: Federal Housing Administration, Farmers Home Administration

FHLBB: Federal Home Loan Bank Board

FHY: fire hydrant

FICA: Federal Insurance Contributions Act

FICB: Federal Intermediate Credit Bank

FIFO: first in, first out (inventory term)

FIG: Federation of International Gymnastics

FIP: fairly important person

FIT: federal income tax

FITW: Federal Income Tax Withholding

FL: Florida

FLB: Federal Land Bank

FLETC: Federal Law Enforcement Training Center

FLTST: flight steward

FM: frequency modulation

FMC: Federal Maritime Commission

FNMA: Federal National Mortgage Association

FO: fuel oil

FOB: free on board

FOC: free of charge

FOR: free on rail (or road).

FORTRAN: formula translation (data-processing term, computer programming term)

FOT: free on truck (business and trade)

FP: floating policy, fully paid

FPC: Federal Power Commission

FPO: Fleet Post Office

FPS: foot-pound-second (system of measurements)

FRA: Federal Reserve Act

FRB: Federal Reserve Bank

FRD: Federal Reserve District

FREC: Federal Radio Education Committee

FRS: Federal Reserve System

FS: final settlement

FSEE: Federal Service Entrance Examination (Civil Service)

FSI: Foreign Service Institute

FSLIC: Federal Savings and Loan Insurance Coproration

FSP: Food Stamp Program

FT: foot (or feet)

FTA: Future Teachers of America

FT-C: foot-candle (illumination unit)

FTC: Federal Trade Commission

FTI: federal tax included

FTLB: foot-pound

FTRF: Freedom to Read Foundation

FUNY: Free University of New York

FWL: Foundation for World Literacy

FX: foreign exchange

FYA: for your attention

FYI: for your information

FYIG: for your information and guidance

GA: Georgia

GAAP: generally accepted accounting principles

GAAS: generally accepted auditing standards

GAD: Grants Administration Division (Environmental Protection Administration)

GAI: guaranteed annual income

GAL: gallon(s)

GAO: General Accounting Office (US Government)

GASP: Greater (name of city) Alliance to Stop Pollution

GATT: General Agreement on Tariffs and Trade

GAW: guaranteed annual wage

GBF: Great Books Foundation

GCA: Girls Clubs of America

GCD: greatest common denominator

GCT: Greenwich Conservatory Time, Greenwich Civil Time

GD: general delivery

GDR: German Democratic Republic (East Germany)

GE: Federal Republic of Germany (NATO)

GESTAPO: Geheime Staats Polizei (Secret State Police)

GFA: general freight agent

GHQ: general headquarters

GI: soldier (wartime slang), government issue

GIA: Goodwill Industries of America

GIGO: garbage in, garbage out (data-processing term)

GM: general manager, General Motors

GMAT: Graduate Management Aptitude Test

GMT: Greenwich mean time

GMV: guaranteed minimum value

GN: Graduate Nurse

GND: ground

GNP: gross national product

GOAT: goes over all terrain (vehicle)

GOP: Grand Old Party (the Republican party)

GOSPLAN: from the Russian for Central Planning Commission

GP: general practitioner

GPA: general passenger agent, grade point average

GPM: gallons per mile

GPO: Government Printing Office

GQ: general quarters

GQA: get (or give) a quick answer

GR: government regulation

GRE: Graduate Record Exam

GSA: Girl Scouts of America

GST: Greenwich standard time

GTC: good till canceled (as in a brokerage order)

GTM: general traffic manager

GU: Guam, gastric ulcer

GW: guerrilla warfare

GZTS: Guilford-Zimmerman Temperament Survey

HAA: Housing Assistance Administration (HUD)

HBP: high blood pressure (medicine)

HD: heavy duty

HDBK: handbook

HER: human error rate

HEW: Department of Health, Education and Welfare

H/F: held for

HF: high frequency

HFR: hold for release

HH: His Holiness

HHFA: Housing and Home Finance Agency

HI: Hawaii

HIAS: Hebrew Immigrant Aid Society

HL: height-length

HLS: holograph letter signed

HMS: Her Majesty's Ship, His Majesty's Ship

HMV: his master's voice (phonograph records)

HON: Honeywell, Inc. (NYSE symbol, formerly, M-H)

HOPE: Help Obese People Everywhere (an organization)

HP: horse power

HQ: headquarters

HR: House of Representatives, House Bill (with number)

HRH: His, or Her, Royal Highness

HS: high school

HSCP: high-speed card punch (data processing term)

HSCR: high-speed card reader (data processing term)

HSPT: High School Placement Test

HT: height

HUD: Department of Housing and Urban Development

HV: high velocity

Hz: hertz (cycles per second)

IA: Iowa, immediately available

IAA: International Advertising Association

IABA: Inter-American Bar Association

IACHR: Inter-American Commission on Human Rights (OAS)

IAEA: International Atomic Energy Agency

IAGLP: International Association of Great Lakes Ports

IATA: International Air Transport Association

IAVG: International Association for Vocational Guidance

IBC: Insurance Bureau of Canada, International Business Corporation

IBI: Interpersonal Behavior Inventory (VA)

IBM: International Business Machines Corporation

IBP: Institute for Better Packaging

IBRD: International Bank for Reconstruction and Development

IBS: International Bach Society

IBT: Irrational Beliefs Test (psychology)

IC: integrated circuit

ICAO: International Civil Aviation Organization

ICBM: intercontinental ballistic missile

ICBMS: Intercontinental Ballistic Missile System

ICBO: Interracial Council for Business Opportunity

ICC: Interstate Commerce Commission

ICFA: Independent College Funds of America

ICFTU: International Confederation of Free Trade Unions

ICG: Interviewer's Classification Guide

ICI: Imperial Chemical Industries

ICMA: Institute of Cost and Management Accountants

ICPI: Insurance Crime Prevention Institute

ICS: International Correspondence School

ICU: intensive-care unit (of a hospital)

ICZ: Isthmian Canal Zone

ID: Idaho, identification

IDA: International Development Association, Intercollegiate Dramatic Association

IDP: integrated data processing

IE: id est (that is)

IEEE: Institute of Electrical and Electronics Engineers

IFC: International Finance Corporation

IFO: identified flying object (Air Force term)

IFS: Irish Free State

IG: imperial gallon

IGCC: Intergovernment Copyright Committee

IGS: Institute of General Semantics

IL: Illinois

ILA: International Longshoremen's Association

ILGWU: International Ladies' Garment Workers' Union

ILO: International Labor Organization

IMBE: Institute for Minority Business Education

IMF: International Monetary Fund

IN: Indiana

INC: incorporated

INP: International News Photos

INRI: Iesus Nazarenus Rex Iudaeorum (Latin for Jesus of Nazareth, King of the Jews)

INS: International News Service

IOC: International Olympic Committee

IOG: Intercollegiate Opera Group

IOU: I owe you (business and trade slang)

IPM: inches per minute

IPS: inches per second

IQ: intelligence quotient

IRA: Irish Republican Army, Individual Retirement Account

IRBM: intermediate range ballistic missile

IRC: Internal Revenue Code

IRS: Internal Revenue Service (Treasury Department)

ISBN: International Standard Book Number

ISC: International Student Conference, interstate commerce

ISME: International Society for Musical Education

ITA: Initial Teaching Alphabet

ITED: Iowa Tests of Educational Development

ITT: International Telephone and Telegraph

ITTF: International Table Tennis Federation

ITU: income tax unit

ITV: instructional television

IWW: Industrial Workers of the World

JA: Judge Advocate, job analysis, joint account

JAIM: Job Analysis and Interest Measurement

JAL: Japan Air Lines

JAP: Joint Apprenticeship Program (Department of Labor)

JB: Juris Baccalaureus (Bachelor of Laws)

JCC: Junior Chamber of Commerce

JCD: Doctor of Canon or Civil Law

JCET: Joint Council on Educational Television

JCL: Licentiate in Canon Law

JCS: Joint Chiefs of Staff

JD: Doctor of Jurisprudence, job description (Department of Labor) Justice Department

JDC: Job Description Card

JDL: Jewish Defense League

JE: job estimate

JET: Jobs Evaulation and Training

JEPT: jet propelled

JFK: John Fitzgerald Kennedy

JI: job instruction

JIS: Job Information Service (Department of Labor)

JM: Juris Magister (Master of Laws)
JOBS: Job Opportunities for Better Skills, Job Opportunity in the Business Sector
JOM: job operation manual
JOR: job order request
JOTS: Job-Oriented Training Standards
JOY: Job Opportunity for Youth (NASA)
JP: Justice of the Peace
JSD: Doctor of Juristic Science (Law)
JQ: job questionnaire
JR: junior
JRC: Junior Red Cross
JUD: Doctor of Both Canon and Civil Laws

K: karat (gold measure), kilo (as prefix meaning multiplied by one thousand)
K9: canine (K9 Corps, Army Dogs, World War II)
KC: kilocalorie, King's Counsel, Knights of Columbus
KD: knock(ed) down (i.e., disassembled)
KELP: Kindergarten Evaluation for Learning Potential
kg: kilogram(s)
KKK: Ku Klux Klan
KO: knockout (boxing)
KP: key punch
kph: kilometers per hour
KPO: keypunch operator
KS: Kansas
kw: kilowatt(s)
kwh: kilowatt-hour
KY: Kentucky

L: Latin; law; ledger; listed (securities), fifty lire law
LA: Latin America, Louisiana, Los Angeles
LAW: Left-Handers Against the World
LB: Labrador, pound
LC: Library of Congress, lower case (i.e., small letters)
LCD: liquid crystal display, lowest common denominator
LCL: less-than-carload lot

LCM: least common multiple (mathematics)
LDC: less-developed countries
LDS: Latter-Day Saints
LEA: Law Enforcement Assistance Program
LED: light-emitting diode
LEM: lunar excursion module
LF: lightface (type), low frequency
LH: left hand
LHD: Doctor of the Humanities, Doctor of Humane Letters
LI: Long Island
L/I: letter of intent
LIAA: Life Insurance Association of America
LIFO: last in, first out (inventory term)
LISA: Life Insurance Society of America
LL: leased line (securities)
LLB: Bachelor of Law(s)
LLD: Doctor of Law(s)
LMRA: Labor-Management Relations Act
LOB: left on bases
LOC: Library of Congress
LOCATE: Library of Congress Automation Techniques Exchange
LOG: logarithm
LOX: liquid oxygen
LP: long play(ing) (phonograph record)
LPG: liquefied petroleum gas
LSAT: Law School Admission Test
1LT: First Lieutenant (army)
LT: letter message (cables), lieutenant
LTD: Limited (British)
LWOP: leave without pay (Civil Service)

m: milli- (a prefix meaning divided by one thousand)
M: one thousand (roman numeral), mega (a prefix meaning multiplied by one million)
MA: Master of Arts, Massachusetts
MAC: Military Airlift Command
MAG: magazine
MAN: Manitoba

MAP: Manpower Absorption Plan (Department of Labor)

MAS: Management Advisory Services

MASA: Mail Advertising Service Association International

MAT: minimal aversion threshold (to noise)

MATS: Military Air Transport Service

MAUDE: Morse automatic decoder

MB: Manitoba

MBA: Master of Business Administration

MBF: thousand board feet (lumber)

MBM: thousand feet board measure

MBO: management by objectives

MC: master of ceremonies, Member of Congress, Military Cross, marginal credit

MCCR: Medical Committee for Civil Rights

MCHS: Maternal and Child Health Service

MCP: male chauvinist pig (feminist term)

MCST: mag card selectric typewriter

MD: Maryland, memorandum of deposit, Doctor of Medicine, months after date

M/D: man day

MDAR: minimum daily adult requirement

MDD: Doctor of Dental Medicine

MDP: malicious destruction of property

MDR: minimum daily requirement (of a vitamin, etc.)

MDS: Master of Dental Surgery

MDT: mean down time

MDTA: Manpower Development and Training Act

MDV: Doctor of Veterinary Medicine

MDW: measured daywork

ME: Maine, mechanical engineer, military engineer, mining engineer, managing editor

MEL: minimum earnings level

MEMO: memorandum

MERC: Music Education Research Council

MERCY: Medical Emergency Relief Care for Youth

MET: magic eye tube

MF: microfiche (sheet microfilm)

MFA: malicious false alarm (firefighting)

MFBM: thousand feet board measure (lumber)

MFC: microfilm frame card

MFD: minimum fatal dose

MFN: most-favored nation (tariff)

MF(p): microfiche (positive)

M/G: miles per gallon

MGM: Metro-Goldwyn-Mayer, milligram(s)

MH: man-hours, Medal of Honor

MHR: Member of the House of Representatives

MHT: mean high tide

MHW: mean high water

MI: Michigan

MIA: missing in action (military)

MICR: magnetic ink character recognition (or reader)

MIG: from Mikoyan-Gurevich, a Russian aircraft

MIK: more in the kitchen (family dinner-table expression)

MIMC: Member of the Institute of Management Consultants

MIN: minimum

MIP: Methods Improvement Program (IBM)

MIRACODE: microfilm information retrieval access code

MIS: Management Information Systems

MISC: miscellaneous

MIT: Massachusetts Institute of Technology

MITS: man in the street (the average man)

MLLE: mademoiselle

MLR: minimum lending rate

MLS: Master of the Arts in Library Science

MLT: mean low tide

MLW: mean low water

mm: millimeter (metric unit)

MME: madame

MMES: mesdames

MN: Minnesota

MO: money order, Missouri
MOG: Metropolitan Opera Guild
MOMA: Museum of Modern Art (New York)
MONY: Mutual of New York (Insurance Company)
MP: Member of Parliament, military police, Mounted Police (Canada)
MPG: miles per gallon
MPH: miles per hour
MPM: miles per minute
MRM: mail readership measurement
MS: manuscript, Master of Science, Mississippi
MSGR: monsignor
MSS: manuscripts
MST: mountain standard time
MT: Montana
MTL: mean tide level
MTST: magnetic tape selectric typewriter
MTU: metric units
MV: mean variation, megavolt(s)
MVD: Doctor of Veterinary Medicine
MWL: mean water level

n: nano (a prefix meaning divided by one billion)
N: north
NA: National Archives (US), North America, not available
NAACP: National Association for the Advancement of Colored People
NAB: National Association of Broadcasters
NABISCO: National Biscuit Company
NABS: National Association of Black Students
NABTE: National Association for Business Teacher Education
NACA: North American College of Acupuncture
NAD: National Academy of Design
NAFMB: National Association of FM Broadcasters
NAGA: Negro Actors Guild of America
NALS: National Association of Legal Secretaries
NAM: National Association of Manufacturers

NAME: National Association for Minority Education
NAPA: National Association of Purchasing Agents
NARA: Narcotic Addict Rehabilitation Act
NARAS: National Academy of Recording Arts and Sciences
NARS: National Archives and Records Service
NAS: National Audubon Society, Naval Air Station, National Academy of Sciences
NASA: National Aeronautics and Space Administration
NASC: National Association of Student Councils
NASCL: North American Student Cooperative League
NATO: North Atlantic Treaty Organization
NATTC: Naval Air Technical Training Center or Command
NAWA: National Association of Women Artists
NB: nota bene (note well), New Brunswick, Nebraska
NBA: National Bankers Association, National Bankruptcy Act, National Bar Association, National Basketball Association
NBC: National Broadcasting Company
NBCU: National Bureau of Casualty Underwriters
NBEDC: National Black Economic Development Conference
NBFU: National Board of Fire Underwriters
NBME: National Board of Medical Examiners
NBS: National Bureau of Standards
NC: no charge, North Carolina
NCAA: National Collegiate Athletic Association
NCADH: National Committee Against Discrimination in Housing
NCEC: National Committee for an Effective Congress
NCEY: National Committee on Employment of Youth

NCH: National Committee on Housing

NCI: National Cancer Institute (of NIH)

NCIP: National Council for Industrial Peace

NCJSC: National Criminal Justice Statistics Center

NCOC: National Council on Organized Crime

NCO: noncommissioned officer

NCSH: National Clearinghouse for Smoking and Health

NCSS: National Center for Social Statistics (HEW)

NCSW: National Conference on Social Welfare

NCTA: National Cable Television Association

NCTE: National Council of Teachers English

NCV: no commercial value

ND: no date (of publication)

NE: northeast, New England

N/E: not exceeding (business and trade)

NEA: National Education Association

NED: New English Dictionary (The Oxford English Dictionary)

NEGRO: National Economic and Growth Reconstruction Organization (black entrepreneurial organization)

NET: National Educational Television

NF: Newfoundland

NFC: National Football Conference

NFL: National Football League

NG: National Guard

NGSM: National Gold Star Mothers

NH: New Hampshire

NHA: National Health Association

NHEF: National Health Education Foundation

NHLA: National Housewives' League of America

NHTSA: National Highway Traffic Safety Administration

NIH: National Institutes of Health

NIRA: National Inter-Racial Association

NIT: negative income tax

NJ: New Jersey

NL: night letter (telegram)

NLRA: National Labor Relations Act

NLRB: National Labor Relations Board

NLT: night letter cable

NM: New Mexico

NMA: National Management Association

NMB: National Mediation Board

NMUC: National Medical Utilization Committee (HEW)

NNPA: National Negro Press Association, National Newspaper Publishers Association

NO: no orders (banking), number

NOA: National Opera Association

NOE: not otherwise enumerated

NOHP: not otherwise herein provided

NOIBN: not otherwise indexed by name (tariffs)

NOW: National Organization for Women

NP: notary public; no protest (banking)

N/P: notes payable

NPC: National Press Club

NPPA: National Probation and Parole Association

NPS: National Park Service

NPU: National Postal Union

NPV: no par value

NQB: no qualified bidders

NRC: National Reading Council

NRS: National Reemployment Service

NS: Nova Scotia

NSAS: nonscheduled air services

NSBA: National School Boards Association, National Small Business Association

NSC: National Security Council, National Safety Council

NSF: not sufficient funds (banking)

NSMS: National Sheet Music Society

NSOB: New Senate Office Building

NSSR: New School for Social Research

NT: Northwest Territories, New Testament

NTL: National Temperance League

NTSA: National Traffic Safety Agency

NTUC: National Trade Union Council for Human Rights

NTX: National Teletypewriter Exchange

NUEA: National University Extension Association

NV: Nevada

NW: northwest, net weight

NWAA: National Wheelchair Athletic Association

NWBA: National Wheelchair Basketball Association

NWH: normal working hours

NY: New York

NYC: New York City

NYME: New York Merchantile Exchange

NYSE: New York Stock Exchange

NZ: New Zealand

OAA: Old-Age Assistance (HEW)

OAB: Old-Age Benefits

OAPEC: Organization of Arab Petroleum Exporting Countries

OAS: Old-Age Security, Organization of American States

OASI: Old-Age and Survivors Insurance

OATS: Office of Air Transportation Security (FAA)

OC: office copy

OCR: optical character reader (or recognition)

OCS: Officer Candidate School

OD: officer of the day, olive drab, overdraft, overdrawn

ODB: Office of Dependency Benefits

OE: Old English (language i.e., before 1150 or 1200)

OECD: Organization for Economic Cooperation and Development

OED: Oxford English Dictionary

OEEO: Office of Equal Educational Opportunities

OEO: Office of Economic Opportunity

OEP: Office of Emergency Preparedness

OIO: Office of International Operations (of IRS)

OIR: Office of International Research (of NIH)

OJ: orange juice

OJT: one-the-job training

OK: Oklahoma, okay

OKA: otherwise known as

OMB: Office of Management and Budget

OMBE: Office of Minority Business Enterprise

ON: Ontario

OPEC: Organization of Petroleum Exporting Countries

OR: Oregon

ORC: Opinion Research Corporation, Officers' Reserve Corps

ORR: owner's risk rates (shipping)

ORUS: Official Register of the United States

OS: out of stock, old style

OSC: Ontario Securities Commission, order to show cause

OSG: Office of the Secretary General (UN)

OSHA: Occupational Safety and Health Act (1970)

OT: Old Testament

O/T: overtime (business and trade)

OTB: off-track betting

OTC: over the counter (stock)

OTJ: on the job

OTS: Officers's Training School

OW: one way (fare)

OWI: operating while intoxicated (traffic offense)

OWM: Office of Weights and Measures (National Bureau of Standards)

PA: purchasing agent, Pennsylvania, power of attorney, press agent, public-address system, particular average, public accountant.

PAC: put and call (stock market)

PACE: Projects to Advance Creativity in Education (HEW)

PAL: Police Athletic League (New York)

PAN-AM: Pan-American World Airways, Inc.

PAR: People Against Racism (Civil Rights Organization), program analysis and review

PATH: Port Authority Trans-Hudson (New York)

PAU: present address unknown

PAYE: pay-as-you-earn

PB: passbook (banking)

PBA: Patrolmen's Benevolent Association

PBR: payment-by-results

PBS: Public Broadcasting Service, Public Buildings Service

PBX: private branch exchange

PC: Peace Corps, put and call (stock market)

PCC: Panama Canal Company

PCEEO: President's Committee on Equal Employment Opportunity

PCEH: President's Committee on Employment of the Handicapped

PCML: President's Committee on Migratory Labor

PCMR: President's Committee on Mental Retardation

PCTS: President's Committee for Traffic Safety

PCV: petty cash voucher

PDF: Parkinson's Disease Foundation

PDQ: pretty damn quick

PE: Prince Edward Island, Physical Education

PER: price earnings ratio

PERT: program evaluation and review techniques

PFC: Private, First Class (army)

PG: parental guidance suggested (movie rating)

PGA: Professional Golfer's Association

PHA: Public Housing Administration

Phar.D.: Doctor of Pharmacy

Ph.D.: Doctor of Philosophy

PHS: Public Health Service

PI: Philippine Islands

PINS: persons in need of supervision

PJ: presiding judge

PKU: Phenylketonuria

P&L: profit and loss

PL: price list

PLO: Palestine Liberation Organization

PLS: Professional Legal Secretary

PM: paymaster, police magistrate, postmaster, postmortem, prime minister, provost marshal, post meridiem (after noon)

PN: promissory note

PNYA: Port of New York Authority

PO: post office

POB: post office box

POD: pay on delivery

POE: port of embarkation, port of entry

POPE: Parents for Orthodoxy in Parochial Education

POPS: People Opposed to Pornography in Schools

POR: pay on return

POW: prisoner(s) of war

PP: pages, parcel post, Planned Parenthood

PPFA: Planned Parenthood Federation of America

PPI: plan position indicator

PPB: planning, programming, budgeting

PR: public relations, Puerto Rico

PRC: People's Republic of China (mainland China)

PROF: professor

PROP: proprietor, proposition

PRS: Performing Right Society

PS: post scriptum (written afterwards, a postscript), public sale

PSF: pounds per square foot

PSI: pounds per square inch

PSL: pressure sensitive label

PST: Pacific standard time

PT: Pacific time

PTA: Parent-Teacher Association

PTO: please turn over (the page)

PUC: Public Utilities Commission

PVR: profit/volume ratio

PW: packed weight, prisoner of war

PWP: Parents Without Partners (an organization)

PX: post exchange

QAR: quality assurance representative

QB: qualified bidders

QC: quality control
QF: quick freeze
QI: quarterly index
QM: quartermaster
QMC: Quartermaster Corps
QMG: Quartermaster General
QT: quiet (or sub rosa, as in "on the QT")
QUE: Quebec
QV: quod vide or quod videte (which see)

R: restricted (movie rating)
3R: readin', ritin', and rithmetic
RA: refer to acceptor
RAAF: Royal Australian Air Force
RADA: radioactive
RADAR: radio detection and ranging
RAdm: Rear Admiral
RAF: Royal Air Force
RAPP: registered air parcel post
RBI: runs batted in
RC: Roman Catholic, Red Cross
RCAF: Royal Canadian Air Force
R&CC: riot and civil commotion
RCIA: Retail Credit Institute of America
RCMP: Royal Canadian Mounted Police
RCT: Rorschach Content Test (psychology)
RD: rural delivery
R&D: Research and Development
RDD: research and development division
REA: Railway Express Agency
RECD: received
REIT: real estate investment trust (generic term)
REM: rapid eye movement
REO: real estate owned (banking)
REV: reverend
RF: radio frequency
RFD: rural free delivery
RH: right hand
RHEO: rheostat
RI: Rhode Island
RIA: Registered Industrial Accountant

RIE: retirement income endowment (insurance)
RIMPTF: Recording Industries Music Performance Trust Funds
RIMR: Rockefeller Institute for Medical Research
RIP: requiescat in pace (may he, or she, rest in peace)
RL: retarded learner (education)
RM: room
RN: Registered Nurse
ROG: receipt of goods
ROT: rule of thumb
ROTC: Reserve Officers' Training Corps
ROW: right of way
RPH: Registered Pharmacist
RPM: revolutions per minute (phonograph records)
RPO: railway post office
RR: railroad, rural route
RS: reformed spelling
RSP: receiving stolen property
RSVP: please reply
RT: released time
RTE: route
RTW: right to work
R/W: right of way
RY: railway

S: signed (before signature on typed copy of a document, original of which was signed), south
SA: South America, South Africa, Salvation Army
SABE: Society for Automation in Business Education
SABW: Society of American Business Writers
SAC: Strategic Air Command
SAE: Society of Automotive Engineers, self-addressed envelope, Society for the Advancement of Education
SAGA: Society of American Graphic Artists
SAI: an incorporated company in Italy
SAJ: Society for the Advancement of Judaism

SALT: Strategic Arms Limitation Talks/Treaty, Sisters All Learning Together (feminist group)

SAM: surface-to-air missile

SANKA: sans caffeine (acronym used as brand name)

SAP: soon as possible

SAR: Sons of the American Revolution

SASE: self-addressed stamped envelope

SASK: Saskatchewan

SAT: Scholastic Aptitude Test

SATB: soprano, alto, tenor, bass (music)

SB: southbound, Senate Bill (state), short bill

SBIC: Small Business Investment Corporation

SBLI: savings bank life insurance

SC: South Carolina

SCAN: Stock Market Computer Answering Service

SCAT: School and College Ability Test (of ETS)

Sc.D.: Doctor of Science

SCL: Senior Citizens League

SCORE: Service Corps of Retired Executives

SCRAP: Society for Completely Removing All Parking Meters

SD: South Dakota

SDBL: sight draft, bill of lading attached

SDR: special drawing right

SDS: Students for a Democratic Society

SE: southeast

SEATO: Southeast Asia Treaty Organization

SEC: Securities and Exchange Commission

SEEK: Search for Education, Elevation and Knowledge

SEN: senator

SG: Surgeon General

SGD: signed

SH: semester hour

SHAME: Save, Help Animals Man Exploits

SHAPE: Supreme Headquarters Allied Powers Europe (NATO)

SI: Sandwich Islands, Staten Island (New York)

SITCOM: situation comedy (television)

SJ: Society of Jesus

SJD: Doctor of Juridical Science (law)

SK: Saskatchewan

SLD: specific language disability (education)

SLR: single-lens reflex (camera)

SMA: Society of Management Accountants

SMOG: smoke and fog

SMR: standard mortality rate

SMSG: School Management Study Group

SN: stock number

SNAFU: situation normal, all fouled up (military)

SODA: Stamp Out Drug Addiction (an organization)

SONS: Society of Non-Smokers

SOP: standard operating procedure

SOPC: sales operations planning and control

SOS: save our ship (or souls)

SP: shore patrol, southern Pacific

SPAR: Coast Guard Women's Reserve

SPCA: Society for the Prevention of Cruelty to Animals

SPCC: Society for the Prevention of Cruelty to Children

SPM: strokes per minute

SPQR: small profits, quick returns

SQM: square meter

SR: senior

SRA: Science Research Associates

SRCC: strikes, riots, and civil commotions

SRI: Stanford Research Institute

SRO: standing room only, single-room occupancy (New York housing term)

SS: steamship, saints (e.g., SS Peter and Paul), Social Security

SSA: Social Security Administration

SSAT: Secondary School Admission Test Board

SSS: Selective Service System

SSU: Sunday School Union

ST: saint, sensitivity training, short ton (2,000 pounds)

STAR: Safe Teen-Age Rocketry

STB: soprano, tenor, bass (music)

STD: Doctor of Sacred Theology, standard

STEP: School to Employment Program

STP: standard temperature and pressure

STS: School Television Service

SU: set up (freight)

SUBS: subscription

SUNY: State University of New York

SUNYA: State University of New York at Albany

SUNYAB: State University of New York at Buffalo

SW: southwest

SWAK: sealed with a kiss (correspondence)

SWALK: sealed with a loving kiss (correspondence)

SWEAT: student work experience and training

SWORD: Separated, Widowed, or Divorced (an organization)

SY: square yard

SYD: Scotland Yard

T: tutti (sing or play together in music)

TA: teaching assistant (in a university)

TAG: The Acronym Generator (an RCA computer program)

TAP: Teacher's Aide Program

TARMAC: tar macadam

TARP: tarpaulin

TARS: Teen-Age Republicans

TAS: Telephone Answering Service (or System)

TB: tuberculosis

TBA: to be announced

TC: Tax Court of the United States

TCPO: Third-Class Post Office

TD: touchdown; time deposit

TEF: Temperance Education Foundation

TEFL: teaching English as a foreign language

TEMP: temperature

TENES: teaching English to the non-English student

TESL: teaching English as a second language

TESOL: Teachers of English to Speakers of Other Languages

TEST: Teen-Age Employment Skills Training, Inc.

TF: till forbidden (i.e., repeat until forbidden)

TGIF: "thank God it's Friday"

THAT: twenty-four-hour automatic teller

Th.D.: Doctor of Theology

TIP: to insure promptness

TKO: technical knockout

TL: trade-last

TLC: tender loving care

TM: transcendental meditation

TMH: tons per man-hour

TML: three-mile limit

TN: Tennessee

TO: table of organization

T/O: Table of Organization

TOP: temporarily out of print

TPQI: Teacher-Pupil Question Inventory

TPRI: Teacher-Pupil Relationship Inventory

TR: tape recorder

TSP: teaspoonful

TT: Teletype

TTP: total taxable pay

TTPE: total taxable pay earned

TTY: teletypewriter

TV: television; terminal velocity

TVA: Tennessee Valley Authority

TWA: Trans-World Airlines, Inc.

TWK: typewriter keyboard

TWX: Teletypewriter Exchange Service (Western Union)

TX: Texas

UA: United Air Lines, Inc., United Artists

UAW: United Aircraft and Agricultural Implements Workers, United Automobile Workers

UC: upper case (i.e., capital letters in typography)

UCLA: University of California, Los Angeles

UDC: Universal Decimal Classification

UFO: unidentified flying object ("flying saucer")

UHF: ultra-high frequency

UK: United Kingdom

UL: Underwriters' Laboratories, Inc.

ULC: Underwriter's Laboratories of Canada

ULI: Underwriter's Laboratories, Inc.

UMW: United Mine Workers

UN: United Nations

UNAUS: United Nations Association of the United States

UNDP: United Nations Development Program

UNESCO: United Nations Educational, Scientific and Cultural Organization

UNGA: United Nations General Assembly

UNICEF: United Nations Children's Fund

UNIDO: United Nations Industrial Development Organization

UNSC: United Nations Security Council

UNSG: United Nations Secretary General

U&O: Use and occupancy

UP: United Press

UPI: United Press International

UPS: United Parcel Service

UPU: Universal Postal Union

URA: Urban Renewal Administration

US: United States (of America)

USA: United States of America; US Army; Underwriters Service Association

USAF: United States Air Force

USBS: United States Bureau of Standards

USC: United States Code; University of Southern California

USCC: United States Chamber of Commerce

USCG: United States Coast Guard

USDC: United States District Court

USDJ: United States District Judge

USES: United States Employment Service

USGLI: US Government Life Insurance

USIA: United States Information Agency

USJCC: United States Junior Chamber of Commerce (JAYCEES)

USLTA: United States Lawn Tennis Association

USM: United States mail, United States Marines

USMA: United States Military Academy

USMC: United States Marine Corps

USN: United States Navy

USNA: United States Naval Academy

USNG: United States National Guard

USNPGS: United States Naval Post Graduate School

USNR: United States Naval Reserve

USO: United States Organization

USOC: United States Olympic Committee

USOE: United States Office of Education

USP: United States Pharmacopeia; unique selling point

USS: United States ship, United States Senate

USSR: Union of Soviet Socialist Republics

USSS: United States Secret Service

UT: Utah

UW: underwriter

V: versus (against)

VA: Veterans Administration; Virginia

VAdm: Vice Admiral

VAT: value added tax

VC: Victoria Cross (British); valuation clause; vice consul

VD: venereal disease

VEEP: vice president

VET: veteran; veterinary

VFD: volunteer fire department

VFW: Veterans of Foreign Wars

VG: very good

VHF: very high frequency (radio)

VI: Virgin Islands

VIP: very important person

VISTA: Volunteers in Service to America

VMD: Doctor of Veterinary Medicine

VNA: Visiting Nurse Association

VOA: Voice of America

VOL: volume

VP: vice president

VS: versus (against)

VT: Vermont

VV: vice versa

VW: Volkswagen

W: west

WA: Washington

WAAC: Women's Army Auxilliary Corps

WAC: Women's Army Corps (formerly, WAAC)

WAF: Women in the (US) Air Force

WAM: words a minute

WAR: "we are ridiculous" (antiwar slogan)

WASP: White Anglo-Saxon Protestant

WATS: Wide-Area Telephone Service

WAVES: Women Accepted for Volunteer Emergency Service (women in the US Navy)

WB: waybill, weather bureau

WCA: Workmen's Compensation Act

WCTU: Women's Christian Temperance Union

WF: wrong font (typesetting)

WHO: World Health Organization (United Nations affiliate)

WI: Wisconsin

WIC: War Insurance Corporation

WIN: Work Incentive Program, Whip Inflation Now, Workshop in Nonviolence

WITCH: Women Incensed over Traditional Coed Hoopla

WMCW: World Movement of Christian Workers

WO: Warrant Officer

WPA: Works Progress Administration

WPM: words per minute

WPS: words per second

WSJ: Wall Street Journal (a newspaper)

W/TAX: withholding tax

WUMP: White, Urban, Middle-Class, Protestant

WV: West Virginia

WWI: World War I

WWII: World War II

WY: Wyoming

X: movie rating for "persons under 18 not admitted"

XQ: cross-question

X-REF: cross reference

XXX: international urgency signal

Y: Young Men's (or Women's) Christian Association

YMCA: Young Men's Christian Association

YM-YWHA: Young Men's and Young Women's Hebrew Association

YT: Yukon Territory

YW: Young Women's (Christian Association)

YWCA: Young Women's Christian Association

YWCTU: Young Women's Christian Temperance Union

YWHA: Young Women's Hebrew Association

Z: zero, Zulu time (Greenwich mean time) zero

ZBR: zero base review

ZIP: Zone Improvement Plan

ZPG: zero population growth